# Communication Theory Through the Ages

*Communication Theory Through the Ages* presents communication theory as a journey through history by way of asking engaged questions. Encouraging intellectual vitality, the authors show students step by step how theoretical ideas are interconnected and lead to an increasingly complex understanding of communication. Students will be motivated to ask questions as they encounter historical figures, social events, and artifacts, resulting in a richer understanding of the biographical, cultural, and social context for communication theories.

**Igor E. Klyukanov** is Professor of Communication in the Department of Communication Studies at Eastern Washington University, U.S.A. He has authored numerous articles, book chapters, and books in communication theory, semiotics, translation studies, general linguistics, and intercultural communication. His works have been published in the U.S., Russia, England, Spain, Costa Rica, Serbia, Bulgaria, India, and Morocco. His textbook *Principles of Intercultural Communication* has been adopted by over 30 colleges and universities in the U.S. His monograph *A Communication Universe: Manifestations of Meaning, Stagings of Significance* won the 2012 NCA Philosophy of Communication Division Distinguished Book Award. He is also the translator and editor of Mikhail Epstein's book *The Transformative Humanities: A Manifesto.* He served as an associate editor of *The American Journal of Semiotics* and is the founding editor of *Russian Journal of Communication.*

**Galina V. Sinekopova** is Professor of Communication in the Department of Communication Studies at Eastern Washington University, U.S.A. She has published articles in such journals as *Journal of Communications, Journal* *of Language and Social Psychology,* and *Listening: Journal of Communication Ethics, Religion, and Culture.* Recently, her chapter (co-authored with Igor E. Klyukanov) on the press in post-Soviet societies has appeared in *The Handbook of Media and Mass Communication Theory.* She has presented her research at conferences in the U.S., Canada, China, Taiwan, Turkey, Russia, and Bulgaria. She served as a guest editor of two issues of *International Journal of Communication.*

# Communication Theory Through the Ages

Igor E. Klyukanov and
Galina V. Sinekopova

Routledge
Taylor & Francis Group

NEW YORK AND LONDON

First published 2019
by Routledge
52 Vanderbilt Avenue, New York, NY 10017

and by Routledge
2 Park Square, Milton Park, Abingdon, Oxon, OX14 4RN

*Routledge is an imprint of the Taylor & Francis Group, an informa business*

*Library of Congress Cataloging-in-Publication Data*
Names: Klyukanov, Igor, author. | Sinekopova, Galina V., author.
Title: Communication theory through the ages / by Igor E. Klyukanov &
    Galina V. Sinekopova.
Description: First Edition. | New York : Routledge, 2019. | Includes
    bibliographical references and index.
Identifiers: LCCN 2018043291| ISBN 9780765646750 (hardback) | ISBN
    9780765646767 (pbk.) | ISBN 9781315718668 (e-book)
Subjects: LCSH: Communication. | Information theory.
Classification: LCC P90 .K5568 2019 | DDC 302.2—dc23
LC record available at https://lccn.loc.gov/2018043291


ISBN: 978-0-7656-4675-0 (hbk)
ISBN: 978-0-7656-4676-7 (pbk)
ISBN: 978-1-315-71866-8 (ebk)


Typeset in Warnock
by Swales & Willis Ltd, Exeter, Devon, UK

For Anya

"Of all affairs, communication is the most wonderful."

*— John Dewey*

# Contents

**2    The Wonder of Polis**                                    **40**
   1.   What We've Got Here is Failure to Communicate   40
   2.   The Polis: Living Together and 'Living Well'   41
      2.1.  Polis as Communicative Space   43
   3.   Polis: The Dark Side of Communication   48
      3.1.  The Politics of Exile   50
      3.2.  Polis: War and Peace   52
   4.   'The Polis of Our Prayers'   53
      4.1.  Polis as an Idea(l)   57
   5.   'We All Came Out of the Polis'   59

**3    The Wonder of God**                                      **66**
   1.   'Everything is Full of Gods'   66
      1.1.  Seeing Gods   69
   2.   'Thou Shalt Have No Other Gods Before Me'   72
      2.1.  Setting Free the Immortal Soul   74
   3.   God Is Not Dead!   75
   4.   'The God-Problem' in Communication Theory   80
      4.1.  Experiencing (the Word of) God(s)   83
      4.2.  Spreading (the Word of) God(s)   86
      4.3.  Listening to (the Word of) God(s)   90

**4    The Wonder of the Body**                                 **97**
   1.   What is the Body?   97
   2.   Body Language   100
      2.1.  Classifying Body Language   103
      2.2.  The Textualization of the Body   106
   3.   The Speaking Body   109
      3.1.  Putting Lived Experience in the Spotlight   110
   4.   The Human Science of Communicology   116
   5.   'The Body Improper'   118
      5.1.  Data Made Flesh   120

**5    The Wonder of the Mind**                                 **123**
   1.   In Search of the Mind   123
      1.1.  What/Where is the Mind?   125

# Acknowledgments

We wish to thank all those who helped us in making this book a reality.

We especially thank Richard L. Lanigan, Thomas Pace, Isaac E. Catt, Deborah Eicher-Catt, Andrew A. Smith, Frank J. Macke, Gary J. Krug, Alexander Kozin, Mikhail Epstein, Alexander Kozintsev: their research guided our thinking in communication theory and helped us to write a proposal for this book.

Richard L. Lanigan read most of the chapters in draft form and offered valuable suggestions, for which we're very grateful.

Suzanne Phelps Chambers was the first person who read and supported the proposal, setting the publication of the book in motion.

We thank John Durham Peters and Ben Peters for their insightful Foreword, as well as for their support over the years.

We thank Richard L. Lanigan, Steven Beebe, Kaarle Nordenstreng, Todd Sandel and Du-Won Lee for their endorsements.

A special thank you is to Michael Williams for attentive and thorough copy-editing and to Meg Lybbert for her helpful suggestions. We thank Felisa Salvago-Keyes, Senior Editor, Christina Kowalski, Senior Editorial Assistant, John Makowski, Editorial Assistant at Routledge's Filmmaking & Photography list, and the entire production team at Routledge/Taylor & Francis Books.

Finally, we're thankful to the many students in our classes who helped us to refine our ideas for the book. And we thank all future students who will read this book and make a journey through the ages of communication theory.

# Foreword

This book builds from a simple and often ignored premise: communication scales to different sizes, shapes, and times. And how does it deliver on that premise! It stands out from a crowded and not terribly distinguished array of communication theory books for its willingness to think with the grandeur the topic deserves. All the big questions are relevant. The book bursts through tired mid-range theories to zoom out to grandiose and zoom into granular scales of thinking. And like all voices worth taking seriously, this work of scholarship does not take itself too seriously: in it, Lewis Carroll's Humpty Dumpty converses with Wittgenstein, asteroids threaten to talk back, and McLuhan butts in on a fascinating back-and-forth between Mead and Vygotsky. Indeed, this book offers a life-raft for the shipwrecked on the sands of self-serious communication theorists. If wit is one anchor for their rainbow of ideas, wonder is the other. This book is on a mission—to understand, to inquire, to probe—and it plays for the highest stakes. It is animated by the spirit—the quest for truth—that should move all scholarship.

A quick glance at the shelves of communication theory texts may leave one feeling stranded indeed. Much of this literature is a bazaar of goods for sale, jumbled together by no greater ambition than to appeal to the undergraduate textbook market or to not leave one's colleagues unacknowledged. Not so here: the method is that of the synthetic essay—or ten of them to be precise. Each chapter tackles a topic that marks a crucial coordinate for organizing human and nonhuman attempts to think about communication. The book has both a synthetic and a collector's spirit. It contains multitudes, spanning aboriginal notions of the eternities to the search for extraterrestrial intelligence in outer space. The wildness of the authors' reach, and the range of their powers of scale, pays dividends. The book introduces a city of over one hundred theorists on communication—from Aristotle to Arendt to Agamben, to stick with just the first letter—that supersedes the smallish bazaar of communication theory.

You hold, dear reader, the general introduction that would have saved us both much grief when we each first encountered the field of communication theory in the early 1980s and early 2000s. Reading this book is like inviting learned friends to tea and listening to them weave fabulous tale after tale with their favorite passages from the impressive library they have lugged to the table. The authors combine the art of interpretation (*hermēneutikē technē*) and the art of judgment (*kritikē technē*) into new syntheses—and the consequence is both original and resonant with ongoing questions. It is a sampler of the full splendor of imaginative communication theory.

The ten chapters take a chiastic architecture. Time (chapter one) and space (chapter ten) are alpha and omega, and mind (chapter five) and language (chapter six) are its pinnacle and primary preoccupation. Polis (chapter two) and community (chapter nine), God (chapter three) and information (chapter eight), and body (chapter four) and culture (chapter seven) weave a clear warp and weft. The book's insistence on key principles such as time as the *a priori* of all other conditions, space as not only social space but outer space, and language not only as meaning but as excess and abundance, would, if taken seriously, make our field much bolder, much grander, and also a bit stranger, all of which we take to be wonderful. We join in congratulating our friends Igor Klyukanov and Galina Sinekopova for the publication of this book and in hoping for more boldness, grandeur, and wonder in all of our work.

Benjamin Peters, The University of Tulsa, USA
John Durham Peters, Yale University, USA
2 July 2018

# 1

# The Wonder
# of Time

Key concepts:

Acoustic space, a priori, ars memoriae, axiology, chronemics, corroboree, empire, erasure, horizontal communication, Global Village, master narrative, media, mediatization, message, mobility, modernity, monochronic time, myth, nihilism, nostalgia, ontology, oral, polychronic time, postmodernity, ritual, ritual view, Self, semantic, semiotic, simulacrum, survivance, time-biased media, totemism, tradition, transmission view, vertical communication, writing.

Key names:

Aristotle, Jan Assmann, St. Augustine, Francis Bacon, Roland Barthes, Giordano Bruno, James Carey, Jean-François Champollion, Émile Durkheim, Albert Einstein, Michel Foucault, Johannes Gutenberg, Jürgen Habermas, Eric Havelock, Martin Heidegger, Heraclitus, Thomas Hobbes, Ivan Illich, Harold Innis, Fredric Jameson, Immanuel Kant, Friedrich A. Kittler, Jean-François Lyotard, Guglielmo Marconi, Marshall McLuhan, Lewis Mumford, Isaac Newton, John Peters, Plato.

## 1. RUNNING OUT OF TIME?

Take a look at the image of the clock in Figure. 1.1.

It looks so cute: one might think it comes from a children's cartoon. Unfortunately, it doesn't. This is the Doomsday Clock that shows a symbolic countdown to the world's end. Created in 1947, the clock has been adjusted more than 20 times by the *Bulletin of the Atomic Scientists* in consultation with its Board of Sponsors, which includes 16 Nobel Laureates. Just recently, the minute hand has been moved again and today the clock is closer to midnight than it has been during the past 20 years. It stands at two minutes to midnight. If you don't quite agree with the opinion of the Science and Security Board of the *Bulletin of the Atomic Scientists*, you can go to its website and take a poll that asks one question: "What time do you think the Clock should read?" Chances are, though, you won't suggest moving the clock back too far. The situation is truly critical: the world faces many complex problems, such as nuclear power and nuclear weapons, and climate disruptions from global warming, all of which are threatening the whole of humanity.

Now what does this have to do with communication? First, and most importantly, the planet is being destroyed by humanity itself. All global problems are the result of concrete human beings who can't communicate successfully with one another and reach an agreement, be it peace talks, political negotiations, or international treaties on climate change. And, second, the information

**Figure 1.1**   Doomsday Clock icon.

about the critical state of the world must be better communicated to everyone. So-called 'risk communication' research addresses social and ecological systems characterized by high levels of uncertainty and complexity, e.g. environmental and health issues. So-called 'crisis communication' focuses on PR problems faced by companies and organizations. And yet, clearly more effort is needed to communicate the message that "modern man is the victim of the very instruments he values most" and that "we have conjured up a genius capable of destroying our civilization" (Mumford, 1944, p. 393). Today the situation is much more critical and so this message must be communicated more clearly and forcefully.

## 2. TIME AND COMMUNICATION

The role of time in communication has, of course, been noted. Communication is usually conceptualized as a process, i.e., "an activity that has many separate but interrelated steps that occur over time" (Ruben & Stewart, 2006, p. 15). The communication process is viewed as "time dependent because no two communication events are the same" (Heath & Bryant, 2000, p. 53); hence, communication is considered to be an ever-changing process. Also, time is identified as a type of nonverbal communication and studied through chronemics, which is concerned with how people communicate through the use of time. However, the importance of time in communication goes much further. In fact, the conceptualization of time in communication theory is considered to be "perhaps more demanding than any other single factor" (Fisher, 1978, p. 222).

There are at least two main reasons why time enjoys a special status in communication theory. First, the starting point in understanding communication is ontological; we must ask the question 'What is the nature of communication?' In the words of Martin Heidegger, "the central range of problems of all ontology is rooted in the phenomenon of time" (Heidegger, 1966, p. 16). And, second, we can understand communication only if we look at its axiology, i.e., identify the values behind human actions, which, of course, change over time. That is why, as William Shakespeare famously put it, "our virtues lie in the interpretation of time" (*Coriolanus*, iv, 7). Thus, we can gain insights into the most fundamental aspects of communication only by paying close attention to the role that time plays in it.

While one can wear a watch in one's pocket or look at a clock, time itself is not a physical object: it is an experience. When we experience time, we respond to the motion of the world in various ways. The importance of this experience can't be overemphasized: "Motion . . . is, in perceptual terms highly salient. . . . After all, survival depends on our ability to detect motion" (Evans, 2004, p. 202). When we experience the world, we try to understand how phenomena succeed one another, e.g. whether one occurs before or after another, or whether they seem to occur at the same time. Thomas Hobbes declared that time is "a phantasm produced by a body in motion" (Robertson, 1886, p. 97).

When we experience time, we routinely use such concepts as 'now', 'an hour', 'two years ago,' etc. Time, as such, however, is not just a general concept; it is a pure form of sensible intuition, or what Immanuel Kant called (along with space) *a priori*, i.e., 'before the experience'. He writes:

> For we should not observe things to co-exist or to follow one another, did we not possess the idea of time *a priori*. It is, therefore, only under the presupposition of time, that we can be conscious of certain things as existing at the same time (simultaneously), or at different times (successively)
>
> *(Kant, 1888, p. 29)*

Time is what makes our experience possible in the first place; it precedes and underlies experience *a priori*. All our concepts, thus, such as 'now', 'an hour' or 'twenty years ago' have meaning only because ultimately they rely on time as an *a priori* intuition.

Time appears mysterious and intangible because it is not a physical being among beings. It is, indeed, not an object, but rather "a mobile image of eternity" (Plato, *Timaeus*, 37d). In other words, we imagine time; it is a product of our imagination. Let's see how time has been conceptualized and has affected communication through the ages.

You must have heard the phrase: 'The Medium is the Message'. This phrase is the title of the first chapter of Marshall McLuhan's book *Understanding Media. The Extensions of Man* (1994). McLuhan was influenced by Harold Innis – another Canadian scholar. Both theorists are considered the founders of the Toronto School of Communication which was interested in the impact of media and technologies on society. Based on their ideas, the history of communication is conceptualized in terms of various stages when certain media would arise and shape the way people understand and organize their world (e.g. Poe, 2011).

Media are often viewed as figure, not ground; in other words, we tend to think of media as something that stands out, e.g. newspapers, radio and television, Internet sites, etc., rather than something that forms the very basis or infrastructure of our lives. Meanwhile, because "forgetting seems to be a key part of the way infrastructure works" (Peters, 2015, p. 36), we must remember that media are the very foundational framework (ground) of our being. Simply put, since we can't communicate by telepathy, we need a medium – an intermediary agency – between others and ourselves. McLuhan understood the importance of media very well; in the phrase 'the medium is the message', however, 'the message' can't be equated with content that supposedly changes depending on the medium in which it is expressed; for example, the expression 'it is raining' does not have two different 'contents' (messages) if it is pronounced orally or written down. Rather, the message of a medium is the sum total of all the changes in the world that it creates: it is our life transformed by a new medium. As McLuhan reminds us, technologies are active processes that reshape both people and other technologies (McLuhan, 1962).

This view of media is very broad and somewhat equivocal: "in effect, all of McLuhan's reasoning is dominated by a series of equivocations very troubling to a theoretician of communication, because the differences between the *channel* of communication, the *code*, and the *message* are not established" (Eco, 1986, p. 234). We must, therefore, clearly differentiate between these terms. The message is content (to be) communicated. The code is a system of units with rules for their combination. The channel is a medium through which a message is communicated. For instance, what you're reading now is a message; created with the help of English as a code; and communicated through a print medium (if you're holding a paper book in your hands) or an electronic medium (if you're reading it on an electronic device such as a computer or an iPhone). It is important to note that a medium can be any intermediary agency between people that allows them to communicate with one another, e.g. fire or sand.

## 2.1. The Signs of the Time

We will use different expressions for the 'medium' and the 'message'. In place of the 'medium' we will speak of the 'The Signs of the Time', i.e., anything that captures meaning and preserves it through time, e.g. songs, dance, paintings, tombs. It is easy to see how this expression covers the medium as such, e.g. human voice or paint; codes, e.g. music or body language; and messages with various meanings, e.g. a song about love.

All such 'Signs of the Time' are meaningful marks and thus semantic and semiotic in nature. Both 'semantic' (relating to meaning) and 'semiotic' (relating to signs) go back to the Greek *sēma* ('mark', 'sign'). The crucial prerequisite for successful communication is "the recognition of the *sēma* 'sign'" (Nagy, 1996, p. 203); an example is a scene from Homer's *Odyssey*: "Penelope's 'recognizing' . . . the *sēmata* [plural of *sēma*] specified by the disguised Odysseus as the clothes given to the real Odysseus by Penelope herself" (ibid.). While the origins of semiotics lie in medical science, the signs used in human communication, unlike natural symptoms such as a rash, are conventional and so can be understood only in specific cultural contexts. That is why "the recognition of the *sēma* implicitly requires an act of interpretation" (ibid.). When we talk about the Signs of the Time, we will look at how they are recognized and interpreted.

We have mentioned 'tombs' as a Sign of the Time. This may not be the first thing that comes to mind when thinking about meaningful marks; and yet, the Greek *sêma* also meant 'a tomb' and 'a grave' and can be considered one of the oldest meaning-storage devices (Peters, 2015, p. 145). Indeed, as long as we can recognize certain structures as tombs and interpret them (e.g. is the tomb a burial of a king or a tribal leader?), the dead are communicating with us through time. It can be said that they have lived to tell the tale – even through death! All Signs of the Time tell a certain tale.

## 2.2. Telling a Tale

Just as we will speak of the 'Signs of the Time' in place of the 'medium,' we will use 'tale' in place of the 'message'. First, a 'tale' means a narrative of real or imaginary events, a story: thus it has a broad meaning. It is important to note that "time becomes human to the extent that it is articulated through a narrative mode, and narrative attains its full meaning when it becomes a condition of temporal existence" (Ricoeur, 1984, p. 52). In other words, humans telling tales and time go hand in hand. Second, a 'tale' means a recital of events or happenings; in other words, it is an imaginative inter-action in which people can actively participate. And, third, the archaic meaning of 'tale' is 'a tally or reckoning, a total'; in this sense, 'tale' stands for anything that matches another thing and is used for an account or reckoning (including the reckoning of time). Overall, the meaning of 'tale' is something like 'an account of things in their due order'; thus, a certain 'medium' tells a certain 'tale' or creates a certain 'message'.

So we will use the expression 'the Signs of the Time' in place of the 'medium' and 'Telling a Tale' in place of the 'message'. It must be emphasized that our view of their relationship is not deterministic. We do not claim that the medium *is* the message; rather, we speak of the medium *and* the message. Let us see how people have dealt with time through the ages by creating certain signs that tell a certain tale.

## 3. LIVING THE DREAMING

Let us begin with the so-called 'Tribal Stage' that McLuhan in *The Gutenberg Galaxy* (1962) identified as the first era in the social evolution of modern humanity, which covers the period from the time that people acquired oral speech to the beginnings of literacy. The word 'tribal' has a number of negative connotations, associated with primitiveness, crudity, backwardness and superstition. 'Tribal' people are often portrayed as savage and irrational: after all, these are the people whose beliefs are centered on the veneration of various objects (totems) such as plants or animal skins. It was assumed, for instance, "that Aboriginal inhabitants were already doomed to a timeless, un-evolving fate" (Leane, 2010, p. 36), leading to the colonization of the indigenous people there. The same reasoning was used to support colonization in other places such as Africa, Americas and New Zealand.

And yet, the words 'tribal' and 'totemism' are very complex in meaning and have deep historical roots. The word 'tribal' came to denote 'modern ethnic groups or races of people' only in the 16th century. The roots of the word go back much further, meaning 'a dwelling', 'being', 'existing', 'coming to be' and 'happening'. Similarly, the word 'totemism' is derived from the term *ototeman* in the Ojibwe language, meaning 'brother-sister kin', with 'kin', in its turn, going back to the root that means 'to produce,' 'give birth' and 'beget'. In this light, such meanings can't be 'crude' and 'backwater'; in fact, we could perhaps learn something from them.

So, how fair is it to talk about the tribal cultures being 'doomed' and in need of 'rescuing'? What is really meant by their 'timeless' nature? The Tribal Stage clearly deserves more attention with a special focus on the role of time in communication. To that end, let us look at the culture of Australian aboriginals. It makes good sense to focus on Australian aboriginals as an exemplar of the Tribal Stage: after all, the Australian aboriginal culture is said to be the oldest continuous living culture in the world. Significantly, the word 'aborigines' is derived from '*ab origine*' and literally means 'from the beginning'.

## 3.1. The Signs of the Time

In the past, the media that we routinely use today, such as print or electronic currents, did not exist. People had to use whatever was readily available to them and what we often take for granted. Let us first turn to sound – "by far the most important medium" (Peters, 2015, p. 73), which is as ubiquitous as breathing.

It is the very sound of a human voice that provides a basis for the culture's continuity and solidifies its group identity. We can mention oral aboriginal stories that include numerous genres, e.g. babies' stories, children's stories, horror stories, love stories, etc. Also, aboriginal songs must be mentioned, with language that is usually markedly different from everyday speech and typically allusive. Songs, too, are characterized by various genres, e.g. sorcerers' songs, 'gossip songs,' which usually complained about sexual infidelity and 'ganhil' – a sort of extemporaneous song, which allowed people to praise or abuse others with impunity (Ross, 1986). Overall, the Australian aboriginal tribes are connected by the so-called 'songlines' – "both traditional songs and invisible tracks which crisscross Australia in a complex web" (Eberle, 1994, p. 82). By following these pathways, the aborigines can navigate the open spaces of the country and, more importantly, have endured through time.

Just like their songs, Australian aboriginal dancing can appear very strange to Westerners. For example, one of the earliest written records of aboriginal dancing in Canada is found in the diaries of Jacques Cartier, who wrote in 1534 of "wild men . . . dancing and making many signs of joy and mirth" (Hopkins, 1898, p. 236). However, similar to music, dancing is integral to Australian aborigines' expression and continues to be practiced today.

What happens to the body when the dance of life stops is also very important; hence the disposal of human corpses as a cultural practice. In Australian aboriginal cultures, the dead were sometimes exposed to the elements for eventual disintegration, e.g. placed in trees, on a raised platform, or covered in native plants, sometimes buried, and sometimes cremated. Cremation and burial were the most common methods of body disposal. New evidence from Lake Mungo in Western New South Wales shows that Indigenous Australians were cremating their dead at least 40,000 years ago.

Stories, songs, music, dance and even burials can be seen as art, in the sense of the Greek *poíēsis*, i.e., 'making', 'production', or 'composition'. For some crafts, as we just saw, aborigines use the media to which they have a direct access – the sound of their own voice and their own body. For other crafts, they use natural media, i.e., those that are literally found in natural environments around them.

To Australian aborigines, music is not something separate from life that must be analyzed in order to understand and enjoy; rather, music is an integral part of life. In making their instruments, Aboriginal Australians use the media that are readily available, e.g. boomerang clapsticks for producing percussive sound, animal skins for drums, or a naturally hollow tree for wind instruments. As a result, the Australian aborigines' music, with its monotonous and somewhat indefinite rhythm, may sound strange to the Western ear, and yet it provides a living fabric for their culture.

Australian aboriginal art is made from bark, flowers, dirt, crushed seeds, etc. and mixed natural earth pigments such as ochre. Aboriginal tribes have been using these materials to create various adornments and paint their bodies for thousands of years. Australian aborigines have also used sand as a medium; drawing from the ground is a famous cultural practice when they just sit, talk and simultaneously draw in the sand, smoothing it over after making a point and starting again (Green, 2014) (Figure 1.2).

While sand drawing may appear to be a mundane and even meaningless pastime, it has been recognized by UNESCO as a Masterpiece of the Oral and Intangible Heritage of Humanity, described as a rich and dynamic means of communication.

Thus, Australian aborigines combine in their communication different media, such as the voice and the body, alongside natural mediums such as sand, to create complex messages. The best example of a communicative event in which all these media find their manifestation at the same time

**Figure 1.2**    Alice Springs Desert Park, aboriginal sand drawing. © Tourism NT.

is the so-called *corroboree* – an important dancing ceremony that often mimics the movements and behaviors of animals, sometimes performed spontaneously, and always with symbolic meaning. At a *corroboree*, "you might have four different totemic clans, from any number of different tribes, all of whom would swap their songs, dances, . . . and grant each other 'rights of way'" (Chatwin, 1988, p. 58). In other words, a *corroboree* is the prototype for communication where meanings are exchanged and the laws of inter-action established. At such events, Australian aborigines interact with the ancestral totemic spirit beings of The Dreaming so their culture is recreated and reinforced. Let us see what tale is narrated by and at the Dreaming.

## 3.2. Telling a Tale

Australian indigenous peoples' life is guided by a complex system of relations – among themselves as well as their relationships with the environment – which is based on the Dreaming when ancestral Totemic Spirit Beings formed the Creation. The Australian aboriginal conception of time is very subtle. The Dreaming is usually presented as atemporal or time-less (TenHouten, 2005, p. 152). However, Australian anthropologist W. E. H. Stanner captured its complexity perhaps best of all when he said that "it was and is everywhen" (Stanner, 1979, pp. 23–24). Thus, since it is 'everywhen', it is more accurate to speak of their culture as timeful: they live in time and do not feel any desire to contemplate it or make predictions about a future. For them, time is literally grounded in place.

Australian aboriginal people place utmost importance on 'the place', or the entire earthly environment made by the Ancestor Spirits. The land, with all its hills, rocks, mountains, etc., is the source of the culture's potency, dreamed into existence.

As we remember, sound is the most important medium of communication for tribal cultures. Such cultures exist in 'acoustic space', which McLuhan calls "the 'mind's ear' or acoustic imagination" (McLuhan, 2004, p. 71). It is important to note that 'acoustic space' has no fixed boundaries and no fixed directionality: the ear "favors sound from any direction. We hear equally well from right or left, front or back, above or below.... There is nothing in auditory space corresponding to the vanishing point in visual perspective" (Carpenter & McLuhan, 1960, pp. 67–68). While the eye pinpoints objects in physical space against a certain background, the ear is open to the entire world and it does not matter from what (back)ground the sound comes. In other words, while "the perspectival world is primarily visual" (Gebser, 1985, p. 146), (the atemporal) acoustic space is aperspectival. When we speak about "putting time into perspective" (Zimbardo & Boyd, 1999), 'perspective' is used in the figurative sense of a 'mental outlook over time', not in the meaning related to the realm of optics. Thus, the aperspectival world is primarily acoustic: "Its resonant and interpenetrating processes are simultaneously related with centers everywhere and boundaries nowhere" (McLuhan, 2004, p. 71).

So, for Australian aboriginal people the Dreaming is not only 'everywhen', it is also 'everywhere'. The place, due to its acoustic nature, is meaningful in its entirety, not just this or that object. In other words, for them it is not a matter of perspective: it all matters. Everything is alive and sacred! Also, the best way to identify with the Dreaming is through listening to the land. When we listen, we don't have to move: we just are. And, when we are aware, we revere and respect everything that is meaningful and are filled with awe for its mysterious potency.

### 3.2.1. Letting the Mystery Be!

The nature of time has always been considered mysterious – elusive and illusive. Tribal cultures never try to discover the secret of time or to demystify it: they are comfortable just being one with it, constantly enacting it. James Carey wrote of two views of communication – the transmission view "directed toward the extension of messages in space" and the ritual view directed "toward the maintenance of society in time; not the act of imparting information but the representation of shared beliefs" (1989, p. 18). Tribal cultures are an example of the second view: their communication is not so much transmitting received knowledge as acts of performance that allow the culture to stay alive and endure. It is important to note that every culture is a holistic system that an individual can never leave and look at the entire system from the outside: people in tribal cultures seem to understand it well and have the wisdom to let the mystery be. The act of 'letting' may appear too simple because it sounds as though it requires little or no effort. However, nothing is as difficult and as important as 'letting it be', i.e., 'allowing to remain'. By letting the mystery be, Australian aboriginal people are allowing everything to remain alive.

Every act of ritual communication as enactment of meaning seems ephemeral and immediate; yet, it is through such fleeting acts as songs, dances and drawing that our very life endures – we endure. Perhaps Shakespeare thought of tribal cultures when he set his *Tempest* on an island and wrote: "We are such stuff as dreams are made on"?

While sound is the most important – and the most immediate – medium, Australian aboriginal people's ritual of using sand for story-telling captures the performative nature of communication best of all. When the Dreaming stories are being told, they are accompanied by drawings on sand that are made and then erased. This is possible because "sand drawing is a form of writing, and erasure is in the nature of the medium" (Brody, 1981, p. 11). It must be noted that sand drawings are different from early cave painting: they are cleared away as soon as the story is complete. Everyone participating in such acts of enactment of meaning is drawn into existence then and there; similarly, everyone is talked, sung and even buried into existence.

While it is common to say that sand drawings are intended to be erased quickly after creation, the verb 'to erase' does not seem to be the best one to describe the ritual. The medium is not really 'removed' or 'scraped out'; rather, sand is 'evened up, 'leveled up' or 'smoothed over'. The difference is very significant because we can then vividly see the egalitarian nature of the culture that endures through time by keeping the playing field level, so to speak. It is in tribal cultures that we find the roots of egalitarianism which is typically viewed as a trend of thought in political philosophy with the key idea of all humans being equal in fundamental worth or moral status. Equality that lies at the basis of egalitarianism goes back to such meanings as 'evenness', 'smoothness' and 'uniformity', and we can physically see those meanings as aboriginal Australians draw their stories in the sand and then even it up, smoothing it over so that the culture can remain uniform where everyone is consonant with others.

So, what is the gist of the narrative told by Australian aborigines? On the one hand, they do not seem to pay much attention to time because their communication occurs 'everywhen'. On the other hand, because of their primarily acoustic word, they seem to interact with one another without boundaries and so their communication takes place 'everywhere'. Both 'everywhen' and 'everywhere' begin with 'every'. 'Every' goes back to the Old English 'æfre ælc' which means 'each of a group,' or literally 'ever each' (Chaucer's 'everich'). Cultures can best endure if each of the group plays an equal role in communication: this is the narrative that the Australian aborigines have been telling us for thousands of years.

Thus, the so-called 'Tribal Stage' of humanity, which we discussed using the culture of Australian aborigines as an exemplar, is characterized by simple and ephemeral mediums, and yet, a complex and lasting message. While concrete messages seem to disappear, similar to sand drawings that are constantly smoothed over, the overall tale is preserved in the embodied form, committed to memory and known by heart: communication connects 'ever each' with 'ever each' in/to one 'drawing' that presents a model or way of behavior. One can see parallels between this view of communication and the concept of Tao, e.g.: "The Aboriginal perspective is in many ways very close to the Taoist viewpoint" (Coward, 1995, p. 11).

The Tribal Stage of *Homo loquens* ('Speaking Man') can be summarized as follows (Table 1.1):

**Table 1.1**    *Homo loquens* ('Speaking Man')

| DOMINANT MEDIUM | ORAL |
|---|---|
| Time Perception | 'Timeful' ('everywhen') |
| Examples of Signs of Time | Songs, music, dance, sand drawing |
| Message | Communication connects 'ever each' with 'ever each'. Cultures can best endure if each of the group plays an equal role in communication. |

## 4. AS ABOVE, SO BELOW

When humans were connected to the place, they didn't try to control it; rather, they listened to their environment where they found meanings and enacted them. In a way, the place had power over people, which they didn't try to challenge or predict; rather, they found it nurturing and mysterious, letting it be.

Gradually, people started to share power with the external world, as it were, adapting to its cyclical nature. According to Émile Durkheim, the rhythm of social life formed the foundation for temporality (1964). However, we should not forget the opposite view, e.g. expressed by Maurice Bloch, that time is grounded in the external world (Bloch, 1977). Time, of course, cannot be completely reduced to environmental, cosmological, biological and natural factors. And yet, "it seems obvious that a civilization that develops in an area with stark, clearly observable weather patterns that determine sustenance might view the world more generally through cycles" (Brettler, 2004, pp. 114–115). On the one hand, in some cases, as in equatorial cultures, little or no variation in the environment cycles can be observed. On the other hand, depending on location there may be too much variation, going well beyond the four-season European climate description of summer, autumn, winter and spring. It is the happy medium, so to speak, when clearly observable weather patterns are not (almost) non-existent and are not too changeable, that gives rise to the cyclical view of the world.

Many ancient cultures share this cyclic view of time; while they may differ in specific details, this perception of time is found in such cultures as Sumerian, Egyptian, Babylonian, Ancient and Classical Greek and Roman, Indian (Hindu, Buddhist), and in the Ottoman Empire. In all these cultures we can see how slowly timefulness gives way to temporality in the form of tangible periodicity. As a result, it becomes possible to measure time in terms of its various extents (periods). For instance, the Hindu cosmic cycle is measured in *yugas*; there are four *yugas* forming a cycle which totals 4,320,000 years (Fagg, 1985, p. 81).

It is common to visualize cyclical time as a circle. However, while this metaphor may be helpful in understanding the nature of temporality that is closed off, it must be noted that cycles are not identical with circles: a cycle is a uniform process of movements from a specifiable point to the same point. For instance, a digital clock displaying minutes from 00 to 59 and then 00 again is an example of a cycle, not a circle (cf. MacDonald, 2013).

In other words, human power presupposes an increase in abstract thinking; the nature of cyclical time, while grounded in the external world, is both perceptual *and* conceptual.

## 4.1. Time in Ancient Egypt

We will focus on Egypt as an exemplar of the cyclic view of time. Time was clearly perceived by the ancient Egyptians as "not a progress but a rhythm" (Boorstin, 1992, p. 156). Where did that rhythm, which found its best manifestation in the successive reigns of the pharaohs, come from?

Above the Earth, the ancient Egyptians admired the perfectly uniform movement of the stars – and tried to measure the time of their activities accordingly. Whereas the Babylonians viewed the moon as the universal measure of time, the Egyptians went beyond the nocturnal cycle by discovering the length of the solar year. In fact, the English word 'hour' is derived from the Latin and Greek *hora*, which in turn originated from the ancient Egyptian 'hor', meaning 'the sun's path', named from Horus – their "god of the dawn" (Penprase, 2011, p. 138). The sun's path, of course, was observed by its shadow using the sundial – an upright stake placed in the ground. Such a seemingly simple tool – a stake pointing upward – was a revolutionary invention: it was an analog clock that allowed people to conduct their regular activities during the daytime (Figure 1.3).

Whereas the Australian aborigines smoothed the sand over after each drawing, keeping the playing field level for everyone, the ancient Egyptians looked up toward the sun; it is here, perhaps, that we can see the origins of the so-called 'horizontal communication' and 'vertical communication'. Horizontal communication, oriented toward equality, takes place within the same level of an organization, while vertical communication occurs between different levels of the organizational hierarchy.

Down on the Earth, the cyclic activities of the ancient Egyptians were determined by the Nile; the welfare of the entire culture literally depended on how its flows were regulated. In the words of Herodotus who visited Egypt in about 450 B.C., "Egypt is the gift of the Nile" (Griffiths, 1966, p. 57). Not surprisingly, solstice and the Nile-flows were considered the turning points of the old Egyptian year. However, there was always the danger of an eclipse of the sun or the floods of the Nile and many rituals were performed to avert such possible evils. In Assyria and Babylonia, for instance, "not only were

**Figure 1.3**    Surf drifts up close to a beach sundial at 1 PM. Photo by Cate Frost/ Shutterstock.com.

royal events fixed according to the scholarly calendar but also great out-lays of wealth and specialist personnel were expended on matters temporal. Enormous and elaborate public rituals . . . were designed . . . to control and manage present and future" (Robson, 2004, p. 82). What were the Signs of the Time showing that communication in ancient Egypt was orderly and thus predictable?

## 4.2. The Signs of the Time

As we saw earlier, during the Tribal Stage living equaled the Dreaming: it was the pattern that connected – through timeful communication – 'ever each' with 'ever each'. This way, by which life was Dreamt or the Dream was lived, can be called 'survivance' (Vizenor, 1999). Whether seen as a combi-nation of 'survival' and 'endurance' or 'survival' and 'resistance', this term captures well how cultures exist in and through time simultaneously. The spectral nature of such existence is rendered by the suffix '-ance' that can't be identified either with the active or the passive voice, i.e., either with the subject or the object. Thus, "the whole experience" was "a kind of dream . . . It was a life without self-examination" (Havelock, 1963, p. 190).

Using Havelock's phrase, it's possible to say that people in such cultures live in a kind of hypnotic trance. What caused them to wake up? The answer is found in the new form of communication – writing, which "is unquestionably the most 'momentous' of all technical innovations in human history" (Peters, 2015, p. 208). Let us see why the eye (reading) became more important than the ear (listening) and why writing is such a momentous innovation by looking at a number of shifts it caused in human lives.

*Shift from commonality to individuality.*    A written word is different from a spoken word; as the Russian saying puts it, 'A (spoken) word is not a sparrow: once it flies out, you can't catch it'. Thanks to writing, however, if you missed it, you can try and catch the word again. You can also spend more time looking at it and thinking about its meaning: "you could as it were take a second look at it" (Havelock, 1963, p. 208). With a spoken word, you can't take a second listen. This seemingly simple difference between speaking and writing is extremely significant. One has now the luxury (or the curse) of separating oneself from the word, unlike the 'immediate' experience of oral communication that is beyond our control in which words are gone the moment they fly out like sparrows. It should be noted, however, that there's always a small temporal gap between uttering and hearing a word and so speech and hearing are not really simultaneous; that's why we can speak about the 'immediate' experience of oral communication only in quotes. But, "our senses are too dull to notice this small gap" (Peters, 2015, p. 93) this small gap. As a result, the whole experience of oral communication appears as a kind of dream. Once writing allows people to separate themselves from the word, they can spend more time dwelling not in, but on, their own communicative experience; thus self-consciousness is born or, to use Havelock's metaphor, "the conception of 'me thinking about Achilles' rather than 'me identifying with Achilles'" (1963, p. 209).

*Shift from remembrance to memorizing.*    As already mentioned, separating oneself from the word can be seen as a blessing or a curse: the most well-known argument for the latter is found in Plato's *Phaedrus* where written marks are viewed as implanting forgetfulness in people's souls. Plato believes that once people start relying on such artificial external marks, they will cease to exercise memory and stop calling things to remembrance from within themselves. Remembrance was at the heart of oral culture and functioned in the form of commemoration when everyone was brought together in a holistic event in which it was impossible to separate oneself from the overall experience (Hobart & Schiffman, 2000). It can be noted that the word 'remembrance' has the same spectral suffix '-ance' as 'survivance', suggesting an experience where no clear-cut boundaries between subjects and objects can be drawn. With writing, and people separated from the word by/in time, a shift occurs from remembrance to memory as a container for information. The art of memory (Latin: *ars memoriae*) now includes various techniques of organizing impressions and improving their recall. Whereas a culture bound together by commemoration as a living entity needs no external aids, now more emphasis is placed on various mnemonic devices to store more information.

*Shift from communication to documentation.*   Plato was critical of writing as a means of direct communication because he saw its purpose as storing and preserving knowledge. Everything that is significant and valuable is reserved for oral communication, whereas writing must be used primarily for the purpose of documentation. Not surprisingly, thanks to writing, annals and chronicles became common; for instance, in ancient Egypt the annual records of the rulers and the fortunes of their kingdoms go back to before 3000 B.C.

*Shift from number to numeral.*   Although in pre-literate cultures people could certainly count, those cultures in which numbers were present as numerals developed what Friedrich A. Kittler calls 'the media of mathematics', i.e., the transformation of numbers as a matter of hearing into numerals as a matter of reading and writing (2006). The ancient Egyptians even had a symbol for infinity and a symbol for zero that was the same as the hieroglyph for beauty! Once people started expressing numbers numerically in various ways, they gained more power in representing their experiences; in this respect, establishing a numerical relationship was "a small leap of the mind" (Havelock, 1963, p. 210).

Thus, with the invention of writing an overall shift was taking place from living in and dreaming the world to its visual representation in various codes, i.e., different systems of writing. The hieroglyphic (non-alphabetical) system, used in ancient Egypt, was unique: it contained not only pictograms but also phonograms – symbols that had phonetic value. Although that system made for considerable versatility in communicating experiences, meaning still was quite open to interpretation that depended on the context: for instance, one and the same symbol can mean 'sun' or 'light'. So, for the most part, the Egyptian hieroglyphic system had a dual nature: some symbols conveyed meaning through pictorial resemblance to objects and some by representing a vocal sound. To avoid confusion in interpretation, the so-called 'determinatives' were sometimes used – symbols that were not pronounced but placed next to other symbols to help in understanding the correct meaning.

A good metaphor for the memory contained within hieroglyphs is the wax tablet widely used in ancient Egypt. While the wax surface was used to represent an object, it couldn't convey all the complexity of information associated with it; also, the inscription in soft wax could be easily erased. Just like a garment, people were 'wearing' memory in the form of a wax tablet (Draaisma, 2000). Thus, the memory contained within hieroglyphs has a dual nature: an external artificial device (a prosthetic), on the one hand, and information stored internally in the mind, on the other.

Although the Egyptian writing system contained phonograms, hieroglyphs were, first and foremost, the visual signs that were sacred; Thoth, the god of writing, was called 'the lord of divine speech' (Figure 1.4).

**Figure 1.4**   Thoth, the god of writing. Image from the Travelers in the Middle East Archive (TIMEA).

Thus, 'divine speech' referred to the visual signs and not to the sounds. Moreover, for the Egyptians, the 'divine speech' that endured through time, while focusing on the graphic nature of hieroglyphic script, was also manifested in two other closely related areas – rituals and art (especially monumental art).

Funerary procedure was one of the most important rituals in ancient Egypt. What may appear to be a simple physical process of putting a dead body in a grave was, in fact, an elaborate ritual of making sure a body is preserved for continuing its cycle in another lifetime. The ritual included mummification – a process of embalming a body; placing the body in a burial tomb; the 'Opening of the Mouth' ceremony when the mourners through prayers symbolically opened the mummy's mouth so that the person could breathe, eat and drink in the afterlife; and, finally, sealing the tomb.

Egyptian art included sculptures, crafts such as metalwork, paintings, and murals that often decorated the tombs of nobles. Naturally, "the visual communicative act depends on the stability of the social framework" and "a common cultural background or a framework of shared knowledge" (Hartwig, 2015, p. 51). But, first and foremost, Egyptian art depended on the stability of the medium: we can now enjoy so many wonderful works because they were made of durable materials such as parchment, clay and, most importantly, stone – what Innis called 'the time-biased media' (Innis, 1971). The most famous and enduring form of monumental art of the Ancient Egyptians is the pyramid – "the sign . . . resisting time, the hard text of stones covered with inscription" (Derrida, 1982, p. 83). And the most famous stone, of course, is the Rosetta Stone on which the writing was carved in three different languages – Hieroglyphics (top), Demotic (middle) and Greek (bottom). The inscription was deciphered only in 1822 by Jean-François Champollion, and "what a joy it must have been [for Champollion] to open this one-way communication channel with another civilization, to permit a culture that had been mute for millennia to speak of its history, magic, medicine, religion, politics and philosophy" (Sagan, 1980, p. 296). What was that message that was silent for thousands of years and that Champollion brought to the world – "a message not across space, but across time" (Sagan, 1980, p. 296)?

## 4.3. Telling a Tale

As mentioned earlier, in the repetition of natural cycles such as the phases of the sun and the seasons, there was always a danger of something outside of the normal (cyclical) flow of time, for instance, an eclipse of the sun or a flood. The ancient Egyptians thus lived with a constant fear of annihilation. It is not surprising, therefore, that they looked for an ordered life with predictability and regularity. Such order was personified by Ma'at – the goddess of truth, justice and harmony who affirmed the balance of things and who was depicted as a woman wearing an ostrich feather on her head – a symbol of the principles she represented.

The social structure of ancient Egypt was structured like a pyramid with the pharaoh at the top followed by several tiers below him: high government officials such as the chief treasurer and the army general; priests and nobles; soldiers and scribes; craftsmen and merchants; farmers and unskilled workers; and slaves. Everything was organized along hierarchical lines; significantly, both 'hierarchy' and 'hieroglyphs' come from the same Greek word *hieros* – 'sacred'; thus, the hierarchy was as sacred to the people of ancient Egypt as the hieroglyphs. This cyclical world order where everyone's life is based on where one is born into the hierarchy can be seen as a kind of the 'wheel of fortune', which taught everyone "to acquiesce and rest satisfied with whatever turns and changes the divine being may allot" (Plutarch, *Life of Numa*, 14.5; quoted in Ewbank, 1842, p. 118) (Figure 1.5).

The pharaoh, as the living representation of Ma'at on Earth, was the ultimate upholder of the universal order. We see the influence of such theocracy, as a form of government on behalf of a deity, not only in antique times but also through the Middle Ages. The following lines from Alexander Pope's poem *Essay on Man*, written at the end of the 18th century, apply to ancient Egypt well: "Order is Heav'n's first law; and this confess'd, / Some are, and must be, greater than the rest, / More rich, more wise. . .". However, we shouldn't forget that Pope continues his poem thus: "but who infers from hence / That such are happier, shocks all common sense". In other words, the richer and the wiser are not happier than their impoverished counterparts because they happen to occupy a different position: happiness is experienced equally. In ancient Egypt everyone, whatever the social tier, had to perform his or her own duties, making sure the social wheel keeps rotating: only that way could the entire world avoid the danger of losing its order and continue to be saved.

What seems to be morbid obsession of the ancient Egyptians with death is, in fact, a part of the journey of life; hence "the intimate relationship between . . . cyclical cosmologies and salvation" (Fagg, 1985, p. 81). Salvation is guaranteed only when the culture goes through another cycle

**Figure 1.5**    Fortune and Her Wheel. Illustration from vol. 1 of Boccaccio's *De Casibus Virorum Illustrium* (*On the Fates of Famous Men*) (1467, Glasgow University Library).

and emerges safe, i.e., intact and whole. While later Christianity interpreted salvation as "the deliverance of mankind from its enslavement to the planetary powers, which determined human fate and fortune" (Brandon, 1972, p. 375), the ancient Egyptians all followed the cosmic order – 'Heav'n's first law'. It is important to emphasize in this respect that "in this cyclical cosmology the concept of salvation has to do not with redemption, but with renewal and 'keeping things going'" (Assmann, 2003, p. 209).

The Egyptians' desire to 'keep things going' shows the duality of their thinking: they tried to have it both ways, as it were, i.e., to *keep* time and to have it *going*. The latter was represented by the kind of time called 'Neheh' – the never-ending cyclical time in accordance with the movement of the heavenly bodies. The former was represented by 'Djet', or the kind of time associated with immutable permanence, or time at a standstill. Such suspended time was the ideal that the ancient Egyptians tried to reach when the earth and the sky become one and time stands still; "in other words, the Egyptians sought security from Time by becoming Time itself" (Brandon, 1972, p. 372). It is no accident that 'pyramid' means 'a place of ascension' – a stairway to heaven, i.e., to salvation.

Thus, ideal security in heaven could be guaranteed by the never-ending cycles of various acts of communication on Earth. Significantly, for the ancient Egyptians the symbol of salvation was the scarab whose pellet they compared to the globe of the sun. As long as the scarab rolls his pellet, the sun comes up and life continues. Thus, for the ancient Egyptians "everything hinged on precise reiteration" (Assmann, 2003, p. 71). Just as the scarab lives in 'Earth's soil', constantly reborn with the sun, on Earth it was the scribe who was central for making sure life continues by repeatedly using written signs to keep records of the ups and downs of their kingdoms. One can say that in ancient Egypt everything hinged on precise reiteration of the written word. In *The Ancient Egyptian Book of the Dead* we read: "That which can be named must exist. That which is named can be written. That which is written shall be remembered. That which is remembered lives" (2006, p. 272).

Although the ancient Egyptians feared various deviations from the cosmic order, they still had complete trust in its overall predictability and regularity. After all, such order was based on cyclical time that was not perceived as a scarce commodity because "there seems always to be an unlimited supply of it just around the next bend" (Lewis, 2006, p. 57). However, although he may have made plenty of time, 'God helps those who help themselves', as they say in the West, and we find the traces of such human agency and self-reliance already in ancient Egypt where people started to try helping God help them reach salvation.

Their efforts were not truly scientific in the modern sense of the word; for instance, many people were preoccupied with the so-called 'philosopher's stone' looking for the elixir of immortality. If, as recorded in Egyptian texts, Thoth and Hermes Trismegistus drank 'white drops' said to keep them immortal (Coulter-Harris, 2016, p. 35), surely that substance could be found! The alchemy laboratory with its experimentations and numerous bottles, herbs, potions and ovens, however, proved not enough to look at time differently. It took Giordano Bruno's poetic vision to challenge the idea that only fixed and regular motion of heavenly bodies was beautiful and acceptable. He dismantled the celestial clock and paved the way for a different view of time.

The Traditional Stage of *Homo scriptor* ('Writing Man') can be summarized as follows (Table 1.2):

**Table 1.2**   *Homo scriptor* ('Writing Man')

| DOMINANT MEDIUM | VISUAL (WRITING) |
| --- | --- |
| Time Perception | Cyclical |
| Examples of Signs of Time | Wax tablet, inscriptions on stone, monumental art |
| Message | Order hinged on precise reiteration of the written word. That which is written shall be remembered. That which is remembered lives. |

## 5. THE CLOCKWORK UNIVERSE

For centuries the cosmic order seemed stable as it went through unchanging cycles the way the scarab rolls his pellet or the scribe writes the sacred script with the same precision. However, it became more and more clear that it was impossible to reach immutable permanence by suspending time completely. The seemingly unchanging order based on cyclic time was first challenged by the Judeo-Christian tradition in which all the events that befell a chosen people were specific – a unique sequence not to be belittled by repetition. Thus, "while the heathens wander around in circles, Christians move toward the consummation represented by redemption" (Assmann, 2003, p. 13). Only by making this passage from beginning to end does it become possible "to set free the immortal soul", in the words of St. Augustine (*The City of God*, XII, 14). As Bossuet puts it so eloquently in his *Discours*, "Egypt, once so wise, stumbles along drunken, dizzy, because the Lord has spread giddiness in its designs; she no longer knows what she is doing, she is lost. But peoples should not fool themselves: When it pleases Him, God will straighten out those who err" (Fabian, 2014, p. 10). For that to happen, time had to be straightened into a line.

For Christians, human life is all about moving toward the consummation when the soul is saved, which has to do with its redemption and not with renewal and 'keeping things going' – the way the cyclical cosmology viewed the concept of salvation. Christianity, therefore, with its teleological conception of life, paved the way for the Modern Age where the linearity of time is fully manifested. In the words of Ivan Illich, "Modernity came into being only because people had experienced the world as lying in the hands of God and so it became possible, later on, to take that world out of God's hands" (Cayley, 2004, p. 69). In other words, modernity not so much invented the linear conception of time as secularized Judeo-Christian Time by generalizing and universalizing it.

The emergence of the linear view of time in the Modern Age was facilitated by a rapid increase in mobility: people now moved not only within a closed cyclical circle and not only following in the footsteps of the Savior, but also across borders. People now circulated more freely from place to place. Significantly, the word 'to circulate' acquires the meaning of 'moving about' only at the end of the 17th century; until then it meant 'to form a circle'. It is no accident that we speak of the circulation, and not the rotation, of money, emphasizing mobility and not simply cyclic movement.

As a result of expanding circulation, people explored otherness and so developed a greater cultural awareness paying more attention to difference, such as national difference, rather than the sameness found in the concept of an empire. The more people travelled and met others, the more they came to see and understand themselves through the others' eyes. Travel, then, was a vehicle for one's self-realization: the main discovery in the Modern Age was that of Self. As Michel Foucault says, 'man' as a concept did not exist during or before the Classical age and came into being only in the 18th century (Foucault, 1970). Of course, this is not to say that human beings as a species didn't exist until then; rather, it was only in the Modern Age that the self-consciousness of 'man' fully developed. The emergence of Self, in which everyone can move freely – across borders as well as in thought – led to "the ousting of religion as a time-setting authority, and as the highest authority in determining time" (Nowotny, 1994, p. 83). It is important to note that religion was simply 'ousted'; only later would God be declared 'dead'. The human, who could now produce anything, including time, occupied the place vacated by God, so a revolution was clearly underway. Although the origins of that revolution lie in the human mind where the idea of a powerful Self first appeared, we must look at the medium that helped to make that idea reality.

## 5.1. The Signs of the Time

As mentioned earlier, time was felt to be plentiful when people lived according to the unchanging cycles of the soil. With the industrial revolution, or the age of machines, things began to change (Figure 1.6).

Tools such as plows and sickles had been used before the industrial revolution, of course. However, their use followed the cycles of nature; in other words, nature drove the worker. The industrial economy not only moved the work environment indoors but also created machines for which the natural cycles were no longer relevant: now the time spent at work could be set by people themselves and so the pace of work could be regulated by/through the machine. As a result, life in the Modern Age became less organic and more mechanized: modern people are said to be those "who would sooner check the weather report than stick their heads out the window" (Peters, 2015, p. 254).

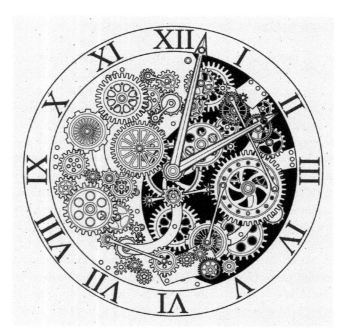

**Figure 1.6**    Clock mechanism with cogwheels. Photo by ONYXprj/Shutterstock. com.

Thus, once the concept of an individual Self was discovered, humans were able to translate its power into the machines that would allow them to exercise control over nature, as well as themselves. In *Technics and Civilization* Lewis Mumford identifies two such machines that exemplify the Modern Age best of all: "the clock was the most influential of machines, mechanically as well as socially. . . . Second to the clock in order if not perhaps in importance was the printing press" (2010, p. 134). Let us look at each separately.

### 5.1.1. The Clock

It is important to note that clocks had existed well before the Modern Age, e.g. shadow clocks (sundials) or water clocks. When Mumford writes about the clock as the most influential invention, he is talking about the mechanical clock that can control time through the mechanism of escapement. This mechanism is driven by the force from coiled springs or suspended weights, allowing the clock's gear train to 'escape' by a fixed amount: such regular advancement moves the clock's hands forward at a certain rate. In other words, whereas in the past humans could not escape the natural cycles of time, or the Order of Nature, now they can 'order nature' and have power over time, allowing it to 'escape' only when and how they choose.

Thanks to the mechanical clock, in the Modern Age time was straightened into a line. It is here that the so-called 'monochronic time' originates – a linear and compartmentalized order essential for the smooth functioning of a complex industrial society. Unlike polychronic time, which focuses more on interpersonal relations and less on pre-set schedules or clocks, monochronic time can be measured in regulated units and becomes crucial for the organization of any activities: it is no accident that monochronic time lies at the basis of organization communication in most contexts of bureaucracy, government and business.

Monochronic time exemplifies the so-called 'absolute or mathematical time', which, as Isaac Newton wrote at the beginning of his *Principia*, "of itself, and from its own nature, flows equally without relation to anything external" (1934, p. 6). It may seem as if monochronic time is a form of external order that originates outside the individual and thus is imposed on humans. However, it was the same mechanical clock that "dissociated time from human events and helped create the belief in an independent world of mathematically measurable sequences" (Mumford, 2010, p. 15). As Mumford goes on to explain: "Abstract time became the new medium of existence. Organic functions themselves were regulated by it: one ate, not upon feeling hungry, but when prompted by the clock; one slept, not when one was tired, but when the clock sanctioned it" (2010, p. 17). It is important to remember that the clock did not sanction human life by itself: behind the clock, the humans were setting various goals and then, based on those goals, setting the clock.

In industrial society the main goal was, of course, the production of goods and making profit: that is how time became a form of commodity in the Western industrialized world. Just like any product, time could now be 'saved', 'given', 'lost' or 'exchanged', and most often time was exchanged for money. As we read in the *Encyclopedia of Time*, "in the machine age, the notion of the linearity of time prevailed because time, following the laws of economics, was equated with money for the first time and thus made into a scarce resource" (Macey, 1994, p. 9). The early capitalists placed the clocks in factories behind closed doors to regulate workers' labor. Since only the factory owners and their representatives had access to the clocks, workers started to worry that the owners would slow the factory clocks to get more labor than they were paying for and soon portable clocks and watches began to appear (Dinwoodie, 2006, p. 334). It should be noted that the expression 'time is money' cannot be limited only to the business sector: in the private sphere (for example, at home) time could be treated as a scarce resource as well. Therefore, the linear conception of time can influence various aspects of both mass and interpersonal communication.

### 5.1.2. The Printing Press

Earlier, we saw how writing, as a visual medium, drastically changed communication and the role of time in it. However, it was print, while still a visual medium, that proved to be truly revolutionary and opened up new modes of communication.

It is important to note that, just like clocks, printing existed well before the Modern Age. Centuries before Johannes Gutenberg's famous invention, so-called 'block printing', in which wooden blocks coated with ink were pressed to paper, was used in China, Japan and Korea. They even tried to develop movable characters out of clay and wood – not the most durable media. Even movable metal type is said to have been invented in Korea almost one hundred years before Gutenberg's, and "one can only wonder if the Korean invention . . . was communicated to Europe, resulting in its re-invention by Gutenberg" (Wilson, 2003, p. 19). So Gutenberg made the printing process more efficient, which, of course, does not diminish its revolutionary nature. With his background as a goldsmith, he developed a press that used movable metal type in which separate characters for each letter, number and punctuation mark could be arranged in any desired order. As a result, the same type could be reused and reset to print mass varieties of standardized texts.

The clock and the printing press were the two most unique and thus important (visual) media of the Modern Age. Unlike all other machines that created tangible products, e.g. textiles or steamboats, the clock and the printing press produced information. Let us now look at the message that the clock and the printing press helped to bring into the world.

### 5.1.3. Telling a Tale

Many significant changes in human life were stimulated by the new media.

*Individuality.*    When a person realizes his or her potential as someone different from others, we talk about individuality (not to be confused with individualism as its egoistic deformation). The Modern Age brought the uniqueness of the individual to the forefront.

*Freedom.*    Every individual is seen as free to reject the claims of any authority; the person is free to think for himself/herself and act accordingly.

*Rationality.*    The individual's actions must be governed by deliberation and calculated thought.

*Mediatization.*    The Modern Age saw consequential interrelations between mass media and socio-cultural changes, including communication between institutions and between institutions and individuals. Unlike mediation, which denotes communication processes in general, mediatization refers to the large-scale processes that change the relationship between media, culture and society.

All these ideas were brought together by the Modern Age into a coherent message known as a grand narrative or a metanarrative, which was meant to give an overall meaning to various socio-cultural phenomena with an appeal to universal values. It is sometimes stated that the grand narrative of the industrial revolution "consisted in the mostly forced and painful habituation of people to the temporal requirements of the machine and its economic conditions of production" (Nowotny, 1994, p. 63). However, this mentions only one side of the Modern Age and does not address the true goal of modernity expressed in its metanarrative: the emancipation and progress that humanity can achieve through technology and scientific knowledge. As Thomas Carlyle put it in his *Sartor Resartus*, he who "had invented the Art of Printing" created "a whole new Democratic world" (1831, p. 85).

The key ideas of this metanarrative are found in the works of two thinkers most directly associated with the advent of the Modern Age – Francis Bacon and Thomas Hobbes. Bacon's major work is *Novum Organum Scientiarum* in which he presents science as the new instrument in the human quest for a true understanding of nature. Only science "would bring together the 'mind of man' with 'the nature of things' *for the advancement of humankind*" (Merchant, 2008, p. 756; emphasis added). Similarly, Hobbes in the introduction to *Leviathan* – his great 'discourse of Common-wealth,' – calls on the reader to 'Know thyself' (Latin: *nosce teipsum*). When he cast individuals as mechanical, he did so for a reason: as machines, people are made up of the same motions and are, therefore, all equal.

Thus, the metanarrative of the Modern Age has a clear message: rational thought, by using the new medium of communication, would lead to full realization of everyone's potential. Human life thus does not go in cycles but progresses in a linear fashion toward that goal. The term 'master narrative', introduced by Jean-François Lyotard (1984) and often used as synonymous with 'grand narrative' and 'metanarrative' captures this message perhaps best of all. The main goal of the Modern Age is the mastery or control of the environment – physical, moral, political, cultural and social. Most importantly, however, it is the mastery of Self that must be achieved and that can guarantee progress in all other realms. It can be said that Self is the main product of modernity: only through self-realization can social equality be achieved.

Without a doubt, the Modern Age brought many benefits to people (and not only economic wealth): expanded individual freedom of interactions and mobility as well as an increased media freedom, new social and political identities including voluntary associations and movements, wider participation in cultural processes, more tolerant treatment of people with different backgrounds, etc. At the same time, there is a dark side of modernity (and also not only in the economic sphere): alienation, reification of social relations (when people are viewed as objects or 'things') and what Jürgen Habermas calls the 'colonization of lifeworld' by the systems of steering media, such as power and money (Habermas, 1989). In this light, it is even sometimes stated that "modernity is nothing but information masked as communication" (Catt, 2011, p. 140).

## 5.2. Running Out of Steam

Every grand narrative functions to legitimize certain power or authority: in the Modern Age it is the power of the human who challenged the authority of nature and God. The more ideas making up this grand narrative are accepted throughout a culture, the more natural it appears. These ideas, which conceptualize various experiences, can be seen as myths – only not as the stories of the tribal or ancient societies, but as what Roland Barthes calls 'the myths of the second order of signification' (1972). Such myths take the existing signs and add to them an additional meaning. For instance, 'the city' denotes a large and permanent human settlement of significant size and importance: this is the first order of signification. In the Modern Age, however, the city began to be mythologized, i.e., to have an additional (connotative) meaning of something civilized and good, as opposed to the countryside. Linear time was mythologized the same way and the more natural it appeared, the longer "the machine age, with its dominant conception of linear time, was able to remain unchallenged" (Nowotny, 1994, p. 83).

However, the writing for the Modern Age was already on the wall, and who would express it better than Shakespeare? The following lines are often quoted as the glorification of 'the modern man': "What a piece of work is a man! How noble in reason, how infinite in faculty! In form and moving how express and admirable! In action how like an angel! In apprehension how like a god!" As he continues, though, Hamlet's monologue gets darker and more sarcastic: "The beauty of the world! The paragon of animals! And yet to me, what is this quintessence of dust? Man delights not me; no, nor Woman neither. . .".

And so the road to the full mastery of Self (and, by the same token, of society at large) was getting more and more bumpy, and the Machine of the Modern Age began to skid. It seemed as if, with every bump on that road, another opportunity to reach the goal of complete self-realization was lost. In this sense, "the search for time lost arises in the throes of the socio-cultural earthquake called modernity" (Brockmeier, 2002, p. 20). Yet, the search was still on, with the hope of finding lost time and finally using it toward the right end. Nostalgia, which is but a wistful longing when hope is no more, will come later (and will be discussed later in the book). However, that search would more and more often take on eschatological or apocalyptical notes, and 'the end is near' sign may be the most representative of the modern times.

The Modern Age of *Homo vestigium* ('Searching Man') can be summarized as follows (Table 1.3):

**Table 1.3**    *Homo vestigium* ('Searching Man')

| DOMINANT MEDIUM | VISUAL (PRINT) |
| --- | --- |
| Time Perception | Linear |
| Examples of Signs of Time | The clock, the press |
| Message | Through the mastery of Self progress in all other realms can be achieved. |

## 6. THE FUTURE (AND THE PAST) IS NOW

No matter how much energy modern societies were putting into the development of practices and institutions, the main goal of the universal order still couldn't be achieved and so the grand narrative remained unfinished. The world couldn't reach the point of saturation in the original meaning of the word – 'sated or full', which goes back to the root *sa- 'to satisfy'. This became especially obvious in the second half of the 20th century. It is no accident that the Rolling Stones released their famous song *(I Can't Get No) Satisfaction* in 1965, referring both to sexual frustration and commercialism. And it is no accident that the 20th century ushered in the age of post-modernity as a reaction against the Modern Age. Although post-modern thought is sometimes equated with the refusal to accept the existence of any meaningful structural conditions, it is more accurate to see post-modernity as an argument against viewing any structures as existing independently of human actions. While 'the modern man' could say, together with Archimedes, 'Give me a fixed point and I will move the world', the 'post-modern man' saw power not in the external structures but in how such structures are articulated; these articulations are the relationships between Self and others, always situated within concrete circumstances. To put it differently, Self can never be outside of the world, and communication is our internal condition.

Not surprisingly, post-modernity called for the reconceptualization of time. While the best minds of the Modern Age were trying to invent more accurate ways to measure time, a clerk in the Bern patent office was reviewing the proposals coming across his desk. The clerk's name was Albert Einstein, and that experience probably stimulated his thinking about time and the eventual formulation of the Theory of Special Relativity (Galison, 2004, p. 325). Whereas Isaac Newton believed in the same universal time for everyone in all locations that can be accurately measured by clocks, for Albert Einstein absolute simultaneity couldn't be reached no matter how hard we tried to apply more energy to our efforts: two events that appear simultaneous for one observer are not simultaneous for observers who are in relative motion. As such, clocks in motion move more slowly than stationary clocks. Thus, what is considered to be time always depends on how it is experienced, and two people in two different systems of reference (motion vs. rest) do not share the same time because they do not experience events simultaneously. In other words, no universal time exists because we all relate to time differently, based on the perspective of our experiences. If no absolute simultaneity can be reached, then no identical or same meaning can be achieved: although the one who perceives the two events as simultaneous and the one who perceives them as taking place at different times are both right, their experiences are still different. No matter how hard we try to control it through the mechanism of escapement, time will escape on its own terms – always contextual and contingent. It is as if the 'id' part of 'identity' – the impulsive and spontaneous time – always breaks loose.

There are many reasons why post-modernity came into its own in the 20th century, including social, cultural, political and personal factors. We're more interested in which media led to the emergence of post-modern thought.

## 6.1. The Signs of the Time

While communication in the Modern Age relied mostly on the visual medium, the clock and the printing press being its two main manifestations, the way to post-modernity was facilitated by the electronic medium. Earlier, communication occurred either in 'real time' (oral communication) or with delayed time (script and printed communication). The telegraph was the first electronic medium that revolutionized long-distance communication by transmitting electrical signals over a wire. It was a faster and easier way to send and receive information over long distances than any other previous modes of communication. The telegraph was followed by the telephone, which allowed people to extend the voice to one another and communicate 'in real time' while physically situated at different locations. Radio, although it can be used for person-to-person communication, was the first true medium of mass communication. It was later replaced by television as the most popular mass communication medium. Today, of course, we live in the network society in which individuals and communities are interconnected by computer networks, exemplified by the Internet.

Two innovations were especially significant for the emergence of the post-modern network society. One was the development of the wireless communication system; instead of using a wire or cable, it became possible to use the air as a medium. Guglielmo Marconi, who used the ideas of Heinrich Hertz about electromagnetic energy moving in the atmosphere, sent the first wireless signal at the end of the 19th century; now Wi-Fi has become ubiquitous in most parts of the world. Whereas a wire is either a line, e.g. a thin metal thread, or an electric circuit, the message sent by the wireless communication system as an electromagnetic wave passes through the air at the speed of light – seemingly formless and ethereal. The line from Karl Marx's *Communist Manifesto*, "All that is solid melts into air", although written with a different message in mind, applies to wireless communication very well. The other innovation is the development of digital binary code: ones and zeroes have replaced paper, radio waves and cable. As a result, we can now read books, listen to the radio, and watch cable television on the Internet. And not only can anyone do this alone, but we can all interact and collaborate with one another online. Similar to Web 2.0 we can talk about 'Tribe 2.0'.

Thanks to wireless and digital communications, "we now live in a global village . . . a simultaneous happening" (McLuhan & Fiore, 1967, p. 63). 'Village', of course, is a metaphor and does not mean a dwelling or settlement; rather, the focus here is on communication processes of retribalization that happen to connect everyone with everyone else across the globe. Since absolute simultaneity can't be reached, however, as discussed previously, it would perhaps be more accurate to call this happening 'instantaneous', emphasizing its immediate and spontaneous character. Every act of communication is but an instant in which we are present. Communication happens simultaneously only *with* something else, whereas every act of communication is instantaneous in itself simply by occurring in an instant, however one defines it. So the main question becomes one of "the linkage of unequal times in the contingent, shifting, and relatively unstable orderings – political, economic, cultural – which make up our entangled world" (Frow, 1997, p. 10). What is the tale told by the post-modern network society? Or does it signify nothing?

## 6.2. Telling a Tale

*Local narratives.*   Post-modern thought does not recognize any grand narratives: any narrative is local and contextual. Electronic media encourage local narratives: one example is the proliferation of 'tourism narratives', e.g. stories from local tour guides, the pre-, on-, and post-tour stories by the tourists themselves, etc. (Bruner, 2005). In 1967 Roland Barthes proclaimed 'The Death of the Author', i.e., the impossibility of imposing any single and final interpretation on the text because everyone has his/her own reading of the text. The reader thus becomes more important than the author; in fact, at its limit, every reader can be seen as an author himself or herself. Online communication makes it very easy for anyone to author any narrative: just write a blog post! According to post-modern thought, "fashioning a variety of *local narratives* about selves might be more highly valued – even if it did not lead to the Truth about Man – than positing timeless, universal truths" (Rubin, 1998, p. 80). However, it must be emphasized that no local narrative can 'lead to the Truth about Man'; as soon as a narrative starts suffering from grandiosity and makes claims for universality, it is deconstructed, i.e., its hidden assumptions are brought to light.

*Erasure.*   We find a similar approach to meaning in communication. No sign for post-modern thought is perfectly suitable for the concept it represents; at the same time, we cannot but use various signs in communication. Signs, such as words, are thus put 'under erasure', i.e., crossed out yet remain legible and in place; this procedure signifies that a sign is 'inadequate yet necessary'. Since meaning both is and is not there, as it were, this procedure brings up a very important question: 'What really exists?'

*Simulacrum.*   If local narratives can be equated with 'the death of the author' and the impossibility of any grand narrative, and erasure with the impossibility of any fixed meaning, the concept of simulacrum takes this line of thought further and argues for 'the death of the real'. In other words, nothing truly real exists, as the single source of things and ideas;

instead, there are only copies without any original. Our reality is merely simulated by electronic media and so we live in the world of hyperreality – the sensory experience of sight, hearing and – increasingly – smell, taste and touch, created by immersive multimedia. Simulacra seem simultaneous: thus, "this weakening of time constraints, in terms of communication between remote places and within the everyday organisation of life, goes even further, offering people a new virtual reality that 'allows "future" or [u]nexperienced experiences to be experienced'" (see: Lee & Liebenau, 2000, p. 50).

Sometimes, post-modern thought is blamed for forgetting of the real; however, it can be said that post-modernity just adds a new – virtual – dimension to reality. People – at least those who create virtual reality – can still tell the virtual reality and real reality apart. Those people understand that communication (still) requires physicality, and we're (still) creatures of flesh and blood – and spirit. Humans are (still) passionate about their lives, and "the passion of time goes by the name of nostalgia" (Parret, 1993, p. 62). Nostalgia is one of the central concepts of post-modern thought; it is no accident that post-modernity gave rise to the field of so-called 'memory studies'. Nostalgia is a very human characteristic, showing how difficult it is for post-modern humans to break with a linear conception of time. The past (still) seems (really) real and humans (still) experience not only instant gratification, immersed in various forms and formats of electronic multimedia, but also nostalgia – a bittersweet longing for home. This longing is different from the search for lost time: whereas the Modern Age had the hope of finding it, post-modernity tells us that 'you can't go home again'. And yet, this longing is still there – just like meaning under erasure (Figure 1.7).

Post-modernity, stimulated by new electronic media and communication systems, is viewed as the product of spatial practices, rather than as a temporal grand narrative. It seems as if we can now experience anything anywhere: space thus is prioritized over time. However, time has not been eliminated by space: it is still very much a part of our communicative experiences. In this sense, the notion of 'timeless time' that is applied to post-modernity (Castells et al., 2006) is an apt label: although seemingly not there, it still is! Just like meaning and human longing, it is only put under erasure – crossed out yet legible and in place, or rather in all kinds of places. We now live in a world of fragmented time – a world of "perpetual presents" (Jameson, 1984, p. 25).

**Figure 1.7**    Time is running out. Photo by RCH Photography/Shutterstock.com

Thus, post-modernity does not really forget the real; rather, it draws our attention to that fine line between the real reality and virtual reality, reminding us that the instant of communication can stretch only as far as the physical signals carry, that in communication "we probe . . .the limits of our instruments" and that "the history of our knowledge is the history of our media" (Peters, 1999, p. 409). Above anything else, communication is experience, i.e., a dangerous search for something meaningful, e.g. the root 'per' in the word 'experience', which carries connotations of danger, trial, or fear (Morris, 1982, p. 1534). Communication will continue as long as we can distinguish simulacra from real reality, and as long as we can feel nostalgic. Once the line between simulacrum and reality disappears – along with the feeling of nostalgia – then, in the words of Michel Foucault, "one can certainly wager that man would be erased, like a face drawn in sand at the edge of the sea" (1970, p. 387).

Post-modernism as a mode of thought is often accused of being nihilistic, which is usually understood as the radical negation of any value. Nihilism is typically associated with despair, meaninglessness and thus a denial of life itself. In this light, communication is often viewed as digital hypermodulation when people are dispersed into countless digitalized micro-experiences

(Pettman, 2016). In spite of all technological advances, we often feel "alone together" (Turkle, 2011).

Post-modern thought, though, can be seen in a positive light, as well; we can recall McLuhan's deep faith in the relationship between the harmony of all human beings and electronic technology. The original thrust of post-modernity is democratizing because it shows that no one can monopolize communication: it must be maintained as an empty space – the arena where everyone can participate. As we have seen, space tries to erase time and keep the place empty, but time can only be put under erasure and so is still there.

The concept of nothing can be disconcerting, just as nil, which initially was a placeholder to represent an empty space (and from which nihilism is derived), was disconcerting and even considered a dangerous idea for many centuries, especially in the West (Seife, 2000). However, our life can be seen as hinging on nothing: "The nature of existence is the nature of the immaterial idea: Words do not matter . . . , but then again, nothing matters . . . The irony here is quite layered: Nothing matters; communication, in modernity, is nothing (*Nullius in Verba*); therefore communication, in this ironic post-modern sense, matters (as the nothing, it is the only thing that can matter)" (Shepherd, 1993, p. 89). If we come to terms with the realization that nothing *is* perfect and keep the arena of communication empty, time may bring new modes of communication, e.g. teleportation, based on research into quantum entanglement and nonlocality that today sounds like science fiction.

The (Re)Tribal Stage of *Homo nodus* ('Man as a network node') can be summarized as follows (Table 1.4):

Table 1.4    *Homo nodus* ('Man as a network node')

| DOMINANT MEDIUM | ELECTRONIC |
| --- | --- |
| Time Perception | Timeless (time under erasure) |
| Examples of Signs of Time | Wireless digital technologies |
| Message | Communication will continue as long as we can distinguish simulacra from real reality. |

The 'timeless time' is said to create "a forever universe" (Castells, 1996, p. 433). But, how long is forever? When Alice asks the White Rabbit this question, he says, "Sometimes, just one second". Better yet, we can say that forever lasts but an instant. Robert Frost's famous poem needs updating: the world will end not in fire nor in ice – should it end, the world will end in an instant. That is why every instant is crucial. As stated earlier, communication is always experience – an exciting yet risky (to various degrees) search for meaning. With virtual reality, created by electronic media, our communication experiences expand dramatically; at the same time, the risk grows of forgetting that each such experience is but an illusion. In other words, there is always a play element in communication (Latin: *ludere* – 'to play'). Around 500 B.C. Heraclitus said, "Time is a child playing a game of draughts; The kingship is in the hands of a child". Today one can't help wondering if the games being played by the grown-ups may end badly – in the end of the world. And one can only hope that the fate of the world is in the hands of a child – a child in the sandbox playing on an iPad.

# 2

# The Wonder
# of Polis

Key concepts:

Acropolis, auditory space, *agōn*, agora, civic memory, demos, dialectic, *eudaimonia*, *homonoia*, the ideal speech situation, justice, logos, public communication, oral speech, ostracism, *parrhēsia*, *politeia*, the public sphere, *phronēsis*, rhetoric, secondary orality, *stasis*, *telos*, topos.

Key names:

Benedict Anderson, Hannah Arendt, Aristotle, Jürgen Habermas, Heraclitus, Hermagoras, Isocrates, Immanuel Kant, Robert W. McChesney, Walter Ong, Plato, Diogenes of Sinope, Socrates.

## 1. WHAT WE'VE GOT HERE IS FAILURE TO COMMUNICATE

You may be wondering about the title of this chapter: 'The Wonder of Polis'.

If you remember that 'polis' has something to do with ancient Greece – a kind of city perhaps – then you might think: why talk about it now? Isn't 'polis' what existed a long time ago? Why would it be of any significance in today's world – so complex, so mobile, so technologically advanced?

And, if you can make a connection between 'polis' and 'politics' (if only by noticing their common root), you'll most likely think: what's so wonderful about that?! Politics has indeed become a dirty word. Many Americans, as well as people in other countries – especially the youth – are losing faith in the political system and are fed up with government institutions. Many people trust private businesses more than they trust their elected representatives. Many have little knowledge of political issues or candidates, and rarely or never participate in political activities such as voting, attending meetings or communicating with their representatives. Political campaigns now resemble marketing communication and brand advertising. Cynicism and apathy toward politics are common. There is widespread loss of public interest in politics and loss of hope that one's voice matters in the formation of public policy. One recent book even talks about "a citizenless democracy" (McChesney & Nichols, 2016).

Everyone seems to be lamenting the sorry state of today's politics, feeling isolated and powerless. In the *Iliad* (22.511) Andromache runs to the city walls and publicly laments the death of Hector, her husband, "who guarded the city" (24.729–30). We, however, in times of trouble or concern, turn more and more often away from public matters to TV and other gadgets. And yet, our private freedoms are shrinking, dominated by the interests of global corporations. We are disengaged, disoriented, disconnected. To use the famous phrase, 'What we've got here is failure to communicate'. In this case, 'failure to communicate' means 'failure to participate in political communication', that is to say, in the life of the polis. The concept of polis did not disappear into the dustbin of history. For instance, Google brings up – in 0.70 seconds – almost 92,000,000 results! So, let's not dismiss the significance of the polis for our own times. As you read this chapter, you will see how the concept of the polis is crucial to our life as well as to the field of communication studies.

## 2. THE POLIS: LIVING TOGETHER AND 'LIVING WELL'

Polis is first of all understood as a city (or sometimes a 'city-state') and that must be taken literally – as a physical settlement. In fact, the Greek word

**Figure 2.1**    Parthenon, Athens acropolis, Greece. Photo by Dimitrios/
Shutterstock.com.

'polis' first of all meant 'citadel', i.e., a fortified hill-top stronghold: the word 'acropolis', coined later, literally means a 'high city' (Figure 2.1).

As a territorial entity, the polis was an urban center with physical structures such as walls, a marketplace, theaters, etc. However, there would be no polis without a people: all physical structures existed to provide public space for people to come together toward certain ends. In this sense, the formation of the polis is a teleological process (from the Greek *telos* – 'end', 'result').

The polis grows from human natural inclinations to live in association with others: first, in families, and then in villages, to meet their everyday needs. Finally, the polis is formed from several communities: as Aristotle puts it, "the polis, in its simplest terms, is a body of such persons adequate in number for achieving a self-sufficient existence" (*Politics*, III.1, 1275b20–21). In other words, people could not exist apart from one another: they could survive and perform their natural functions only in the polis.

However, not every 'body of persons' constitutes the polis: there must be something present that is higher than the Acropolis, something more important than the needs of a family or a village. The polis is founded on higher principles than just a physical place and goes beyond mere survival. The end of the polis is 'living well' – a noble life that is ethically and spiritually good. Aristotle draws very clearly the distinction between the origin of the polis and its continued functioning: the polis "comes to be for the sake of life, and exists for the sake of the good life" (*Politics*, I.2, 1252b27–30). It is in the light of this end goal that we must understand Aristotle's famous definition of 'man' as a 'political animal' (*zōon politikon*): people live in the polis because it provides the necessary conditions for everyone's self-realization. In other words, you're not a complete person unless you live in the polis.

Thus, the polis is a community that allows people to lead their ordinary lives but also to promote virtuous lives. Plato, for instance, identified four main virtues – wisdom, courage, temperance, and justice – as the capacities for action that must be realized by everyone in the polis. Justice in a sense is the culmination of the other virtues: by practicing wisdom, courage and temperance, everyone can, and must, do what is just for the entire polis. In other words, justice implies that *everyone* makes their specific contribution for the good of the polis. This way, not only can the highest good be achieved for all, but each person can also achieve what the Greeks called *eudaimonia*, i.e., 'good spirits', 'psychic harmony' and 'happiness'. For "he who leads the pleasantest life is the happiest" (Plato, *Laws*, II, 662d). One can 'live well', therefore, only by living well with others. The 'good life' is the life lived for the common good, and no common good can exist without communication.

## 2.1. Polis as Communicative Space

The polis was a community just large enough and small enough to achieve self-sufficiency; such autonomy implied the people's right to administer justice and establish laws by themselves. The polis, therefore, was a self-sufficient and self-governing community. It was by gathering in a shared territory and talking about the matters of common concern that the citizens of the polis practiced self-government and made decisions. It was a revolutionary idea to realize that a society is not imposed from the outside but is created by people themselves from inside the polis – from inside the city walls and from within one's soul: by voicing one's own concern and hearing the voices of others.

According to Aristotle, nature does nothing in vain and so equipped humans with speech and reason. As Socrates says in one of Plato's *Dialogues*, "let us construct a polis from the beginning, through logos" (*The Republic*, II, 369c). Or, in the words of Isocrates, "generally speaking, there is no institution devised by man which the power of speech has not helped us to establish. For this it is which has laid down laws concerning things just and unjust, and things honorable and base; and if it were not for these ordinances we should not be able to live with one another" (Isocrates, *Antidosis*, 254–255).

People as 'political (polis-dwelling) animals' are able to communicate their ideas and create a society where everyone can realize themselves as best as possible. Communication, therefore, lies at the very heart of the polis. In fact, "to belong to a community was to share in the spread of information in that community: misanthropy, in the Greek tradition, took the form of cutting oneself off from all forms of contact. . . . Refusal to communicate removed one from society" (Lewis, 1996, p. 5). Thus, the polis is not only a physical territory and a political entity; it is, first and foremost, open space for communication and decision-making.

In ancient Greece that open space was predominantly auditory space: most matters of the polis were conducted orally through public communication. It is important to emphasize that "auditory space has no point of favoured focus. . . . The eye focuses, pinpoints, abstracts, locating each object in physical space, against a background; the ear, however, favours sound from any direction" (McLuhan, 1997, p. 41). Oral speech is the most immediate medium and does not discriminate: it is ideal for democracy because no one can monopolize voice. It is no wonder that oral communication is viewed as the pre-requisite for the very possibility of public life. The ideal polis, therefore, is the space where everyone can hear everyone else's voice. It is interesting to note that even ancient amphitheaters to this day are considered an acoustic marvel because they carry voices to everyone, all the way to the back row (Figure 2.2).

The main gathering place for all citizens of the polis was the agora: that is where the assemblies of people were held and decisions made on such matters as going (or not) to war, electing officials, etc. Through the assembly, all citizens, regardless of their property status, could exercise their power, especially the 'little people' or demos (hence, 'democracy'). The agora, however, was not only a place for political assemblies, but also a center for the commercial, religious and cultural life of the city (Figure 2.3).

Public communication was conceived as different from other forms of interaction such as mundane conversations in the family: it belonged to the list

**Figure 2.2**    Tourists on the amphitheater (Coliseum) in Ephesus, Turkey on April 13, 2015. Ephesus contains the largest collection of ancient Roman ruins in the eastern Mediterranean. Photo by Nuamfolio/Shutterstock.com.

of technical, or productive arts. The rhetorical art of persuasive speech was considered a political faculty – an essential technical skill for participating in the life of the polis. The importance of rhetoric was expressed very well by Isocrates: "[P]eople can become better and worthier if they conceive an ambition to speak well, if they become possessed of the desire to be able to

**Figure 2.3**    The Roman agora in Athens, Greece. Photo by Anastasios71/Shutterstock.com.

persuade their hearers, and, finally, if they set their hearts on seizing their advantage" (*Antidosis*, 275). Rhetoric in the ancient polis was especially important: supporting an opinion from probability was given much credibility because "some kinds of information were hard to find out, especially on matters outside the polis" and so "the lack of accessible information led to greater reliance on rhetorical arguments" (Lewis, 1996, p. 111).

Rhetoric alone, however, is not enough for successful communication in the polis: after all, one can persuade one's hearers just by learning how to skillfully manipulate arguments. Classical rhetoric views communication as a linear process of presenting a message to an audience in order to cause a certain effect: in this sense, "rhetoric is regulatory rather than constitutive, i.e., it modulates a meaning which is already there, rather than creating it anew" (Sonesson, 1996/1997, p. 50). It is well known that Plato was critical of rhetoric because it can be equated with fabrication, which, of course, can never pave the way for a healthy polis. In his famous 'Simile of the Divided Line', Plato introduces the idea of 'dialectic' – "that which logos itself grasps by the ability to engage in dialogue" (*The Republic*, VI, 511b). This ability is higher than the faculty of rhetoric because it allows people to search for truth and inquire into issues through reasoned arguments.

Communication as the dialectical process of inquiry requires the ability to ask questions and refute contradicting points of view. One can possess the art of rhetoric (and be successful at persuasion) without any true knowledge of the issue, but it is only by engaging in a dialogue that people can move closer to understanding the true essence of things. When people engage in a dialogue, communication is a *joint* search for truth in which meanings are constantly created and recreated. Dialectic is crucial in the life of the polis because "democracy and dialectics alike demand the ability to see things from another's perspective" (Ober, 2001, p. 159).

Communication is thus an ever-changing process; one can recall Heraclitus' famous phrase *panta rhei* – 'everything flows'. Communication, too, keeps flowing and never stops. Unlike rhetorical skills, therefore, one can never learn dialectics: one must 'go with the flow' and constantly engage in a dialogue with others. There is no set of skills as a bag of tricks that one can learn before one starts communicating and use them in any situation: one must engage in communication and move toward understanding an issue through questions and answers. It is very important to remember that people "cannot decide what to say just by knowing what might be said; they must also know what has just been said by others and what goes without saying for their audiences" (Bialostosky, 2004, p. 406). It must be emphasized that we cannot predict all situations that may arise and demand action from us; in other words, we cannot develop a definitive set of skills for responding to communication before the very act of communication. To put it differently, we do not know what is good or bad for us until we are faced with a concrete situation and engage in dialogue with other people. Thus, "it is only when we are confronted by the demands of action in the context of a particular set of circumstances that we get a true understanding of what our ends really are . . . Action in the particular circumstances of life is a continuing dialogue between what we think our life is about, and the particularities of moral and practical exigency" (Beiner, 1983, p. 24). In this light, communication in the polis is always a process of dealing with the pressing needs of the situation and making decisions accordingly, and always doing so together with other people.

If one approaches communication dialectically, one must constantly make decisions: in this respect, dialectic is linked to *phronēsis*, which is not simply a crafty procedure toward achieving a certain end, but the ability to reflect upon and decide that end, making practical decisions in constantly changing situations. *Phronēsis* is reasonableness or practical wisdom. Each phronetic decision is an "act with regard to the things that are good and bad for man" (Aristotle, *Nicomachean Ethics*, VI.5, 1140b4). Communication as action is a continuous process of doing the things that are good for you and others; it's easy to see why dialectics and *phronēsis* are crucial in the life of the polis.

It must be clear by now that the polis is formed and stays vibrant not only through the (spoken) word but also through action. Hannah Arendt captures the communicative basis of the polis very well when she writes: "[i]n acting and speaking, men show who they are, reveal actively their unique personal identities and thus make their appearance in the human world" (Arendt, 1998, p. 179). In the final analysis, then, the polis, as communicative space, is "the space of appearance in the widest sense of the word, namely, the space where I appear to others as others appear to me, where men exist not merely like other living or inanimate things but make their appearance explicitly" (1998, pp. 197–198). The agora is not simply a place for gathering together and spreading information about political matters: it is the space where citizens come forth, in speech and action, showing who they are for one another (Figure 2.4)

**Figure 2.4**    *Pericles' Funeral Oration*, by Philipp von Foltz.

Communication in the polis, thus, is not based only on the technical skills of persuasion, but also on the embodied ability to face a situation and other people and make decisions together with them. Life in the polis requires of its citizens 'being there'.

## 3. POLIS: THE DARK SIDE OF COMMUNICATION

The nature and effects of dysfunctional and destructive communication have been examined by scholars from a variety of perspectives, often labeled 'the dark side of communication'. Various areas of family and interpersonal communication have been investigated most often, e.g. criticism and complaints, teasing and bullying, transgressions and revenge, etc. (Olson et al., 2012; Spitzberg & Cupach, 2007). Recently, more attention has been paid to organizational, computer-mediated, and health communication contexts, focusing on the topics of sexualization, cyberstalking, bereavement, and various illnesses (Gilchrist-Petty & Long, 2016). All such forms of communication, which undoubtedly deserve scholarly attention, are examples of behaviors at the micro-level of interaction. We must not forget, however, about the large-scale forms of public and political communication, which deal with the matters of common concern and which are often dysfunctional and destructive as well, e.g. techniques of repression and manufacturing consent; political disengagement and lack of deliberation; message control by media; increasingly intractable conflicts, etc. To understand how such problems can be avoided or overcome, we must take a closer look at the life of the ancient polis.

You may be surprised to hear about the polis and the dark side of communication in one sentence: wasn't the polis a peaceful, nice, and stable place, where people deliberated and made all decisions together? Yes, but only in the ideal society such as Plato's *Republic* – his *kallipolis* – where reason governs each individual's actions and no one's soul is ever in conflict with itself, the whole society being harmonious as a result. In real life, though, there was a dark side to the polis. For one thing, women, slaves, and non-citizens were excluded from the process of deliberation and decision-making. Those who did take part in the life of the polis disagreed vehemently and violently: the polis thus was often torn apart by conflicts. Internal strife was so frequent that the ancient Greeks considered it to be inherent to the polis and gave it the name of *stasis*, i.e., conflict among citizens within the civic space of the polis. As Socrates puts it in *The Republic*, *stasis* is "a polis which is internally divided" (*The Republic*, V, 470d). *Stasis* applied to internal divisions of various kinds: usually between the elites and wealthy (oligarchy) and the common, poor citizens (the demos), but also between different ethnic groups living side by side in the same polis.

*Stasis*, as civil strife between different factions that disrupted the healthy functioning of the entire polis, was seen as a disease of the body politic. Both the polis and the body were seen as governed by the same principle of balance between various elements: like any disease, *stasis* is caused by one element overpowering all others and thus upsetting the overall balance. Plato compares the sick body (*sōma nosōdes*) and the divided city as two entities that are subject to *stasis* (*The Republic*, VIII, 556e). And Herodotus writes: "Miletus, at the height of her fortunes, was the glory of Ionia. Two generations before this, however, she had been very greatly diseased by *stasis*, until the Parians made peace among them" (*The Histories*, 5.28.1).

Peace in the polis is the healthy condition when every citizen works toward just ends: such a sense of 'oneness of mind' was known in ancient Greece as *homonoia*. Consider the following conversation between Socrates and Thrasymachus from Book I of *The Republic*: "Injustice, Thrasymachus, causes civil war [*stasis*], hatred, and fighting among themselves, while justice brings friendship and a sense of common purpose [*homonoia*]" (I, 351d). The condition of the polis known as *homonoia* is based on the four virtues mentioned earlier: justice, courage, temperance, and wisdom. For instance, in Book IV of Plato's *Republic* wisdom is presented as "a kind of knowledge belonging to some of the citizens that counsels not about the affairs connected with some particular thing in the city, but about how the city as a whole would best deal with itself and the other cities" (IV, 428c–d).

So the opposite of faction is *homonoia*, which calls on citizens to agree on how to conduct the matters of common concern. The ancient polis dealt with the problem of *stasis* first of all by addressing its causes and making sure *homonoia* was maintained. The polis sought to prevent the appearance of factions by keeping any form of individualism at bay, especially economic differentiation. The agora was not only the political center of the polis, but also performed the function of a marketplace. While viewed as a necessity, however, the marketplace was also perceived as a potential threat to *homonoia*; as a result, laws were created to stave off the potentially corrupting influence of the marketplace.

### 3.1. The Politics of Exile

In addition to such legal measures, citizens of the polis resorted to more symbolic actions that were communicative in nature. One such action was the ritual of ostracism, also aimed at avoiding the explosion of factional strife. Ostracism was practiced to send into exile those political figures who may have gained too much power. Those individuals were sent into exile for ten years, but kept their property and could return at the end of that period. While no deliberation took place, a quorum was required for an ostracism to be held. During the ritual, each citizen marked potsherds (*ostraca*, hence the name of the procedure) with the name of a person he wished to see expelled from the polis and put the *ostraca* into an urn inscription-side down. The person whose name appeared most frequently would be ostracized from the polis (Keegan, 2014) (Figure 2.5).

Ostracism was supposed to prevent open confrontations between different factions; also, it was through ostracism that the demos could exercise their power against elites, keeping the latter's actions in check. However, the mechanism of the 'politics of exile' was not always effective: the instrument of ostracism often deprived the ancient polis of its prominent leaders

**Figure 2.5**   Ancient ceramics used for democratic voting in Athens in the 5th century B.C. Museum of the ancient agora in Athens, Greece. Photo by Andronos Haris/Shutterstock.com.

at critical times. Sometimes the exiled elites called on foreign forces to help them return to their polis and take revenge on those who sent them into exile. One more reason why the mechanism of ostracism was not always effective might have been its use of writing rather than oral speech, which made the communicative practice disembodied and thus more detached from real life. Citizens were present there not in person, but in the form of their anonymous *ostraca* only.

Open communication, of course, was considered a more effective way of dealing with the effects of *stasis* and various methods were designed for discovering the key points of the controversial issues and suggesting the most appropriate means for dealing with them. One example of such a method is the Rhetorical Stasis Theory, credited to the Greek rhetorician Hermagoras, who in the late 2nd century B.C. identified four stages of the public decision-making process. According to that theory, people can make the best judgment only if they go through the following four stages: conjecture or fact (What happened?), definition (What do we call it?), quality or value (Was it blameworthy?), and policy or procedure (What shall we do? How shall we proceed?) (Walker, 2000). However, not all methods of communication worked, either. After all, when citizens appear in front of one another, "they engage in a constantly fluctuating process of real communication. They bathe in each other's noise. That's what a community is, and it's not something that you make happen: it's something that just happens" (Sartwell, 2002, pp. 56–57). And so the loud noise often silenced the most common-sense judgments, leading to the literal violence in the struggle for power in the polis.

## 3.2. Polis: War and Peace

Just as *stasis* was inherent to the ancient polis, tensions between various poleis were always high and often resulted in war. When Solon, the famous Athenian legislator, formulated his law on *stasis*, he included in it the obligation of every citizen to take up arms in the case of conflict. It is important to remember, though, that the ancient Greeks distinguished between war (*polemos*) and civil strife (*stasis*). As Plato says in *The Republic*, Greeks and barbarians "are enemies by nature, and this hatred must be called war; while when Greeks do any such thing to Greeks, . . . this kind of hatred must be called faction" (V, 470c). Naturally, hatred for the enemy justified modes of warfare that were far more atrocious. Many violent wars were fought between neighboring poleis, such as Corinth against Corcyra, or Athens against Megara; the most well-known example, of course, is the Peloponnesian War between the Delian League led by Athens and the Peloponnesian League led by Sparta (Figure 2.6).

**Figure 2.6**    Destruction of the Athenian army in Sicily during the Peloponnesian War, 413 B.C.: wood engraving, 19th century.

Even during violent and bloody wars, however, communication between the opposing sides took place involving the so-called 'heralds'. The herald performed a number of important tasks, such as declaring war or peace, requesting the bodies of the dead, and carrying various oral messages. The herald also reported all military engagements back to his own polis. The warring sides understood the need for communication very well and so the status of the herald was considered inviolable. When the conflict was especially intense, a polis might refuse to send heralds or to accept them from the enemy; this would result in *polemos akēruktos* – 'undeclared war' or 'war without heralds', which denoted a war of particular violence, with even contact by herald suspended (Lewis, 1996). Unfortunately, numerous examples of both *stasis* (civil strife) and *polemos* (foreign war) can be found throughout history since the times of the classical polis.

One might think that *stasis*, as internal conflict, is a lesser evil than *polemos*, as external war. After all, as Plato says, Greeks, being Greeks, will not "ravage Greek territory nor burn habitations, and they will not admit that in any city all the population are their enemies, men, women and children, but will say that only a few at any time are their foes, those, namely, who are to blame for the quarrel" (*The Republic*, V, 471 a–b). And yet, while undoubtedly less desirable than peace, war is waged by all citizens thinking as one; it encourages virtue; and it allows for neutrality and negotiations. Civic strife, however, is a greater evil because it undermines the polis from within. It is a disease that metastasizes to all parts of the political body (one clearly sees 'stasis' in 'metastasis'). No healthy polis will wage war against its neighboring poleis provided they are healthy as well. It is clear then why every effort was made to either avoid *stasis* or get rid of it by purging it from the soul and speech of all citizens of the polis. And so it is understandable why, in Aeschylus' *Eumenides* (976–8), we hear the Chorus sing: "I pray that Stasis, insatiable of evil, shall not thunder in the polis." We know that those prayers were not heard, and the 'good life' in the ancient polis unraveled because of internal strife. External conflicts, beginning with the Peloponnesian War, also led to the decline of the polis. However, while the ancient polis may have disappeared over two thousand years ago, to say that it is no longer relevant would be wrong.

## 4. 'THE POLIS OF OUR PRAYERS'

While the polis was an autonomous entity that could by itself establish and administer justice, it was also conceived as a natural entity that must function in harmony with the cosmic order. At least "since the days of Solon, men had seen a mutual correspondence between the order of the polis and the order of the universe" (Meier, 1990, p. 91). Thus, the polis contained within itself the idea of a large unity of all beings living in the world together. That idea was first articulated by the Greek cynic Diogenes of Sinope, who is perhaps better known today for choosing to live in a tub (Figure 2.7). When asked where he came from and what his native city-state was, Diogenes famously answered that he was *kosmopolitēs* – literally, 'a citizen of the cosmos or universe'.

The idea of cosmopolis was further developed by the Greek and Roman Stoics. Later, this idea influenced the intellectuals of the Enlightenment, when it was introduced into modern languages, e.g. such words as 'cosmopolitan', 'world citizen', 'Weltbürger', and 'Citoyen du monde'. Immanuel Kant was the most significant and consistent thinker who promoted the cosmopolitan idea. This may seem strange, considering that Kant, although he did not live in a tub, still hardly left his native city of Königsberg during his lifetime. And yet, Kant was a true philosopher who traveled in his thought and whose vision embraced the entire universe, e.g. one of his most

**Figure 2.7**    *Le tonneau de Diogène*. Image from Biblioteca de la Facultad de Derecho y Ciencias del Trabajo Universidad de Sevilla.

famous phrases: "Two things fill the mind with ever new and increasing admiration and awe, the more often and steadily we reflect upon them: the starry heavens above me and the moral law within me. . . . I see them before me and connect them immediately with the consciousness of my existence" (Kant, 1996, p. 269). Making this crucial connection, Kant called for universal hospitality, which "means the right of a stranger not to be treated with hostility when he arrives on someone else's territory" (1991, p. 105). He spoke of a universal community that must solve all matters through civilized discussions. To that end, every individual must have the moral duty to think and behave like a citizen of the world. "Only under this condition can we flatter ourselves that we are continually advancing towards a perpetual peace" (1991, pp. 107–108).

We can see how the polis is not only a physical self-sustained entity; it is rather the space where the universe and the existence of each individual connect, forming a new consciousness that is (ideally) harmonious and perpetually peaceful. Such collective consciousness comes into being as a result of connection through various mediums. We remember that the classic polis was a setting where citizens appeared in front of one another to discuss matters of common concern: the public forum in the agora took the form of face-to-face oral communication. Later, ideas were disseminated and debated in the public sphere through the mass media based on writing and print, as discussed by Jürgen Habermas in his book *The Structural Transformation of the Public Sphere* (1989 [1962]). Today, of course, electronic communications have added a new dimension to the concept of cosmopolis since the decision-making process is now dispersed along numerous networks. The civic potential of new media and electronic technologies has found its manifestation in such phenomena as technopolitics, satellite politics, e-democracy, cyberdemocracy, virtual polis, etc. (Roberts, 2008). In light of this, "the public sphere is a common space in which the members of society are deemed to meet through a variety of media: print, electronic, and also face-to-face encounters; to discuss matters of common interest; thus to be able to form a common mind about these" (Taylor, 1995, pp. 185–186).

The concrete space of the classic polis turns into a more abstract public sphere where communication is mediated through various technologies, institutions and structures. The modern public sphere, therefore, can be viewed as an imagined community. The concept of 'imagined community' became popular following Benedict Anderson's book *Imagined Communities: Reflections on the Origin and Spread of Nationalism* (2006). As can be seen from the title, imagined communities are considered to be the products of modern nationalism: simply put, such communities are imagined "because the members of even the smallest nation will never know most of their fellow-members, meet them, or hear them, yet in the minds of each lives the image of their communion" (Anderson, 2006, p. 6). However, the concept of an 'imagined community' can also be connected with the polis of the ancient world. In fact, Anderson himself admits that "all communities larger than primordial villages of face-to-face contact (and perhaps even these) are imagined" (Anderson, 2006, p. 49). Indeed, the people of ancient Athens, for instance, imagined themselves as members of a self-governing political entity, e.g. the following titles: *The Athenian Experiment: Building an Imagined Political Community in Ancient Attica, 508–490 B.C.* (Anderson, 2003) and *Cosmopolis: Imagining Community in Late Classical Athens and the Early Roman Empire* (Richter, 2011). It is important to emphasize that "the imagined public is not . . . imaginary" (Peters, 1995, p. 16). 'Imaginary' means something that exists only in the imagination, unreal. 'Imagined', however, means 'forming a mental picture of something, making a guess or conjecture'. The difference between these two meanings is significant: 'imaginary' is make-believe detached from reality, while 'imagined' is the product of a creative and visionary process aimed at transforming reality. Emily Dickinson captured this key difference very poetically: 'To treat your facts with imagination is one thing, but to imagine your facts is another'.

Any community, therefore, whether the polis in the traditional sense or (especially) the cosmopolis, requires imagination. The word 'imagination' goes back to 'imago', which means 'an image, a likeness': hence, a community is formed because every individual tries to discover his or her likeness with all other individuals, to identify with them. (It is no coincidence that the words 'likeness' and 'like' are derived from the same root *lik-, meaning 'same'. That is why we usually 'like' those on Facebook who are similar to us, or those who we wish we were like (role models and other people we aspire to be like). If, however, as Aristotle says, the polis attempts "as far as possible to be entirely one, . . . as it becomes increasingly one it will no longer be a polis. For . . . it would destroy the polis. Now the polis is made up not only of a number of human beings, but also of human beings differing in kind; a polis does not arise from persons who are similar (*ex homoíon*)" (*Politics*, II.2, 1261a15–24).

It is crucial to imagine, therefore, how we can all be alike and different. As a rule, more emphasis is placed on thinking alike or being of the same mind;

at worst, we can always 'agree to disagree'. Such an arrangement accom-
modating different views is known as *modus vivendi* (Latin, meaning 'way
of living'). The modern phrase 'agree to disagree' is said to have been first
used in 1770 by John Wesley, who wrote a memorial sermon for George
Whitefield where he downplayed their doctrinal differences. After he says
"we may agree to disagree", though, John Wesley continues: "But, mean-
time, let us hold fast the essentials" (1831, p. 477). In other words, while
there will always be "doctrines of a less essential nature" over which we may
all "agree to disagree", there is something truly essential that must be held
by everyone, and that is our willingness for 'disagreeing to agree'. Nothing is
more important than being open to one another and engaging in an honest
exchange of ideas with the view of agreeing on what is good for everyone.
What is good for everyone, therefore, is communication itself: everything
else may be open for debate! Thus, what everyone 'must hold fast as the
essentials' is public communication. As such, public communication is not
simply a part of the life of a polis, but its very essence. Every individual must
be equally able to participate in communication and have a say in collective
decision-making on matters of common interest. No decision can be made
prior to communication: it is only through interaction with others that we
can learn their opinions and make joint decisions.

We all know, of course, that the communicative use of public reason has not
always been successful. Habermas showed how the public sphere, as a part of
people's lifeworld, is colonized by the market economy and media systems.
Even the Internet, proclaimed at one time as a new public sphere in which
democracy can flourish, is far from the ideal of social integration, being
transformed by centralization and commercial interests. As the title of one
of the articles looking at 'mediated cosmopolitanism' puts it, "Mediapolis,
where art thou?" (Lindell, 2015). And yet, we're still talking about the polis,
and we still view "the wise man as a *kosmopolitēs*, as a citizen of the world"
(Sloterdijk, 2013, p. 6). By now you probably can see why this is the case: the
polis is, first and foremost, an idea(l). Let's discuss this in more detail.

## 4.1. Polis as an Idea(l)

As an idea, the polis is a normative concept: in this sense, the polis is
theorized in terms of values and principles that could best guide our life,
presenting a view of what the ideal polis ought to be. Obviously, there will
be different ideas about the ideal polis, i.e., how people could organize their

life into what was known in classical Greece as *politeia*, which can be translated as 'constitution" or 'regime'. *Politeia*, by the way, was the original title of Plato's famous book commonly known in English as *The Republic*. It must be remembered that Plato did not write about a republican form of government as it is understood in modern political science; instead, he presented his view of the ideal way of creating the 'common entity' or 'the people's thing' (Latin: *res publica*). In his *Politics* Aristotle also talks about his view of 'the best regime'. While he never gives it a name, Aristotle mentions its "defining principle" as "a good mixture of democracy and oligarchy" (IV.9, 1294b14). Most recently, a normative approach to *politeia* has been developed by Habermas who, in one of his works (1994), discusses three models of democracy – proceduralist, liberal, and republican – and then introduces his own conception. Habermas grounds his conception, known as the Theory of Communicative Action, in the view of communication as a rational activity: all participants in this open interaction must be able to present good reasons for their actions or defend what he calls 'validity claims'. Ideally, the four types of validity claims – to comprehensibility, truth, normative rightness, and sincerity – must be defended by every participant, i.e., recognized and accepted by everyone else. Habermas calls this situation of perfect communication "the ideal speech situation" (2001).

It is important to remember that "no two historical poleis were exactly the same" (Manville, 1990: 38). Therefore, we must view the polis not only as a normative concept, but also describe the specific forms of *politeia* as practiced in real socio-cultural circumstances. As Aristotle puts it, "one should study not only the best regime but also the regime that is [the best] possible" (*Politics*, IV.1, 1288b37). The descriptive approach is all about facts: it explains what the polis is and how it came into being as a result of specific processes of communication. There are always tensions between normative standards and the practices through which the polis comes into being. Today, for instance, the European Union is a good example of such tensions. However, it is still noted that, in spite of extensive descriptions of practical methods of constituting citizenship, a clearer normative justification for European integration is needed (Neuvonen, 2016).

Thus, in understanding the polis, the importance of normative theory should not be underestimated. When Aristotle writes that, "It is easy enough to theorize about such matters: it is far less easy to realize one's theories", he says so because we talk about the ideal polis "in terms of our wants; what actually happens depends upon chance" (*Politics*, VII.13, 1331b18). For him, the ideal polis is "the polis of our prayers" or, literally, "according to prayer"

(*Politics*, IV.11, 1295a29). Yet, while putting ideas into practice is hard and actual legislating falls short of the ideal, theorizing 'about such matters' is not simply harder; it is essential. Without ideas about what the ideal polis ought to be, there would be nothing to 'pray for'! In other words, it is as an idea that the polis starts – and continues all the way to cosmopolis.

The relationship between the polis and Greek religion was very important and complex and so 'the polis of our prayers' can be understood literally, i.e., prayed for by all citizens of the classical polis. At the same time, if we recall that the verb 'to pray' goes back to Latin *precari* – 'to ask earnestly' – the meaning of the phrase takes on a broader meaning: 'the polis of our prayers' is the space where we constantly engage in communication and ask one another earnestly how to live well together. We must describe this space, which is continuously defined and redefined, as best as we can. And we must also keep 'theorizing about such matters': the ideal polis is the light on the horizon that beckons and guides us. Each time new ideas are put forward by someone, the world appears in a new light and new perspectives are opened up for action. We can never reach this horizon but only move toward it. And so we must see the light on the horizon to keep moving. Without the light of the polis, and without our constant social movement toward it, darkness will set in.

## 5. 'WE ALL CAME OUT OF THE POLIS'

Some may argue that the situation of the ancient world is ancient history and that the polis is too different from modern society. And yet, most would agree that the Western societies have been shaped by classical Greek and Roman traditions, which are present in government, legal systems, trade, the economy, the arts, religion, mythology, sports, fashion, etc. As far as communication theory is concerned, one can say that 'we all came out of the polis', somewhat modifying the phrase attributed to Fyodor Dostoevsky who said, "We all come out from Gogol's *Overcoat*", referring to the influence of a short story by Russian author Nikolai Gogol on all of Russian literature. Few, if any, would disagree that the entire field of communication has roots in the classical world where communication was practiced and examined within the complex framework of the polis.

It is no accident that the study of communication goes back to the ancient polis: as *politeia*, it was a community of people organized through communication, beginning with complex relationships between the polis and the family as fundamental forms of social integration. While derived from the naturalness of the family as a kinship group, the polis also provided the necessary conditions for all citizens to realize their full potential. Hence the mutual influence and tensions of the family and the polis, addressed by both Plato and Aristotle in their works (Hittinger, 2013). In a similar vein, although women were excluded from political decision-making, the gendered nature of the polis was quite complex, informing the role that gender constructions play in the life of modern democracies.

The communicative organization of the polis emphasized the role of many symbolic forms used to draw people together into a community, including the material and technological means of city-building. The polis was the place for establishing, legitimizing and maintaining power between people as well as for setting up the parameters by which city and nature could exist in harmony, including various settlement patterns, architectural constructions and other visual markers. It must be noted that the modern Urban Communication Foundation, which promotes our understanding of communication patterns in the urban environment, emphasizes the role of such communicative freedoms in the city as spaces to argue, places for human interaction, free-speech rights and zones, civic and cultural places to gather, etc. The Foundation's Communicative City Award, which was recently given to Amsterdam, specifically noted its richness and variety of places of interaction, including the liveliness of politics and civil society (Aiello & Tosoni, 2016).

The ancient polis was not only a physical settlement, but also a space of memory: as Hannah Arendt succinctly puts it, "the organization of the *polis* . . . is a kind of organized remembrance" (1998, p. 198). The polis overcomes the frailty of human affairs and continues to live in the form of civic memory, commemorated in stories as well as public statues of gods, leaders, sporting champions, etc. (Figure 2.8).

Collective memory is crucial for public discourse and decision-making: if the polis fails to organize itself into a coherent remembrance, the next generation may forget what constitutes the good life, leading to the disintegration of the polis. It is important to emphasize the active nature of memory: only by appearing before others, i.e., being seen and heard, can people organize themselves into the polis, growing stronger both as a community and as individuals. So the nature of the polis, as the space of appearance, is inherently performative. In other words, "the Polis, properly speaking, . . . is the organization of the people as it arises out of acting and speaking together" (Arendt, 1998, p. 198). Thus, in addition to being

**Figure 2.8**  The Lincoln Memorial in Washington, D.C. Photo by Tim Evanson.

organized through families, settlement, and memories, the polis is organized, above all, through speech and as deeds, showing to us, using the title of a famous book, *How to Do Things With Words* (Austin, 1975).

All exigencies of the polis were addressed through public communication when justice was tested and enacted. Since the decisions were never made before the actual communication took place, *homonoia*, as a community of mind, called for active and creative debate and deliberation. Every citizen of the polis was expected to engage in self-reflection and display the art of speaking effectively in public arenas, which included not only speaking in the assembly but also other roles, e.g. the herald who spread the news within and outside of the polis by carrying a precise oral message. Thus, practices of public speaking were central to the life of the polis and it is out of such practices of oratory and debate that the idea of rhetoric emerged in ancient Greece. It is no accident that the rhetorical tradition is considered to be the oldest tradition of communication theory: the polis was a rhetorical community *par excellence* (Miller, 1993).

All conceptualizations of rhetoric related in one way or another to the life of the classical polis: in Aristotle's words, rhetoric "dresses up in the form of politics" (*Rhetoric* I.2, 1356a27–30). Of course, the main treatise on the

art of persuasion was, and still is, Aristotle's *Rhetoric*. Its relation to the
polis may not always be visible. However, he talks about *topoi* as the lines
of reasoning and thus the substance of deliberation. If we remember that a
topos is literally a place where those lines of argument are found, it becomes
clear that rhetoric was the basis of the polis. The well-known three kinds
of rhetoric identified by Aristotle – deliberative, forensic and epideictic –
may not sound like place-names to the modern ear, but in Aristotle's times
they did: "the deliberative is called *symbouleutic* or *demagoric*, referring
to the Boule or the agora, and the forensic is called *dikanic*, suggesting a
*dikasterion* (literally, place of justice). *Dikanic* topoi are the ways that juries
deliberate in the *dikasterion*" (Bilansky, 1999, p. 223). Another conceptualization of communication is Rhetorical Stasis Theory, mentioned earlier,
identifying four stages in the stopping and the starting process of argumentation. Parallels between these stages and Aristotle's common *topoi* have
been noted (Fahnestock & Secor, 1985).

Public communication in the polis required of the speaker many rhetorical skills and also physical abilities such as muscular and vocal control:
participation in the life of the polis was essentially an oral communication
event. Today, of course, the situation is different as we live in the world of
various mass media including newspaper, television, and the Internet. And
yet orality still plays an important role, now called 'secondary orality', i.e.,
the re-emergence of oral speech in modern societies. Clearly not identical
with the orality of pre-literate cultures, or the 'primary orality', 'secondary
orality' coexists with the media of writing, print, and electronic recording
and transfer. However, according to Walter Ong, who coined the term 'secondary orality', it is more deliberate and self-conscious in its expression
and "fostering of a communal sense", but "generates a sense for groups
immeasurably larger than those of primary oral culture – McLuhan's 'global
village'" (Ong, 1982, p. 136). As a result, 'secondary orality' is viewed as a
means of communication through which the original sense of community
can be recovered.

Overall, rhetoric clearly operated in the background of the polis. Moreover,
it is fair to say that "the historiography of rhetoric strongly shows that the
practice and study of rhetoric have never known a more friendly environment" (Bilansky, 1999, p. 222).

Every event of public communication in the polis was an example of the rhetorical *agōn*, i.e., it was a contest against a rival in front of an audience: every
speaker tried to persuade those assembled toward his position. The audience

thus could lack the ability to make an informed decision, swayed by a popular leader (a demagogue) or carried away with emotions. Since the outcome depended on the skills of persuasion, and anyone could be trained in that art, then one could think that rhetoric is nothing but "cookery in the soul", as Plato called it (*Gorgias* 465d.). The situation was not perceived as a laughing matter, though: if such things as the good, the true, the beautiful, etc. do not really exist and are 'mere words', then the polity itself may be in danger of losing its integrity. To rectify the situation, a special method of dialectical inquiry was developed by Socrates and promoted by Plato. While rhetoric is concerned mostly with particular topics, dialectic is concerned with general questions and provides real knowledge of the nature of Self, the world and the relationship between Self and the world. Dialectical inquiry, following Socrates, is considered to be the "quintessential activity of the true philosopher" (Nightingale, 2004, p. 78). It is important to note that the dialectical method requires the examination of all concepts through dialogue with others: it begins by questioning basic assumptions underlying the concept and proceeds by critically assessing its definitions and thus moving toward the truth. The dialectical method is the process of inquiry into reality itself that is carried out by people wrestling with and resolving contradictory views and leading the polis to the common good. Everyone can live a virtuous life in the polis through self-examination, questioning and considering opposing beliefs and then modifying their own beliefs in accordance with the common good. All ethical virtues can be elicited only through a continuous process of dialectical inquiry; also, as mentioned earlier, the polis can remain vibrant only if the bases of its ethos of the good life are passed down from generation to generation.

It is in the dialectical method that the origins of Critical Communication Theory can be found. It was not simply common for citizens in the polis to be asking questions that bring contradictions to light in the process of discussion and reflection, it was expected of every citizen: those who did not want to take part in the life of the polis were proclaimed to be *apoleis* – those outside of the polis. It was understood that the citizens could arrive at the truth by constantly telling the truth, i.e., exposing weaknesses of the assumptions underlying the polis in order to make them stronger. This was done through various forms of communication – from performing comedy on stage to the practice of speaking truthfully and boldly even in the face of danger or powerful people, known as *parrhēsia* or the 'right to say all' in any situation, be it on stage or in political deliberations. "In parrhesia, the speaker is supposed to give a complete and exact account of what he has in mind so that the audience is able to comprehend exactly what the speaker thinks" (Foucault, 1983). Without *parrhēsia*, one could not be considered a full citizen of the Greek polis.

Thus, the life in the polis called for creative deliberation and a joint search for truth because "it is not in the nature of man to attain a science (*epistēmē*) by the possession of which we can know positively what we should do or what we should say" (Isocrates, *Antidosis*, 271). When people spoke and acted together in the polis, they did so by using both rhetoric and dialectic, which are counterparts because they are both concerned with questions that cannot be resolved scientifically. The polis can remain a dynamic space of appearance only as long as the process of dialectical inquiry and decision-making through public communication continues.

As you can see, the field of communication studies clearly came out of the polis, which was formed through various forms of communication practice, examination and instruction. Just look at the divisions and interest groups that make up the two largest associations – the National Communication Association (NCA) and the International Communication Association (ICA) – and you will see how the rich legacy of the polis is present – explicitly or implicitly – in those areas of inquiry, for example: Argumentation and Forensics; Communication Ethics; Communication Law and Policy; Critical and Cultural Studies; Feminist and Women's Studies; Group Communication; Language and Social Interaction; Mass Communication; Organizational Communication; Performance Studies; Philosophy of Communication; Political Communication; Public Address; Public Dialogue and Deliberation; Public Diplomacy; and Rhetorical and Communication Theory. The influence of the classical polis on modern Western societies is beyond any doubt. As noted earlier, the polis is, above anything else, a normative concept guiding our thinking about how to live together for the common good.

Critics may point to the aforementioned dark sides of the polis, such as the exclusion of women from politics or the use of slaves for hard labor and even domestic chores. However, those were general arrangements in all polities at that time. Besides, if we look at the role of women in societies later in history, we'll see that in Russia, for instance, explicit commitments to promote the equality of men and women were made only following the Socialist Revolution of 1917, and women's right to vote was secured in the U.S. only in 1920 by the Nineteenth Amendment to its Constitution. As for slavery, we shouldn't forget that in Russia the system of serfdom was abolished only in 1861, and slavery in the U.S. only in 1865. At the same time, it must be noted that it was Socrates who first questioned the assumption of his fellow citizens that slaves could not speak or participate in democratic life (Plato, *Meno*, 84b–c).

The classical polis was not ideal but it showed us how we can move toward the ideal of the common good. In spite of its negatives, the polis was still a wonderful thing: "the wonder of the polis . . . lay in dialogue, the active life which was always the public life" (Shorris, 2000, p. 71). We learned from the polis that our well-being depends on the involvement of every citizen in the creation of the good life. We must take this lesson to heart because of the predicament in which we find ourselves: at stake today is the entire globe, and we, as the citizens of the cosmopolis, must put everything into question, including our own assumptions, openly deliberate every issue of common concern and make prudent and ethical decisions together. The word 'polis' literally means 'a fortified place in a city', 'a stronghold', or 'a final retreat'. We must understand that our world, even as the cosmopolis, is a very small place and each of us is a part of it. We cannot retreat from the world because for each of us the final retreat is oneself and one cannot escape from oneself. We must not retreat from the world, then, but rather treat it as the space in which we live – with wisdom, courage, temperance, and justice. It is only through communication that we can not only survive but live well with others – live for the common good.

# 3

# The Wonder
# of God

Key concepts:

Analogic communication, polytheism, monotheism, diacritical, digital communication, divination, divine, epiphany, interdiction, hermeneutics, homiletics, Inter mirifica, 'I-It', 'I-Thou', listening, logos, mythos, noetic, oath, oracular communication, positivist sociology, proselytizing, religious, ritual, science, the scientific method, spiritual, travel narratives, worship.

Key names:

Giorgio Agamben, Aristotle, Thomas Aquinas, St. Augustine, Martin Buber, Kenneth Burke, James Carey, Auguste Comte, Nicolaus Copernicus, Charles Darwin, Émile Durkheim, Galileo Galilei, Martin Heidegger, Homer, Ivan Illich, William James, Johannes Kepler, Isaac Newton, Friedrich Nietzsche, St. Paul, Charles S. Peirce, John Peters, Thales, Paul Watzlawick, Frank Wilczek, Ludwig Wittgenstein.

## 1. 'EVERYTHING IS FULL OF GODS'

In Homer's epic poem, Odysseus is trying to escape the wrath of Poseidon and find safe shore on which to make landfall when he sees a river and asks its god to pity and rescue him: "Hear me, lord, whoever you might be. . . I come to your stream, to your knees, after many trials" (*Odyssey* 5.445–450). Odysseus spoke – and the river stopped the waves in front of him, and Odysseus was saved. The way Odysseus speaks to the god of the river is not the same as prayer in the modern sense of the word, i.e., a devout petition to God usually at a religious service; rather, it is an urgent request entreating someone with whom Odysseus comes face to face in a concrete situation. That Odysseus does not address the god by name ("whoever you might be") shows that it is an unknown god – one of many (Hexter, 1993).

Many people – from the Thracians to the ancient Egyptians to the ancient Greeks to the Maori to the Native Americans – have worshipped a variety of gods and goddesses (Figure 3.1).

History and cultural anthropology provide a wealth of evidence for the existence of such a polytheistic world-view: see, for example, a book entitled *A World Full of Gods: An Inquiry into Polytheism* (Greer, 2005) that shows well how this view fits diverse human experience. The expression 'A world full of gods' can be traced back to a famous statement attributed

**Figure 3.1**    *Gods and Goddesses in a Landscape.* Metropolitan Museum of Art. The Elisha Whittelsey Collection, The Elisha Whittelsey Fund, 1951.

to Thales – a pre-Socratic Greek philosopher – who said, "All things are full of gods" (*panta plērē theōn*). As Aristotle explains, "some say that it [soul] is intermingled in the universe, for which reason, perhaps, Thales also thought that all things are full of gods" (*De Anima*, I.5, 411a7). Thales thought water to be the divine source of everything in the universe (something that Odysseus in the earlier example would relate to). Thales was already looking for the *archē* – the first principle or element that endows all things with moving power.

True polytheism, though, does not attempt to determine the *archē* as the source of everything else: it recognizes the existence of many gods and goddesses, each invoked in his or her own sphere and in accordance with various life experiences – from fishing to building to planting to harvesting, etc. As a result, their existence "in the world renders it alive, dynamic, unpredictable, enigmatic and yet not alien nor merely awe-inspiring, since none of the gods assumes an absolute status, but as multiple and transmutable, eternal and mortal, may even be partially discovered in man's living forces themselves" (Goudeli, 2002, pp. 94–95). In such a dynamic world, human beings and supernatural beings live side by side and can form living relationships.

Because of this closeness, it was often natural to model the gods and goddesses as human beings: in ancient Greece, for instance, they normally took the shape of humans and exhibited human traits – in other words, looked and acted like humans (Figure 3.2).

Thus, interaction between human beings and supernatural beings predominantly had the character of analogic communication, in which something is "represented by a likeness" (Watzlawick et al., 1967, p. 61). Since "analogic communication can be more readily referred to the thing it stands for" (Watzlawick et al., 1967, p. 62), it can be relied upon more effectively "for the contingencies of relationship" (Watzlawick et al., 1967, p. 63). And, since

**Figure 3.2**    *Jupiter with gods and goddesses on Olympus* by Paolo Veronese. Boston Museum of Fine Arts.

in analogic communication we find "the lack of the simple negative, i.e., an expression for 'not'" (Watzlawick et al., 1967, p. 65), all human beings, gods and goddesses were just themselves and so their interaction had a more natural (positive) character: only later would the moral purpose of every communicative act come to the foreground and humans find themselves not as ideal as God and thus "rotten with perfection" (Burke, 1966, p. 16).

## 1.1. Seeing Gods

Communication between human beings and supernatural beings went in two directions. On the one hand, the initiative for communication comes from the gods and goddesses, as in the case of divine epiphany: "the awe-inspiring moment in which a divinity reveals him- or herself or manifests his or her power to a mortal or group of mortals, whether in a dream or a 'waking vision'" (Cioffi, 2014, p. 3). This way, for example, Athena – the goddess of wisdom, military victory, and the patron of the city of Athens – appears to Achilles at the beginning of the *Iliad* (1.197–200). On the other hand, humans initiate communication with divine beings in order to appease those that are benevolent and to ward off those that are not, which could be done through prayer, sacrifice, various forms of magic such as incantation, etc. Here, communication most clearly reveals its nature as semiosis, or a process of sign interpretation: people looked for meaning in what seemed random and arbitrary, finding a message from the gods and goddesses in a flight of birds (augury) or the entrails of sacrificial animals (extispicy). A special case of divination is communication with a god or a goddess through a third party, e.g. an oracle. On the one hand, oracles would directly communicate with a deity through an actual experience in order to respond to an inquiry from someone: the most famous oracle in ancient Greece, for instance, was the Pythia – a priestess at Delphi who was believed to receive messages from Apollo – the god of prophecies (Figure 3.3).

On the one hand, oracles would spontaneously receive messages from a god or a goddess that had nothing to do with an original inquiry: many visitors to Delphi were awarded such epiphanies and such "spontaneity . . . underscores the significance of their messages" (McGlew, 1993, p. 68). Thus, oracular communication would gravitate either towards human interpretive effort or divine epiphany. These two ends of human–divine communication can be identified, respectively, with the so-called "inspired divination . . . caused by the supreme power of the gods", and "inductive divination" that is "a largely 'human' endeavor", i.e., "depends upon human interpretation" (Addey, 2014, p. 241).

**Figure 3.3** The Oracle of Delphi. Attic red-figure kylix, 440-430 B.C. Kodros painter. Photo by Zde.

Another way to approach these two types of divination is to view them, following the Stoics' views, as 'natural' and 'artificial': the former "owes nothing to specialized training and instruction" whereas the latter is "the kind of expertise which is acquired by instruction and training" (Allen, 2001, p. 162).

Thus, in polytheistic cultures the human world and the world of divine beings were closely intertwined, forming numerous sites of interaction. Sometimes, human-divine communication was more natural – direct, immediate, and contingent: Odysseus, for instance, does not even address the god of the river by name since it was an unknown god. More often, though, their communication would be more artificial – ritualized in the form of complex practices: for example, it was believed that "when the totem animal is sacrificed, the gods and the people eat in a common meal. Such a meal is considered as a sacrament, and they believed that it brings a bond of union among them" (George, 2008, p. 8).

In all these cases, an encounter takes place when human beings and deities show themselves to one another. This contact highlights the nature of theory in which the meanings of seeing (*thea*, ancient Greek) and god (*theos*, ancient Greek) are interrelated. On the one hand, theory (*theōria*, ancient Greek) refers to watching a spectacle: in ancient Greece, envoys, called *theōroi*, were sent to participate in various shows: "paradoxically, then, the word and concept of 'theory' stems from the festival culture of antiquity" (Burkert, 1987, pp. 29–30; see Fischer-Lichte, 2014, p. 99). On the other hand, theory refers to contemplative contact with the divine because those envoys performed acts of worship at such festivals. Thus, "if Greek philosophy elevated this concept to the 'theoretical' realm it was because the abstract 'show' of thinking seemed to them to be something celebratory" (Burkert, 1987, p. 30; see Fischer-Lichte, 2014, p. 99). It is important to note that, in this festive polytheistic world, "everything shows itself (by itself), and the natural attitude of the protagonists – gods and human beings both – consists in the contemplation, in theoretical bliss, of the appearing that accrues to them" (Gasché, 2007, p. 203). In this sense, one of the items quoted earlier has a very apt title – *Seeing Gods* (Cioffi, 2014): similar to the famous title of Heinz von Foerster's collection of essays – *Observing Systems* – it shows that gods, just as humans, are not only viewed, but are also viewers.

In that never-ending festive show, human communication with deities was not based on any logically conceived and legislated doctrines, any dogma, or any sacred written texts. Rather, the world was kept in motion through mythos – imaginative stories that gave meaning to life experiences. Such stories were not so much abstract narratives as forms of practical knowledge, constantly reenacted and orally passed from generation to generation. In that respect, stories generated through mythos were more lived than told, i.e., actions performed in concert with others. Mythos "lacks the explicit distinction between true and false" (Anderson, 2004, p. 61); in spite of this, or perhaps because of it, its articulation could provide people with an enduring appeal.

Communication between human beings and divine beings was woven so naturally into the fabric of mythos that everyone took it for granted. The world was seen to be dynamic and festive yet ordered, with the human fate determined by complex interactions with gods and goddesses. Such an order was based on cyclical time, e.g.: "in this cyclical cosmology the concept of salvation has to do not with redemption, but with the renewal and 'keeping things going'" (Assmann, 1996, p. 209). It would only be much later that the concept of salvation was introduced by Christianity; when Odysseus is trying to find safe shore on which to make landfall, he is not seeking salvation – he simply wants to be saved from the dangerous water currents.

## 2. 'THOU SHALT HAVE NO OTHER GODS BEFORE ME'

As time went on, it was becoming more and more difficult to 'keep things going'. The world proved too dynamic, life experiences too diverse, and so the search for one reasoned explanation of everything was under-way. Gradually, a shift from polytheism to monotheism was taking place (Figure 3.4).

**Figure 3.4**    *The promulgation of the Law on Mount Sinai.* From Gerard Hoet et al., *Figures de la Bible,* published by P. de Hondt, The Hague, 1728.

The seemingly eternal and unchanging order was first challenged by the Judeo-Christian tradition, which replaced many gods and goddesses with one God: "In the beginning was the Word, and the Word was with God, and the Word was God" (John 1:1). 'The Word' is a translation of the Greek word *Logos:* the mythological stories, which gave meaning to various life experiences and did not draw any distinction between true and false, were replaced with logos as one true account of the world, grounded in reason and rationality. The emphasis shifted from mythos to logos. Whereas stories generated through mythos were more lived than told, logos brings everything into one story, e.g. the Bible as the greatest story ever told: it is important to note that this story is more told than lived.

The transition from polytheism to monotheism was facilitated by the appearance of the alphabet. Every monotheistic religion has one 'greatest story' in which the word of God is contained: the Torah and the other books that comprise the Old Testament were written in Hebrew, the Qur'an was written in Arabic, and the books that comprise the New Testament were written originally in Greek. Most systems of writing allow people to create digital messages where the relation between the sign and what it stands for is based on convention, not likeness: for that reason, "digital message material is of a much higher degree of complexity, versatility, and abstraction than analogic material" (Watzlawick et al., 1967, p. 64). It became possible to develop more abstract thinking, moving away from concrete situations in which deities were involved, to abstract concepts, such as 'God', 'omnipotence', 'morality', etc. Thus, communication with God took on a more symbolic nature; for instance, when Protestant churches use bread and wine (or grape juice) for communion, they symbolize the body and blood of Christ. Even many Roman Catholics, according to a Gallup poll, think that the bread and wine they are receiving at Holy Communion (Figure 3.5) symbolize the spirit and teachings of Jesus and, in so doing, are expressing their attachment to His person and words (D'Antonio et al., 2001).

Whereas in analogic communication we find "the lack of the simple negative, i.e., an expression for 'not'" (Watzlawick et al., 1967, p. 65), digital communication, with its high degree of complexity, versatility and abstraction, makes it possible to refer to something that is not: in this case, God. Unlike the never-ending festive show of the polytheistic world, with monotheism the focus shifts to something in which one can only have faith. St. Paul famously defines faith as "the conviction of things not seen" (Hebrews 11:1); similarly, the Qur'an "is guidance . . . for those who believe in the unseen" (2:3–4).

**Figure 3.5**    The mystery of Holy Communion. Photo by Janbies.

## 2.1. Setting Free the Immortal Soul

Although God was not seen, and humans were not – could never become – like God (and, of course, God could never be imagined acting like humans), the resulting conviction was even stronger because it was based on faith rather than fate. No longer was the world taken for granted: instead, the relationship between God and humans in all monotheism is established through a special covenant. It is a highly symbolic arrangement between God, who is omnipotent and holy, and people, who are sinful and flawed. If people take responsibility for their actions and live in accordance with the word of God, thus fulfilling their side of the covenant, God will fulfill his by providing redemption for people so that their soul is saved. With this new teleological view of the world, when human life is conceptualized as moving forward to the final goal (*telos*), people aim not at what "fate or cyclic and natural determinism allows, but at something beyond fate, something we call 'higher' or 'the transcendent'" (Visser, 2002, p. 23). This way, a new – linear – concept of time was introduced: only by morally going through life from beginning to end is it possible "to set free the immortal soul" (St. Augustine, *The city of God*, XII, 14).

Thus, the transition from polytheism to monotheism took the form of a number of shifts: (a) from many gods and goddesses to one; (b) from concrete practices to symbolic actions; (c) from analog communication to digital communication; (d) from the seen to the unseen; (e) from fate to faith; (f) from stories lived to stories told; (g) from mythos to logos; (h) from the world taken for granted to the world based on covenant and morality; and (i) from cyclical time to linear time. As a result, the emphasis in the human-divine connection shifted: whereas earlier 'everything was full of gods' and deities appeared to human gaze, now faith moved inside the human mind, as it were. However, the human–divine connection was still oriented toward the same realm of more elusive experience providing a perspective on issues of ultimate significance.

## 3. GOD IS NOT DEAD!

At the same time, another perspective on the world was being developed: it tried to explain things scientifically – not by invisible superhuman powers, but by observable natural causes. Logos, as a logical account based on reason and rationality, proved instrumental for identifying the causal principles by which the world operates. In the history of Western civilization, beginning with Thales who believed that the world was made up of a natural substance (water), numerous scientific advances were made in geometry, astronomy, geography, botany, physics, etc. Since then, science has been exploring the world's frontiers, providing answers to various experiences in the form of laws and principles, and not imaginative stories about the word of god(s).

Scientific discovery was based on the explorations not only of the ancient Greek 'natural philosophers', like Thales, but also Islamic as well as medieval and Renaissance European thinkers. Scientific progress was spurred by translation as a form of intercultural communication; for instance, many scientific writings of early scholars in the ancient Near East, Egypt, Greece and Rome, who studied medicine, astronomy, mathematics, etc., were translated into modern European languages (Imhausen & Pommerening, 2016). Also, there was a growing movement of people across local, regional, national and continental borders. Whereas ancient Greece had *theōroi* as observers of sacred spectacles where gods and people showed themselves to one another, as time went on people in their travels focused more and more on objects and events that they encountered in their daily life. The diminishing role of divine presence is reflected in many travel narratives in which scientific reasoning is increasingly used to explain the world. For example, in the introductory note to *The Voyage of the Beagle* Charles Darwin states:

"As far as I can judge of myself, I worked to the utmost during the voyage from the mere pleasure of investigation, and from my strong desire to add a few facts to the great mass of facts in Natural Science" (1909, p. 1). Thus, people in the Modern Age were drifting further away from god(s).

Modernity has differentiation at its core: if everything in traditional (pre-modern) societies is intermixed and blended, to a modern person the world is neatly organized into separate domains such as 'culture' and 'nature', 'science' and 'magic', etc. In a similar fashion, modern science developed its own method, which the American 19th-century pragmatist philosopher Charles S. Peirce described as follows:

> There are real things, whose characters are entirely independent of our opinions about them; those realities affect our senses according to regular laws, and . . . by taking advantage of the laws of perception, we can ascertain by reasoning how things really are.
>
> *(1992, p. 120)*

This method is consistent with the meaning of the word 'science' that is derived from the Proto-Indo-European root *skei-* 'to cut, to split'. In this sense, the scientist is separated ('split') from 'real things' as the object of study.

The scientific method has a number of fundamental characteristics. First, scientific inquiry relies on direct sensory experience or observation of the world: as a result, 'the conviction of things not seen' is clearly outside of this method. Second, all empirical findings must be rationally and logically explained. Third, observations made through the scientific method must be verifiable, i.e., either confirmed for regularity or refuted: for example, the statement "with no air resistance all objects, regardless of their mass, fall to the ground at the same rate", is scientific, while the statement "God loves all people" is not. Fourth, those who use the scientific method aim at collecting evidence that is measurable. Interestingly, the word 'modern', meaning 'now existing' or 'relating to the present time', is traced back to Latin *modus* – 'manner, measure'. Thus, both science and modernity desire, as it were, to exist now and measure everything. In the pre-modern cyclical world, time was not a scarce commodity because "there seems always to be an unlimited supply of it just around the next bend. As they say in the East, when God made time, He made plenty of it" (Lewis, 2006, p. 57). However, during the scientific revolution time "was equated with money for the first time and thus made into into a scarce resource", leading to "the ousting of religion as a time-setting authority" (Nowotny, 2005, p. 83).

As a result, it was discovered "that many questions, formerly obscured by the fog of metaphysics, can be answered with precision" (Russell, 2009, p. 283). Thanks to these (and other) important characteristics of its method, modern science proved itself indispensable in studying phenomena that are material in nature and providing humans with understanding of how the events in the world can be controlled.

So, God's influence was undermined first of all by the findings of natural science that started in ancient Greece, continued through the Middle Ages, and culminated with the scientific revolution of the late sixteenth and seventeenth centuries. In the history of Western Civilization such thinkers as Nicolaus Copernicus, Johannes Kepler, Galileo Galilei, Isaac Newton and many others produced scientific breakthroughs that provided rational explanations for many phenomena previously unexplained. Of special significance was Darwin's Theory of Evolution, which explained the world's development and diversity by natural selection: in the words of Stephen Jay Gould, "[n]o scientific revolution can match Darwin's discovery in degree of upset. . . Evolution substituted a naturalistic explanation of cold comfort for our former conviction that a benevolent deity fashioned us" (2001, p. xi). All these scientific findings and their profound influence on human thought are well documented (Mason, 1953). With these breakthroughs, natural science encroached on God's territory and challenged the accounts attributing many events, including the creation of the world, to divine forces. The concept of scientific laws seemed to leave no room for God's action.

Social science, modeled after natural science, also looked for the laws by which the world operates so that people's interactions could be understood and controlled. The view that the scientific method can be applied to the study of society is best represented by the positivist sociology developed by Auguste Comte in the 19th century. From biology he borrowed the concept of consensus, which he viewed as the interconnectedness of all parts of the social system – a social order based on common beliefs and ideas. By using scientific tools such as surveys and statistics, the law undergirding this social order can be uncovered. Comte called this law 'The Law of Three Stages' and believed that it was applicable to all societies. According to the law, humanity passes through three successive stages: the theological stage, based on the will of God; the metaphysical stage, based on abstract speculative concepts such as freedom; and the positive stage, based on scientific thinking. Thus, all social phenomena are no longer explained by supernatural forces, and all theoretical concepts become positive, i.e., limited to scientific laws that reveal cause and effect relationships.

Comte's ideas proved very influential. Building on his positivist approach to society, Edward Burnett Tylor, one of the founders of modern anthropology, argued that humanity progresses through three stages: savagery, distinguished by hunting and gathering; barbarism, distinguished by agriculture and nomadic herding; and civilization, distinguished by industrialism and urban life. In a similar fashion of positivist thinking, Sir James George Frazer, another founder of modern anthropology, claimed that humankind had passed through three stages: magic, characterized by a false causality between social and natural events; religion, when social phenomena were attributed to divine intervention; and science, which discovers the true causes by which social events can be controlled.

Thus, with its emphasis on observable evidence, logical rigor, precise measurement, and avoidance of metaphysical ambiguity, science helped to uncover many laws underlying the natural and social world, which appeared as an intricately tuned mechanism. With the rapid development of science, the world seemed to have changed irrevocably, separating us from our primitive, pre-modern ancestors: as a result, faith was losing its luster and God was increasingly pushed into the margins. Ironically, the idea of God contained within itself the seeds of its own destruction: as Ivan Illich put it, "modernity came into being only because people had experienced the world as lying in the hands of God and so it became possible, later on, to take that world out of God's hands" (Cayley, 2004, p. 69).

Indeed, in 1882, in his collection *Die fröhliche Wissenschaft* (*The Gay Science*, also translated as *The Joyful Pursuit of Knowledge and Understanding*), Friedrich Nietzsche famously declared: "God is dead. God remains dead. And we have killed him" (Nietzsche, 1974, Book 3, Aphorism 125). In other words, the idea of the divine stopped being the source for all morality, value, and order; as a result, people faced a profound crisis of established ideals and truth. It is important to emphasize, as Martin Heidegger points out, that Nietzsche's pronouncement does not mean there is no God: "The pronouncement means something worse: God has been killed" (1977, p. 105). Of course, it was the natural scientists who were blamed for that in the first place: in this respect, the following book title is very telling: *God Is Dead! Don't Blame Nietzsche: It Was Carl Sagan and Stephen Hawking Who Killed Him* (Pafumi, 2013). As we saw earlier, though, social scientists contributed to the demise of God as well. Comte, as a young boy, "naturally ceased to believe in God", and this "necessary emancipation" (Pickering, 2006, p. 34) later formed the basis for his positivist thinking. Émile Durkheim, another social scientist, focusing on the disorganization of European economic, political, and social institutions, proclaimed that "the old gods are growing old or already dead" (1954, p. 427). It must be noted, however, that Nietzsche blames humankind for the death of God: all people are "murderers of all murderers" (Nietzsche, 1974, Book 3, Aphorism 125). Indeed, since the beginning of history, humans have been responsible for terrible horrors – many committed in the name of God: crusades, slavery, apartheid, religious and genocidal wars. . . Had Nietzsche lived to see the horrors of the 20th and 21st centuries – millions killed in the First and Second World Wars, concentration camps, annihilation of thousands in Hiroshima and Nagasaki, daily murder and violence today – he would become even more convinced that "God remains dead". How can God – if in fact God does exist – remain silent in the midst of such evil and suffering?! And so, instead of sustaining all this the way Job did, people lose their faith. Thus, if anyone is to blame for the death of God, it is nobody else but us: it is at our hands that God has become "unbelievable" (Nietzsche, 1974, Book 5, Aphorism 343).

It was no surprise, then, when on April 8, 1966, *Time* magazine came out with one of its most iconic covers ever produced. The cover read simply, 'Is God Dead?' However, five decades later, *Time* published an article entitled 'Rumors of God's Death Have Been Greatly Exaggerated' (April 7, 2016). Indeed, in spite of a vast amount of knowledge generated by science, the existence of God or some kind of divine force has hardly been disproved. On the contrary, one can read, for example, about "the God upgrade" (Korngold, 2011). Even polytheism remains a presence in modern society (duBois, 2014). Belief in God is still strong all over the world: according to a 2014 Pew Research Center survey, nearly 90% of Americans believe in God or some kind of universal being; even the majority of those who are religiously unaffiliated say that they believe in God or a universal spirit. About 68% U.S. adults do not see any conflict between science and belief in God: in fact, they are seen as the two sides of the human impulse to understand our place in the world and to marvel at the wonder of life (Pew Research Center, 2014; Aczel, 2014). The list of famous scientists who believed in God includes Nicolaus Copernicus, Johannes Kepler, Galileo Galilei, Isaac Newton, Max Planck and Albert Einstein. Today, when asked if science makes belief in God obsolete, the opinions of many scientists range from 'No' to 'It depends' to 'Yes' to 'Absolutely not!' (see: https://web.archive.org/web/20161108232749/templeton.org/belief ). According to Frank Wilczek, an American theoretical physicist, mathematician and Nobel laureate, there are questions that take us beyond the borders of physics into theology (Wilczek, 2017). This includes not only specifically scientific questions such as "Why is a hyper-compressed description of the universe's operating system possible?", as mentioned by Frank Wilczek, but also questions about the meaning of human existence and the nature of the universe. Bruno Latour, a French philosopher, anthropologist and sociologist, appears to be right: we have never been modern (Latour, 1993), i.e., we have never separated ourselves from our pre-modern ancestors whose life was driven by mythos. Moreover, perhaps, since we cannot eliminate the metaphysical stuff such as imaginative stories and faith, can we never become modern?

Be that as it may, we still believe that there are more things in heaven and earth than can be explained by science. Also, just as science can be used for either harmful or good purposes, people's belief in God can move people in various ways affecting their communicative behavior. On the one hand, it can cause conflicts in interfaith marriages (Soliz & Colaner, 2014); by the same token, "You can't understand three-quarters of the conflicts in the world unless you recognize that God is a central player" (Rothman, 2016). On the other hand, as Pope Francis put it, "true faith in the Son of God is inseparable from self-giving, from membership in the community" (Francis, 2013, paragraph 88). When Dante ends his *Divine Comedy* by talking about "the Love that moves the sun and the other stars", we should remember that his masterpiece "is set within medieval cosmology. In that cosmos the Love of God directs the heavenly bodies like the sun and the stars musically in their orbits" (Fischer, 2004, p. 85). Without a doubt, the wonder of God enriches the human experience!

Thus, what we call 'God' still points to an infinite transcendence captivating our minds and hearts. Just as Horatio, a model of rationality in Shakespeare's *Hamlet*, is having a hard time dealing with a ghost, we continue to struggle coming to terms with the wonder of God. Or, in the words of Ludwig Wittgenstein, one of the most influential philosophers of the 20th century, "to believe in a God means to see that the facts of the world are not the end of the matter" (1979, p. 74).

## 4. 'THE GOD-PROBLEM' IN COMMUNICATION THEORY

It is commonly thought that the wonder of God has no place in communication theory, which is secular and does not address all those mysterious and transcendent aspects of the human condition. We hear about "the alarming impertinence of a Christian theory of communications" in "many quarters of communications scholarship" (Fackler, 2014, p. 875). We read that it is hard to imagine a textbook on public speaking that views communication not as a mechanistic process emphasizing technique, but as "a significantly serendipitous process" (Schultze, 2005, p. 6). It is argued that contemporary communication theories are secular and ignore the role of human spirituality: as a result, we are missing an essential component of practical discourse (Sabourin, 2003). Similarly, it is noted that scholars have ignored "the role of divine inspiration in the communication process" (Kaylor, 2011, p. 77). While we need to distinguish between 'religious' as referring to the structures and beliefs of organized denominations, 'spiritual' as more personal connection to faith in any supernatural phenomena, and 'divine' as related to deity, they all can be brought together under the concept of God pointing to the most elusive, mysterious and animating forces that lie beyond the physical facts of the world.

Just as the rumors of God's death have been greatly exaggerated, the alarm sounding God's absence in communication theory seems to be exaggerated as well. It must be pointed out that the 1966 article in *Time* magazine, published half a century ago, did not proclaim the death of God: instead, it called for the new approaches to the problem of God and the new language to discuss it. In other words, God was not killed but problematized. In fact, although it may have been found subversive by modernity's agenda, "historically speaking, the God-problem was one of the most recurring themes in communication studies" (Schultze, 2005, p. 1). This problem is addressed in many different ways.

*Associations.* There are several academic societies formed by people interested in the study of the God-problem. For instance, the Religious Communication Association brings together those who share a common interest in understanding the nature of religious speech, media, performance and other communication. It is important to note that the association is an interfaith scholarly and professional organization open to diversity of religious beliefs, subject matter concerns, and methodologies. One of the academic divisions within the National Communication Association (NCA) is the Spirituality Communication Division aimed at promoting an understanding of spirituality from a communication perspective and focused on the uncertainties and mysteries of everyday life.

*Journals.* There are a number of journals dedicated to the analysis of the God-problem in the context of communication and media studies. According to the content analysis of 29 journals over a 10-year period conducted by Stephen Croucher and his team (Croucher et al., 2016), at least 15 main themes related to religion and spirituality are covered in these journals, including communication traits and behaviors, media use and preferences, organizational behaviors, communication about health related issues, and intercultural and interracial interactions. While the overall academic discourse of 'religion' and 'spirituality' is significant, there are two leading journals which provide most of the coverage of these issues: the *Journal of Communication and Religion*, published by the Religious Communication Association, and the *Journal of Media and Religion*. Another journal that must be noted is the *Journal of Management, Spirituality & Religion* (*JMSR*), which positions itself as the first port of call for academics interested in the spiritual and religious aspects of managing and organizing. Also, some communication journals publish special issues on topics that deal with the God-problem: an example is a special issue on religion and spirituality published by the *Journal of Applied Communication Research* (2011).

*Reference works.* Many such topics find coverage in communication encyclopedias and handbooks. For instance, one of the articles in the *SAGE Encyclopedia of Communication Theory* is entitled 'Religious Communication Theories' (Schuetz, 2009). Many aspects of divine-human communication are discussed in the article on Christianity published in *The International Encyclopedia of Communication Theory and Philosophy* (Horsfield, 2016). *The Handbook of Media and Mass Communication Theory* contains a chapter on Jewish communication theory (Cohen, 2014) and another one with a telling title: 'God Still Speaks' (Fackler, 2014).

*Dissertations.* One can find in-depth coverage of the relationship between God and communication in many dissertations, e.g. such recent titles as *Voices in Concert: Communication Ethnography of Pentecostal Worship* (Coats, 2012), *Why the Passion? Bernard Lonergan on the Cross as Communication* (Miller, 2008), and *In Defense of Communicating God's Word: Conversational Preaching. How an Understanding of Interpersonal Communications Theory Can Improve Our Preaching* (Sowards, 2017).

*Books.* There are numerous books dedicated to various aspects of the God-problem from diverse communication perspectives, e.g. *Religion as Communication. God's Talk* (Pace, 2011), *Communication Theory for Christian Witness* (Kraft, 1991), and *Communicating God's Word in a Complex World: God's Truth or Hocus Pocus?* (Shaw & Van Engen, 2003).

*Articles.* Every year, hundreds of articles are being published addressing the God-problem in communication studies. For example, the content analysis of the journals mentioned earlier found 468 articles that made references to issues related to 'religion' and 'spirituality' (Croucher et al., 2016). Naturally, when the agency of God within human communication is considered broadly, the number of articles increases significantly, e.g. the following titles: 'Human Communication Revisited – A Biblical Perspective' (Ayee, 2013), 'God-Man Communication in the Quran: A Semiological Approach' (Gheituri & Golfam, 2009), and 'Chaos, Communications Theory, and God's Abundance' (Huchingson, 2003).

## 4.1. Experiencing (the Word of) God(s)

Experience can be broadly conceptualized as any instance of undergoing or encountering something that has had an effect on you. Experiencing (the word of) god(s) may be defined more specifically as "feelings, perceptions and sensations . . . involving some communication, however slight, with a divine essence, that is, with God, with ultimate reality" (Stark & Glock, 1974, p. 15). Such experiences are very common, according to a number of recent studies that examined people's perceived interactions with God and their effects. Let us take a quick look at some of the most important kinds of these experiences.

One is divine revelation as direct communication from God to humans. Revelation, derived from the Greek word *apokalupsis*, meaning 'unveiling', is understood as an "intense or unusual experience that the recipient interprets without a doubt to be a direct communication from God . . . and regardless of whether the recipient understood/understands the meaning of the message clearly" (Sigler, 2014, pp. 149–150). God's self-revelation is said to take many forms, e.g. through natural elements, miracles, or prophecy. This way, people say they hear the voice of God: this does not need to be taken in its materialistic sense, but, rather, as becoming aware of God's presence, i.e., as a mystical perception of God's inner workings in one's soul and body. Such inner illumination must not be equated with receiving divine instruction in the form of complete sentences, what is known as 'the propositional view of revelation': rather, it must be understood as the most immediate and authentic encounter with God. At the same time, this encounter cannot be reduced only to an emotional state, as we still get a new, non-discursive knowledge that is immediately and intuitively perceived. In other words, experiences of divine communication do not so much pop into people's heads, but much rather *happen* to them (Immink, 2016). Thus, when criteria for a model for direct divine communication are suggested, they include the experiences' noetic character, briefness, and spontaneity, which set such experiences apart from an effortful process of reasoning.

Every experience relates to something else, i.e., is an experience of something, and the more effort it requires, the more it is based on intentionality of consciousness. By intentionally directing our consciousness to something that is not given in the experiencing act itself, one is able to transcend oneself: this way, one can experience God through worship (Figure 3.6).

While god(s) can be worshiped through many forms, e.g., songs and dances, the most common is prayer, whether private or communal, an example of the latter being the so-called 'gathered' or 'covered' meetings of Quakers (Molina-Markham, 2014). Prayer can be a matter of words or silence,

**Figure 3.6**   Child worshiping God in Patan, Nepal. Photo by Deshpremiraj.

The Wonder of God   85

e.g. "the inclusion of silent, individual prayer within the communal sharing of the Word of God of the liturgy" (Stewart, 2008, p. 208). Prayer has
received much scholarly attention as a unique phenomenon of human
communication in which God is addressed and thus experienced (Benson
& Wirzba, 2005). Often, prayer is analyzed from the perspective of ethnography of communication, e.g. a study on child-God communication in
Northern Italy (Zanatta et al., 2011) or an ethnography of the private performance of the five daily prayers of Islam (Haeri, 2013).

It must be noted that people's experiences of sensing god(s) are met with
doubt in our secular age, whether they are viewed as divine revelation that
occurs seemingly without any human effort or as intentionally directed to
god(s) – the former being met with more doubt than the latter. Such doubts
can be justified if experience is treated within the bounds of reason, reduced
to statements that can be understood by a process of logic and capable of
empirical verification. At the same time, as William James put it, in the
human consciousness there may exist "a sense of reality, a feeling of objective presence, a perception of what we may call 'something there', more deep
and more general than any of the special and particular 'senses'" (1903, p. 58).
Such objects of human experience may be more or less abstract, are not
demonstrable in a concrete way, yet are real in that they influence people's
actions. Real experience, then, is what appears in our consciousness, and
so we must focus on the realm of phenomena or what is actually given in
experience. This view places the emphasis on the lived experience, which
is always something unique, personal, and affective. In this view, experiencing (the word of) god(s) can be best theorized by phenomenology, which,
as a systematic study of consciousness and subjective human experience, is
an interpretive approach to communication focusing on people's life experiences and their meanings (Croucher & Cronn-Mills, 2015, p. 53). The
phenomenological tradition is grounded in the idea of communication as
an authentic and genuine connection to otherness – an inner awareness of
the other that resists empirical claims. Much work has been done in this
light, showing how the word of god(s) can be experienced: one very recent
example is a topical issue of Open Theology, *Phenomenology of Religious
Experience* (Louchakova-Schwartz & Crouch, 2017), prepared by the Society
for the Phenomenology of Religious Experience (SOPHERE) – an international organization for advancing knowledge of religious experience in its
historical, theological, sociological, philosophical, and psychological aspects.

Unlike the scientific view of communication that analytically breaks communication down into empirically verifiable steps, the humanistic view is

synthetic in that it emphasizes the whole person experiencing the Other – in this case, god(s) – both cognitively and corporeally, in a dynamic and living process of communication. A well-known example of 'this' view is the human encounter with God or the 'eternal Thou' as conceptualized by Martin Buber. Only in this encounter can the 'I' develop as a whole being, going beyond what he calls the 'I-It' relation. While it may be tempting to see the 'I-It' relation as denigrated by the 'I-Thou' experience, our journey begins with the genuine gift of the 'I-It' making the 'I-Thou' possible: thus, neither can be ignored by communication theory (Arnett, 2016).

It is no surprise, then, that calls are made for intensified study of various forms of experiencing the word of god(s), emphasizing the need for more synthesis of existing knowledge (Sigler, 2014). Not only do such experiences impact people's ability to function in everyday life, but they prove themselves to be meaningful, useful and necessary. They are found to be normative and so differ phenomenologically from pathological experiences found, for example, in schizophrenia (Luhrmann, 2012). Experiencing the word of god(s) must be viewed as "the very movement itself of the soul, putting itself in a personal relation of contact with the mysterious power of which it feels the presence – it may be even before it has a name by which to call it" (James, 1903, p. 464). It is through such experiences that we can feel the emotions of wonder and joy that "have organic, cognitive and – in the case of, for example, religious or metaphysical wonder and joy – social dimensions (including, for example, social relations with the community and with the sacred)" (Petersen, 2014, p. 816).

## 4.2. Spreading (the Word of) God(s)

It is common to draw a distinction between non-missionary (non-proselytizing) and missionary (proselytizing) world religions, Hinduism often presented as an example of the former and Christianity of the latter. Broadly understood, though, we take the concept of god(s) as pointing to those experiences that transcend the physical world and, while non-demonstrable, are real and of ultimate significance. In this sense, the word of god(s) is a message that cannot be equated only with organized religion. Furthermore, if we take into account that "the archaic meaning of 'message' actually is 'mission' and in the oral tradition, messengers also were the missionaries for a godly cause" (Krippendorff, 1990, p. 6), then it becomes even more clear that propagation lies at the heart of the word of god(s) as a form of communication. Any such message for a godly cause is like a seed that is cast by someone. In this light, communication appears as dissemination: anyone who spreads the word of god(s) is like the biblical sower who is not being selective but freely disseminates his seeds, "speaking into the air" (Peters, 1999).

Thus, whenever we see the word of god(s) spreading across space, we can talk about the transmission of that message. In fact, according to the so-called 'transmission view', the origins of communication are seen in religious ideas transported "across geography for the purpose of control" (Carey, 1989, p. 18). An example of such transportation is the contact of European Protestants with "the heathen community of the Americas . . . seen as a form of communication with profoundly religious implications. This movement in space was an attempt to establish and extend the kingdom of God, to create the conditions under which godly understanding might be realized, to produce a heavenly though still terrestrial city. The moral meaning of transportation, then, was the establishment and extension of God's kingdom on earth" (Carey, 1989, p. 13). In this light, whenever we discuss political, economic, or technological innovations, this meaning should not be overlooked.

The discussion of *what* is contained in the word of god(s) as message, is outside of the scope of this chapter: it has been extensively covered within the frameworks of theology, history, anthropology, etc. Our focus here is on *how* message is communicated to achieve some anticipated outcome: this is addressed by several communication theories.

The theory that must be mentioned in the first place is Information Theory, which reduces communication to a probability function and is concerned with "only the efficient transmission of messages through communication channels, not what those messages mean" (Hayles, 1999, p. 54). According to this theory, just as mail can carry from a sender to a receiver all kinds of messages, "in the same manner, priests bring the voice of god closer to believers" (Krippendorff, 1990, p. 1). In Christianity, for example, the missionary, evangelist, or pastor can be identified as the one bringing the voice of God, while "God and Jesus Christ are the source of the message" (Schnabel, 2008, p. 402). Another example is the "hierarchical partnerships" in writing religious treatises that "enable God's message to be transmitted efficiently from the top down" (Benedict, 2004, p. 20). Yet another way to apply this theory is to measure the surprise content of a sermon (Sheridan, 2014). Also, a conciliar document created by the Second Vatican Council in 1963, known as *Inter Mirifica* (The Decree on the Means of Social Communication), "tends to present communication as a process of transmission. . . . It is formed from a metaphor of geography of transportation. . . . *Inter Mirifica*'s analytical presentation of an instrumental approach to social communication is illustrated by constant use of this vocabulary: 'senders', 'receivers', and 'exchanges'" (Kappeler, 2009, p. 66).

One of the main modes of spreading the word of god(s) is preaching as a form of communication (Figure 3.7).

While there may be many factors involved in preaching, "the underlying model is bound to involve a sender, receivers, and the transmitting of a message through signs" (Buttrick, 1988, p. 175). Whereas "a message transmitted mostly by the spoken word" is at the heart of preaching, it is noted that in this area, "the impact of new forms of media" on preaching "effectively has yet to

**Figure 3.7**   *St. Paul Preaching in Athens*, by Raphael. Located in the Victoria and Albert Museum. From the Royal Collection of the United Kingdom.

be thoroughly measured and/or evaluated" (Cutié, 2016, p. 3). That this effect needs to be 'thoroughly measured' must be especially emphasized because, in this view, communication is treated in terms of one's freedom of choice when selecting a message to be transmitted. It must be also emphasized that new communication technologies, from the telegraph to the computer, have extended God's kingdom on Earth further, including not only preaching but other forms of communication.

With the introduction of feedback, information flows become receptive to environmental influences and capable of adapting to them for various purposes. How information is controlled and regulated in such open systems is theorized by cybernetics, which can also shed light on spreading the word of god(s). For instance, the so-called 'ecclesial cybernetics', related both to traditional ecclesiology and to modern communication theory, is aimed at discovering the operative principles by which communication occurs between all levels in the church and between the church and its total environment. To that end, ecclesial cybernetics uses such concepts as 'input', 'output', 'channels', 'feedback loop', etc. Once church communication is viewed in terms of how the decision-making process is controlled, conclusions can be made about making information flows more effective and democratic (Granfield, 1973). Another area where the ideas of cybernetics could be used is the theory of regulation of religious communications, which is considered "still woefully incomplete" (Price, 2007, p. 105). There are many issues that deal with people's rights to receive and impart information, from the regulation of sermons to the control of campaigns for conversion. While the concepts of power, ideology and freedom of expression are usually addressed by critical communication theories, cybernetics is focused on the nature of strategic communication, system architecture, satellite channels, etc.

Last but certainly not least, classical rhetoric needs to be mentioned as a communication theory covering the symbolic techniques used in propagating and reinforcing the word of god(s). Homiletics, or the theory of preaching as a unique form of communication, is based on rhetorical concepts, from the invention of the message to the modes of its effective delivery. It is important to emphasize that these concepts come from classical rhetorical theory, which fits well into the transmission view of communication as moving "in a linear way. . . from preexisting situation to text to audience effect" (Combs, 2005, p. 11). In other words, this approach "remains defined by a linear, cause-and-effect model in which an object receives some unintended, meaningful action" (Vivian, 2004, p. 59). At the same time, it must be remembered that this approach "can be useful to distinguish pragmatically between communication sources and receivers, to map the flow of information through systems, or to think of messages as containers of meaning or of communication as an intentional act performed in order to achieve some anticipated outcome" (Craig, 1999, p. 137).

## 4.3. Listening to (the Word of) God(s)

Earlier, two extreme forms of divine–human communication were mentioned – the so-called 'inspired divination', caused by the power of the gods, and 'inductive divination' that calls for human effort in understanding the gods. The former was widespread in the times when the world was full of gods and every encounter with a god was felt as immediate and authentic; the latter became common as a transition was taking place from polytheism to monotheism and thus from concrete practices to symbolic actions. Not only was God's kingdom on Earth being extended farther and farther across space, but the meaning of God's word was harder and harder to understand as more and more time elapsed. Thus, more and more ambiguities were involved in trying to understand and evaluate events, claims and cognitions presented as the word of God. Since a gap still exists between God and humans, we can only, in the words of the Apostle Paul, "see through a glass, darkly" (1 Corinthians 13:12). Because "a sacred text does not magically interpret itself for human beings" (Schultze, 2005, p. 14), human effort in understanding God's word is needed. Such effort finds its best manifestation and explication in hermeneutics as a key interpretive approach to communication.

The term 'hermeneutics' is related to the Greek god Hermes (Figure 3.8) whose task was to provide an interpretive bridge between the divine realm and the human realm, thus offering to human beings the possibility of a communion with the divine.

The Greek verb *hermēneuō* refers to the process of explaining or translating the meaning of obscure messages. In this sense, the process of translation from one language to another has special significance. This mode is present whenever an original text is translated into a new context: for instance, "translatability became the characteristic mode of Christian expansion through history" (Sanneh, 1989, p. 214). Of course, hermeneutics must

**Figure 3.8**  Hermes – *Greek mythology systematized* (1880).

be understood very broadly, i.e., as an interpretive procedure necessary to understand the meaning that is not transparent and make it intelligible to the people of a different time and place.

Hermeneutics, which has its origins in the interpretation of the divine, received its first systematic formulation in trying to understand the meaning of the word of God as expressed in the Bible. The early Christian authors were concerned with establishing the procedures for differentiating between apocryphal, or doubtful of authenticity, and true versions. Whenever they came across a word or a passage deemed significant, however not quite transparent in its full meaning, they would place signs above, beneath or next to those words or passages: through this diacritical operation, meaning was interpreted by being glossed, edited, amended or commented upon (Alloa, 2015). While hermeneutics in its early stages was text-based, it did not always operate in the form of visual signs. For example, because the Hebrew of the Torah lacked vowels, it was the responsibility of the reader to scan the roots of the words, adding vowels: any variation in vowels could produce different meanings from the same root. The reader had to look at all possible meanings and make sure that the word that was created as a result of adding vowels would be understood in the context of the entire message: "thus, every pronunciation of a biblical word is already an interpretive act of major consequence" (Cherry, 2007, p. 12).

The construction of hermeneutical frameworks made it possible to establish a canon of scriptural texts, to summarize the essence of shared beliefs, or to determine the relative authority of different communication genres: for instance, "in regards to prayers which are not psalms, the taxonomy based on communication theory allows those who read biblical prayers to analyze and classify them in more accurate and informative ways" (Neyrey, 2004, p. 353). Overall, hermeneutic procedures allow people to determine which messages can be evaluated and authorized as valid communication from God.

It must be emphasized that, as Heidegger recognized, "to interpret is first to listen" (Palmer, 1980, p. 6). When focusing on listening as a cognitive process, we must not forget that, from the perspective of philosophical hermeneutics, people listen to various messages in order to interpret their meanings: once understood and accepted, the meaning becomes a part of your being. In this sense, "listening requires the submission of spirit, soul, and body to God" (Ime, 2013, p. 91). A close link between obedience and listening can be found in many cultural traditions and reflected in such languages as Greek, Latin and Hebrew. It is important to note that obedience is a self-reflexive process, i.e., involves a free meaningful choice. It is as if, after listening to someone, one comes back to himself/herself: only this way can true connection be established. This is clearly seen in the Russian equivalent for the verb 'to obey' – *slushat'sya*, which literally means 'to listen to oneself'. It is interesting to note that this self-reflexive nature of obedience is found only in listening and not in the other forms of communication: e.g. such words as *govorit'sya* ('*to speak oneself'), *pisat'sya* ('*to write oneself') and *chitat'sya* ('*to read oneself'). Listening as commitment is never forced; that is why it plays a central role in the ethical constitution of the subject. Thus, it is through listening that people are drawn together in fellowship and commit to the same meaning: "we become one when we listen together" (Lipari, 2010, p. 350).

Whatever people obediently listen to, i.e., follow and share, is sacred because it appears natural: "In any given cultural community, the sacred is whatever it treated as unquestionable, 'beyond interdiction,' as Durkheim puts it" (Rothenbuhler, 1998, p. 24). One may wonder how this fits into the framework of hermeneutics which consists in asking questions about the meaning of a message. Being a part of something that is sacred, though, is not questioning it in the sense of challenging or contesting it; rather, it is trying to openly and lovingly find meaning. In fact, "the ability to ask questions well is nothing other than a certain love of λόγος [logos]" (Ewegen, 2014, p. 46). In other words, once we have found a meaningful answer to a question, our action becomes 'beyond interdiction'. Such actions take the form of rituals, which are non-instrumental action, i.e., "not useful for specifically technical purposes" (Rothenbuhler, 1998, p. 11). Besides, "in a ritual . . . authors are unimportant" (Krippendorff, 2009, p. 61). However, it is in this seeming unusefulness and anonymity that ritual reveals its profound significance: it is a form of communication in which meaning is revived through constant transformation. Because ritual highlights "the transformative, efficacious quality of the liminal" (Crosby, 2009, p. 9), every time an act of listening takes place, the invisible threshold between humans and god(s) is crossed (it is worth remembering that Hermes is the god of boundaries and crossroads).

Thus, when humans listen to the word of god(s), they are drawn together by certain meanings that are constituted within various symbolic activities, some of which are interpreted as sacred and take the ritual form: it is such practices that are then symbolically enacted – time and time again. We find this approach in the so-called 'ritual view of communication' that focuses on the representation of shared beliefs and maintenance of society in time (Carey, 1989). Significantly, this view highlights such routine (i.e., most frequent) symbolic actions as religious festivities, song and prayer: these activities (re)create a meaningful and ordered world, which becomes the framework for human action. This symbolic world, shared by those with collective memory and cultural identity, is sustained as long as people continue listening to the word of god(s).

When we read that "the word 'God' embraces an ultimate reality and gives it a significant interpretation" (Gräb, 2011, p. 163), we must remember that this is a general statement. In real life, messages are interpreted and made relevant to a particular place and time, i.e., are "processed hermeneutically within a community, which . . . applies God's Word to its reality" (Shaw & Van Engen, 2003, p. 17). Therefore, many different interpretations exist and each is significant in its own way. There are numerous examples of how interpretation will differ between communities, affecting communication in and between people from those socio-cultural orders; consider, for instance, the area of illness and healing. It is noted that for neo-Pentecostals in an Episcopalian church, certain communicative behaviors are interpreted and accepted as indications of the presence of the Holy Spirit, while some frenzied or violent outbursts are not recognized as acceptable. The phrase 'Thou shall not heal by the arm of the flesh' can be interpreted in these communities as a rationale against immunization and deaths from diphtheria in nonimmunized children as 'acts of God'. Another example is the difficulty getting rural fishing villagers in India to accept the smallpox vaccination as they believed that smallpox was caused by the goddess Kali and not by a virus: when vaccination was promoted as a mark of respect to that goddess, the acceptance of immunization was no longer a problem (Putsch & Joyce, 1990). As we know only too well, though, not all conflicts in which the word of god(s) generates different interpretations, can be resolved so easily or at all, e.g. the so-called 'intractable conflicts' (Smith, 2016). Let us not forget, though, "that hermeneutics is one of the most promising approaches for interreligious dialogue" (Hustwit, 2014, p. x) and use its theoretical framework towards making that dialogue more successful.

We must remember that God is an ultimate reality that can only be invoked. In fact, the English word 'god' can be traced back to the Proto-Germanic *guthan, from Proto-Indo-European *ghut- 'that which is invoked'. For example, whenever the Athenians "pronounced the name of their city, they thereby invoked the name of the goddess Athena, their divine protectress" (Colaiaco, 2001, p. 121). It may seem that invocation is a very abstract form of communication far removed from our daily life; this, however, is not the case, for invocation is, first and foremost, an oath.

While not a communication theorist but a sociologist, Émile Durkheim captured its essence very well, noting that, when words are "pronounced in ritual form and ritual condition, they take on a sacred (and therefore emotional) character by that very act. One means of giving them this sacred character is the oath, or invocation of a divine being. Through this invocation, the divine being becomes the guarantor of the promise exchanged. Therefore the promise . . . becomes compulsive, under threat of sacred penalties of known gravity" (Durkheim et al., 2013, p. 200). Thus, an oath has a complex nature. First, it is affirmation, since God can never be signified completely, being 'a sea of existence indefinite and indeterminate', according to Thomas Aquinas; God can only be affirmed as a name. Second, God is invoked as a witness to the words of the one who takes an oath. And, third, to take an oath is to curse oneself in the event of not doing what one swore to do or doing what one swore not to do:

**Figure 3.9**    *The Oath*, by Kristjan Raud. Sourced by Vapsid.

"the violation of the oath disturbs the communication between the human and the divine sphere" (Schroeder, 2001, p. 137). The oath, therefore, is a combination of three components – an affirmation, the invocation of God as witness, and a curse directed at perjury. If "the oath is the most ancient thing, no less ancient than the gods" (Agamben, 2017, p. 314), then communication, as such, begins with the oath: it is a force that binds together words and actions, humans and gods, and humans and humans (Figure 3.9).

So, in the beginning was the Word and in the beginning was the Act: when God speaks, it is done, with no interval between the two. That is what God teaches us and that is what humans are striving for. Were it not for God, there would be no humans: may the force be with us all!

# 4

# The Wonder
# of the Body

Key concepts:

Apperception, body language, the body image, chronemics, communicology, existentialism, flesh, the grotesque body, gustorics, haptics, intercorporeality, kinesics, the lived body, the living body, nonverbal communication, olfatics, paralanguage, perception, performance, phenomenology, posthuman, *Prägnanz*, proxemics, *res cogitans*, *res extensa*, semiotics, sensation, speech, textualization, virtual communication.

Key names:

St. Thomas Aquinas, Mikhail Bakhtin, Ray L. Birdwhistell, Kenneth Burke, Charles Darwin, René Descartes, Edward T. Hall, Katherine Hayles, Hippocrates, Edmund Husserl, Richard L. Lanigan, Bruno Latour, Gottfried Wilhelm Leibniz, Michel Foucault, Albert Mehrabian, Maurice Merleau-Ponty, John Peters, Jean-Paul Sartre, Charles S. Peirce, Plato.

## 1. WHAT IS THE BODY?

In *Phaedo*, Plato laments that "it is not possible to have pure knowledge of anything so long as we are within the body" and so "if we are ever to have pure knowledge of anything, we must get rid of the body and survey things alone in themselves by means of the soul herself alone" (*Phaedo*, 66d–e). Indeed, if only we could be like angels – those "messengers between ourselves and God" who need "no earthly food or drink" (James, 1909, p. 164)! Un/fortunately, we can't communicate like angels since they have no fleshly bodies – and we do; 'un/fortunately', because it "is a tragic fact, but also a blessed one" (Peters, 1999, p. 29). It is what makes us humans, i.e., earthly beings that do have bodies.

That the human body draws much scholarly attention, then, is not surprising. The body of studies on the body is vast and growing day by day. In fact, there is a field of 'body studies' which is interdisciplinary in nature. Within this field, such topics are addressed as 'Body, Self and Society', 'Religion and the Body', 'Medical Regimes and the Body', 'Gender, Sexualities and Race', and 'Technologies and Body Modification' (Turner, 2012). Key concepts related to the body range from 'the affective body' to 'the sleeping body' to 'corporeal capital' to 'healthism and the body' to 'horse-human relations' (Blackman, 2008).

What first comes to mind when we speak of the body as a communication phenomenon is, of course, body language as a form of nonverbal communication (Figure 4.1).

**Figure 4.1**    Expressing disagreement with body language. Photo by STUDIO GRAND OUEST/Shutterstock.com.

It is common to consider the verbal as "implicitly the norm while 'non-verbal modes' can too easily be pictured as merely secondary adjuncts to speech" (Finnegan, 2002, p. 37). However, "what is called, rather diminishingly, non-verbal communication is clearly older than language" (Peters, 2015, p. 271). It is difficult, therefore, to agree with those who say that the importance of nonverbal communication in human behavior was discovered only "in recent years" (Buck, 1997, p. 322) or that most of the public become aware of the existence of body language, as a part of nonverbal communication, only in the 1970s (Pease & Pease, 2008). In fact, much of what we know about ancient cultures we have learned from nonverbal communication, e.g. cave paintings or relief drawings. It is thanks to the relief drawings found in an Egyptian tomb, for example, that we know how to make bread as the Egyptians did during the Old Kingdom. We basically followed the instructions as shown in the ancient drawings: this is how you leave a container with the wet dough outdoors and this is how you put the dough into pots when it is ready (Calero, 2005). Or, take dance, which has been a form of nonverbal communication and social organization from australopithecines to *Homo sapiens*, as Judith Hanna shows in her book *To Dance is Human: A Theory of Nonverbal Communication* (1987). Or, take music: like dance, it goes back in time and, like dance, due to its rhythmic nature, it provided the early humans with an evolutionary advantage, as argued by Steven Mithen in his book *The Singing Neanderthals: The Origins of Music, Language, Mind, and Body* (2005). All these human activities, as well as and many others, including the Bacchanalia – those Roman festivals of Bacchus – or sports spectacles in the ancient world (Kyle, 2015), or meditation and yoga as "forms of intrapersonal communication" (Cushman & Kincaid, 1987, p. 20), have one thing in common: they can't take place without the body.

When we read that, "since communication studies was founded as a discipline in 1915, the discipline has not consistently acknowledged bodies" (Thornton, 2016), we can agree with the statement only if we accept the status of the study of communication as an institutionalized (in the U.S.) discipline and the date when it was founded. If, however, we look at it more broadly, we can quickly see how, through the ages, the body has been recognized as an object of communication theorizing. For instance, in ancient Greece athletic and rhetorical practices overlapped, and many philosophers such as Isocrates and Demosthenes provided their insights into the realm of such bodily arts (Hahee, 2004). Another philosopher – Alcidamas, who was Plato's contemporary – says that "an oral speech holds more intrinsic appeal for an audience that a written one, even if the product is somewhat less polished, as real bodies have more appeal than polished and perfect statues" (McCoy, 2007, p. 170). We also know that, when the early Greek scientist-philosophers wanted to understand human behavior, they often looked inside the body: for instance, Hippocrates explained human health and temperament by the (im)balance of the body's four humors. While many people find these ideas outside the scope of modern science they still have similarities with traditional medicinal practices in some cultures, suggesting that there may be some validity to Hippocrates' theory: that is why, perhaps, his ideas endure to this day. As another example, we can recall how Gottfried Wilhelm Leibniz found the harmony of things in the beats or vibrations of sounding bodies that meet at specific intervals (Leibniz, 1890), anticipating future research into the effects of nonverbal synchronization on the processing and acceptance of messages (Woodall and Burgoon, 1981). A major study of body language that is often considered to be the most influential pre-20th-century academic work in nonverbal communication is Charles Darwin's *The Expression of the Emotions in Man and Animals*, published in 1872.

As time went on, the role of the body was theorized more and more actively, with an explosion of research in the second half of the 20th century when Ray L. Birdwhistell published his book *Introduction to Kinesics: An Annotation System for Analysis of Body Motion and Gesture* (1952); and when Edward T. Hall published his research on how people use space and time in human communication, e.g. *The Silent Language* (1959), *The Hidden Dimension* (1966) and *The Dance of Life: The Other Dimension of Time* (1983). At about the same time, Albert Mehrabian was developing his ideas about the nature of nonverbal communication (1971). Today, no one will say that the body is missing from communication theory. It is common to treat communication as embodied practice and consider incarnation to be the very condition of human life (Marvin, 2006). While the importance of the body in and for communication is widely recognized, though, it can be theorized very differently.

## 2. BODY LANGUAGE

In most discussions of the body as a communication topic, a common point of departure has been René Descartes, who famously proclaimed: *Cogito, ergo sum* – 'I think, therefore I am.' In other words, we can be certain of our existence because there is no doubt that we think. Thus, our mind – *res cogitans*, or 'the thinking thing' – is a substance that is separate from the body, which is *res extensa*, or 'the extended thing'. As a result, consciousness became disembodied, with most of the attention focused on the human reason and rationality. At the same time, because mental and corporeal substances were positioned as separate, one could now pay attention to "the body proper, the object body that became a subject for systematic investigation" (Lock & Farquhar, 2007, p. 19).

Descartes' division of the human universe into two separate realms is, in a way, appealing: it is counterintuitive to identify oneself with one's body. When we think of our personal identity, we usually take it to be the realm of our unique ideas, values, beliefs, etc. That's what we mean when we refer to oneself as 'I', and not the body. We even speak of the body as something separate, the way we speak about other objects, e.g. 'my body', 'my bicycle', etc. In other words, here the subject of knowledge ('I') is something separate from the object known ('body', 'car'). Additionally, one may argue, when we start to examine the physical realm of the human, we can't find something specific that would be "a bearer of that peculiar, interior dimension that each of us experiences as consciousness" (Harris, 2005, p. 208); therefore, consciousness must be its own separate realm.

While Descartes' dualism initially appears appealing, it faces a serious obstacle: the mind and the body, as two supposedly separate realms, are still the two parts of the human being. And, as Descartes admits himself, these two parts interact because the mind, which is incorporeal, can move the body; at the same time, the mind is affected by the brain. This is known as the problem of mind-body interaction and Descartes tried to solve it by finding "a language for expressing these realities, and a model for explaining them, that do not compromise the distinctive natures of mind or body" (Clarke, 2003, p. 136). Although Descartes is known (and criticized) for his dualism, he in fact brought in a third entity to explain the connection between the mind and the body: since both are God's creations, they work independently as the parts of God's perfectly harmonized clock movement (Boorstin, 1983). Of course, today most people will find this explanation inadequate because we still fail to understand how the mind and the body interact, i.e., why the mind thinks the way it does and why the body moves the way it does. For instance, if we ask why we think the way we do and are told that this is because God made us such, we can then ask why God made us such thinkers and not thinkers of some other kind; "and if the answer is that God's reasons are beyond our understanding, then nothing is really understood" (Bailey, 2005, p. 38). And yet, it's important to remember that Descartes, although often blamed for viewing the body as machinelike, still tried to explain the interaction between the mind and the body, albeit by bringing in God. It was only later that the separation became complete when "post-caretesians, who removed God from the system, came to emphasize control and . . . mechanical thinking" (Bailey, 2005, p. 71).

According to Descartes, everything received by the senses is inspected by the mind which alone can understand essences (Figure 4.2). That all knowledge of the real world ultimately rests on the mind as 'the thinking thing' is exemplified by Descartes' famous phrase *Cogito ergo sum*: 'I think, therefore I am'. It's important to emphasize that, while he "prized the mind above flesh" (Shilling, 2012, p. 211), Descartes never denied that the senses are a part of the process of human existence; since the body can be viewed as a separate object of scientific study, its sensory organs cannot be overlooked. Thus, when his ideas are taken as a point of departure in discussions of the body, Descartes cannot only be criticized for his dualism but also must be commended for drawing scientific attention to the body and its role in communication. In fact, all the main types of nonverbal communication that one can find today in most textbooks, are based on

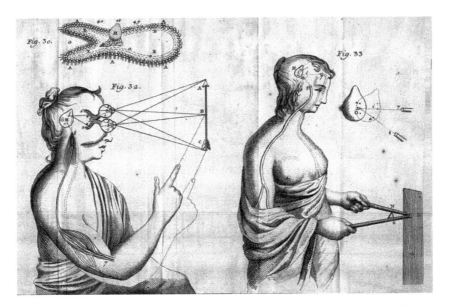

**Figure 4.2**    Illustration from *L'homme du René Descartes, et la formation du foetus* . . . (Paris: Compagnie des Libraires, 1729). Image from Historical Medical Books at the Claude Moore Health Sciences Library, University of Virginia. Reproduced by McLeod.

the five main senses for identifying nonverbal communication, what is known as "the fivefold sense classification" (Finnegan, 2002, p. 37).

## 2.1. Classifying Body Language

We find sound as a basis for paralanguage, i.e., such vocal characteristics that contribute to meaning in communication but are not considered to be a part of the verbal language system, such as tempo, pitch, volume, rate of speech, and rhythm. The study of paralanguage is known as 'paralinguistics'. Olfatics is focused on smell, and gustorics on taste. The study of visible arm and body movements, gestures, facial expression, posture and gait is known as kinesics (or, sometimes, kinesiology: Lanigan, 2010; Meline, 2010). "Included consistently in the canon of communication theory" (Padula, 2009, p. 581), this last forms of nonverbal communication has been extensively researched because it depends on sight, from which our brain receives more than 75% of all information.

It must be noted that kinesics (or kinesiology) is the study of body movements: that is why attention is focused on different parts of the body and it isn't easy to agree whether they are a part of kinesics (or kinesiology). For instance, some scholars write that their "theoretical work has proposed major differences between the face and body, particularly when there is conflict about communication" (Ekman & Friesen, 2008, p. 275). In another book, we find one chapter on 'Facial Expressions' and another on 'Body and Gestures' (Matsumoto et al., 2013). Does that mean the face is not a part of the body? In yet another book, we find two separate terms: *facsics* for "the study of how the face communicates", and *ocalics* for "the study of how the eyes communicate" (Berko et al., 2004, pp. 64, 66). Does that mean the eyes are not a part of the body and that eyes are not a part of the face? And what about eyebrows: are they a part of the body (and so fall under kinesics or kinesiology), or are they a part of the face (and so outside of kinesics or kinesiology)? We could continue focusing on other parts and create labels for their study, e.g. 'aurisics' for the study of the ear movements (from the Latin *auris* – 'ear'), or 'nasusics' for the study of the nose movements (from the Latin *nasus* – 'nose'), or 'osics' for the study of the mouth movements (from the Latin *os* – 'mouth').

We can talk about body movement (not movements), as studied by proxemics and haptics. Proxemics looks at the entire body moving through space as it crosses various distances, from public to intimate; going all the way results in touch, and then haptics takes over. Touch, as St. Thomas Aquinas put it, "is diffused through the whole body" (1946, p. 609). The most elusive form of nonverbal communication is time, studied by chronemics. Time does not have a separate sense organ and so cannot be seen, heard, touched, smelled, or tasted: it can only be felt. Thus, it requires the entire body, more so than proxemics and haptics.

It must be pointed out that there is more to nonverbal communication than meets the eye. While the movements of the body (parts) are visible with the naked eye, all other forms of nonverbal communication cannot take place without movement. For instance, paralanguage can't function unless the diaphragm and the rib cage draw air into the lungs, making it possible for the airstream to pass between the two vocal folds that vibrate and produce noise, which is converted by the resonator system – the throat, nose, and mouth – into sounds communicating meaning. Similarly, there is no touch without some mechanical deformation of the nerve endings that transmit signals to the cerebral cortex: we can capture their movement by using a video camera (just like we can capture on video the movement of vocal cords). The same goes for the smelling nose, which only appears to lack movement: in real life, when certain scent molecules fit specific receptors, this triggers changes in cells and a specialized message is sent to the brain. The tasting mouth, supposedly devoid of movement, is all about the taste buds actively forming a complex network, i.e., accepting, rejecting or modifying signals before sending them to the brain. Thus,

> whether a body is near or far, the only way in which it affects the organism so as to occasion sensation is through motion. The motion may be of the whole mass, as when something hits us; it may be in the inner particles of the thing, as when we taste or smell it; it may be a movement originated by the body and propagated to us through vibrations of a medium, as when we hear or see. But some form of motion there must be.
>
> *(Dewey, 1916, p. 30)*

Based on these ideas, communication can be viewed as an exchange of messages that "requires some sort of 'transmission' of 'information' in respect to states of the parts of the body" (Sereno & Mortensen, 1970, p. 78). This view is found in most textbooks, where the body language is a system of the body parts (a 'vocabulary') and their combinations formed by moving those parts (a 'grammar'); this way, messages are sent and received: "for example, we all tend to raise our eyebrows when we express surprise" (Berry, 2007, p. 16). Or, take the gesture for sleeping that involves "moving the head into a lateral position, perpendicular to the body, with or without bringing one or both hands below the head as a kind of pillow" (Ekman & Friesen, 2008, p. 283). Viewed this way, it is common to discuss how to make body language more effective in various situations of communication (Thompson, 2003).

If the body is conceptualized as a "skin-bounded, . . . biomechanical entity" (Lock & Farquhar, 2007, p. 2), then it appears machinelike and not different from animals who are remarkably similar in their physiological and anatomical makeup: that are also bounded by skin and can also move in many ways. Descartes even thought that, "if there were machines with the organs and appearance of a monkey, or some other irrational animal, we should have no means of telling that they were not altogether of the same nature as those animals" (Descartes, 1954, p. 41). The language of the body is often taken as the main evidence for animals' ability to communicate. In fact, looking at how the body moves and sends messages, one can talk about other types of communication in the natural world, including those among plants and insects, e.g. "Insects were found to have rich mental lives; they can learn, remember, think and communicate" (Snyder, 2017).

Human communication, however, goes beyond a process of mutual influence through messages: humans are clearly human animals whereas animals are hardly animal humans. When people speak about human uniqueness because of the ability to make free choices, they speak about a moral sense that goes beyond just a response to external stimuli: while "animals respond to stimuli directly; human beings interpret the events" (Gusfield, 1989, p. 9). It must be remembered that, as Kenneth Burke put it, animals "simply do as they do – and that's that" (Burke, 1989, p. 286). On the contrary, the symbol-using animal – the human – can respond to any given situation "with a disobedient No" (Burke, 1989, p. 286). In other words, human body language is an ability not only to move the body in certain ways, but also an ability *not* to move it in certain ways: for instance, standing still as the opposite of moving the body can often be a case of very meaningful communicative behavior. Also, humans can choose to act, or not to act, on the world, including their own body: for instance, one can see many animal tattoos on humans but no human (or any other) tattoos on animals. In the same vein, although "the communication systems of all living creatures are programmed to some extent by genes" (Friend, 2004, p. 7), genetic engineering is solely a human undertaking.

## 2.2. The Textualization of the Body

When communication is equated with a process of sending and receiving messages that supposedly contain meaning, we bypass several important questions, such as 'How did meaning get there?' and 'Why do people often fail to extract the correct meaning out of a message?' We can begin to answer these questions when we start conceptualizing communication in a more complex way, i.e., as a process of creating and interpreting meaning. In this light, the view of the body and its role in communication starts to become more complex, as well. It becomes clear that there is no 'body in itself' as a static object of inquiry because

> body cannot be described outside of the different discoursive practices that define it: to forget this implies the risk of hypostatising the body, as if it were endowed with an inherent essence, independent of the different practices, discourses and cultures that shape it.
>
> *(Violi, 2008, p. 54)*

As a result, the body appears dynamic rather than static, constantly constructed and reconstructed through symbols rather than machinelike and fixed.

Even when the natural sciences present it as a stable object that can be described by sophisticated technologies, such as radiography or magnetic resonance imaging, the body is still not an essence permanently captured but, rather, a result of socio-cultural construal represented in symbols. Similarly, the body in medicine may appear as a natural entity possessing an inherent essence, and yet, it may be construed differently by different cultures, along with the concepts of illness and healing (Stibbe, 1996). The social sciences and humanities, of course, examine the body more directly as a phenomenon of different discursive practices and text representations. Often, it is those whose idea of the body does not fit into the accepted view who refuse to take it for granted, e.g. research on differently abled bodies (Barnes, 2017), feminist scholarship on images of women's bodies across diverse media (Carilli & Campbell, 2005; Charles, 2016), or investigations of political technologies used to control the body (Cisney & Morar, 2016). Thus, it becomes clear that the body is not a simple instrument for sending and receiving messages: rather, the body is something that is constantly technologized, medicalized, (dis)abled, regulated, etc. In other words, people construct the body as they see fit: in the words of Anthony Giddens, "we have become responsible for the design of our own bodies" (1991, p. 102). It must be noted that the view of the body focused on sending and receiving messages is concerned primarily with the effectiveness of communication rather than its power dynamics and ethical aspects.

Thus, we see that the body can be viewed not only as an entity with clear structures and boundaries, but also as a more fluid construct created and interpreted through different discourses. On the one hand, this view is welcomed by many because it provides new opportunities: now the body can be liberated from one fixed identity and become dispersed and multiple. On the other hand, the more fuzzy the boundaries of the body, the more difficult it is to determine what the body means. Whereas earlier the body could be opposed to the text, with textualization "presented as overcoming the material limitations of the human body" (Marvin, 2006, p. 69), now the body itself becomes more and more like the text – a sign invested with meaning rather than a skin-bounded biomechanical entity. Moreover, it turns out that people can literally inscribe meaning into "the mother of all media, the body" (Peters, 2015, p. 187), tattoos being an example of such inscription (DeMello, 2000). Thus, the body as an inscriptive surface literally becomes the text (Figure 4.3).

So, whereas earlier it was possible to distinguish between the real world that is present (and the body as its crucial part) and the text as the representation of the world (and the body), now that distinction has been erased: everything is text or, as Jacques Derrida famously put it, "there is nothing outside of the text" (1997, pp. 158–159). But then if the text, including the body, is nothing but a sign, then it can continue absorbing meaning from different discourses until it no longer seems to be attached to any reality: it becomes one of many empty signifiers "because they signify nothing and represent nothing more than what is made of them" (Dosse, 2011, p. 204). And so the body seems to disappear in the constant post-modern play of floating signifiers. What seemed at one point objective and physically defined, having lost its self-evident immediacy, became mediated to the point of obliteration. Thus, the body has moved from theorized as just being, to being constructed, to being deconstructed – possibly out of existence. Taking this line of theorizing to its extreme, "the postmodern wave of theorizing . . ., has, in its own forgetfulness of being, forgotten the phenomenon of lived-body experience" (Macke, 2015, p. 61). If we conceptualize communication as limited to sending and receiving messages, then the body must be viewed as nothing but an object that moves in the world without interacting with it. If we conceptualize communication as a play of signs, then at some point we must admit that "the body itself, as a unified entity, is . . . an empty totality that organizes the world without participating in it" (Jameson, 2003, p. 713). How can we think

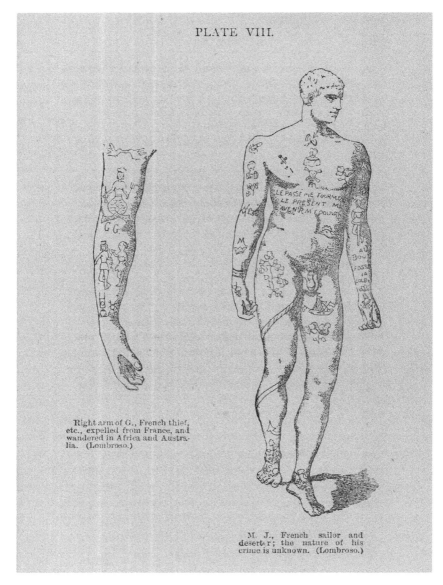

PLATE VIII.

Right arm of G., French thief,
etc., expelled from France, and
wandered in Africa and Australia. (Lombroso.)

M. J., French sailor and
deserter; the nature of his
crime is unknown. (Lombroso.)

**Figure 4.3**    Left – Tattoos on the right arm of a French thief expelled from France.
Right – Tattoos on the body of a French sailor and deserter. From the
Wellcome Collection gallery (L0033860).

of the body not only in terms of moving parts, but also participation in the
world? How can we look at the body that not only is, but also lives? How
can we see that the body is not only language, or discourse, or text, but also
speech – living in the here and now?

## 3. THE SPEAKING BODY

As noted earlier, both humans and animals are biological organisms that come to know the world by sensing it: here, "sensations are forced upon us . . . Over their nature, . . . we have . . . no control" (James, 1907, p. 593). When you open your eyes, it is not up to you what you see: it is just what is in front of you. Also, sensations "are neither true or false: they simply are" (ibid.). We can recall Burke's words about how animals respond to the outside stimuli, which equally apply to humans: both "simply do as they do – and that's that" (Burke, 1989, p. 286). It is important to note that sensations provide us with very rich information about the world: that we cannot conceptualize every sensation only testifies to the richness of the stimuli we receive. Moreover, the world we come to know this way is real for every single organism: there is no 'individual' reality! This kind of knowledge is sometimes known as "knowledge by acquaintance" (James, 1890a, p. 217); it can also be labeled 'knowledge from reality'. Simple as it may seem, this knowledge is crucial for the survival and reproduction of the organism – both human or animal.

However, the biological organism, identified with the living body, is not the same as the experiencing subject, identified with the lived body (Husserl 1989; Merleau-Ponty, 2012). By the same token, sensation is not the same as perception, although the two are often used interchangeably: perception is an active process and not just passive reception of stimuli. For instance, when you open your eyes, it is up to you what you choose to focus on, and this is how your interaction with the world begins. Overall, perception can be understood as a process of interaction between the world and the Self, beginning with the body: this is how we become conscious of the world. In this sense, communication is always embodied: a striking reminder of that is the early Christian ritual of *conspiratio*, when, as we are reminded by Ivan Illich, in addition to a communal meal of bread and wine, or a *symposion*, "there was also a breathing into each other's mouths so the community was constituted in flesh, blood and spirit" (Cayley, 2004, p. 85).

It is important to emphasize that we perceive not so much things as relationships, always looking for a whole rather than its parts. Moreover, we often experience things that are not a part of our simple sensations, as demonstrated by Gestalt psychology, e.g. the law of closure when we perceive something in its complete form despite the absence of one or more of its parts. Significantly, the most general Gestalt law is *Prägnanz*, which although sometimes equated with the sense of something being 'pregnant with meaning', simply means that something is 'in good form' – and people are driven to experience the world in as good a form as possible. So, when the body is directed towards whatever it perceives, a body image is formed, i.e., proprioceptive and self-referential awareness of one's own body, which allows people to act purposefully in and on their surroundings (Gallagher, 2005). This conceptualization of the body image is clearly different from the one in message-oriented conceptualizations when it is equated with a 'media representation', e.g. representations of female body images in women's magazines (Charles, 2016).

Perception is always focused on whatever content the body provides us: we are always conscious *of* something – whatever may appear in our consciousness here and now. Whereas you sense the reality that is known by cognition and ostensibly has been and will be forever (and for everyone), you perceive the world as it exists here and now (and only for you): every communication experience, therefore, is an actual experience known by sensation. We could define flesh as the body that (really) is, and the body as the flesh that (actually) exists. The knowledge we receive this way is sometimes called 'knowledge about', "and this knowledge admits of numberless degrees of complication" (James, 1890b, p. 2); it all depends on the interaction between the body and the world. Thus, when we speak of perception, it means that an individual becomes aware of something that appears in his/her consciousness and posits it as actually existing: the intentional object of perception, therefore, has two characteristics – "self-presence and actuality" (McKenna, 2012, p. 8). All these ideas found their manifestation in phenomenology, which focused on lived experience and gave prime attention to the body as a source of the subject and society.

## 3.1. Putting Lived Experience in the Spotlight

Phenomenology focuses on individuals' subjective experiences, which appear in one's consciousness in the process of interaction with the world. While going back to ancient Greek philosophy, e.g. such concepts as *eidos* ('idea', 'form'), *noēma* ('thought', 'content'), etc., phenomenology took its modern shape in the early 20th century when Edmund Husserl published *The Crisis of the European Sciences and Transcendental Phenomenology* (1970), in which he argued that all scientific explanations of the world are not direct representations of the real but only abstractions from it. To overcome this forgetting of the real, we must focus on our lived experience in every act of interacting with the world.

Phenomenology thus made it possible to go beyond the instrumental view of the body as an 'extended thing' used to send and receive messages. The body is "rather the very nexus of our experience and our way of being-in-the-world" (Crossley, 2012, p. 142). We tend to focus too much on our ability to use symbols and develop ideas; our existence, however, begins with the body as it experiences the world. In fact, "the first act of civilization is wagering on whether to open the hand or reach for a weapon" (Kearney, 2015, p. 17); at stake is coping with the world, i.e., one's very survival. It is crucial to remember that "coping is phenomenologically prior to theorizing, or indeed the conceptual identification of any objective 'thing' including our own [mind or] . . . body" (Weinberg, 2012, p. 148). The importance of the body, therefore, cannot be overestimated: "the sentient lived body is a . . . starting point for examining the complex intersection of nature with culture, the individual with the social and the psyche with the somatic" (Blackman, 2008, p. 87). No one has done more for examining these intersections than Maurice Merleau-Ponty, who extended Husserl's ideas and put the body in the spotlight of scholarly investigations.

For Merleau-Ponty, the body is not simply an external object (cf. Descartes' view of the body as 'an extended thing'); it is also a subject of experience through which we connect to the world and one another. Based on this premise, Merleau-Ponty "revolutionized phenomenology with his fine-grained analyses of the body as a crucial medium for human being-in-the-world" (Weinberg, 2012, p. 148).

In his analyses of the body, Merleau-Ponty focused on perception, which, as noted earlier, is an active process: we become aware of objects of our perception only insofar as we are aware of our body and how it interacts with the world. In other words, "to perceive we must take up a bodily relation to what we perceive" (Crossley, 2012, p. 132). Perception, therefore, is not simply a passive response to stimuli: it is always a new experience that appears as the body senses and organizes its interactions with the world. It is tempting to equate perception with representation, e.g. any scientific model that explains a certain object. However, "the whole of perception . . . cannot be exhausted by an explanation" because experience "is informed and organized in accordance with my body. That is, it is literally *organ*-ized" (Haas, 2008, p. 36). It is important to emphasize that Merleau-Ponty does not focus on separate organs as tools used for sending and receiving messages. He writes that "our organs are no longer instruments; on the contrary, our instruments are added or joined organs" (Merleau-Ponty, 1993, p. 138).

Thus, when we speak of experience as 'organ-ized', it is the entire body that is conceptualized as an organ. Unlike the analytical view of the body that breaks it down into parts (separate organs or senses), Merleau-Ponty's approach to the body is synthetic and holistic. Perception is multi-sensory and full-bodied experience. It is the entire body that never leaves us (even if separate organs can be removed and senses can be blunted or go away). We can exist only in/as our body. It is no coincidence that these ideas resonate with existential thought, as captured by Jean-Paul Sartre: "The body is the totality of meaningful relationships to the world" (Sartre, 1995, p. 344).

So, our 'being-in-the-world' is always bodily existence: it is through the body that we begin to perceive the world and give meaning to it. Our body is not only an object whose senses respond to outside stimuli but also a subject of experience. Merleau-Ponty provides a phenomenological account of how we become aware of our subjectivity: "when I press my two hands together, it is not a matter of two sensations felt together as one perceives two objects placed side by side, but an ambiguous set-up in which both hands can alternate the role of 'touching' and being 'touched'" (2012, p. 95). This shows the body's capacity to be both an object (touched) and a subject (touching): the relationship of touching–touched is reversible and constantly oscillating (Figure 4.4).

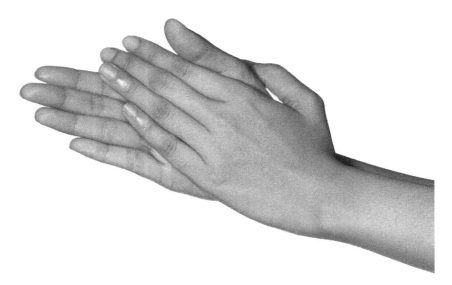

**Figure 4.4**    Cropped view of a woman's hands with palms rubbing together. Photo by Wanchai Orsuk/Shutterstock.com.

Because the body can be a subject of its own experience (called apperception), it can relate to other bodies: this way, intersubjectivity is formed. Merleau-Ponty calls this relation 'carnal intersubjectivity' and illustrates it by the handshake:

> [W]hen I shake his hand . . . [the other man's] hand *is substituted for my left hand*, and my body *annexes* the body of another person . . . My two hands 'coexist' or are 'compresent' because they are one single body's hands. The other person appears through an extension of that compresence; he and I are like organs of one single intercorporeality.
> *(Merleau-Ponty, 1964a, p. 168)*

While the handshake is also reversible, it presents limits to one's capacity because "I cannot experience the Other's hand touching my own" (Daly, 2016, p. 80). It is more accurate to say, perhaps, that one *can* experience it, just not as fully as touching one's own. What is more important to keep in mind, though, is that, since the body is not only an object but also a subject, it allows us to recognize and experience other embodied subjects (Figure 4.5).

**Figure 4.5**   A handshake.

Moreover, because our bodily awareness from the very beginning is oriented toward otherness, we can experience empathy (which is another concept, just like ethics, absent from most discussions of body language). However, there is an optimum distance from which an object is best perceived and appears in consciousness as a phenomenon in its entirety, just "as for each painting in an art gallery, there is an optimal distance from which it asks to be seen" (Merleau-Ponty, 2012, pp. 315–6). Once we are outside of that distance, we lose sight of the flesh of the world: that is why most people do not feel such objects as insects (too small) or galaxies (too large). Since the word 'feel' goes back to the meaning of touch, it can be said that we are out of touch with (those objects of) the world.

When attempts are made to overcome the view of the body as an object, performance studies are usually mentioned as a notable exception: this field is said to have been consistently "invested in the live body" (Shaffer et al., 2015, p. 187). Without a doubt, performance studies pay special attention to the materiality of the body; it must be noted, though, that performativity has its limits because it focuses on how certain positions are enacted in communication rather than on a concrete subject whose lived experience calls for reflexivity and its theorizing. Small as the different emphases of performance studies and phenomenology may appear, they are significant. The former, as previously noted, are invested 'in the live body', whereas the latter focuses on the lived body (it is no coincidence that we speak about 'live performances', not 'lived performances'). Also, communication as performance assumes a certain role to be enacted; the meaning of the verb 'to perform' implies carrying something out, finishing or accomplishing something. 'To act', in its turn, goes back to the meaning of 'drawing out or forth, moving'. This difference is reflected in that the former is used most often as a transitive verb, e.g. 'to perform a role', whereas 'to act' is used mostly as an intransitive verb. In other words, you do not perform something, you just act. Of course, as correctly argued by the editors of the volume entitled *Performance and Phenomenology: Traditions and Transformations*, "performance *can be* a privileged object of phenomenological investigation as well as a means of developing phenomenological practice" (Bleeker et al., 2015: 2; emphasis added). Thus, while communication can be carried out (and theorized) as performance, it is always (inter)action. Sometimes, communication is performance art; always, "it is the art of guiding one's body into discourse . . . the struggle involved in the insertion of agency – wound and bow, death and life – into discourse" (Bhabha, 1994, p. 184). Communication is always a process of acting or 'drawing out or forth, moving', with the body always as "the last frontier of authenticity" (Peters, 1999, p. 221).

One might find phenomenology, as the study of structures of consciousness, too abstract for real-life application; however, this is not the case. The phenomenological method has been used in many situations in which individuals reflect on the experience of their bodies interacting with the world. One such study looked at the lived body as the essential dimension in social work practice, mostly from the perspective of food and eating (McCormick, 2010). Another study undertook a phenomenological approach to the lived world of an autist, paying special attention to the perception of play and time (Rasmussen, 1991). Yet another described the intimate lived relationship between human bodies and the physical worlds in which they find themselves in the light of such spatial qualities as street configuration, population density, and mix of activities (Seamon, 2013). One more example is the research into the lived body in places of learning such as classrooms (Alerby et al., 2014).

Thus, there is more to the body than just its language. Body language, like any code, is lexicon and grammar, in this case – in the form of the body parts and their combinations: this is how messages are produced. The body is not simply given to us as an object so we could communicate in this world by sending and receiving messages. Even when it is stated that the body is discursively constructed, the body appears as an object, albeit a more dynamic and fluid one: it still does not speak for itself. We must not forget that "the body is a natural power of expression" (Merleau-Ponty, 2012, p. 187). In other words, the body is a medium of communication through which the world is revealed to us: it is the body that speaks. We should understand speech not only as a form of oral communication but broadly, i.e., as the means through which we become aware of ourselves: in this sense, "the speaker does not express just for others, but also to know himself what he intends" (Merleau-Ponty, 1964a, p. 90). Communication, therefore, "is not the goal of speech, but its very structure, since expression happens in the weighty" (Landes, 2013, p. 134). And the weighty is the body – our sole means of communication.

We can't understand anything other than by living in it, i.e., experiencing the world through our body. Because we must interact with the world – through our body – for our existence to become meaningful, the experience of the lived-body is inherently ambiguous: as Merleau-Ponty puts it, "expression is like a step taken in the fog – no one can say where, if anywhere, it will lead" (Merleau-Ponty, 1964b, p. 3). In this light, when it is stated that today we live in precarious times due to neoliberal policies (Bates et al, 2017), or hear about precarity within the age of digital media (Heidkamp & Kergel, 2017), we need to remember that communication overall is a risky enterprise: the meaning of the word 'experience', after all, goes back to the Proto-Indo-European root *per-* – 'to try, risk'. Communication is never just motion, it is always an act: it is not communication when we simply go through the motions. And it is impossible to 'go through actions'!

When we perceive the world through the body, our experiences are grouped together into concepts as cognitive categories: conceptualization is our capacity to capture patterns in the flow of experience so that such mental representations can then be used in the process of communication and identification of objects. Concepts are generalizations that denote objects by abstracting their characteristics, which find their manifestation in symbols, including nonverbal symbols. Whereas sensations provide 'knowledge of', or perception, 'knowledge about', or conceptualization, is the realm of understanding or 'know-how'. We should never forget, though, that it is thanks to the body, as an object and a subject, that we can form concepts and know things. In place of Descartes' *Cogito ergo sum* – "I think, therefore I am", we need to state: 'I am (my body), therefore I think.'

## 4. THE HUMAN SCIENCE OF COMMUNICOLOGY

The body as an object has received much attention in discussions of nonverbal communication focused on message production and reception. The body as a subject has been theorized mostly within phenomenological, performance, and critical studies, which are more preoccupied with how meaning is experienced, enacted, and interpreted. There is one approach, however, aimed at bridging a gap between these two perspectives on the body: communicology, "a recent and substantially different theory" (Littlejohn et al., 2017, p. 55). The human science of communicology makes its key premise very clear: "absent a body to experience it, there is no information, no message, no meaning, no self, no society, and no culture" (Catt, 2011, p. 134). The body is foregrounded in the study of all levels of human discourse: (1) the intrapersonal level (or psychiatric/aesthetic domain), (2) the interpersonal level (or social domain), (3) the group level (or cultural domain), and (4) the intergroup level (or transcultural domain) (Lanigan, 2015; Catt & Eicher-Catt, 2010; Smith et al., 2017).

Communicology as a new theory of communication views the body as an elaborately coded affair (Eagleton, 1996). This focus is rooted in semiotics, the study of signs, which goes back to the 5th century B.C. when Hippocrates established 'semiotics' (*sēmeiōtikē*, derived from the Greek *sēmeiōtikos*) as a branch of medicine. The decision about the state of a patient was made on the right discerning of bodily symptoms: hence semiotics appeared as "the art of reading a body" (Alloa, 2015, p. 200). However, communication is not only an act of discerning, i.e., distinguishing between different representations, but always an act of the lived body: that is why communicology focuses not only on the semiotic analysis of communication but also the phenomenological experiences of the body to gain deeper insights into human agency and intention. Thus, communicology as semiotic phenomenology makes clear that "the movement from body to sign is recursive, the body knows itself only as sign, but the sign occurs exclusively in embodiment" (Catt, 2017, p. 62).

Based on these theoretical premises, communicology develops its own method as a series of three steps that need to be taken towards understanding the human condition of embodiment. The first step is the description of pre-consciousness (awareness), which accounts for the absolute human condition of Subjectivity. The second step is the reduction of consciousness (awareness of awareness), which accounts for the absolute human condition of Intersubjectivity. And the third step is the interpretation of experience (representation of awareness of awareness), which accounts for the absolute human condition that Subjectivity is Intersubjectivity (Lanigan, 2015). The theoretical framework and method of communicology have been used in the study of gender and organization (Ashcraft & Mumby, 2004), sexuality (Martinez, 2011), interpersonal relationships (Macke, 2015), ecological communication (Catt, 2017), etc. It is important to emphasize that in all these studies communicology accepts contingency as an inherent characteristic of communication experience: it is due to such contingency that the body is always "a body of infinite variability and creativity" (Broadhurst & Price, 2017, p. 2).

Thus, communicology provides a complex and unifying view of communication. First, communicology is a human science, i.e., it brings together the humanities and social sciences into one coherent framework. Second, it brings together semiotics, on the one hand, and phenomenology, on the other. Third, it brings together a theory of communication, i.e., semiotic phenomenology, and a method, i.e., a series of three steps, briefly discussed in the previous paragraph. Fourth, it brings together the ideas of North American thinkers, such as Charles S. Peirce, and Continental thinkers, such as Maurice Merleau-Ponty. And, finally, it brings together the two separate perspectives on the body into the unified science of embodied discourse.

## 5. 'THE BODY IMPROPER'

We see that humans are complex beings whose communicative behavior in the world can be presented as a synthesis of three processes (Table 4.1).

Three things need to be especially noted here. First, the table analytically breaks down into three supposedly distinct realms what in fact is one holistic and simultaneous process of human life. Second, all three realms are equally important: for instance, some may denigrate sensations as the level when we are not 'fully human', while others may find conception to be out of touch with our true nature, e.g. John Keats' longing 'for a life of sensation rather than of thoughts!' Third, and most important for our discussion here, it is the body that holds together and mediates between the other two realms.

Some believe that the human body is still "remarkably stable . . . in the midst of the radical changes in the technological and social-cultural context" (Renson, 1997). A more accurate statement, though, would be that the body constantly "needs anchoring" (Marvin, 2006, p. 68); as we saw earlier, the body is porous and permeable, negotiated and constituted through different discourses, especially today when we hear about collective bodies, cyborg bodies, pharmaceutical bodies, etc. In fact, the body is often viewed as "arguably the most fluctuating signifier in the history of cultural expression" (Jordan, 2004, p. 327). The best example of this is the post-modern body that appears to us freed from physical constraints: it is not actually present and we experience it in its effect.

With bodies further and further removed from natural flesh and blood, we move into the world of "a lively carnality suffused with words, images,

**Table 4.1** Metaphysics of the Body in Communication

| SENSATION | PERCEPTION | CONCEPTION |
| --- | --- | --- |
| Body | Flesh | Mind |
| Knowledge of | Knowledge about/from | Understanding (Know-how) |
| Action / Reaction | Interaction | Transaction (Transformation) |
| Sensible | Sentient | Synergism |
| Being | Existence | Essence |
| Actuality | Reality | Potentiality |
| Singular | Particular | Universal |

senses, desires, and powers" (Lock & Farquhar, 2007, p. 15). It all sounds like a great party – a carnival, one could say. We usually associate a carnival with public revelries that involve costumes, dancing, music, etc. However, at the basis of a carnival lies the carnal body: it's no accident that both words – 'carnival' and 'carnal' – sound so similar. The carnival body is always playful to the point of being grotesque, e.g. the concept of 'the grotesque body' put forward by Mikhail Bakhtin, who saw it best exemplified by the Renaissance carnivals as described in François Rabelais' novels such as *Gargantua and Pantagruel*. At such carnivals, frivolity and ambiguity ruled, making it possible to invert the normal social order in new ways: communication thus appeared as a process of "unruly biological and social exchange" (Bakhtin, 1984, p. 46). While the Renaissance carnivals are perhaps the best example of the inherently unstable and undefined body (and certainly the best theorized, thanks to Bakhtin's works), we find such grotesque realism throughout history – from the emergence of the physical body in ancient Greece (Brooke, 2010) to vulgarity, ambiguity and the body grotesque in *South Park* (Thorogood, 2016). It can be said that the body has always been grotesque because it has always been the nexus of nature and culture: in the words of Merleau-Ponty,

> For man, everything is constructed and everything is natural, in the sense that there is no single word or behavior that does not owe something to mere biological being – and, at the same time, there is no word or behavior that does not break free from animal life.
>
> *(2012, p. 195)*

In this light, life is always a carnival, just more grotesque in some situations than in others. And, it is our own body that "continuously breathes life into this visible spectacle" (Merleau-Ponty, 2012, p. 209). Today, the terrain of the body keeps being contested as it takes on grotesque forms, with the boundaries between nature and culture being blurred. And yet, even when we talk about a transformation of substances and a dissolution of forms into the so-called 'body without organs', which is immediate and fluid and "does not end at a precise point" (Deleuze & Guattari, 1987, p. 121), we're still talking about 'body'. We may view the body as never fixed and full of possibilities, or we may mourn the forgetting of the body, but we're still aware of our body on a physical level and the body as a sign in different discourses. Most of us are still certain that "it is the body and its functions which just cannot be deconstructed out of existence" (Volkman, 2003, p. 303). Enter the post-human.

## 5.1. Data Made Flesh

Communication is a process in which our bodily awareness is inherently oriented to otherness. It is believed that theory, as the contemplation of an object in all its order and beauty, can be traced back to out-of-body experiences practiced in ancient mystery cults (Peters, 2005, p. 23). However, every act of communication is an out-of-body-experience as we're constantly tempted "to be raptured out of the bodies" (Haraway, 1999). In a way, when one communicates, one can't help having a feeling of floating outside one's body, which is not that unnerving and can even be sought: if you were to choose between two states of existence – being 'out of your body' and being 'out of your mind' – which one would you choose?! It is important to note, though, that communication as out-of-body-experience assumes leaving one's body and then returning to it. In some translations of the expression into other languages this is made very clear: for instance, in Russian 'out-of-body-experience' is known as *vnetelesnoe perezhivanie*, where the word *perezhivanie* means 'experience', 'feeling', 'trial' and – most importantly – 'living through'. In other words, human communication is what we live through thanks to our body.

The post-human, though, is a different realm. The post-human is often conceptualized as referring "to the destabilization and unsettling of boundaries between human and machine, nature and culture, and mind and body that digital and biotechnologies are seen to be engendering" (Blackman, 2008, p. 117). However, the post-human view is ultimately aimed at overcoming the human being as a biological substrate, which calls not simply for the extension of the body but its merging with informational patterns. Thus, "in the posthuman, there are no essential differences or absolute demarcations between bodily existence and computer simulation, cybernetic mechanism and biological organism, robot teleology and human goals" (Abbas, 1999). In other words, one will no longer be able to distinguish between the real body, present in the flesh on one side of the informational hardware such as a computer screen, and the informational patterns that make up its software – what William Gibson in *Neuromancer* calls "data made flesh" (Gibson, 1984, p. 16). As a result, the post-human moves beyond the phenomenological aspects of human embodiment (Figure 4.6).

The goal of the post-human enterprise is developing the technologies powerful enough to conquer the human body (Tratnik, 2017). When Bruno Latour says that "the opposite of body is not emancipation, it is not soul, it is not spirit, it . . . is death" (Latour, 1999, p. 141), we need to remember

**Figure 4.6**    The post-human body. The dawn of the machine age.

that he talks about the human body. The human world is still a biological world, even if it is always shaped by politics: in this world, one can still hear the echoes of citizens forming a community and facing one another in the flesh just as they did in the ancient polis. The post-human world is one of biotechnologies and bioinformatics, in which communication is reduced to informational circuits; in such a world, "the body ceases to exist as living being and becomes dead living matter" (Giblett, 2008, p. 34). It is no longer the body that lives and breathes in the human sense (and so it is 'dead'), but it is still 'living matter' – or whatever it ends up being labeled as.

Our interaction with the world is never perfect: our perception often fails us. For instance, you may be strolling on the beach and mistake a rock for a crab (Bueno, 2013). At the same time, if all objects appeared to everyone in the same way, we would not be creative and there would be no poetry. For the post-human 'living matter' this is no problem at all: first, its object recognition can by far surpass our perception, and, second, progress is being made towards overcoming the ultimate challenge in artificial intelligence and robotics – creating machines that are creative. Virtuality, without a doubt, creates new possibilities for communication. However, in all virtual communications, capable of producing certain effects maximally removed from the physical existence of the body, one can still discern the human presence; after all, 'virtual' goes back to the Proto-Indo-European root *wi-ro*, meaning 'man'. Thus, the human is the ghost present in every machine. The realm of creativity is not that of (perceived) reality or (sensed) actuality, but of (conceived) potentiality: with the post-human, the world becomes one of pure potentiality, i.e., powers and forces constantly (trans)formed by informational patterns. In this light, Descartes' dualism has not been overcome; if anything, we are becoming more Cartesian as we treat the body as a machine. For instance, "the current definition of brain death is Cartesian through and through: if nothing happens in the mind, then personhood ends, and the corpse is ready to be surgically disassembled" (Ecks, 2009, p. 156). In the post-human world, such problems won't exist because the body won't exist – only pure forms, meaning the ultimate triumph of Platonism. This will be a world of Morpheus, one of dreams constantly formed and transformed.

Meanwhile, we still live in the world where the body holds us together and connects us to the emerging world, just like the hyphen connects 'post' and 'human'. More and more often, though, we come across 'posthuman' without any hyphen; one day, it may give way to another word, something like 'morphean', and the human will disappear, along with its body. In the words of Michel Foucault, "if some event of which we can at the moment do no more than sense the possibility – without knowing either what its form will be or what it promises – were to cause them to crumble, . . . then one can certainly wager that man will be erased like a face drawn in sand at the edge of the sea" (1970, p. 387). However, it does not have to be just one event: 'the erasure of the human' may be a result of our own incremental actions. After all, according to Kenneth Burke's famous definition, "man is the symbol-using . . . animal . . . separated from his natural condition by instruments of his own making" (Burke, 1966, p. 16) and so can finish the job without any external help.

For the time being, though, we continue living in/through our bodies and dreaming about the post-human world. Everyone can probably relate to these words by Katherine Hayles, a famous theorist of humanities and media technologies:

> If my nightmare is a culture inhabited by posthumans who regard their bodies as fashion accessories rather than the ground of being, . . . my dream is a version of the posthuman that embraces the possibilities of information technologies without being seduced by fantasies of unlimited power and disembodied immortality, that recognizes and celebrates finitude as a condition of human being, and that understands human life is embedded in a material world of great complexity, one on which we depend for our continued survival.
>
> *(1999, p. 5)*

What is your nightmare and what is your dream?

# 5

# The Wonder
# of the Mind

Key concepts:

The brain, cultivation, empathy, the extended mind thesis, externalization, gesture, ideology, internalization, the mind, *res cogitans, res extensa, mens auctoris*, mirror neurons, neuroimaging, propaganda, the semantic triangle, symbol, *tabula rasa*, telepathy, quantum entanglement, vicarious.

Key names:

Theodor Adorno, Aristotle, Francis Bacon, Mikhail Bakhtin, Gregory Bateson, Edward Bernays, Noam Chomsky, Charles Horton Cooley, René Descartes, Jürgen Habermas, Edward Herman, Max Horkheimer, Immanuel Kant, Friedrich A. Kittler, Alfred Korzybski, John Locke, Karl Marx, G. H. Mead, Marshall McLuhan, C. K. Ogden, John Peters, Plato, I. A. Richards, Friedrich Schleiermacher, Charles S. Peirce, Socrates, Lev Vygotsky, Wilhelm Wundt.

## 1. IN SEARCH OF THE MIND

Human life is a meaningful life and there can be no meaning without mind; no one will deny that being human is being mindful. Mind allows us to find meaning in the physical world; in our own actions (ethics); in the things we

make (art); and in its own workings (philosophy or logic). The mind's awareness of itself is perhaps the most wonderful characteristic of being human.
Thanks to its self-conscious nature, the mind has been contemplated by
many great minds throughout history.

Talking about the mind has a long tradition that goes back to ancient animism: "in its belief habits the human mind has emerged from jungle magic. . .
Sorceries, incantations, mystic ceremonies, magic prescriptions, totems,
and taboos express the primitive supernatural. . . . This is what is meant
by animism – that the primitive world is a soul-world" (Jastrow, 1935,
p. 9). The psyche drew the attention of Plato, who famously portrayed it
as a charioteer (reason) and two horses – one white (spirit) and one black
(appetite) (*Phaedrus*, 246e–247e): the rational charioteer is clearly closer to
the mind in its modern sense and plays a crucial role in guiding people's
ascent to divine heights. Aristotle put the mind (*nous*, usually rendered as
'intellect' or 'reason') in the center of a human nature that desires knowledge
and understanding (*De Anima*, III.4, 429a10–11); moreover, human mind
can contemplate things (the 'theoretical mind'), and act following deliberation (the 'practical mind') (*Nicomachean Ethics* VI.11 1143a35–b5). René
Descartes conceptualized the conscious mind as a separate entity – *the res
cogitans*, or 'a thinking thing' that he saw as "a thing which doubts, understands, [conceives], affirms, denies, wills, refuses, which also imagines and
feels" (Descartes, 1911, vol. 2, p. 153). Immanuel Kant put the human mind
in the spotlight as constituted by the faculties of sensibility, understanding
and reason, which are prior to experience and form a basis necessary for
all human behavior (Kant, 1899). It was Wilhelm Wundt who established
psychology, i.e., the scientific study of the mind as the sum of our inner
experiences: thus, the mind came to be conceptualized as a unified realm
of mental phenomena, distinct from the physical realm (body) and the spiritual realm (spirit). The mental realm of the mind includes such capacities as
thinking, intentions, judgments, knowledge, memory, etc.

While psychology is traditionally viewed as "the science of mind" (Cacioppo
& Freberg, 2016), the mind draws the attention of many academic disciplines.
For instance, the SAGE Center for the Study of the Mind at the University
of California, Santa Barbara, brings together scholars from philosophy, economics, anthropology, linguistics, computer science, ecology, marine biology,
mathematics, physics, chemistry, geography, religious studies, English, and
yes, communication. As we'll see later, communication theory provides an
important, if not crucial, perspective on the nature of the human mind.

Still, despite so many great minds having made so many efforts, understanding *what* the mind is and *where* the mind is causes much debate.

### 1.1. What/Where is the Mind?

It is common to equate the mind with the brain, especially in the light of rapid developments in brain imaging technology. It is tempting to claim that brain scans can capture the mind in action: then, it could be possible to use the results of brain imaging in many areas of human communication – from political campaigns to marketing to forensic practice.

However, the mind is not equivalent to the brain. Indeed, "biology gives you a brain. Life turns it into a mind" (Eugenides, 2002, p. 479). Important as the neurobiological basis may be, human behavior cannot be understood without our life experiences – such socio-cultural and psychological factors as group identity, motivations, stress, etc. In other words, humans always exist in an environment, and we rely on that context in our communicative behavior. Our mental activity is not caused only by a set of neurons (the brain), but also by judgments, inferences, etc. (the mind). Based on that we decide, for instance, whether certain external stimuli are a cause for fear or not: a man taking quick breaths and sweating will communicate one thing if he's wearing a jogging suit and something very different if he's wearing a groom's tuxedo (Levitin, 2017).

Similarly, empathy as a communication phenomenon can hardly be explained by neurobiological factors alone. Much research has been conducted on mirror neurons as a mechanism underlying empathy – special nerve cells that are said to enable people to mirror the emotions of others. It seems only natural to suggest that empathy can be mirrored through various chemicals as affect transmitters between people sharing the same physical context (Heinrich, 2012). In other words, all we need to do to develop empathy is to share the same physical context – and mirror neurons will take care of the rest. And yet, while many of our experiences are vicarious, whereby people's conceptions of reality are influenced "by what they see, hear, and read" (Bandura, 2001, p. 271), our communicative behavior cannot be fully understood "without direct experiential correlates" (ibid.). The more direct our experiences, the more they influence communication, especially empathy: that's why empathy is usually associated less with sight or sound as the 'high' senses, and more with touch as one of the 'low' senses.

Obviously, no one can share the same physical context with everyone else: simply put, one can't directly occupy another person's body. Everyone's conception of reality is to some degree unique, determined by one's past experiences. In this light, empathy in communication cannot be completely explained by the brain faculty of mirror neurons: being empathic is being mindful, which is rooted in socio-cultural and psychological factors. For instance, empathy can be affected by in-group/out-group bias: research shows that people show a reduced neural response to pain when it is inflicted on ethnic out-group members. Also, such factors as one's attitude towards the other person, or one's relationship with the other person, can increase or decrease empathy, sometimes causing an almost complete blockage of empathic responses (Lamm & Majdandžić, 2015).

As we can see from the examples of fear and empathy in communication briefly described here, the mind and the brain cannot be equated, and not all social, cultural and emotional aspects of human communication can be explained by applying techniques from neuroscience. Thus, brain scans cannot be identified with the mind; there is clearly something else to the mind that goes beyond neuroimaging. In fact, the very hardware and software used in brain imaging, e.g. computed tomography (CT) or magnetic resonance imaging (MRI), are tools created by the mind: thanks to these tools, we can see neurons in the form of color images. It is important to realize that these are just images, i.e., symbolic representations of neurons: had different tools been created by the human mind, we might have their different representations, i.e., different images of neurons.

At the same time, there can be no doubt that "neuroimaging could be a valuable way to study topics in communication as well as assess the effects of such things as media exposure, communication trait modification, cultural issues, and communication education trainings" (Brefczynski-Lewis, 2011, p. 197). One more promising area where brain imaging technology can be applied is the assessment and treatment of human communication disorders (Ingham, 2007). It is important to remember, however, that while the brain and the mind are two different frameworks, both are essential for explaining and understanding human communicative behavior. Not only can communication theory learn from brain studies, but also "the field of social and affective neuroscience would clearly benefit from the decades of social interaction research generated by scholars in communication studies" (Brefczynski-Lewis, 2011, p. 197).

The evidence of the symbolic mind at work goes back thousands of years in history: many scientists refer to the Upper Paleolithic as the 'big bang' of human culture, marked by cave paintings and statues of animals, decorated tools and pottery, personal ornaments such as beads and pendants, etc. (Gabora, 2007). Of special significance are burials, which show how a physical event (death) takes on a highly symbolic meaning: "We remember people after they are gone, we imagine the existence of unseen worlds where they may now reside, and we can project our minds into the future to see the inevitability of our own deaths as well as those of the people around us" (Petzinger, 2016, p. 45). Burial sites, perhaps more than anything else, testify to the human mind in action as a realm of thinking, intentions, memory, imagination, etc.

By now it must be clear that the mind is not the same as the brain (Figure 5.1).

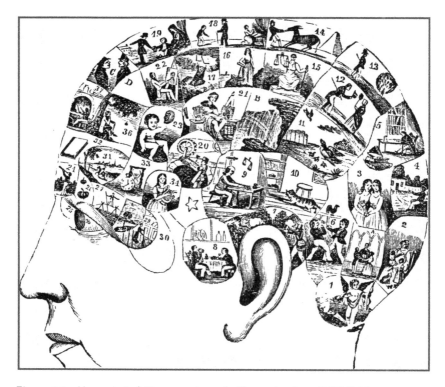

**Figure 5.1**   *Human mind, Human universals.* Illustration from S. Well, *New physiognomy: or signs of character, as manifested through temperament and external forms, and especially in "the human face divine"* (New York: Fowler & Wells, 1889) p. 132. Scan by the Harold B. Lee Library, Brigham Young University.

This, however, tells us what the mind is *not*. Defining what it *is* is a more difficult task: whereas the brain forms an anatomical part of the human body, the mind is an awareness of embodiment in the physical world. The mind as an awareness, however, is mysterious and elusive: we cannot have direct access to it the way we can take a picture of the brain. Thus, it is not surprising that, throughout the centuries, the mind has been conceptualized metaphorically, i.e., by using figures of speech applied to something to which words or phrases are not literally (directly) applicable. One of the earliest and most famous metaphors is Plato's comparison of the mind to a block of wax, which he considered to be "the gift of Memory, the mother of the Muses" (*Theaetetus* 191d-e). Our thoughts are imprinted upon it, and we remember them as long as an image lasts. In a similar fashion, John Locke conceptualized the mind as 'white paper' (*Essay Concerning Human Understanding*, II, 1.2), i.e., as a 'blank slate' (*tabula rasa*). In the 16th–18th centuries the mind was metaphorically viewed as a book, as a theatre, or as a museum: "in this vision, the mind is primarily conceived as a space able to mirror and contain the external world" (Albano, 2005, p. 845). In the 18th century the mind was also characterized in terms of coinage, court, empire, inhabitants, rooms, and writing (Pasanek, 2015). In the 19th century the mind was represented by such new metaphors as 'landscape of the consciousness' and 'soulscape', emphasizing the totality of an individual's mental realm (Kearns, 1987). In the 20th century the mind was described as a sponge, as a computer, as a Swiss army knife, and as a cathedral (Mithen, 1999). The metaphor of a cathedral paved the way for the view of the mind as a special architecture formed by various modules (Carruthers, 2006). We can see that all such metaphors are spatial in nature, presenting the mind as an entity that exists in or moves through space. On the one hand, such a view is a step toward answering the question 'What is the mind?'; on the other hand, answering that question becomes more and more difficult as we try to answer another question, 'Where is the mind?': it seems to be growing, e.g., from a wax block to a cathedral to a landscape. In other words, the mind is extended further and further into the world. This view is found at the basis of the so-called 'extended mind thesis'.

The extended mind thesis fits into the framework of 'active externalism' developed within environmental constructivism, niche construction, developmental systems theory, etc. (Greif, 2017). The proponents of the 'extended mind thesis' claim that it cannot be reduced to what exists within the confines of the organism's skin and skull; rather, the mind goes beyond those boundaries into the physical and socio-cultural environment. In other words, it is argued that the human mind is a result of structures and processes located outside the human head (Figure 5.2).

**Figure 5.2**   The over-extended mind. Image by Camilo Rueda López.

The extended mind thesis, contra Descartes, views the mind not as something that transcends materiality but as a thing extended in space – a kind of *res extensa* (Rickert, 2013). For instance, such objects as pens, paper and personal computers are so thoroughly enmeshed with our mental realm that they are now a part of its very machinery (Kiverstein et al., 2015). The same can especially be said about the role of the smartphone that is now deeply ingrained in our lives – so deeply, in fact, that it reaches all the way to our mind. As a result, for instance, not only are our mental skills diminished, such as problem-solving and creativity, but our communication also suffers, including the development of relationships, interpersonal closeness, and trust (Carr, 2017).

In a way, this view focuses on the mind as it is connected to the materiality of the world with its various media. Plato, who emphasized the nature of the mind as the gift of memory, himself contributed to this view by comparing it to a block of wax. Yet, the other view of the mind – as an aviary – he offers in the *Theaetetus* (196d–200c) is more airy and dynamic. And, of course, in the *Phaedrus*, he conceptualizes communication in a truly transcendent sense, speaking about "a speech living and ensouled. . . the written version of which would justly be called an image" (*Phaedrus*, 276a). This speech is not simply an image (a representation) available to everyone, but that 'living and ensouled' something "which is able to defend itself and knows to whom it should speak, and before whom to be silent" (*Phaedrus*, ibid.). That view of the mind, understood in terms of the presentation of living memory, is not prevalent in spatial metaphors, and we need to be re-minded about the nature of the mind as 'the gift of Memory, the mother of the Muses'.

## 2. COMMUNICATION AS MATCHING OF MINDS

Based on this discussion, we can identify three principal elements: the mind, symbols, and the world. It is through their interrelations that meaning in communication is formed, which is usually presented in the form of the semantic triangle that brings together 'thoughts', 'symbols', and 'things' (Suto, 2012) or 'the human mind', 'the world', and 'language' (Riemer, 2010). The semantic triangle model is associated with the work by C. K. Ogden and I. A. Richards, although its ideas go back to Aristotle's *De Interpretatione*. As can be seen from Figure 5.3, "each side of the triangle signifies a relation and each vertex signifies a *relatum* in the relation" (Suto, 2012, p. 32).

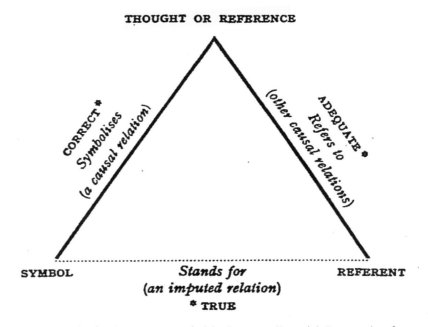

**Figure 5.3**   Ogden Semiotic Triangle (aka Semantic Triangle). Figure taken from C. K. Ogden & I.A. Richards, *The Meaning of Meaning: A Study of the Influence of Language upon Thought and of the Science of Symbolism* (1923), p. 11.

In this view, to quote I. A. Richards, "communication takes place when one mind so acts upon its environment that another mind is influenced, and in that other mind an experience occurs which is like the experience in the first mind, and is caused in part by that experience" (1928, p. 17). We can see that the (similar) meaning that occurs in two minds is identified by referring to the experience of environment. This meaning is semantic meaning, i.e., one that appears in the mind as a relation between symbols and the reality they represent.

C. K. Ogden and I. A. Richards' work, including their semantic triangle, paved the way for General Semantics, developed as a coherent theoretical framework by A. Korzybski, S.I. Hayakawa et al. It is no surprise that in the view of general semanticists, people in communication must pay more attention to extensional orientation to the actual physical world ('the territory'), instead of relying too much on intensional orientation of symbols, i.e., the presented real world ('the map'); e.g. "meanings of words . . . are best expressed by extensional definitions – i.e., by references to actual existents in the process world" (Gorman, 1962, p. 81). It must also be noted that General Semantics is conceptualized as "a new extensional discipline which explains and trains us how to use our nervous systems most efficiently" (Korzybski, 1958, p. xxxviii). It is explicitly positioned as a scientific approach to communication (Korzybski's major book is tellingly titled *Science and Sanity*). If humans used language symbols so that 'maps' could accurately represent as 'real' the actual world ('the territory'), there would be no misunderstanding in communication either by mistaking the map for the territory, or the territory for the map: once we can use our nervous systems efficiently, different human minds will see meaning in the same way or similar ways, leading to an improved human condition ('sanity').

This view is consistent with C. K. Ogden and I. A. Richards' ideas: for them,

> a language transaction or a communication may be defined as a use of symbols in such a way that acts of reference occur in a hearer which are similar in all relevant respects to those which are symbolised by them in the speaker. From this point of view, it is evident that the problem for the theory of communication is the delimitation and analysis of psychological contexts, an inductive problem exactly the same in form as the problems of the other sciences.
>
> *(1989, p. 315)*

We can see how every act of communication is 'an inductive problem', supplying more and more evidence for the truth of the general conclusion; this way, it 'trains us how to use our nervous systems most efficiently'.

This approach is the same as in the other sciences (e.g., natural sciences) – a process of specific observations that results in a general conclusion. For instance, the Principles (of Nonidentity, of Non-Allness, and of Self-Reflexivity) with which Korzybski replaced Aristotle's Laws (of Identity, of Excluded Middle, and of Non-Contradiction, respectively), still provide a basis for understanding language use.

It must be emphasized that "communication for Ogden and Richards was not the coordination of action or the revelation of otherness, but a matching of minds, a *consensus in idem*" (Peters, 1999, p. 14). The goal of ideal communication is congruence (Nöth, 1995, p. 72) – two entities being identical in form, coinciding exactly when superimposed (Figure 5.4). The reason you cannot really see Mind 2 in the figure is because it is identical to Mind 1. In this sense, the semantic triangle, employed by General Semantics, is an example "in a long line of geometrical models of meaning" (Nerlich, 1992, p. 208).

Korzybski realized that such an ideal in human communication can't be reached because of the changing nature of reality, wherein nothing is identical to itself: that is why he replaced Aristotle's Law of Identity with

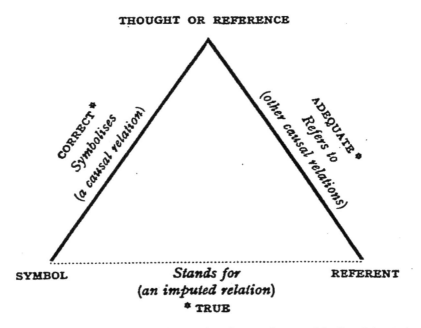

**Figure 5.4**　The semantic triangle (2). Thought or Reference (Mind) 1 = (identical to) Thought or Reference (Mind) 2.

his Principle of Nonidentity. So, in his statement about "an ideal human relational language [being] of structure similar to that of the world *and* to that of the human nervous system" (Korzybski, 1958, p. 259), it is more accurate to speak about 'the most effective language' or something along those lines rather than 'ideal'. As mentioned previously, the ideal of communication is complete matching of minds or congruence.

## 2.1. Communication as Shaping Minds

When C. K. Ogden and I. A. Richards speak about the acts of reference (to actuality) that produce similar thought (reality) in the hearer and the speaker (ideally, two being of 'one mind'), they call such communication 'a language transaction'. However, it is hard to see how such a process of matching of minds is a 'transaction', i.e., 'management or settlement of affairs'. (A theory such as Coordinated Management of Meaning would be a better example of that, viewing communication as a process whereby people are interacting and constructing meaning). It is difficult to characterize a process of interpersonal communication (between the hearer and the speaker) thus casually conceptualized as transactional. It is even more difficult to look at mass communication that way. When such messages are transmitted to a mass audience, communication can be especially effective; not surprisingly, it is in the process of mass communication that "the battle of the human mind is largely played" (Castells, 2007, p. 239). In fact, even "torturing bodies is less effective than shaping minds" (Castells, 2007, p. 238).

One of the most obvious cases of communication aimed at shaping minds is, of course, propaganda, and "shaping the public mind is a full-time job" (Kirsch, 2016, p. 36). The nature of propaganda has been widely theorized, from Edward Bernays who viewed it as a process in which "our minds are molded" (Bernays, 1928, p. 9) to the idea that "the mass media could fire magic bullets of information capable of shaping public opinion" (Pratkanis, 1997, p. 137) to Edward Herman and Noam Chomsky's 'propaganda model' (1988). As Chomsky emphasizes while sympathetically reviewing Bernays' ideas, mass media can regiment "the public mind every bit as much as an army regiments their bodies" (Bernays, 1928, p. 25).

Communication as a process of shaping minds goes beyond 'propaganda models' and can be conceptualized by the so-called 'Media Effect Theories': as the name suggests, these theories study what effects communication has on mass audiences. Let's briefly discuss three such theories.

Agenda Setting Theory posits that there exists a correlation between the emphasis placed by media on certain issues, e.g. their relative placement in news or the amount of their coverage, and the importance people attribute to these issues. As stated by the scholars who originally developed those ideas, "in choosing and displaying news, editors, newsroom staff, and broadcasters play an important part in shaping political reality" (McCombs & Shaw, 1972, p. 176). These ideas have proved to be influential in analyzing the relationships between media and publics in many areas of life, from economic to psychological. A special journal – *The Agenda Setting Journal. Theory, Practice, Critique* – dedicated to the analysis of such issues is published by the John Benjamins Publishing Company.

Priming Theory is often viewed as an extension of Agenda Setting Theory: whereas the latter focuses on how certain issues are made more salient in people's minds, the former emphasizes how mass media shapes people's judgments about those issues. Priming Theory shows how mass media shapes human minds in terms of personality traits, knowledge organization, memory storage, etc. For instance, it has been shown that priming can shape people's stereotyped perceptions of certain groups (Hansen & Hansen, 1988) and their political judgments about those stereotyped groups (Dixon, 2006). Several important characteristics of priming have been identified that relate to how knowledge is stored in the form of memory nodes: e.g., the effects of mass media are stronger if the primes are more intense (frequent), more recent, or last longer (Higgins, Bargh, & Lombardi, 1985).

Framing Theory, unlike agenda-setting and priming theories which focus on the accessibility of information, is based on the assumption that information is usually presented by mass media using certain meaningful frameworks (Scheufele, 2000). It is by invoking such schemas in people's minds that their understanding of all sorts of issues and events is shaped, ranging from social protest to government spending to European Union integration (Lecheler & de Vreese, 2012). Framing Theory is often used to explain how the media shapes people's minds in understanding politics. One of the best-known examples of how foreign policy events can be framed is the analysis by Robert Entman (1991) of news coverage of the 1983 Soviet shooting down of a Korean civilian airliner and the 1988 U.S. shooting down of an Iranian civilian airliner: the first was portrayed as a deliberate attack ('a murder in the air'), while the second was portrayed as an unfortunate and tragic mistake. The two strikingly different frames were visually reflected on the covers of *Newsweek* (September 12, 1983 and July 18, 1988, respectively).

One more theory that must be mentioned here is the well-known Cultivation Theory (Gerbner & Gross, 1976). While not everyone agrees that it is an 'effects' theory, pointing to the claims made by those who first developed it, this theory has been very influential in analysis of media effects on people's minds, e.g.: "cultivation is arguably among the most important contributions yet made to scientific and public understanding of media effects" (Shanahan & Morgan, 1999, p. 5). Cultivation Theory posits that the effect of massive television exposure over time shapes or 'cultivates' our perception of social and cultural reality.

However, there is a difference between the meanings of 'shaping' and 'cultivating': the former refers to a process of molding or cutting something that exists to give it a desired shape, whereas the latter has the meanings of promoting growth, encouraging or fostering, refining as by education, and even seeking someone's acquaintance or goodwill, as occurs when a club cultivates its new members. These meanings of 'cultivating' are consistent with the meaning of 'cultivating' as an old gardening principle in which one loosens the soil, taking care to not disturb plant roots or cause any other damage to the plant. It is this meaning of carefully cultivating or tilling the ground that we find in the word 'culture' (Berger, 2000). Thus, 'cultivating' suggests that we take care of the Other, while 'shaping' focuses on molding something to give it a shape desired by the Self. Taking all this into consideration, it is very difficult to speak about 'cultivation' as conceptualized in Cultivation Theory; rather, its focus is on shaping people's minds (so, in a way, Cultivation Theory is a misnomer). On a larger scale, we can see how difficult it is to decide whether minds are matched, shaped, molded, cultivated, etc. In its essence, propaganda is a process of dissemination – spreading ideas to large numbers of people. It is difficult, though, to agree with the statement that "a clear-cut definition of propaganda is neither possible nor desirable" (Doob, 1989, p. 375). It is crucial to determine when a process of mass information dissemination re-presents facts (education, news), represents facts (advertising), or mis-represents facts (propaganda). We must combine a scientific analysis of media effects with a humanistic understanding of such delicate matters as 'care', 'love' and 'goodwill' – all that stuff that 'dreams are made on'.

## 2.2. The Over-Extended Mind

As communication takes on a more mass, and less interpersonal, character, the mind seems to extend further and further into the world. Not only is

**Figure 5.5**    Silhouette of a man with a cane. Image by Madeleine Price Ball.

it located beneath the surface of one's skin, but it also reaches out into the environment: thus, it is embodied and embedded (Haugeland, 1998). In support of their views, the proponents of the extended mind thesis often discuss Gregory Bateson's example of a blind man navigating through the world with a cane (Figure 5.5).

There is no doubt that the ease of the man's navigation is a matter not only of nerve endings in the cortex, but also of the fingertips and the cane. What is overlooked, though, is "that this object is not simply conjured out of the blind person's mind, but has been made by someone" (Graves-Brown, 2015). In other words, human actions, such as navigating through the world with a cane, do not appear out of nowhere: their locus is (also) joint action or interaction through which objects and meanings are produced. In the case of a blind man, "the individual, the child, is not simply thrown into the human world; it is introduced into this world by the people around it, and they guide it in that world" (Leont'ev, 2009, p. 117). Such guidance can take the form of producing a stick of a certain shape or painting it a certain color: for instance, the walking stick is usually painted white, which comes to represent blindness of its bearer (Graves-Brown, 2015). We can't, therefore, simply presuppose the existence of a walking stick as a part of one's cognition without explaining its nature and role in communication.

If we accept the line of reasoning taken by the proponents of the extended mind thesis, we can go well beyond the cane of a blind man. That mind functions within a socio-cultural context can be clearly seen, for example, in the way we remember or forget things. What comes into, or goes out of, our mind depends on who we are communicating with – their social status, credibility, etc., our relations with those people, or the nature of conversations in which remembering takes place: "from this perspective, what is remembered is governed by what is communicated. Remembering is, if you like, communicating" (Hirst et al., 2014, p. 375). However, just like the walking stick of a blind man, the mind here is taken for granted – "an abstract version of an unproblematic property" (Morton, 2005, p. 569). In other words, the mind is simply presupposed as given, instead of being problematized and explained. As a result, the mind appears as something separate from communication – a view that does not do justice to either of them. In this view, the mind "has the responsibility to achieve knowledge. And after it has knowledge, then it may, if it has sufficient time on its hands, decide to communicate what it knows to others" (Ramsey & Miller, 2012, p. 14). To understand the dialectical relationship between the mind and communication, we must realize that every action is at the same time not only an interaction, but a transaction as well, by which tensions are managed and meaning settled, if only temporarily (Graves-Brown, 2015). When communication is equated with an act of reference to the world that produces similar (ideally, the same) thought in the minds of the hearer and the speaker – communication that C. K. Ogden and I. A. Richards call 'a language transaction' – that view does not address their interactive engagement in a process that can be difficult, deliberately uncooperative, and characterized by a degree of uncertainty.

If we want to draw a line between the mind and the world, it is reasonable to say that the mind does not really extend outside our head; note the neuroscientific recognition that "the mind is located 'everywhere and nowhere' in the brain" (Bhandar & Goldberg-Hiller, 2015, p. 13). At the same time, if we understand extension as an act of stretching out, then we can talk – in a more metaphorical meaning – about the extended mind. In this sense, a parallel can be drawn between the extended mind and Marshall McLuhan's treatment of 'the extensions of man' as the technological simulation of consciousness extended to the whole of human society (1994). To look for a line that separates an individual (human mind) from the whole of human society is misguided and counterproductive; instead, we should focus on how the mind and society emerge together through communication in a social process (Mead, 2015).

## 3. THE MAKING OF THE MIND

As stated previously, the mind can't simply act on the world: the individual mind can exist only insofar as its every action is at the same time an interaction with other people in which meaning is transacted, i.e., initiated, negotiated, and shared. This view of the mind was best developed (independently and at about the same time) by two thinkers – George Herbert Mead and Lev Vygotsky. Parallels between their ideas have been noted by many scholars (e.g. Wertsch, 1985). Let us look at the main parallels in their thought.

First, both thinkers emphasized that the mind cannot exist separately from the human brain and central nervous system. Mead stated that the physiological organism is a necessary but not sufficient condition of mental behavior (2015). In his turn, Vygotsky saw human development as the transformation of the biologically given 'lower mental functions' and the socially constructed 'higher mental functions'. Echoing Mead's statement, he argued that "no higher form of behavior is possible without lower forms, but the presence of lower or secondary forms does not exhaust the essence of the main form" (1997, p. 82). We are human *animals*, but we are also *human* animals.

Second, both thinkers emphasized that the mind exists not as an entity but as a social activity. According to Mead, "the individual mind can exist only in relation to other minds with shared meanings" (1982, p. 5). Vygotsky similarly saw the individual as a "social microcosm, as a type, as an expression or measure of the society" (2004, p. 317). If we take the existence of the mind as a given – something that exists before any human experience – then its nature remains mysterious. If, however, we view the mind as emerging in the dynamic social process that constitutes human experience, then it becomes clear that the nature of the mind is inherently dialogical: it is through participation in the social act of communication that the mind is formed.

Third, both thinkers emphasized that interaction in which the mind emerges is symbolic: human interaction is mediated by signs such as language signs or gestures. In other words, the mind emerges through "communication by a conversation of gestures in a social process or context of experience" (Mead, 1934, p. 50). For Mead, a gesture is any symbol that becomes significant for an individual because it allows one to view oneself (internal embodiment; proprioception) from the perspective of other people (external embodiment; exterioception). When I interpret the actions of others, I point out to myself that they have this or that meaning to me. This process of self-indication is a "communicative process in which the individual notes things, assesses them, gives them a meaning, and decides to act on the basis of the meaning" (Blumer, 2004, p. 81). Communication starts at the social (intersubjective) plane and ends up with an individual capacity to use signs that have shared meaning. As individuals are developing this capacity in a joint activity, social relations are transformed rather than simply transmitted into meanings. Both Mead and Vygotsky emphasized the importance of play (transposing internal and external embodiment) in this activity: by transitioning from play to game, the individual mind develops from 'me' to 'us' as the social mind.

When "the self comes to use the signs, once directed to others or received from others, in relation to the self" (Holland & Lachicotte, 2007, p. 108), meaning has been internalized. A well-known example of internalization is Vygotsky's analysis of the emergence of (the meaning of) pointing. Initially the child tries and fails to grasp something out of reach; at this stage, we can't talk about communication because the child is not self-conscious of pointing. However, "in response to the unsuccessful grasping movement of the child, there arises a reaction not on the part of the object, but on the part of another person" (Vygotsky, 1997, p. 105), e.g. the child's mother hands the object over to the child. It is only when the child can reflect on the meaning of that gesture that grasping becomes pointing. Henceforth, the child will be pointing to an object out of reach instead of trying to grasp it, knowing that someone who shares the same meaning will hand it over. From that perspective, communication can be viewed as a process of externalization (of internal meaning).

### 3.1. Taking the Perspective of the Other

Thus, every individual action is at the same time a symbolic interaction and a joint transaction. We become who we are by 'taking the perspective of the other' (Mead) or through 'reverse action' (Vygotsky). In this light, communication is a process in which, to use Charles Horton Cooley's famous phrase, "I imagine your mind, and especially what your mind thinks about my mind, and what your mind thinks about what my mind thinks about your mind" (Cooley, 2017, p. 100). It is important to note that individuals *interpret* one another's actions, which involves an element of imagination (choice of context). The relationship between signs and objects is never direct: meaning is a result of synthesizing one's past experiences with the present situation and anticipating future actions. In this sense, "the time field for action extends both forward and backward" (Vygotsky, 1980, p. 36).

Both Mead and Vygotsky thought that the capacity to take the perspective of others by interpreting symbols and acting on the world is a uniquely human capacity. It is this capacity for reflexive thinking (our mind) that distinguishes humans from other animals. For humans, objects are not mere external stimuli as they have a socially assigned meaning (objects are named and remain in time as names). According to Vygotsky, "society is the bearer of the cultural heritage without which the development of mind is impossible" (Miller, 2011, p. 199). In a similar vein, according to Mead, "an animal as opposed to a human form, in indicating something to, or bringing out a meaning for, another form, is not at the same time indicating or bringing out the same thing or meaning to or for himself; for the animal has no mind, no thought, and hence there is no meaning here in the significant or self-conscious sense" (1964, p. 168). At the same time, Mead's work includes examples of animals using significant gestures and has much to offer animal studies (Wilkie & McKinoon, 2013).

When conceptualized in terms of matching or shaping minds, communication appears as a mechanical process of one person (or people) acting on another person (or other people). This view overlooks one of the main human characteristics – our desire to understand other minds, which can be carried out only through a process of interpretation. We can understand others because we can view things from their perspective. Our ability to understand other minds is linked "with our capacity to transform ourselves imaginatively into an occupant of the other person's point of view" (Stueber, 2010, p. 10). As Friedrich Schleiermacher showed in the Romantic era, one must, as it were, step outside of oneself and take the other's position so that to interpret a literary work and discern the author's mind (Latin: *mens auctoris*) (Schleiermacher, 1977). In the same vein, Charles S. Peirce spoke about "communication from an uttering mind to an interpreting mind" when "the person divides himself into two parties" and "thinking takes the form of a dialogue" (1967, p. 498). As 'the father of pragmatism', Peirce highlighted the (pragmatic) relation between signs and their interpreting minds. Unlike semantic meaning, which is concerned with the relationship between signs and objects (and is the focus of General Semantics, as already discussed), "pragmatic interpretation is ultimately an exercise in mind-reading, involving the inferential attribution of intentions" (Sperber & Wilson, 2002, p. 3). While misinterpretation is its unavoidable part, the pragmatic view presents a more complex and adequate picture of the nature of communication. Just like that of Schleiermacher and Peirce, Mikhail Bakhtin's work is based on the "idea of the interpretive mind" (Brockmeier, 2005, p. 436). For him, every utterance as a unit of communication is inherently dialogic: "that is, it is personal, it has a voice, the voice of someone's mind" (ibid.). The better we can hear those multiple voices, the better we can understand other minds – and our own.

The making of the mind, as based on the previous discussion, is reflected in Figure 5.6. As we can see, one has the capacity to view oneself both as a subject (Self) and an object (Other). In this light, every act of communication is an interaction in which the Self takes the role of the Other: when viewed

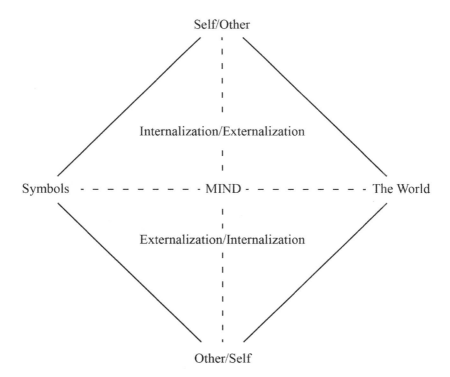

**Figure 5.6** The interactive mind. Image created by the authors.

as a process going from the Other to the Self, it is internalization, and, when viewed as a process going from the Self to the Other, it is externalization. Communication, of course, is one holistic activity in which these two processes exist together and simultaneously as reversible, reflexive and reflective: everything is just a matter of perspective.

As individuals interact with one another, their selves emerge, which is to say a society emerges. In Cooley's words, *"self and society are twin-born, we know one as immediately as we know the other"* (1998, p. 19; emphasis added). The birth of self and society would be impossible without the making of the mind. On the one hand, the mind is formed (made) through symbolic interactions (internalization); on the other hand, the mind is what creates (makes) a human society (externalization). In both cases, the mind is an activity – either as an act of meaning being formed by interacting individuals using symbols that represent the world, or as "an act of bringing forth not only the world but also the human actor" (Stetsenko, 2016, p. 270). In both cases, the mind appears as "a simultaneous and bidirectional spiral of mutual becoming" (Stetsenko, 2016, p. 270). The apexes labeled 'Self' and 'Other' in Figure 5.6 represent the individual minds, while the space in between is the social mind. "At the most basic level, the mind is the ability to step outside oneself as a means to reflect on one's actions. At the most developed level, the mind represents the highest functioning of the self when people assume the attitudes of an abstract community" (Hallett et al., 2009, p. 491); note the space between the two apexes. Of course, the two can be separated only for the purpose of discussion; in real life, it is one spiral of the emergence of actual meaning. Overall, it is through communication that we become mindful, and it is by being mindful that we can communicate.

## 4. WORLD WITHOUT THE MIND?

In a recently published book *World Without Mind: The Existential Threat of Big Tech* (Foer, 2017), we read about the impact on today's society of the big technology companies, such as Amazon, Facebook and Google. However, the call made in the book is not for giving up all technology, but rather for understanding the ideology behind it and the motivations of the big tech companies. What the author advocates is that we seek to make informed decisions on accepting and using technological innovations. To that end, we must think for ourselves, i.e., develop an independent and critical mind.

Devotion to technology without contemplating its nature and effects is often conceptualized as "a form of idolatry" (Barbour, 1992, p. 14).

It is stated that "our idols of technology are the false notions that have grown up around modern society's fervent commitment to technological progress" (Leiss, 1990, p. 5). In the work of Francis Bacon we find the best-known discussion of such "false appearances that are imposed upon us by the general nature of the mind" (1861, vol. 3, p. 396). These false appearances, according to Bacon's *Novum Organum*, take the form of (a) the Idols of the Tribe – false concepts as distorted reflections caused by the structure of human understanding that is but a crooked mirror; (b) the Idols of the Cave – preconceived doctrines individuals have due to their education, custom, and other experiences; (c) the Idols of the Market Place – false conceptions that enter our minds through a combination of words in the realm of public communication; and (d) the Idols of the Theater – prejudices developed from our traditional philosophical systems. Bacon calls for our understanding to be "thoroughly freed and cleansed" (Bacon, 1861, vol. 4, p. 69) from these idols of the mind.

Bacon distinguished between the (false) idols of the human mind and the (true) ideas of the divine mind. His goal was to replace these idols with the true science: the new empirical method, introduced in *Novum Organum*, is aimed at operating inductively without any preconceived ideas. The roots of such critical thinking in the Western tradition go back to ancient Greece when Socrates questioned people's unproblematized claims to knowledge (he famously declared that 'the unexamined life is not worth living') and when Plato saw in images but imperfect reflections of the true ideas: "idolatry, according to Plato, is the mistake of conflating knowledge of the imperfect image with the perfect nature to which the nature refers" (Cort, 2010, p. 260). However, when it comes to what is understood in the Western tradition as the scientific method, "it was Bacon who began the movement for a critical scrutiny of the human mind" (Eby & Arrowood, 1946, p. 238). On the one hand, for Bacon the true ideas are those of the divine mind; on the other hand, if human understanding is empirically freed from the idols of the mind, knowledge can be achieved. Thus, Bacon balanced theology and science in his thought. The empiricists (including Bacon) took seriously the idea that human attempts at recovering their divine birthright are inherently tainted by their animal origins (Harrison, 2007). It was rationalists who further advanced the primacy of the mind. In this respect, it is hard to overestimate the role played by Immanuel Kant, who emphasized the active and productive nature of the mind (and who dedicated *The Critique of Pure Reason* to Bacon). While Kant is usually viewed as a philosopher exemplifying abstract thought, he was invested in the social realm of human interaction. His work exhibits a rhetorical sensibility and an interest in public discourse, including aesthetics and politics. In this light, it becomes possible to speak about Kant's philosophy of communication (Ercolini, 2016).

## 4.1. Ideas Vs. Idols

When discussing the workings of the human mind and their impact on human social interactions, it is impossible to ignore the ideas of Karl Marx, for whom socialism as "the actualization of man's essence, by overcoming his alienation . . . is the fulfillment of the prophetic aim: the destruction of the idols" (Fromm, 2013, p. 53). This aim can be fulfilled by means of a revolution that brings about a structural change in the economic conditions of a society as its base. A revolution is a result of class struggle or different ideologies as systems "of the ideas and representations which dominate the mind of a man or a social group" (Althusser, 1971, p. 120). Such systems form the superstructure: its main goal is to reinforce the ideology of the ruling class – those who own the means of production. This suggests that the superstructure plays a secondary role in society. However, the significance of what takes place in 'the mind of a man or a social group' cannot be minimized. In a letter to Thomas Jefferson (August 24, 1815), John Adams talks about the nature of a revolution. He notes that his ideas "may be peculiar, perhaps Singular" and says:

> What do We Mean by the Revolution? The War? That was no part of the Revolution. It was only an Effect and Consequence of it. *The Revolution was in the Minds of the People,* and this was effected, from 1760 to 1775, in the course of fifteen Years before a drop of blood was drawn at Lexington.
>
> *(Cappon, 1959: 455; emphasis added)*

In other words, it can be argued that all physical means of production first take shape in the minds of the people. It is appropriate to view base and superstructure as a system or an interactive whole. Marx seemed to understand that himself when he wrote:

> *The ideas of the ruling class* are in every epoch the *ruling ideas,* i.e. the *class* which is the *ruling* material force of society, is *at the same time* its *ruling* intellectual force. The class which has the means of material production at its disposal, has control *at the same time* over the means of mental production
>
> *(Marx & Engels, 1970, p. 64; emphasis added)*

Just as Kant's ideas are now viewed from the perspective of philosophy of communication, we now hear about 'the forgotten' Marxist theory of communication and society (Holzer, 2017), showing how communication relates to work (living wages), production (sustainable ecology), and profit (social value), and identifying the relationships between ideology and everyday communicative practices and media contents.

The ideas of Marx were developed by a group of sociologists at the University of Frankfurt am Main, Germany, known as the Frankfurt School of Critical Theory. Three generations of the Frankfurt School can be noted (Anderson, 2000). The first generation (identified with the reaction to the rise of National Socialism and its effects) is represented by such thinkers as Max Horkheimer and Theodor Adorno, who analyzed the roots of totalitarianism in mass culture and brought to light its effects on the individual. The second generation (identified with the revelations of Nazi crimes and the social transformations of the 1960s) is represented most notably by Jürgen Habermas, who developed his theory of universal pragmatics based on the role of communication and rational argument. The third generation (identified with the fall of the Berlin Wall and the spread of globalization) is represented by such thinkers as Axel Honneth, who are skeptical about universalistic categories and point to the importance of emotions and the unconscious in human life. With each generation, there is more and more emphasis on the role of language, culture and the workings of the human mind.

Informed by the ideas of all these (and other) thinkers, from Socrates to today's scholars, communication within the critical tradition is conceptualized as a process of discursive reflection (Lanigan & Strobl, 1981). This conceptualization starts with intrapersonal communication because "while we call eloquent those who are able to speak before a crowd, we regard as sage those who most skillfully debate their problems in their own minds" (Isocrates, *Antidosis*, 256). The critical tradition has also been used in the analysis of group communication, e.g. interaction within families (Turner & West, 2014); organizational communication (Mumby, 2012); and mass communication, in which a shift from 'idols of production' to 'idols of consumption' was noted between 1900 and 1940 (Lowenthal, 1944). Today, in the age of the Internet, the ideas of critical theorists are applied to the analysis of social media and technology (Allmer, 2015; Fuchs, 2016).

The critical tradition in communication theory is well documented (Allen, 2017). We just want to emphasize a key point: in any critical view of communication, it is the mind itself that can, and must, "consider the false appearances that are imposed upon us by the general nature of the mind" (Bacon, 1861, vol. 3, p. 396).

## 5. ALL IS THE MIND?

As noted earlier, although it cannot be identical with the brain, it is common to believe that the mind cannot exist separately from the human brain and central nervous system, indeed, the whole synergistic body. When the mind is viewed as extended into the environment, the focus is on how it is shaped by our engagement with other people and socio-cultural artifacts. This thesis is not taken to mean that the mind really extends outside the surface of one's skin. Thus, the mind, whether treated as an individual's brain activity, or its metaphorical extension into environment, is still conceptualized to be something bounded in space and time – more so in the first case and less so in the second.

These conceptualizations are developed within the frameworks of philosophy of the mind, cognitive science, logic, and metaphysics. However, there are theories, grounded in neuroscience and quantum physics, that view the mind as non-local – literally unbounded in space and time (Figure 5.7) (Herbert, 1987).

In this view, all our interactions with others are unmediated (no connecting signal is involved), unmitigated (the strength of the interactions does not diminish with distance) and immediate (not limited by the velocity

**Figure 5.7**　All is mind. Image by nednapa/Shutterstock.com.

of light). The mind, therefore, is not a stand-alone entity but a process-field that exists in a dimension higher than our three-dimensional space and one-dimensional time world. All minds as such fields are interconnected with one another via quantum (subatomic particles) movements such as resonance, entanglement, and tunneling. In this sense, communication is no different from two particles which, although separated by immense distances, are 'synced' together in such a way that one affects the other instantaneously: communication is thus entanglement. In a recent paper, the four-dimensional field of the mind is presented shaped as a torus in which "various communication mechanisms . . . are clearly *interrelated*" (Meijer & Geesink, 2017, p. 68).

The conception of the mind as a non-local, interconnected higher-dimensional field might explain what are considered psychic or extra-sensorial phenomena such as precognition, clairvoyance and telepathy. For instance, "even though the impossibility of *immediate communication* between minds may be a fundamental psychological fact" (Peters, 1999, p. 5; emphasis added), numerous telepathy trials with positive results – in human as well as interspecies communication – have been noted, including controlled experiments (Erickson, 2011). All such entanglements, e.g. promoting the healing of distant individuals or animals, acquiring detailed information about scenes and situations at global distances, etc., can be viewed as forms of mind-to-mind communication. These interactions are immediate, unmitigated and unmediated; one can say that here the message is the medium.

Earlier, it was shown that there can be no world without the mind. Now it appears that we cannot really speak about an individual mind, even if it is extended, because a demarcation line is still presupposed between the mind and its environment. Both modern science and the first principle of the ancient hermetic philosophy say the same thing: 'All is Mind'.

The implications of this view of the mind for communication are mind-boggling. Humans will be able to become, in Shakespeare's words, 'infinite in faculty! . . . In action how like an angel! In apprehension how like a god!' In more prosaic terms, the entire history of media can be viewed as overcoming human limitations, becoming more and more able to communicate across space and time. According to Friedrich A. Kittler, the history of analog media is structured by the disability theme: for example, the telephone and the gramophone were invented for the deaf, and the typewriter for the blind. Moreover, "in Kittler's earlier narrative, *media* that help us *see*, *hear* and write better *were developed by* and for *those who saw* and *heard less*" (Winthrop-Young, 2015, p. 81; emphasis added). It must be noted that telepathy is experienced in extreme situations such as anxiety or emergency, i.e., those reaching a limit of (mediated) communication that can only be overcome through an immediate transmission over distance ('tele-') of feeling or suffering ('-pathy') (Glasser, 1967, p. 21). Kittler speaks of analog media which communicate meanings as continuous patterns resembling reality: in other words, analog communication (choice of degree: both more and less) is based on likeness, emphasizing such meanings of the word 'like' as 'having the same characteristics or qualities as; similar to', and 'feeling attraction toward or taking pleasure in'. In this respect, the power of new digital (choice of kind: either one or none) technologies is overrated. In fact, it may well be those who are 'disabled' (measured against the 'able' criterion set by modern humans) – visually impaired, deaf or hard of hearing, autistic, etc. – who are more powerful. As well as animals – 'our little brothers'. They may be more powerful because less is more, and what is needed perhaps is not to increase Gross Domestic Product but to quiet the mind and open it to the cosmos. Paraphrasing Matthew 5:5, we could say: 'Blessed are the 'disabled': for they shall save the earth'.

If 'All is Mind', some people are concerned that we may lose our identity and our communication may still fail us: "for instance, how does a mother who senses that her faraway child is in danger know that it is her child who is involved and not some other child somewhere else in the world?" (Dossey, 2013, p. 2). However, the prognosis is mostly optimistic (Erickson, 2011, p. 51): the human world will become one of more openness, transparency and empathy. We will be able to feel the sufferings of nonhumans as well as their joy. This "full democracy would be transspecies, transgender, transrace, transregion, transclass, transage, transhuman: what Emerson called 'the democracy of chemistry'" (Peters, 1999, p. 260). One can only hope that we are ready for that. But then, to quote Shakespeare, 'All things are ready, if our mind be so.'

# 6

# The Wonder of Language

Key concepts:

Conversation, conversational implicature, dyad, discourse, ethnomethodology, ethnolinguistic vitality, 'face', the ideal speech situation, intersubjectivity, language ecology, language game, linguistic landscape, private language, the public sphere, referentiality.

Key names:

Aristotle, St. Augustine, Kenneth Burke, José Ortega y Gasset, Hans-Georg Gadamer, Harold Garfinkel, Howard Giles, Herbert Paul Grice, Jürgen Habermas, Einar Haugen, Wilhelm von Humboldt, John Locke, Martin Buber, Plato, Ferdinand de Saussure, Tzvetan Todorov, Ludwig Wittgenstein.

## 1. LANGUAGE PROBLEM(S)

For centuries people have been trying to understand the wonderful phenomenon of language. Thousands of years ago the problem of language attracted the attention of many thinkers who pondered its nature and use in communication. In Plato's *Cratylus*, two main speakers – Cratylus and

Hermogenes – debate whether names belong naturally to their objects or are purely conventional signs and thus reveal nothing about the nature of things. In other words, "Cratylus wants names to be meaningful in themselves and by nature (the realist), and Hermogenes wants them to signify by convention (the nominalist)" (Bliss, 2008, p. 14). This debate on the nature of language, started by Plato, continues to this day.

Plato himself favors the position of Cratylus: this can be explained in part by the fact that, in those times, words were viewed as immediately influencing reality; in a way, people were not conscious of language as something external, taking it for granted as a part of their own life. Only gradually did the distance between words and things begin to increase and the symbolic use of language start to emerge. Today, of course, language is commonly considered a symbolic instrument that can be used for whatever purpose desired. Thus, over the centuries, we have traveled a long path: "from the complete unconsciousness of language that we find in classical Greece, the path leads to the instrumentalist devaluation of language that we find in modern times" (Gadamer, 2004, p. 422).

As a result, it is now more common to speak of language problems – the instances when language fails us in our communication – rather than to address the problem of language, i.e., problematize its nature and use. Whereas in the past our attention was directed to the problem *of* language, today more attention is paid to various problems *with* language. Such failures to communicate start as occasional troubles and grow into problems when they become systemic within a society, with various institutions brought to bear.

Language problems in social interaction are traditionally associated with racism, sexism, poverty, crime, delinquency, homelessness, mental illness, and other devalued or deviant communicative behaviors. Thirty years ago, in his article *Language, Interaction, and Social Problems*, Douglas W. Maynard (1988) listed such examples as service encounters, male-female interaction, conversation in a doctor's office, conflicts between racial groups in school settings, abuse of status and power in organizations, and the role of media in claims-making. To these problems, which still exist today and are perhaps even more acute that before, others can be added. For example, romantic encounters may end badly (Robbins & Dowty, 2016); people complain that because of text messaging "we never talk any more" (Kluger, 2012); bullying in schools is now wide-spread (Smith et al., 2004); mental illnesses such as dementia, now on the increase, are often characterized by language problems (France & Kramer, 2001); language is connected to poor academic performance (Ballard, 2003); and the problem of language endangerment is increasingly alarming (Rogers & Campbell, 2015). This list can go on and on.

To provide "a deep understanding and potential solutions to language problems in a society" (Muraoka, 2009, p. 151), the concept of 'contact situation' is suggested. It usually refers to situations where several languages come into contact and are often used simultaneously by various speakers – what is traditionally discussed under the rubric of language policy and planning. However, every act of communication is a contact situation, whether it is a contact of oneself with oneself (e.g. internal conflict), or a contact with a friend, or a contact with several people within a group, or an intercultural contact. Whenever we communicate and use language, we can always say: 'We are in a situation here'. Unlike the phrase 'We have a situation here', which people do not like to hear because it means that something has gone wrong and needs fixing, the phrase 'We are in a situation here' is neutral: it simply means the combination of circumstances at a given moment or a certain state of affairs. Just as we cannot not communicate, we cannot not be in a situation. Thus, it is necessary to view "the speech situation as an inalienable ground for any . . . inquiry into language" (Stawarska, 2015, p. 183). We will discuss four speech situations in accordance with four interconnected levels of interaction experience: intrapersonal, interpersonal, group, and intercultural.

## 2. THE INTRAPERSONAL COMMUNICATION SITUATION

While until recently it had amounted to little more than a mention in a sentence (Cunningham, 1995) with calls made for its theoretical grounding (Vocate, 1994), intrapersonal communication now enjoys serious scholarly attention (Macke, 2014). Conceptualized as "self-talk" (Martinez, 2011, p. 77) or "conversation with the self" (Alderson-Day et al., 2016), intrapersonal communication "occurs in the absence of other people" (Barnlund, 1968, p. 8). It plays an important role in one's communicative behavior, from problem solving to evaluating and planning one's actions to emotional balance. The therapeutic function of intrapersonal communication is especially noted; any language disorder affects an individual's ability to function normally and maintain one's identity. Interestingly, the intrapersonal therapeutic function is addressed by departments of communication disorders, whereas departments of communication mostly focus on problems as social exigencies.

Since intrapersonal communication occurs in the absence of other people, how one talks to oneself is entirely up to an individual. In a well-known scene from *Alice in Wonderland*, Humpty Dumpty says: "When *I* use a word, . . . it means just what I choose it to mean – neither more nor less". When questioned by Alice if he "*can* make words mean so many different things", Humpty Dumpty replies: "The question is . . . which is to be master – that's all. . . . *I* can manage the whole lot of them!" (Figure 6.1).

Just like Humpty Dumpty, an individual can manage the whole lot of language; in this sense, one's language is a private language. The idea of a private language was made famous by Ludwig Wittgenstein who wrote: "The words of this language are to refer to what can be known only to the speaker" (Wittgenstein, 1953, §243).

To talk meaningfully about the world, it seems only natural to name all its parts. Then, this will be a language in which "every word has a meaning. This meaning is correlated with the word. It is the object for which the word stands" (Wittgenstein, 1953, §1). Every situation in the world, of course, is

**Figure 6.1**    Humpty Dumpty by Clara E. Atwood, from Charles Welsh, *A Book of Nursery Rhymes* (Boston: D. C. Heath, 1901), p. 119.

made up not only of isolated objects but also of states of affairs and facts; thus, language must relate to the world not only through names but also predicates or propositions (lexicon and grammar, or semantics and syntactics). Thus, language "in its essential principle, is a nomenclature, that is, a list of terms corresponding to things" (Saussure, 1986, p. 65); here, by 'terms' we understand words and phrases, and by 'things', objects, states of affairs and facts. In this view, language represents reality; if 'terms' corresponds to 'things', then an individual can function successfully in one's world. One can then rightfully say: "I am my world" (Wittgenstein, 2002, 5.64).

## 2.1. Language as Representation

The representational view of language in the Western European tradition goes back to Aristotle, who in *De Interpretatione* argued that "the letters are signs of sounds, the sounds are signs of mental experiences, and these are signs of things" (Heidegger, 1971, p. 97; cf. Aristotle, *De Interpretatione*, 1, 16a3–8). This view is considered classical, manifested in the works of John Locke, St. Augustine, Ferdinand de Saussure, and Ludwig Wittgenstein, among others. The word 'classical' can be traced back to the Proto-Indo-European root *kelǝ-, meaning 'to call, to shout'. In this sense, an individual calls on one's language whose terms are neatly organized (classified) and accurately represent reality.

Such a language appears ideal as it presents a clear picture of the world. It is such a language that the members of the British Royal Society had in mind when they envisioned "a world where people would speak of things *as they really were*, . . . in plain language as clear as glass – *so many words for so many things*" (Bizzell & Herzberg, 2001, p. 795; emphasis added). 'Plain language' must be conceptualized not so much as 'clear glass' but as a mirror, i.e., a glass surface coated with a metal amalgam that reflects a clear image. Language thus presents a picture of the world by reflecting its objects, states of affairs and facts. However, even though one appears to be a master of one's language, language problems still exist; it is as if language resists all attempts to be reduced to a mirror. It is as if language is saying to an individual: 'OK, if you want me to just reflect the world, go ahead and live in it'. And so, in the words of Wilhelm von Humboldt, "man lives primarily with objects, indeed, since feeling and acting in him depend on his presentations, he actually does so exclusively, *as language presents them to him*" (Humboldt, 1999, p. 60; emphasis added). Thus, the tables are turned: now language is the master, for it *allows* an individual to see the world only in a certain way. If we want communication to be more successful, we must stop viewing it only as a mirror that presents a picture (and blaming this mirror for all problems). We must admit that "what is to be done with the picture, how it is to be used, is still obscure. Quite clearly, . . . it must be explored *if we want to understand the sense of what we are saying. But the picture seems to spare us this work*: it already points to a particular use. *This is how language takes us in*" (Wittgenstein, 1953, §115; emphasis added). In other words, unless we admit that more work is required from us to understand language, it will continue taking us in, in more than one sense of the word.

So, language cannot be conceptualized as a private tool managed by an individual; if nothing else, language cannot be reduced to an instrument because "we cannot, for instance, pick it up and set it aside at will" (Crusius, 1999, p. 162). What one can do is make language represent objects and name them any way one wants. Let us look at three cases when an individual adopted this approach to language.

The first case is a story from the Old Testament when "Adam gave names to all cattle, and to the fowl of the air, and to every beast of the field" (Genesis 2:20, King James Version) (Figure 6.2).

**Figure 6.2**   A Byzantine fresco depicting Adam naming animals. Photograph printed in *The Orthodox Weekly Bulletin*, Vestal, Cliffwood, New Jersey, U.S. (1999, Sept. 12–19). Scan by Michael Romanov.

In this situation, the cattle, the fowl and every beast do not speak; "they only receive the apposite labels which enable man to organize God's creations. Adam himself is alone; he knows neither intimate companionship nor human society" (Stawarska, 2015, pp. 33–34). That Adam feels alone is clear if we read the entire verse: "And Adam gave names to all cattle, and to the fowl of the air, and to every beast of the field; but for Adam there was not found an help meet for him". Or, as translated in the English Standard Version of the Bible, "But for Adam there was not found a helper fit for him". In other words, none of those creatures could be a suitable companion for him.

The second case is Columbus's encounter with Native Americans as discussed by Tzvetan Todorov in his well-known book *The Conquest of America: The Question of the Other* (1999). According to Todorov, Columbus's goal was to reaffirm his picture of the world, and so he was only interested in which Spanish word every object corresponded to: "Columbus addressed his language, accordingly, directly to nature, to the referent" (Pinchevski, 2005, p. 144). Not only did Native American cultures suffer subjugation based on such a view of language, but Columbus's reputation suffered as well, if only posthumously; it is no accident that today more and more people in the U.S. want to replace the traditional Columbus Day holiday with Indigenous People's Day.

The third case is the story of Humpty Dumpty who, as all know, sat on a wall, had a great fall, and all the King's horses and all the King's men could not put him together again. In Lewis Carroll's telling he is a self-described master of words, which mean what he chooses for them to mean: it is not surprising that scholars note "his loneliness" and his "insisting on being an 'Adam'" (Tekdemir, 2007, p. 209). They also note his "obsession with referentiality" and his "desire to control language and communication" (Schwab, 1994, p. 164). Significantly, when he falls, it is this (his) side of the wall. In Humpty Dumpty's mind, it was a safe fall because he could count on 'all the King's horses and all the King's men'; in *Alice in Wonderland*, he says: "They'd pick me up again in a minute, they would!" He takes it for granted, just as he takes for granted the words of his language to mean whatever he wants. And yet, they failed to help him.

These three cases have several things in common. First, in all three cases language is taken to be an instrument, with words referring to things. Second, this approach to language turns out to be problematic. And, third, the reason for those failures to communicate lies in the main characters' failure to admit that language can be different if used in other situations by other people: in other words, they failed to see the otherness of language. It is argued that, when Adam names the cattle, the fowl, and every beast, "the name is the essence of the thing [and more than just a] device for identification. If the Chinese call a cat something like a meow (it sounds much like it) and if we've named a bird a chickadee (after its call) – these are sure signs that the creature was not named at Eden by our first human ancestors" (Mozeson, 2018). And yet, those names for a cat and a bird *are* different from those in Hebrew. Columbus failed to recognize the diversity of Native American languages: "in Columbus's view, there was no human subject on the other side" (Pinchevski, 2005, p. 144). The same could be said about Humpty Dumpty: had he fallen on the other side of the wall, he might have had a softer landing or, if not, might have been put together by other men (or women) who were caring and more experienced in such matters than all the King's horses and all the King's men.

These three cases have one more very important thing in common, albeit implicitly. They all show that, no matter how hard one tries "circumventing the dimension of intersubjectivity" (Pinchevski, 2005, p. 144), one is always drawn to the Other, whether it is every beast of the field, other cultures, or something/someone on the other side of the wall. These tensions, inherent in language, are demonstrated best of all by Humpty Dumpty who comes closest to coming out of his shell. In Lewis Carroll's book, he sat on the wall "looking away from Alice as he spoke"; "his eyes were steadily fixed in the opposite direction, and he didn't take the least notice of her". As a result, "Alice didn't know what to say to this: it wasn't at all like conversation, she thought, as he never said anything to *her. . .*". It was as if he were talking to himself; later, of course, he addresses Alice, "looking at her for the first time". Humpty Dumpty wants to be a master of his language, yet can't help looking at others and talking to them. Although "Humpty Dumpty has developed his own absurd philosophy of a private language . . . – a philosophy that guarantees him absolute sovereignty over language and communication" (Schwab, 1994, p. 164), he still talks to Alice who is entrapped "in weird language games" (ibid.) because Humpty Dumpty controls the rules of the game, changes them spontaneously or invents new ones. And yet, Alice engages in those games with Humpty Dumpty. In fact, "the most complicated game that Carroll and Alice play in the Alice books is the game of language itself" (Susina, 2010, p. 426).

## 2.2. Language in Use

The concept of the 'language game' was introduced by Ludwig Wittgenstein, who wanted to explore the nature of language more fully by going beyond its representational view. We cannot fully understand the nature of words and expressions if we only view them as supposedly objective pictures of reality. Language is not simply an abstract system of 'terms' that refer to 'things', and meaning is not an objective property of language. One can never completely define every single word and expression, thus making language one's own. One can, though, engage in various practical activities with others. Thus, "language does not exist by itself in a static system of definitions and syntax, but is intimately caught up in our activities and practices" (Blair, 2006, p. 8). It is in such activities that words and expressions come alive and language reveals its nature as a living organism. And it is such activities in which it is used by people that Wittgenstein called 'language games'.

Since the meaning of a word or an expression can never be limited to its fixed definition (as a picture reflecting reality), it must be examined in a specific context of use. Wittgenstein emphasizes that innumerable activities can be considered language games, as long as the contexts of their use are similar, forming 'family resemblances', e.g., reporting something, telling a story, making a joke, being ironic, criticizing, objecting, guessing, joking, greeting, etc. There is one crucial thing that language games have in common: "they are related to one another in many different ways. And it is because of this relationship, or these relationships, that we call them all 'language'" (1953, §65). Therefore, language is not simply a unidirectional reflective mechanism referring to something or representing something. The nature of language is inherently relational, as it brings together two or more concepts, objects or people. A relation is always *between* two or more entities, for example, between different contexts of language use.

Every language game is a result of relations between different people who use language in this or that context. No game, however simple, can circumvent the dimension of intersubjectivity. Consider Wittgenstein's description of a primitive language in which there are only four words and each represents a certain object:

> Let us imagine a language . . . meant to serve for *communication between a builder A and an assistant B*. A is building with building stones: there are blocks, pillars, slabs and beams. B has to pass the stones . . . in the order in which A needs them. For this purpose they use a language consisting of the words 'block', 'pillar', 'slab', 'beam'. A calls them out; B brings the stone which he has learned to bring *at such and such a call*. Conceive this as a complete primitive language.
>
> *(1953, §2; emphasis added)*

As we can see, even this language, when used, becomes a game, for it is based not only on each word referring to an object but, more importantly, on a relationship between a builder A and an assistant B, the latter doing something at such and such a call of the former. In other words, language is not simply a (unidirectional) way in which 'terms' correspond to 'things' but also a (bidirectional) way in which one person calls to another and that other person responds. What lies deep within language is its power to allow people to establish a relationship of response-ability; communication, as language in use, is our ability to be responsible, i.e., to respond to one another.

In this light, a language game is not a contest in which one wins and another loses. We do not play language games *against* someone, we play them *with* someone. If we go back in history, we find in the word 'game' such meanings as 'fun', 'amusement', 'glee', 'pleasure', 'merriment', 'participation', 'communion', and 'a sense of people together'. It was only later that the meaning of 'contest for superiority' was attested. When language is used successfully, it is a win-win situation because a relationship between people is maintained and the game of language continues. The word 'win' goes back to the Proto-Indo-European root *wen-, meaning 'to desire', 'to strive for'. One can, therefore, play a language game with oneself, communicating intrapersonally, as long as one still has a desire to continue and keep striving for something.

For example, chess "does not exclude the possibility of playing it against oneself provided such solitary games are not regarded as paradigm instances of chess" (Candlish & Wrisley, 2014). In most cases, however, at some point one loses any interest in winning against oneself, i.e., loses any desire to continue; that's why chess is essentially a game for two players. It takes at least two people – yourself and someone else – to play language games that are more desirable. One can sit on the wall only so long: sooner or later, one takes the plunge. And, if one doesn't have a very soft landing, one will hopefully be put together again through some caring and responsible activity.

Thus, it is possible to speak about relationships between different contexts of language use and relationships between different people who use language in this or that context. It is impossible, however, to speak about either of them without identifying one more crucial relationship, i.e., the one between language and people using it. Whereas the view of language as representation is focused on semantics, or correspondences between language signs and what they stand for, and syntactics, or the formal arrangements of language signs, the view of language as game highlights its pragmatic aspect focusing on "how to do things with words" (Austin, 1975). In this view, meaning is not what is reflected in/by language but *a result of our reflection* on the use of language in a specific context: "it is *upon reflection* . . . that *we* arrive at a conceptual understanding of reality in so far as it can be articulated in *meaningful* discourse" (Graeser, 1977, p. 378; emphasis added). It is important to emphasize that the meaning of a word or an expression emerges only through its use when reflected upon by people in specific circusmtances.

When the focus is on the relationship between language signs and people using them, the question is not 'which is to be master'. Care should be taken to avoid two extremes. On the one hand, we should avoid a 'managerial' attitude toward words and expressions, summed up by Humpty Dumpty: "*I* can manage the whole lot of them!" On the other hand, we should avoid treating language as something extraordinary, existing outside of the fabric of human life and supposedly capable of ideally reflecting the world. As Wittgenstein writes,

> we are under the illusion that what is peculiar, profound, essential, in our investigation, resides in its trying to grasp the incomparable essence of language. That is, the order existing between the concepts of proposition, word, proof, truth, experience, and so on. This order is a *super*-order between – so to speak – *super*-concepts.
>
> *(1953, §97)*

We seem to want – perhaps in our subconscious desire – to make language do all the work, and yet we end up spending more and more effort trying to discover that 'super-order', failing each time. Or, we give up our efforts and admit that language is beyond the control of our intention and interpretation and that, as Friedrich Schlegel put it, "words often understand themselves better than do those who use them" (1971, p. 260). In that case, there is but one step to stating that "language is not a tool used by an individual to deliver messages; rather, language is a universe in which individuals (addresses) emerge when called" (Rasch, 2000: 70). If that is the case, it is not really a builder A calling an assistant B, but language calling out both.

The truth, as always, is in the middle, i.e., in the relationship between language and people using it. On the one hand, contrary to what Humpty Dumpty thinks, no one 'can *make* words mean so many different things'; rather, you can only "*let* the use of words teach you their meaning" (Wittgenstein, 1953, §212; emphasis added). Then, in return, words will allow meaning to emerge. Thus, no one and no thing is extraordinary. We may think of language as this 'super-order' with 'super-concepts', "whereas, of course, if the words 'language', 'experience', 'world', have a use, it must be as humble a one as that of the words 'table', 'lamp', 'door'" (Wittgenstein, 1953, §97). Likewise, one may think of oneself as a master of language, but that is not so: words are not one's private army of men and horses, or the cattle, the fowl, and every beast. Wittgenstein and other thinkers "emphasized a more humanistic attitude, central to which was a deep respect for language as it is used in its everyday context. These are the so-called 'ordinary language philosophers'" (Avramides, 2017, p. 720). Both language and people are ordinary ('humble'), which is wonderful because together they create order, i.e., something when and where everything and everyone fit together. It must now be clear that language is not only representational but also constitutive: "it is the way humans co-construct the worlds we inhabit" (Stewart, 1998, p. 34). Notably, Wittgenstein viewed language games as forms of life. For him, the language game "is not reasonable (or unreasonable). It is there – like our life" (1969: §559).

When Wittgenstein raised the question of the possibility of a private language, he took it "to refer to what can be known only to the speaker; to his immediate, private, sensations" (1953, §243). However, while one's sensations, such as pain, are undoubtedly private and cannot be felt by others, one "can only talk about it using the expressions commonly used to talk about pain" (Blair, 2006, p. 9). In other words, no matter how private a language may appear, it is always derivative of language use in a language game. "When one says 'He gave a name to his sensation'", writes Wittgenstein, "*one forgets* that a great deal of stage-setting in the language is presupposed if the mere *act of naming* is to make sense" (1953, §257; emphasis added). What we forget is that 'the mere act of naming' is itself a language game, perhaps the most important one. Upon reflection, we can see how intrapersonal communication that supposedly "occurs in the absence of other people" (Barnlund, 1968, p. 8), can only be understood "in terms of a human language shaped by the exigencies of human intercourse" (Polanyi, 1962, p. 3).

## 3. THE INTERPERSONAL COMMUNICATION SITUATION

Intrapersonal communication is easy to conduct because one talks to oneself; in different contexts one still identifies oneself as the same person with the same body. As long as this sameness is maintained, intrapersonal communication is successful: it is only when this normal state is upset that communication disorders arise. Yet, intrapersonal disorders are not as wide-spread as communication problems that arise between people and, first of all, between one person and another person. Such problems are more common because a person faces someone who is different, both in mind and in body. Whereas intrapersonal communication occurs in the absence of other people, interpersonal communication occurs in the presence of another person. The first act of civilization is said to be wagering "on whether to open the hand or reach for a weapon" (Kearney, 2015, p. 17). If that is the case, then every act of communication – and especially interpersonal communication – is wagering on whether to say something to another person or not, and if yes, what and how.

The interpersonal communication situation is usually understood as talk between two people. It is focused on "how we *talk* to others, how others hear what we say and how our communication affects our relational outcomes" (West & Turner, 2008, p. 225; emphasis added); on how people "interact and what they can *talk* about" (Wood, 2015, p. xvii; emphasis added); and on "what drives *interpersonal communication* and why . . . people *talk* about certain things rather than others" (Berger, 2014, p. 586; emphasis added). 'Talk', however, covers a wide variety of communicative acts, from such mundane activities as greeting a neighbor or chit-chat with workmates during a break, to such events as talk in classrooms, in courtrooms, meetings in offices or surveys in call centers, to communication "at the center of world-changing events: summit meetings between world leaders, policy decisions in board rooms of multinational companies, international conferences on environmental policies" (Gardner, 2008, p. 262). Talk can go well beyond an interaction between two people into the public realm, e.g. R. Craig's article entitled 'How We Talk About How We Talk: Communication Theory in the Public Interest' (2005). Mass communication can't be studied without analyzing TV and radio talk shows (Peck, 1995).

## 3.1. Falling into a Conversation

Thus, 'talk' can hardly be viewed as a distinguishing characteristic of interpersonal communication: rather, here "the paradigmatic instance of language is conversation, verbal-nonverbal exchange between humans in real time, either face-to-face or mediated . . . That is the activity humans engage in characteristically, routinely, naturally, and constantly" (Stewart, 1996, p. 21). One can see several important differences already in the usage of the words 'talk' and 'conversation'. First, it is possible to use the verb 'to talk' with both 'to' and 'with'; although slight, the difference is significant: 'to talk to' suggests a unidirectional act when someone is perceived as an object of talk and a response may not be expected. And, although the verb 'talk' is used with both 'to' and 'with', the former seems to be more common, e.g. the phrase 'Nice talking to you!' 'Conversation' is clearly bidirectional: one cannot '*converse to someone', only 'with', i.e., conversation is a reciprocal process. Second, one can talk to/with someone who is similar or familiar, whereas one usually converses with someone different; communication that occurs in the absence of other people is self-talk, not self-conversation. And, third, unlike conversing, one can talk not only to another person but to a group of people or a country (Grant, 2018). Therefore, that conversation is a form of talk that stands apart (Figure 6.3).

**Figure 6.3**   *The Conversation* (Calgary). Photo by Danielle Scott.

Let us discuss in more detail why conversation is a paradigmatic (i.e., exemplary or model) instance of language use in interpersonal communication.

Conversation is commonly characterized as 'casual'. For example, we find a book entitled *Analysing Casual Conversation* (Eggins & Slade, 2005); we read that individuals are "more skilled in some communication activities (e.g., making casual conversation) than in others" (Greene, 2009, p. 138), or that some of "our talk exchanges . . . leave very considerable latitude to the participants (as in a casual conversation)" (Grice, 1989, p. 26). However, if a form of talk is not casual, then it is planned, deliberate, or premeditated. If someone says, 'Let's have a talk', the assumption is that there is a specific topic to be discussed – and most likely a serious one. '*Let's have a conversation' does not sound right precisely because it cannot be planned, deliberate or premeditated. People do not '*have a conversation'; rather, they strike one up – spontaneously and casually. In other words, conversation cannot not be casual. Thus, it is more appropriate to speak simply about conversation, or conversation as a form of casual communication, but not about 'casual conversation'.

Conversation is an occasion of communication that happens to us by chance; it is a happening. That is why "it is generally more correct to say that we fall into conversation, or even that we become involved in it. The way one word follows another, with the conversation taking its own twists and reaching its own conclusions, may well be conducted in some way, but the partners conversing are far less the leaders of it than the led" (Gadamer, 2004, p. 385). You certainly do not plan to be with someone in the same café or in an airport terminal or next to someone on the same bus at the same time: you just happen to be there. In this sense, conversation as a form of interpersonal communication is "that which befalls us" (Klyukanov, 2012). And, because one person happens to be with another person in real time, either face-to-face or in a mediated fashion, "we are bound together in existential and lived ways before we even open our mouths to speak" (Peters 1999, p. 16). Our future is wagering on whether you say something to another person or not, and if yes, what and how.

It is noted that conversations are usually identified with verbal interactions which are "at least tacitly homogeneous with respect to age, class, rank, physical ability, sexual orientation, and other attributes" (Gaudio, 2003, p. 666); in other words, communication here is presumed to focus on sameness. If heterogeneity is acknowledged, it is said to hinder normative expectations that characterize 'casualness' (ibid.). However, while we can predict to a degree our communication with those similar or familiar to us, conversation happens by chance: unlike someone who happens to sit next to you on a bus, you do not happen to be with your family members in the same house every day: you expect them to be there. Conversation happens without any formality; what is considered 'normal' emerges out of the interaction itself. Conversation is not simply a relaxed chit-chat but an event, an opportunity (Latin: *casus*). Conversation perhaps captures best of all the essence of language games since "you must bear in mind that the language-game is so to say something unpredictable. . . . t is not based on grounds . . . . It is there – like our life" (Wittgenstein, 1969: §559). Once we fall into a conversation, it is there and must be communicated through.

Because conversation presupposes heterogeneity (otherness), it exemplifies the nature of every act of interpersonal communication as a face-threatening act. In most cases, interpersonal communication is literally a face-to-face encounter; even in mediated contexts, it is one's 'face', i.e., one's self-concept, that is put in front of the Other. One's face (and 'face') is exposed in any interpersonal interaction, not only, e.g., through criticizing or disagreeing: even a simple request for information is face-threatening because one presumes some right of access to the Other's time, energy, and attention (Morand & Ocker, 2003), something that the other person may be unable to provide and thus lose his/her 'face'. Communicative acts may threaten the Other's need for independence and non-imposition ('negative face') or for solidarity and fellowship ('positive face'). Hence, conversation is always a process of 'facework' whereby one orients one's messages to the Other's 'negative face' or 'positive face'.

In human conversations, people assume that in such interpersonal interactions some general principles are followed. One well-known example is the Cooperative Principle, proposed by H. P. Grice, which states: "Make your conversational contribution such as is required, at the stage at which it occurs, by the accepted purpose or direction of the talk exchange in which you are engaged" (1989, p. 26). Since in conversations not everything is explicitly stated and something is left unsaid (implied), based on these general maxims of conversation, people can infer the intended meaning or work out the so-called 'conversational implicature': many jokes are based on one's failure to do so, e.g.: "The programmer's wife tells him: 'Run to the store and pick up a loaf of bread. If they have eggs, get a dozen.' The programmer comes home with 12 loaves of bread". Thus, every conversation is a process not only of 'facework' but also 'brainwork'.

As can be seen, conversation is not a simple interpersonal chit-chat in which people go through verbal motions, but a process that requires a lot of work. In this process, "participants constitute themselves in conversational practices" (Krippendorff & Bermejo, 2009, p. 123). Conversation, therefore, is by nature a creative form of communication – this cannot be emphasized enough. For instance, Kenneth Burke famously compared the drama of human affairs to an 'unending conversation'. Yet, when he describes it, he never talks about 'conversation', e.g. the following often-quoted passage:

> You come late. When you arrive, others have long preceded you, and they are engaged in a heated *discussion*, a *discussion* too heated for them to pause and tell you exactly what it is about. In fact, the *discussion* had already begun long before any of them got there, so that no one present is qualified to retrace for you all the steps that had gone before. You listen for a while, until you decide that you have caught the tenor of the argument; then you put in your oar. Someone answers; you answer him; another comes to your defense; another aligns himself against you, to either the embarrassment or gratification of your opponent, depending on the quality of your ally's assistance. However, the *discussion* is interminable. The hour grows late, you must depart. And you do depart, with the *discussion* still vigorously in progress.
>
> *(1973, pp. 110–111; emphasis added)*

Unlike 'conversation', though, 'discussion' is a detailed examination of a specific topic: it is an analytical process, deriving from Latin *discutere*, which means 'strike asunder, break up'. In conversation, no specific topic is presented ahead of time to be examined; instead, people strike up a conversation and create a certain order, which is always a synthesis.

It is difficult to converse: "Conversations, as they tend to play out in person, are messy – full of pauses and interruptions and topic changes and assorted awkwardness. But the messiness is what allows for true exchange" (Garber, 2014). What is a true exchange, though? What makes conversation as an interpersonal communication encounter successful? In the words of Hans-Georg Gadamer, "a genuine conversation is never the one that we wanted to conduct. . . . No one knows in advance what will 'come out' of a conversation" (2004, p. 385). No one knows in advance not only what will 'come out' of a conversation but also how one will come out of it: in this light, "genuine conversation is characterized by a stance of openness to the meanings offered by the other, . . . and by a willingness to be transformed through

the revised understanding of the topic that emerges from the encounter"
(Binding & Tapp, 2008, p. 123). Thus, while one never knows in advance
how one will come out of a conversation, if it is a genuine conversation,
one always comes out of it transformed. When Grice writes that we need
"to allow for the fact that subjects of conversation are legitimately changed"
(Grice, 1989, p. 27), by 'subjects' he means the topics of a conversation;
however, this statement equally applies to its participants as subjects. It is
because of this transformative nature that conversation is difficult. When
calls are made for saving the lost art of conversation (M. Garber, 2014), it
must be noted that we can teach the basics of Conversation Analysis and
the main forms of its organization, such as adjacency pairs, turn-taking,
repair, etc. However, no matter how skillful one can be at identifying those
forms, each conversation is different because it befalls us. If we insist on
creating more and more 'safe spaces' for communication, it will be more
and more difficult to save conversation for it is not just a skill but a form of
life. To converse – and not just talk, chat, discuss, etc. – we must be open to
otherness and not be afraid to be transformed. Conversation is a very intimate form of interaction: that is why it is "sometimes referred to as verbal
*intercourse*" (Moon, 2011, p. 72; emphasis added).

Thus, while it does not cover the entire range of interpersonal communication, conversation reveals its nature most adequately. When two people
interact, they create a certain space in which they dwell: as early as the 16th
century, 'to converse' meant 'to communicate with', and before that, in the
mid-14th century, 'to move about, live, dwell'. The word 'conversation' is
derived from Latin *conversatio*, meaning 'an act of living with'. In this sense,
every act of interpersonal interaction is an attempt to create a common
home. Not all such attempts are successful: some end up in failures when
a relationship falls apart, leading to animosity, divorces, etc. Interpersonal
relationships are especially unstable because they are too dynamic, too
interactive: as they say, from love to hate there is only one step. And, it is
someone who loved us before that can hate us 'more successfully' than anyone else because s/he knows us so well and thus can really hurt us. In other
words, whereas the home created through interpersonal communication
may be beautiful, it is also fragile.

Conversations seem to be spontaneous, carried out just by two persons
and without any external influences. However, conversation is subject
to all kinds of social forces – political, economic, cultural – especially
today when so many interactions are mediated by modern technologies

(Gaudio, 2003). In other words, the interpersonal communication situation is subject to what happens outside. While this situation may be a paradigmatic case of language and social interaction, it does not cover the entire realm of communication. This, though, is a blessing in disguise for those engaged in interpersonal interactions. When something from the outside enters their home, so to speak, while a distinction between the individual and the other is maintained, "the mediating third overcomes this binary opposition and binds each dyadic social relation together to form an organic cohesive whole. With this, relations between individuals in the group-in-fusion take on a new meaning. . . . The spontaneous common activity of the group-in-fusion overcomes the other-ness of the other and allows the individual to determine that he and the other have the same interests" (Rae, 2011, p. 100). With this, we move to another level and find ourselves in a different communication situation.

## 4. THE GROUP COMMUNICATION SITUATION

It must be noted right away that already "at the purely informational level of communication, the group level is much more complex than the interpersonal level" (Martinez, 2011, p. 83). At the same time, the group level has parallels with the intrapersonal level because both deal with sameness or 'oneness' (unlike the interpersonal level that focuses on otherness). In both cases, we deal with an individual communicating as one/self (the intrapersonal level) or a group communicating as if one (the group level). Groups are commonly described as self-defining, self-organizing and self-regulating.

At this level, communication becomes 'ethnic' since "*ethno* refers to the people who make up a group or interact in a given context" (Wright, 2017, p. 608). Every group is ethnic because it brings together people of the same kind. How such an order is created by the members of a group is studied by Ethnomethodology. Interestingly, although Ethnomethodology is primarily associated with Conversational Analysis, when Harold Garfinkel was developing this methodology in the 1950s, he was studying jury deliberations in the U.S., i.e., how (such) groups of people came to their decisions.

It can be debated whether to consider two people a group. The word 'dyad' is ambivalent: that is why, perhaps, there are two words in English with different meaning. 'Pair' refers to two equal or well-matched people, e.g. 'two of a kind', while 'couple' refers to two who are together through some tie or connection. The former suggests sameness and is thus easier to identify with a group, whereas the latter highlights difference and is thus easier to conceptualize in terms of interpersonal (not group) relationship. For instance, two people who tie the knot are a (married) couple and not a pair. It is not always easy to say whether a married couple can be called a family, i.e., a group. If the family is considered "a self-defined group of intimates who create and maintain themselves through their own interactions and their interactions with others" (Turner & West, 2013, p. 9), then any two persons who are married can be called a family (or, for that matter, any 'group of intimates' who define themselves as such). It is more common, though, to conceptualize family as a social group consisting of parents *and* their children. As Zygmunt Bauman puts it, "Society *sensu stricto* begins with the Third" (1993, p. 112).

### 4.1. Society *Sensu Stricto*

Thus, the group communication situation consists of more than two participants, with the upper limit determined by their shared goal, e.g. a study group vs. a large corporation. It is important to note that "social groups are not fixed entities, but are actively defined and negotiated through intra- and intergroup communication" (Keblusek et al., 2017, p. 632). The group level is focused on intra-group communication, that is, on how groups are formed through various interactive patterns among individuals (Figure 6.4).

Naturally, "language plays a central role in this" (Keblusek et al., 2017, p. 632). Of course, communication at the interpersonal level also exhibits recurring language behaviors. However, these patterns constantly change with every interaction; that is why, perhaps, the analysis of conversations is usually limited to a notational transcription of their formal structure: for example, the length of each conversational turn, pauses between them, interruptions and overlaps, etc. Interpersonal interactions are just too diverse and dynamic to provide a lasting social order.

A communication order, therefore, is a truly social phenomenon. (Even conversations, as mentioned earlier, are subject to social forces: we may not realize this or try to forget about this, but every interpersonal interaction takes place within a certain society). A communication order of a social group is grounded in meaning and thus goes beyond recurring formal structures of language. Many theories explain how groups are formed through interactive patterns among individuals. For instance, Decision Emergence Theory (DET) describes how decisions emerge in a group from its members' verbal

DISCUSSING THE WAR IN A PARIS CAFE.
SEE PAGE 364.

**Figure 6.4**   *Discussing the War in a Paris Café* by Fred Barnard (1846–1896) – a scene from the brief interim between the Battle of Sedan and Siege of Paris during the Franco-Prussian War. From the *Illustrated London News*, 17 September 1870.

interactions but still are formed within stage development (Fisher, 1970). Symbolic Convergence Theory (SCT) shows how individuals form a cohesive group through the sharing of dramatized messages, called fantasy themes (Bormann, 1982). The Theory of Coordinated Management of Meaning (CMM) presents communication as a process of "making social worlds" (Pearce, 2009). In all these theories, communication is conceptualized as a process of individual actions creating a dynamic whole (a group). It is shown how people play certain roles and follow certain rules as they use language for coordinating their individual efforts toward making a social world, no matter how small or large.

There is a significant difference between the intra- or interpersonal situations and the group communication situation: in the former cases, "by definition, the message is unavailable for public examination" (Cunningham, 1995, p. 6). 'Public' is concerned with people and thus presupposes everything open to general observation. The intrapersonal situation, by definition, is made up of just one person who obviously cannot observe oneself. In the case of interpersonal communication, one has another person in front of oneself; this, however, cannot be identified with examination or observation: rather, two persons can see each other. 'Observation' is a careful examination of something that requires some detachment from what is observed as well as more time to think about what is observed. "You see, but you do not observe" Sherlock Holmes tells Dr. Watson in 'A Scandal in Bohemia'. Two persons in a conversation are too involved in their interaction: for them to switch from 'seeing' to 'observing' would require stepping back and trying to decide what each of them has just observed. This goes against the very nature of interpersonal communication. In the situation of group communication, not only is the message available for public examination but its public consideration is necessary. When Socrates states that "the unexamined life is not worth living" (Plato, *Apology*, 38a5–6), the idea is that, for one's life to be truly meaningful, it must be observed and examined by others.

Communication, thus conceptualized, is most famously addressed by Jürgen Habermas in his Communicative Action Theory. According to Habermas, if individuals interact on the basis of common understanding, they can recognize themselves as a group and act in accordance with the norms developed through interaction. It is crucial that claims made by everyone must be open for examination and, if challenged, must be defended. In other words, everyone must consent to his/her use of language being publicly examined by all. This way, individuals can organize themselves into a group with openly established social norms – what Habermas calls 'the public sphere'. He sees this unified arena of communicative action as an 'ideal speech situation' (Habermas, 1962).

'Speech' at the level of group communication does not mean the same as 'speech' at the level of interpersonal communication. Although both share the meaning of 'articulating sounds to utter words with the ordinary voice', speech at the interpersonal level takes the form of interaction: when two persons speak, they converse. When more than two people start speaking, their communication goes beyond interaction and becomes a matter of transaction: now, through an exchange and management of messages, a decision needs to be made by all involved. Here participation is crucial, although individuals do not always contribute equally to group decision making. In such cases, it is suggested that groups need to break into smaller configurations, which function as 'discursive groups' rather than 'conversational groups' (Waller et al., 2011). At this level, individuals do not converse but discuss or discourse: significantly, the article just cited focuses on group decision making during jury deliberations. When interacting, two persons do not really deliberate.

Speech at the group level takes the form of discourse, i.e., language use through which social order of a group is constituted and maintained. Discourse is always civic because those taking part in it are all citizens, that is, inhabitants of a certain public sphere. As a member of a group, everyone has the moral obligation to follow its norms; at the group level, the moral nature of communication, as discourse, comes to the foreground. As Habermas writes, "A norm is valid when the foreseeable consequences and side effects of its general observance for the interests and value-orientations of *each individual* could be *jointly* accepted by *all* concerned without coercion" (Habermas, 1998, p. 42; emphasis added). Ideally, individuals form one whole in which they can keep their own identities. In other words, one stands for the group just as the group stands for one. Or, as the Latin phrase goes, *Unus pro omnibus, omnes pro uno* ('One for all, all for one').

## 5. THE INTERGROUP COMMUNICATION SITUATION

Earlier, it was noted that groups are defined through intra- and intergroup communication. Communication always "separates, sets apart, 'particularizes' its members from members of other communities, as much as it unites them and makes alike inside its own boundaries" (Bauman, 1993, p. 40). Intragroup communication focuses on sameness as it presupposes its individual parts sharing the same meaning. These parts can be individuals or sub-groups: it is crucial to understand, though, that they all work toward a common goal; thanks to their coordinated efforts, the group functions as a whole. In that sense, there are no differences between such parts, and the boundary is around the entire group.

As they evolve, groups become more differentiated. It becomes more difficult to maintain group stability from the inside: such efforts are too labor-intensive. At some point, a group may become too heterogeneous and complex: differences outweigh similarities, and its stability is upset.

No longer is it one entity made up of individual parts: now there are (at least) two different groups. Whereas intragroup communication focuses on sameness (no matter how many individual parts, they all form one 'We'), intergroup communication differentiates between 'Us' and 'Them'. Intergroup communication focuses on differences that can include ethnicity, political ideology, age, race, gender, etc. In all cases, intergroup communication focuses on communication between dominant and subordinate groups (Giles et al., 2010). In other words, differences are grounded in power and voice, as in e.g. the Muted Group Theory (Kramarae, 2009).

Intergroup communication is latently present within intragroup communication, with sub-groups being the prototypes for different groups: it is all a matter of where boundaries are drawn. In the intergroup communication situation, two groups, although different, always "coexist with comparative others" (Giles, 2012, p. 13), i.e., within a common boundary. Such a boundary may be more difficult to identify, since the focus is on differences, but it is always potentially out there as long as the groups are both separated and drawn to one another (just as Columbus and his crew were drawn to those in the East Indies). After all, we are all human, which, unfortunately, is often lost on people when different groups are fighting to death.

Groups' boundaries are predominantly marked by language. What lies outside of the boundaries of a group is not the same as what, for Wittgenstein, lies beyond the bounds of language; hence nonsense cannot be put into words. What exists beyond the boundaries of a group is very much sayable, just by others whose language is foreign, strange, barbaric. It is known that the Greek *barbaroi* meant 'all that are not Greek'. Since then, practically every group has assigned the status of 'barbarians' to groups that are different and whose language is unintelligible; therefore, it was not worth engaging in communication with such groups (Boletsi, 2013).

Language at the level of intergroup communication has been theorized by many disciplines, including sociolinguistics, sociology, social psychology, anthropology, etc. Such multidisciplinary attention to the role of language in intergroup communication is not surprising: the focus here is not so much on interaction or discourse, but rather on the speech codes shared by the entire group and used by its members to produce and understand texts. Such 'archetypes', as they are sometimes labeled in the Coordinated Management of Meaning Theory, are the broadest and most intangible rules to follow: identifying and conceptualizing them requires the joint effort of many disciplines. There are no individual authors behind such rules; the same goes for texts, which, in their purest form, are impersonal, produced by the entire group.

One example of the use of language at the intergroup level is 'linguistic landscape', understood as the "visibility and salience of languages on public and commercial signs in a given territory or region" (Landry and Bourhis 1997, p. 23) (Figure 6.5).

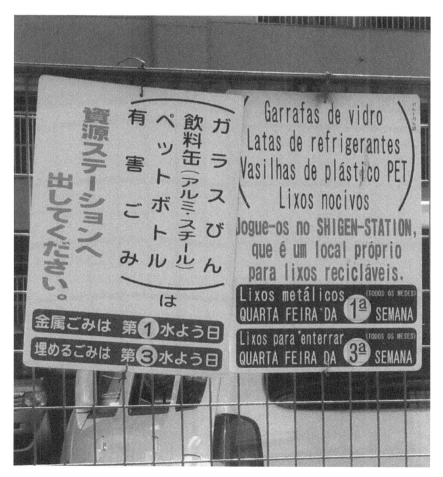

**Figure 6.5**    Signs in both Japanese and Portuguese in the Homi housing complex in the Homigaoka district of Toyota City, Japan. Photo by Arthurmelo.

In creating a linguistic landscape, more powerful groups "will define language policies that are likely to serve their own ends" (Giles et al., 2010, p. 126). Linguistic landscape is the public space, constructed by symbolic means such as language, that can be distinguished only by members of an out-group: just as fish do not know they are in water, members of an in-group do not know they are in a certain 'linguistic landscape'.

Not surprisingly, the concept of linguistic landscape is linked to ethnolinguistic vitality – "a group's ability to maintain and protect its existence in time as a collective entity with a distinctive identity and language" (Ehala, 2015, p. 553). Ethnolinguistic vitality arises and is theorized in situations of intergroup communication, e.g. the cases of linguistic imperialism or minority language maintenance. The degree of ethnolinguistic vitality is usually predicted by attitudes to three factors of comparison between the in-group and one or more out-groups: group strength (numbers, in-group marriage, etc.); social status and prestige; and support from social institutions (media, government, education, etc.) (Gallois et al., 2012). All these practices are enacted through various texts, language laws and other policies.

Group identities are enacted, of course, through other forms of language use, such as labeling and naming, stereotypical talk, linguistic intergroup bias, prejudice toward the out-group, etc. (Giles, 2012). In all such situations, group speech codes are activated. Consider, for example, the employment situation when a cafeteria at a British airport had hired food servers from India and Pakistan, and both supervisors and customers were complaining that these new employees were surly and uncooperative, presented as an intercultural encounter (Gumperz, 1982; see also: Tannen, 1984). This, however, is a situation of interpersonal communication, since there are two persons interacting whose interaction is clearly influenced by their group membership. As Howard Giles notes, "Henri Tajfel had always argued . . . that at least 70% of so-called interpersonal interactions were actually highly intergroup in nature" and adds that "this could perhaps even turn out to be an underestimate" (Giles, 2012, p. 3). It must be noted, though, that *all* interpersonal interactions are intergroup in nature simply because everyone belongs to a group: after all, people are social animals. In other words, communication cannot not be intergroup. The level of archetypes (in Coordinated Management of Meaning Theory) has the strongest logical force: we are compelled to use language in a certain way not because of the episode of interaction or our relationship with another person, but because of the rules of the group to which we belong.

When this highest level of speech codes is reached, communication seems to stop, since "feedback is impossible because there is no point at which the message is outside of the system of codification" (Martinez, 2011, p. 77). However, it is precisely at this level that intergroup communication occurs: groups are constantly redefined through feedback from one another. This way, they develop greater complexity and maintain their dynamic stability.

## 6. LANGUAGE AS BE-LONGING

So, what is language? Where does it begin and end? Recall one of Wittgenstein's famous theses, usually translated as "The limits of my language are the limits of my world" (see e.g. Williams, 2008, p. 363). Most often, this statement is applied to private language (intrapersonal communication): in other words, an individual ('I') seems to hold absolute sovereignty over language and communication. What about two persons in conversation, though? Aren't the limits of their language the limits of their – interpersonal – world? This certainly applies to the group, as well, since its members could say, in a collective voice, "The limits of *our* language are the limits of our world". Ditto for the intergroup communication situation. Who does language belong to, then? Whose world does it limit? And what are those limits?

We see how language can change its form: now it is a word or a phrase, now a conversation, now a discourse, now a text. Each time, the limits of the world change. However, each time it is still one and the same language, one and the same world. It is said that "[A]ll communication is to some extent intrapersonal communication" (Blake & Haroldsen, 1975, p. 25). By the same token, though, all communication is to some extent interpersonal, intra-group, and intergroup. It is all a matter of perspective, i.e., it all depends on where we draw boundaries. We can view the intrapersonal communication situation as a microcosm of the intergroup communication situation, or view the intergroup communication situation as a macrocosm of the intrapersonal communication situation.

There is no use in arguing which situation is ideal. As was discussed earlier, Habermas identified the ideal speech situation with group communication because in the public sphere people communicate completely rationally and freely. However, every situation – intragroup, interpersonal, and intergroup – could be conceptualized as ideal because there is something 'unique' and 'undistorted' about each of them. It is important to realize that an ideal situation does not really exist and can only be imagined. And yet, "although it is an imaginary situation, it is rooted in the real nature of language. . . . [T]he ideal speech situation shows us the . . . potential of language – a potential implicit *in all uses of language*" (Inglis, 2013; emphasis added). Language, therefore, has no single master, as it belongs to everyone and all. Its nature is such that "language needs no central authority to control usage, it needs only the day-to-day interactions of its native speakers to establish and retain its meaning" (Blair, 2006, p. 14) – and that includes all and everyone. Thus, the 'my' in Wittgenstein's famous thesis refers not to any individual(s), "but to the transcendental subject whose language fixes the logical space of the *possible worlds*" (Stegmüller, 1970: 420; emphasis added). Language is not so much what is, but what can be. The more common translation of Wittgenstein's thesis – "The limits of my language *are* the limits of my world" – does not capture this nature of language very well. A better translation is "The limits of my language *mean* the limits of my world" (Wittgenstein, 2002, 5.6). In the original text – *Die Grenzen meiner Sprache bedeuten die Grenzen meiner Welt – bedeuten* means 'to mean', 'to signify', 'to indicate', 'to stand for' and even 'to bode'. Language thus is never 'fixed' ('is') but always 'means', i.e., it is a meaningful activity that can bode well – or not bode well.

All limits of language, therefore, are not constraints but openings: "Language does not arise from a need to escape but from a desire to enter, not from frowns of impotence but from a surplus of vitality and wonder" (Harrison, 2014, p. 27). In every situation of communication, we enter the liminal space of language where meaning is constituted and participants are transformed.

All such situations can be brought together under the framework of Language Ecology. According to Einar Haugen, who is regarded as the founder of this field, it focuses on relations between any given language and its environment, where "the true environment of a language is the society that uses it as one of its codes" (1972, p. 325). In this view, language appears as something surrounded by society and so "the ecology of a language is determined primarily by the people who learn it, use it, and transmit it to others" (ibid.). However, to be more consistent with the meaning of 'ecology', derived from the Greek *oikos* – 'house, dwelling place, habitation' – it is more productive not to treat people as the environment of language, but, rather, to conceptualize language as society's 'dwelling place'. In this sense, when we study language ecology, we assume that "language is the ultimate 'place' of human habitation" (Harrison, 1992, p. 200). Whatever the situation of communication – intrapersonal, interpersonal, group, or intergroup – we find in it an abode for our life. Both 'situation' and 'home' go back to the same Proto-Indo-European root *tkei-* – 'to settle, dwell, be home'.

Wittgenstein famously compared language to "an ancient city: a maze of little streets and squares, of old and new houses, and of houses with additions from various periods; and this surrounded by a multitude of new boroughs with straight regular streets and uniform houses" (1953, §18). This spatial metaphor, though, should not mislead us: language is never only about space but also about people's actions, which always take time. Language takes all kinds of forms of life, as discussed earlier; "we live in our language in the same way that we live in our cities. We find our way about our cities *by doing things,* that is, by *engaging in day-to-day activities*" (Blair, 2006, p. 14; emphasis added).

Thus, language is the home in which the human dwells. Human language is a highly-developed system used to communicate a myriad of meanings; however, it is not the only one. Viewed broadly, communication is a semiotic process in which something can function as a sign to an organism. In this light, language as home grows to the size of semiosphere or biosphere, calling for the possibilities of interspecies communication to be explored (Nollman, 2002). This shows again that the dwelling place of language is never fixed, but always liminal, always in transition. If we conceptualize communication phenomenologically, then the Other

> can be an animal, a plant, a stone. No kind of appearance or event is fundamentally excluded from the series of the things through which from time to time something is said to me. Nothing can refuse to be the vessel for the Word. The limits of the possibility of dialogue are the limits of awareness
>
> *(Buber, 1965, p. 10)*

If we take language to be any semiotic code, then the limits of its ecology expand dramatically, for now humans share that dwelling place with other species. Such a view, based on the "proliferation of codes[,] leads to the ancient but still bewildering question about the bonds – arbitrary or natural – that link language to reality.... A question, ultimately, about the *logos*" (Harrison, 1992, p. 240). It should not be forgotten that the word 'ecology' combines the Greek *oikós* with 'logos'. Usually translated as 'language', its meaning is much wider: first and foremost, 'logos' is a relation that binds together. Thus, we do not dwell in nature but always in our relation to nature. Likewise, one does not dwell in one's own world but always in one's relation to others. "In this sense *oikos* and *logos* belong together inseparably, for *logos* is the *oikos* of humanity" (Harrison, 1992, p. 200–201).

The limits of language, then, never simply 'are' but always mean something: communication is search for meaning, and each attempt to pinpoint it with reference and enclose it within semantic walls fails because language is "not a linguistic word but the *logos* of human transcendence" (Harrison, 1992, p. 229). As we dwell in it, language moves us beyond the containment of words and phrases. In language, we can belong together, i.e., we can 'be' and 'long' for meaning. Only in our be-longing can we feel at home. Poets can feel it better than most: "Time pares me down like a coin, And there is no longer enough of me for myself" (Mandelshtam, 1991, p. 49). Whatever the situation of communication – intrapersonal, interpersonal, group, or intergroup, once you think you've captured meaning, it is no longer enough.

It must be clear by now that we cannot solve the language problem. We can, though, keep solving language problems in day-to-day activities. And not only can but must, because "we may not always be at school or in church, but we are always 'in' language, just as much as language is 'in' us" (Stawarska, 2015, p. 61). In language, we are at home everywhere and everywhen. We want closure but in each act of communication only cross a threshold with the door always open. Language as the house of Being is an open house.

# 7

# The Wonder
# of Culture

Key concepts:

*A priori*, begging the question, culture, *dialektikē technē*, dialogue, *elenchus*, explication, expression, factish, fusion of horizons, *hermēneutikē technē*, *kritikē technē*, nature, psychagogue, *rhētorikē technē*, ritual, synthetic, society, *technē*, tectonic.

Key names:

Aristotle, St. Augustine, Francis Bacon, Gregory Bateson, Kenneth Burke, James Carey, Wilhelm Dilthey, Edward Hall, Martin Heidegger, Hans-Georg Gadamer, Clifford Geertz, Immanuel Kant, Richard L. Lanigan, Bruno Latour, Claude Lévi-Strauss, Jurgen Ruesch, Plato, Socrates, Steve Woolgar.

## 1. WHAT CULTURE IS — AND IS NOT

In 2014, *Merriam-Webster's Dictionary* named 'culture' as the Word of the Year. However, if we look at the Words of the Year for 2015 – '-ism', 2016 – 'surreal', and 2017 – 'feminism', they all clearly pertain to 'culture'. To pick a word as 'the winner' based on how many people look it up is one thing; to define what it is is another. In fact, the more frequent its usage, the broader the meaning is and thus more difficult to define. This fully applies to 'culture', which is often viewed as too vague and too hard to grasp, let alone to measure. To understand what it is and what it is not, let us look at culture as it relates to several other fundamental concepts. Most often, culture is discussed in relation to nature, society and communication.

## 1.1. Culture vis-à-vis Nature

Nature is typically understood as the physical world, including plants, animals, the landscape, etc. This understanding goes back to the Greek word *phusis* meaning 'to grow, to become'. It can apply to nature in general and to a specific thing, e.g., a tree: in both cases, the process of growth is intrinsic, i.e., essential to nature or to (the nature of) a thing. Nature is what grows and becomes by itself, without any external or extrinsic influence. It is an ecosystem that did exist, can exist and perhaps will exist without humans in it. Nature, therefore, is the world without us (Weisman, 2007).

Humans are also a part of nature: biologically speaking, humans are also animals. Genetically, we are not very different from other primates: for example, humans and gorillas share 98.4% of their DNA. Even more strikingly, we share a quarter of our genes with a grain of rice; also, we have a common genetic heritage with rhinos and reef coral (Zimmer, 2013). It is not really genes that make us human; rather, it is culture that is viewed as separating us from the living world of nature. Contrasted with the concept of *phusis*, human culture is typically conceptualized as *technē*, i.e., the ability to make something. Thus, everything around us that does not grow by itself but is a result of *technē*, can be viewed as culture.

*Technē* is linked to the Greek *tiktō* meaning 'to bring forth, to produce'. Culture, then, is something engendered or generated by people. Focusing on *technē as* the human ability to make something, it is easy to forget its "origin that is nature" (Irigaray, 1999, p. 86). All cultural objects and modes of existence are inherently dependent on natural ecosystems: whereas nature can exist without humans, human culture cannot exist without nature; e.g., we can enjoy Shakespeare's genius because the First Folio preserved eighteen of his plays, and to print them, trees had to be cut and turned into paper.

Through *technē*, something concealed in nature is revealed or brought forth into unconcealment. As Martin Heidegger reminds us, *technē* in its essence is "a letting-appear" (1977, p. 14). It is important to note that the action of 'letting-appear', while not as active as most other actions, such as 'causing', 'prohibiting', 'determining', etc., is still an action. In other words, while it is self-revealing and self-producing, nature appears transformed by humans. For instance, Claude Lévi-Strauss (1969) showed how, through cooking, raw food as part of nature is transformed by people into cooked food as part of culture. Thus, *technē* brings about a transition from nature to culture, and "the transition takes place as expression" (Waldenfels, 2007, p. 94; see also: Cassirer, 1996). We become human as we come to express ourselves and create meaning. Culture, therefore, is human self-expression or, rather, constant and various self-expressions (Flanagan, 1996).

We can now define culture vis-à-vis nature: conceptualized as a product, culture is nature transformed, and, conceptualized as a process, culture is the transformation of nature.

### 1.2. Culture vis-à-vis Society

If there is a group of people whose behaviors and interactions can be observed, and such behaviors and interactions are repeated over time toward a common goal, then we have an organized whole in the form of a social system or a society. A system of meaningful resources, produced in the process of such behaviors and interactions, can be conceptualized as culture. In the words of Clifford Geertz, "culture is the fabric of meaning in terms of which human beings interpret their action" (1973, p. 144). 'Fabric' here is not limited, of course, to cloth produced by weaving or knitting textile fibers; rather, it means anything fabricated by the human as *Homo faber* by fitting things together. Culture as the fabric of meaning is very broad: "virtually anything shared (or assumed to be shared) among members of a historically recognizable group can rightfully be called culture" (Hall, 1992, p. 52) (Figure 7.1).

Culture is not only the works of literature, history, and art; nor is it only the artifacts created by the human: what is created by people through *technē* refers less to a class of objects than to the human ability to make (Shiner, 2003).

Thus, society, although it is understood in terms of behaviors and interactions, is something more stable and tangible than culture, which is a more

**Figure 7.1**    Banksy rat graffiti, Liverpool, UK.

dynamic and fuzzy phenomenon. Culture is the living fabric of meaning formed by (the people of) society whose behaviors and interactions are bounded by geographical borders. Culture, unlike society, is not limited by any borders; it can exist anywhere. For instance, U.S. society exists inside clear borders whereas the borders of U.S. culture are invisible and porous: one can find this culture in many parts of the world, as witnessed by e.g. the concept of 'Americanization'. It is no accident that one usually speaks about American society and its culture but not American culture and its society.

The difference between society and culture is significant and often overlooked. Sometimes, for instance, scholars search for the 'location of culture'

(Bhabha, 1994). Yet, it is society that is located inside certain borders. Culture, in its turn, is not located but, rather, present wherever the fabric of meaning formed and shared by a group of people exists. For example, on can certainly find American culture, but not American society, present in other countries. Also, we read that "in our culture there is an intense desire for presence enhanced by contemporary communication technologies" (Gumbrecht, 2004, p. 139). However, culture cannot really desire anything, only the people of a society can. Finally, we come across statements about or messages transmitted from one culture to another. Yet, cultures cannot communicate, only concrete people can.

We can now define culture vis-à-vis society: conceptualized as a product, culture is all of the meaningful resources produced by society, and, conceptualized as a process, culture is the social production of such resources.


### 1.3. Culture vis-à-vis Communication

The terms 'culture' and 'communication', although clearly two distinct words, are often used interchangeably. For instance, the title of James Carey's well-known book is *Communication as Culture* (1989); the opposite, obviously, is implied, i.e., *Culture as Communication*. Even more famous is Edward Hall's claim that "culture is communication and communication is culture" (1959, p. 217). Hall's statement is sometimes interpreted to mean that the relationship between communication and culture is one of synecdoche where the part (communication) stands for the whole (culture). Hence, communication is treated as being subordinate to culture (Hall, 1992, p. 60).

However, while one can speak about 'cultural communication', the opposite is ill-formed: '*communicational culture'. Communication, thus, appears to be broader in meaning than culture. Along with 'cultural communication', one can speak about 'social communication' or 'interpersonal communication'. In this light, culture and communication can hardly be equated because culture seems to begin only at a certain point of communication. We should bear in mind that, unlike behaviors, "'culture' as such cannot be observed directly; it only exists in the form of generalized statements made by social scientists about people, which include . . . their language and systems of symbolization, their conventions and traditions, and all objects, buildings, and monuments which convey some message from the past" (Ruesch & Bateson, 1951, p. 147).

184 **The Wonder of Culture**

When we look at interpersonal communication, we find speech at its most fluid: its nature is that of *hic et nunc*, for this one occasion only. As Gadamer writes, "speech and conversation are not statements in the sense that they consist of logical judgments whose univocity and meaning is confirmable and repeatable; rather, they have their occasional side" (2007, p. 63). The beauty of conversation is that it is never one and the same speech: it is the most natural form of communication, which seems to grow by itself. The best conversation is "never the one that we wanted to conduct. . . . No one knows in advance what will 'come out' of a conversation" (Gadamer, 2004, p. 385). Conversation as a form of interpersonal communication is maximally devoid of craft (*technē*), and *technē* is what creates culture through numerous acts that make meaning confirmable and repeatable. We should, therefore, be more precise and speak about interpersonal interaction(s) rather than interpersonal communication: the former is simply a process of going back and forth, while the latter is a process of uniting, joining or making something common. This applies even more to forms of group communication that can hardly be considered 'conversations': it seems more appropriate to call them 'interactions', 'exchanges', or 'discussions'. So, at best we could say that culture is latently present within interpersonal communication, starts to take shape within group communication, and it is only "inter-group communication that stabilizes norms (forms a culture)" (Lanigan, 2013b, p. 71).

Every interpersonal interaction is a separate case of communication; when such interactions are repeated over and over, it becomes possible and necessary to look for their commonalities. With each interaction, we discover something new about the world and ourselves that we can then rely on in the future: here, we approach life inductively. This inductive approach, which is used in Conversational Analysis, is aimed at identifying the categories that form cultural patterns. As communication involves more people, it becomes increasingly complex and requires various technologies to keep the track of our interactions. Without such technologies, we would rely on our natural memory only; Plato would welcome that, but then his works might have never reached us. With such technologies, our natural memory is supplemented and even augmented; it grows and becomes public and cultural. In this respect,

> *techne* of any type whatsoever – whether arrow-making, harp-playing, mathematics, poetry – is a residue of innumerable and immemorable acts of discovery by bygone individuals, retained in cultural memory as deposits of potential power with which new generations can then be endowed
>
> *(Staten, 2006, p. 575)*

We do not know how many individuals interacted with one another, and their individual interactions may be long gone, but the meanings discovered in the process of communication are retained as a cultural pattern – a model for new generations to follow.

We can now define culture vis-à-vis communication: conceptualized as a product, culture is memorable communication, and, conceptualized as a process, culture is communicated memory.

## 2. CULTURE: THE PATTERN THAT CONNECTS

As mentioned earlier, through *technē* a transition from nature to culture takes place: this way, people express themselves by bringing forth something that is meaningful to them. One of the first human acts was literally clearing out a place from wilderness and preparing it for dwelling – an act that required the use of an axe or similar tools. As *technē*, that act consisted in making space that can be occupied or where something can be done. Opening up space was also opening up opportunity: it was the act of "clearing-away the place from nature but at the same time expressing the given conditions in the construction activity" (Katona, 2010, p. 20).

Thus, the origins of culture lie in human tectonic activity. The word 'tectonic' is derived from Greek *tektōn* – 'builder, carpenter, woodworker'. As time went on, the meaning of the word came to include not only a specific and literally physical activity, but also a more general and symbolic notion of construction (Frampton, 2001). The connection between *tektōn* and *technē* cannot be missed. Later, the geological meaning of the word was recorded: 'pertaining to the structure of the Earth's crust'. One can note parallels between the cultural and geological meanings of 'tectonic': the word 'human' is derived from the Proto-Indo-European root *dhghem-*, – 'earth'. Humans are literally 'earthly beings' – those who live on the Earth. Both cultural and geological tectonics focus on large-scale dynamics: the latter deals with those affecting the structure of the Earth's crust, the former with those created by people and affecting their own life. In both cases, tectonics present a big picture of their object: for instance, although the Earth is in a constant state of change, it is common to speak about 'tectonic shifts'. The same can be said about culture: while it constantly changes, it is possible and necessary to speak about its tectonics and tectonic shifts.

Just as there is a connection between *tektōn* and *technē*, we find a relationship between *tektōn* and 'text' (Leski, 2015). Text is anything that is literally or symbolically joined together into some tangible texture, regardless of material: it can be a coherent whole made up of written or printed words on a page or electronically represented on a computer screen. We must go beyond what is considered natural language and adopt a broad semiotic approach, focusing on signs, i.e., in the words of St. Augustine, that which "all living creatures make, one to another, to show, as much as they can, the moving motions of their spirits, that is, everything that they feel and think" (*De Doctrina Christiana*, II, 2.3). Thus, anything concrete, cohesive and coherent that has symbolic meaning to people can be viewed as text, from a poem to a painting to a city. The more mediated the meaning is, the more unstable it is: a good example is Wikipedia as a textoid a –text-like entity (Epstein, 2012).

Sometimes, calls are made to broaden the notion of 'text' to include the spoken word (Hoffman, 2009). However, what is known as 'oral literature' is in fact an oral form of communication that is textualized: "strictly speaking, ... the term 'oral text' is just as much of an absurdity as is 'oral' literature'" (Kenner, 1992, p. 145). In this sense, we can hardly call 'text', for instance, the defense of a dissertation known as *viva voce* or 'in the living voice'. Voice is the most transitory medium: as the Latin saying goes, *Verba volant, scripta manent* – 'spoken words fly away, written words remain'.

Overall, culture is whatever (meaning) remains: "from a semiotic point of view . . ., in every culture 'a unit' . . . is simply anything that is culturally defined and distinguished as an entity" (Eco, 1976, p. 67). Once people have had enough time to interpret something joined together into some tangible texture as meaningful and put their interpretation into some meaningful tangible texture, it can be considered a cultural unit and can be passed down the generations. Obviously, something recorded has better chances of becoming a part of culture than an oral conversation, discussion, or a nonverbal performance: however, all such forms of communication are grist to the human mill. The main thing is for them to have some trace: we can thus view "culture as a means of tracing the meanings and operations of social forces" (Banet-Weiser, 2010, p. 289).

### 2.1. *Dialektikē Technē*

*Dialektikē technē* is "the art of the argumentative usage of language" (Popper, 1963, p. 295). This kind of *technē* is specific to oral speech as it relates to ideas, or, as Plato puts it, "the living speech, the original, of which the written discourse may fairly be called a kind of image" (*Phaedrus*, 276a). In this sense, *dialektikē technē* is the art of dialogue: it operates as a back-and-forth argumentative conversation, in which two (*dia*) people exchange their thoughts in the form of words (*logos*). Derived from the Greek *dialegomai*, *dialektikē technē* as dialogue is speaking thoughts through from one side across to the other: also, it can take the form of internal dialogue.

This kind of *technē* is usually associated with Plato's works (called *Dialogues* for a reason) and the Socratic Method (questions to discover answers) that Plato made famous. In his *Dialogues*, Plato presents Socrates in conversations with contemporaries, which consist in a step-by-step process of eliciting truth by asking and answering questions – what is known as *elenchus* (Figure 7.2).

The nature of this 'elenctic' method is in examining statements for purposes of refutation – questioning someone to test the consistency of what he or she has said; not surprisingly, it has legal connotations and resembles

**Figure 7.2**   Socrates using his Socratic method.

interrogation, sometimes perhaps even conducted under torture (duBois, 1991). This method is viewed as "superior to solitary discourse, at least 'when the other party to the conversation is tractable and gives no trouble'" (duBois. 1991, p. 113; Plato, *The Sophist,* 217d). In other words, when it comes to searching for truth, dialogue is the best form of communication.

*Dialektikē technē* as practiced by Socrates was aimed at furthering our understanding of the nature of the ethical life by examining concepts such as 'justice', 'virtue' or 'piety'. Just as it applies to focusing on the world of thoughts, the same kind of *technē* lies at the basis of examining the natural world; the Socratic method is close to what is described as the 'scientific method', when accounts of empirical observations are questioned and explanatory theories are constructed (Popper, 1963). This way, nature is interrogated. We can recall that Francis Bacon, who is considered to have developed the scientific method, was influenced by the ideas derived from the courtroom (note the legal connotations of *elenchus*, mentioned earlier). Also, parallels are suggested between his views of nature as female and the witch trials, including the mechanical devices used to interrogate and torture witches. Although this way of obtaining knowledge is often considered benign, identified with the goal of modern science, it is also possible to see it as a practice of subjugation and legitimation for the human domination of nature (Merchant, 2006).

So, natural science, although often presented as the opposite of art, is in fact also a cultural enterprise since its practice contains the elements of *dialektikē technē*. What takes place between humans and nature is a process of asking and answering questions. Planting a seed (by humans) is a kind of question, while the seed sprouting is a kind of answer (by nature), or, if the water in rivers is not clean, this is like nature asking us to help it keep its water clean; or, not contaminating rivers by harmful chemicals could be a human answer. Thus, "the exchange with nature comes across as a sort of conversation with nature, but a conversation that balances accepting, learning from, and even celebrating nature with a fair amount of arguing with nature, for the gardener has a legitimate quarrel with nature – her weeds and storms and plagues, her rot and death" (Kaebnick, 2014, p. 122). This form of exchange has the same ethical underpinnings as when Socrates and his contemporaries were examining concepts such as 'justice': the goal is to elicit truth in terms of how humans and nature can continue to coexist and continue to carry on their conversation. In this sense, just as in any conversation between two people, what takes place between humans and nature could be analyzed in terms of Conversational Analysis; this way, such structural patterns could be identified as adjacency pairs, turn-taking, repair, etc. The focus here is not on the interpretation of the *meaning* produced in the process of conversation, but on how order is created through sequences of actions: what matters is to find out what makes this conversation continue.

Science wants to get rid of any cultural (read: subjective) elements and to operate as strictly objective. The gold standard of science is the controlled experiment: only in this way can we extract true knowledge from nature and thus come to control it. However, whatever number of people we choose to make a control group, they are still people, and, in the final analysis, are just like us: simply put, we are all human. We can't remove ourselves, as subjects, from a scientific experiment; hence, it is never completely objective. In a sense, life overall is one uncontrolled experiment that lacks a comparison group.

We should not forget that scientists are people and they, too, have back-and-forth argumentative conversations with one another. This form of *dialektikē technē* does not have any metaphorical connotations that could be identified in calling what takes place between humans and nature 'conversations': here, the focus is on real (living) speech between scientists. It is such speech that Bruno Latour and Steve Woolgar analyze in their book entitled *Laboratory Life: The Social Construction of Scientific Facts* (1979), where they show how scientific objects and results do not exist outside of scientists' conversations about them (Figure 7.3).

Latour further argues that there are no objective facts: just like fetishes, facts are fabricated and so need to be labeled 'factishes' – a combination of 'fact' and 'fetish' (2010). A close examination of their fabrication requires "the rigour of '*conversational analysis*'" (Latour & Woolgar, 1979, p. 184; emphasis added): here, we are on more familiar ground because the analysis focuses on how order is created through words, not sequences of actions such planting a seed.

Thus, the elenctic practice of science is a form of cultural practice: "what is involved in both cases is a test, something like . . . *elegkhos*" (Foucault, 2005, p. 299). This way, people's views are examined and tested – exactly what Socrates did in dialogues with his contemporaries and what Plato did in his *Dialogues. Dialektikē technē* as the artful use of argumentative language

**Figure 7.3**   Two scientists (Caucasian female and Asian male) examine a vial at the National Cancer Institute (NCI) laboratory in Frederick, Maryland. Photo by Bill Branson.

elicits truth; as a result, people become enlightened. In this light (pun intended), an act of examining (testing) should not be understood as forceful interrogation but, rather, as making a plea. A plea is an act of communication made with conviction in an urgent, emotional and sincere manner. Also, it goes back to Latin *placere* – 'to please, give pleasure, be approved'. A plea, then, is 'something pleasant', 'something that pleases both sides'. It is hard to miss the erotic connotations of communication thus conceptualized; *dialektikē technē* is *erōtikē technē* (Griswold, 2010). *Dialektikē technē* is a process of interrogation as loving questioning, a process of inquiry – seeking knowledge and making discoveries. It is most appropriate to speak about love in this case as *eros* and *ludus* – a game-playful desire. Every act of communication in this sense is a passionate language game.

Thus, *dialektikē technē* is not just a method of examining statements for purposes of refutation (note legal connotations) or conducting experiments to discover natural laws (note scientific connotations); it is a process of loving interrogation aimed at finding truth and 'pleasing both sides'. This process may be torturous, but it is sweet torture.

## 2.2. Rhētorikē Technē

When Socrates asks Gorgias in which *technē* he is an expert, Gorgias says that he is an expert in rhetoric (*Gorgias*, 449a), i.e., the art of the orator. Thus, "from its inception, rhetoric does not claim to be anything but artificial; indeed, it is its artificiality that renders it transferable and teachable" (Brooke, 2000, p. 784). As is well known, the first teachers of rhetoric were the sophists (Figure 7.4), and it is such expert rhetoricians that Plato attacks, presenting Socrates to be a different, and true, master – an expert in dialectics.

For Plato, rhetoric as the use (and teaching) of symbolic means for the purposes of action, is too involved with the phenomenal and always changing world, instead of focusing on the noumenal and eternal world of ideas. If you do not search for truth, then it becomes easy and even tempting to play to the senses and emotions of people in various situations: the sophists were known for teaching both sides of an issue or making the weaker argument stronger (Aristotle, *Rhetoric*, II.24, 1402a23–5) – whatever the issue. As result, in Plato's view, *rhētorikē technē* is not a genuine skill because it provides mere gratification and not the actual good. Also, it leads to relativism,

**Figure 7.4**  *The Sophists* by Daniel Nikolaus Chodowiecki. Located in the Los Angeles County Museum of Art.

which is particularly dangerous in the moral realm: for Plato, knowledge is singular and so you either know what virtue is or you do not. In a way, his approach was scientific, focusing not on ethical behavior but on epistemology: what matters is the knowledge of virtue. The search for truth, however, while based on argument, is not beyond *rhētorikē technē*, which cannot simply be wished away. For instance, the motto of the Royal Society is *Nullius in verba* – 'Take nobody's word for it' (Figure 7.5). And yet, you cannot seek knowledge and make discoveries without taking other people's words: as noted earlier, scientists do talk to one another.

So, communication can't be reduced to an exchange of pure argument, as if two fleshless angels were conversing in some realm not of this Earth. It is certainly important and thrilling to be taking steps toward truth by asking and answering questions; as mentioned earlier, such a process of inquiry

**Figure 7.5**    Bookplate of the Royal Society (Great Britain). Motto: *Nullius in verba*. Photo by the Providence Online Project.

is driven by *eros* and *ludus* – a game-playful desire. However, this conversation can never be concluded, i.e., no concept can be defined decisively and with final authority. *Dialektikē technē* is always 'to be continued'. Yet, communication is not just a practice of argumentation; it requires practical action. Even those engaged in an exhilarating process of inquiry must at some point stop and take such simple actions as eating or bathing. In this light, ethics is not so much talking about virtue: it is a doing.

While *dialektikē technē* is focused on ideas, *rhētorikē technē* is focused on how symbolic means lead to action; as Kenneth Burke put it, 'the basic function of rhetoric [is] the use of words by human agents to form attitudes or to induce actions" (Burke, 1969b, p. 41). The essence of *dialektikē technē* is an argument about definition, i.e., a conversation between two people of differing opinions on some matter. The essence of *rhētorikē technē* is a claim in a dispute or a debate, i.e., a communication among several people on an important topic: a common understanding of what is being disputed or debated is required. A conversation, while conducted with another person ('com', meaning 'with, together'), is aimed at highlighting similarities and differences of opinion; that is why it never ends. A dispute or a debate, while focusing on thoroughly examining something from different angles (Latin: *dis-*, meaning 'separately' and *de-*, meaning 'down, completely'), is aimed at highlighting sameness: we can stand together only by resolving differences. While the goal of *dialektikē technē* is to question everything and to find something different in every concept, the goal of *rhētorikē technē* is to find practical answers for the sake of the public good, thus identifying with others, hence 'identification' being the key term in Burke's rhetoric.

Any symbolic action is a result of a decision. When practical wisdom is presented as acting well, i.e., knowing what to do in concrete circumstances, it should not be forgotten that each such action is not only a doing but also a making. What is made in every situation is a decision: in other words, people make choices what to do. Thus, rhetoric must be understood as the use of symbolic means for the purposes of making decisions on how to act. *Rhētorikē technē*, therefore, is a communication process of dispute or debate in which decisions are made. In fact, the original meaning of 'decision' is 'settling a dispute'. In phrases such as 'I decided' or 'I made a decision' what is really meant is 'I chose to act in a certain way'. There is a difference between a choice and a decision: the former is an individual act selecting one of several alternatives whereas the latter is a group accomplishment – a conclusion reached on a course of action after considering the pros and cons of acting. Of course, choosing and deciding are interrelated: one must be free to choose to decide.

The connection between freedom and making lasting decisions is very important, including the need for a free and open space for a dispute or a debate. The best example of such a space is the agora of the classic Greek polis, where citizens assembled coming forth in speech to make decisions on matters of common concern. The Greek agora, as the Assembly of the People, was opposed to the Council of Chiefs: we find these two forms of communication – one horizontal, one vertical – to this day, manifested, for example, in the square and the tower (Ferguson, 2018). In more authoritarian societies power is concentrated in the tower, where most decisions are made top-down; there is little place for debate side-by-side in the square.

As we can see, *rhētorikē technē* operates in public settings where communication involves a rhetor, a message, and an audience, i.e., a group of listeners or viewers (when the word 'audience' is applied to one person, the meaning is different: 'a formal hearing, as with a religious or state dignitary'). It is in front of an audience that every rhetor makes his/her case with a certain goal in mind, and a debate as a form of public discourse takes place. One makes a case by using, to cite Aristotle's classical definition of rhetoric, "the faculty of observing in any given case the available means of persuasion" (Rhetoric, I.2, 1355b27–28). A case can be made only if it has been previously discovered – through *dialektikē technē* – what is at issue in that case: that is why, as Aristotle notes, "rhetoric is a counterpart to dialectic" (*Rhetoric*, I.1, 1354a). Thus, dialectic sets a context by posing questions, while rhetoric suggests a choice by posing answers.

One makes a claim by making a speech. Making a claim is a process of calling out or shouting, considering the original root of the word. Additionally, when one makes a claim, one asks or demands something by virtue or authority, which is different from making a plea: for example, in a conversation, no one really makes any claims. In all situations of public discourse, one communicates to form opinions and induce action. As is well known, Aristotle identified three such situations. In forensic rhetoric, someone's past actions are debated and a decision is made on his/her guilt or innocence. In epideictic rhetoric, claims are made to address whatever virtues or vices are fit for display in the here-and-now ceremony focused on cultural standards of comportment. And in deliberative rhetoric, one makes claims on expediency of a future action. Although *rhētorikē technē* can operate in relation to the past, present, or future, its overall goal is still to induce action, which will have an impact on communication in one way or another. For instance, if a person is found guilty, s/he will go to jail; if a person is shamed, s/he may stay out of the public eye; and if an imminent danger is proven, a heightened level of security may be introduced. In all situations, therefore, *rhētorikē technē* consists in making a case by making a speech, thus making a decision to be acted on.

*Rhētorikē technē* is most often associated with deliberative rhetoric. In this respect, leadership is considered an especially important communication skill: usually, we hear about 'political leadership'. In any situation, though, a rhetor acts a psychagogue – from *psuchē* ('mind') and *agagein* ('to lead'); thus, a rhetor is always in a sense drawing out his/her audience toward a goal. Acting as a psychagogue is sometimes opposed to the method of *elenchus*: the former leads toward positive beliefs while the latter is a negative way of refutation (Johnson, 2007). Yet, as noted earlier, *elenchus* is a dialectical process of loving questioning, love understood as *eros* and *ludus*, as desire and playfulness. In a way, the dialectician is a practitioner of *elenchus* while the rhetorician is an expert psychagogue. To speak about *rhētorikē technē* as a loving use of the symbolic means for the purposes of action is possible perhaps in terms of *philia* and *agapē*, i.e., fellowship and concern. Whatever the case, true leadership starts at the level of interpersonal interaction (a desire to engage) and grows out of love as playful desire. In this light, dialectic is also a counterpart to rhetoric.

It is difficult, of course, to draw a line between different forms of love because both *dialektikē technē and rhētorikē technē* are forms of *erōtikē technē*. The question here is, "How intimate is a techne?" (Mifsud, 2007, p. 99). If leadership begins with *dialektike technē*, then, "understood as the art of arousing and directing desire (*erōtikē technē*), . . . rhetoric becomes 'a kind of soul-moving power (*psychagōgia*) of discourse'" (Yunis, 2010, p. 82; Plato, *Phaedrus*, 261a); here, one is not so much a leader as a conductor of minds. A true leader brings something forth while a conductor brings something together by managing or directing behavior. Be that as it may, the study of 'communication leadership' can only benefit by examining what role love plays in it (Miller, 2006).

## 2.3. *Hermēneutikē Technē*

Natural scientists sometimes believe that only their efforts are a worthwhile process of inquiry because it produces knowledge. They look at the humanities with a condescending air as a form of entertainment; in their view, the humanities do not make anything. However, it should not be forgotten that the humanities also produce something very important – understanding; the role of *hermēneutikē techně* can't be overestimated because the purpose of hermeneutics is to make meaning understandable (Grondin, 1994). This was stated very clearly by Gadamer: "Hermeneutics is the practical art, that is, a *techne*, . . . the art of understanding, . . . particularly required any time the meaning of something is not clear and unambiguous" (2007, p. 44).

Understanding as making an interpretation (applied knowledge) consists of two interconnected processes – explication and expression. First, we need to try and interpret what does not lie on the surface but rather is implicitly present in a message; and, second, we need to speak (taking speaking in broad terms, as a conceptual code, not only as oral speech), i.e., put that inner meaning into some external form. Hence, "the utterance (*hermēneia*) is always a translation of the soul's (that is, inner) thoughts into externalized language" (Grondin, 1994, p. 21). These two processes take place simultaneously because understanding is explaining by expressing: nothing can be perceived until it has been expressed. It is important to emphasize that understanding is not a simple process of discovering meaning as if it were something hidden and waiting to be found; rather, understanding is an active search in which meaning *is made understandable.* If meanings were discovered, then, once you find a meaning, it no longer requires understanding: your work is done and you can move on to looking for other meanings. In real life, however, everything requires explication and expression over and over, generating meaning that can never be fully understood without a context of expression (Figure 7.6).

*Hermēneutikē techně* would be unnecessary if all meanings were literal and manifest. The origins of hermeneutics are usually associated with problems of applied translation among languages. For example, there are issues with the Biblical exegesis or interpretation of the texts of the Scripture, the meaning of which became often ambiguous as time went on and thus called for interpretation. Soon, hermeneutics extended to other texts and came to be "involved in such things as preaching, [and] interpreting other languages" (Gadamer, 2007, p. 44), among other things. *Hermēneutikē techně* is activated whenever we come into contact with something or someone whose meaning is not clear and unambiguous. Understanding, therefore, is always understanding someone/something other than yourself, including yourself as someone other than yourself.

**Figure 7.6**   Frontispiece by Pierre Giffart, after Pierre Monier. From Jean Mabillon, *De re diplomatica* (Paris: L. Billaine, 1681). Located in the Bibliothèque Municipale de Reims. Scan by G. Garitan.

*Hermēneutikē technē* is a process that requires effort, imagination, and courage: it can be compared to a journey in which we meet texts and human beings that call for our interpretation because of their otherness. Fortunately, although it may not be easy, understanding is possible in principle because we can "project our experienced life into every sort of expression of our own and others' lives" (Dilthey, 2002, p. 109). Moreover, "there are important features in common between making sense of human beings and understanding texts. In particular, a certain kind of circularity attaches to both types of account" (Taylor, 2016, p. vii). We understand meaning only by going through what is known as the hermeneutical circle when we must constantly interpret the whole (text/experience of otherness) in terms of its parts and its parts in terms of the whole (text/experience of otherness). Any change in our understanding of a part impacts our understanding of the whole, and any change in our understanding of the whole impacts our understanding of a part: interpretation is a kaleidoscope that never rests.

The hermeneutical circle must not be identified with the circular argument. The latter is a notorious logical fallacy – a type of reasoning in which the proposition is supported by the premise, which is supported by the proposition, etc.: as a result, reasoning keeps going in a circle and no new meaning is created. A common form of circular reasoning is 'begging the question', where the conclusion is assumed in one of the premises. The hermeneutical circle differs from circular reasoning because it is not a form of argument but rather at attempt at understanding meaning. By going through the hermeneutical circle, one does not really present any reasons or cite evidence in support of how meaning is understood; instead, one simply makes meaning intelligible as best one can, i.e., makes an inference to the best explanation, i.e., abduction (a probability judgment). One does not 'beg the question'; instead, one gives an answer to one's encounter with otherness. Here, unlike the case of circular reasoning, new meaning is created: in this sense, the hermeneutical circle is a virtuous circle. In other words, it is an open circle for it is impossible to reach the 'closure of meaning': no matter how good one's interpretation is, "it is always possible that someone could propose a better one" (Taylor, 2016, p. viii). Hence, communication scholars prefer the image of a helix rather than a circle.

If *hermēneutikē technē* is a journey that takes the form of a circle, then there arises a question where to start. And the answer is very simple: anywhere – simply because one must start somewhere, so "a spiritual or intellectual journey may imaginatively originate at any point on the hermeneutical circle" (Paparella, 2012, p. 11). What is crucial, though, is eventually coming back to where one started, making full circle. Understanding is not simply going in circles, it is making full circles in space and time (helix movement). Hence, one may visit a childhood home, but new times will have changed the "same old place"! When one goes in circles, nothing changes (circular reasoning). When one makes a full circle, one makes a journey, completing a cycle of transition from one lived experience to a different one. Understanding is coming back to where one started with new meanings. Or, putting it more poetically, "we shall not cease from exploration, and the end of all our exploring will be to arrive where we started and know the place for the first time" (Eliot, 1943).

Interpretation always starts at a point when/where understanding becomes a problem – and important; hence, one starts from the point when/where one is – here and now. This situation provides a horizon of interpretation and so understanding is always perspectival. Just as without the limitation of a horizon there would be no seeing, so without the starting point of one's tradition there would be no understanding. It is crucial to emphasize the open and dynamic nature of horizons; as Gadamer says, "horizon is. . . something into which we move and that moves with us" (2004, p. 304). Understanding requires that, as a result of a communication encounter, neither your own horizon nor that of the Other is left intact: true understanding involves transformation or what Gadamer calls 'fusion of horizons'. We change with the horizon, becoming a part of a new whole. We start with our own culture but search for new, different meanings. Understanding, thus, is not reaching the horizon but reaching *for* the horizon; it is an active and constant process of experiencing otherness and making that experience meaningful.

In this process, every experience does matter; in fact, we can only speak of *téchnē* "as oriented toward a singular creation" (Foti, 1999, p. 178). Only by examining the singular experiences of every individual can we understand the ever-changing human nature. While natural science is concerned with the universal laws or what is, hermeneutics as a human science is focused on our experiences; "thus [*hermēneutikē*] *technē* is ordered toward an understanding of what it means to be in general" (Rojcewicz, 2006, p. 64). There is no room for interpretation of nature as something that simply 'is'. 'What it means to be in general', though, by definition, calls for interpretation as it can have different meaning to different people. That is why, as Wilhelm Dilthey famously put it, "we explain nature; man we must understand" (Dilthey, 1990, p. 144).

Through *hermēneutikē technē*, we try to understand what it means to be both oneself – a singular creation – and (hu)'man', in general. We can do this only by interpreting our experiences and making expressions, i.e., making known our thoughts and feelings to ourselves and others. One understands an experience only when one has put it into one's own words, thus allowing the experience to speak in a new way. Each of us is an author producing new and newer interpretations of our experiences; this way, each of us makes oneself and culture, in general. Overall, culture is a text that is constantly (re)produced by everyone and all. Even though many concrete texts have individual authors, culture is a collective creation. In various situations, each of us tries to make meaning understandable. Once it is made understandable, it becomes practicable and can be used in social interaction. Now it can function on its own, as it were: a gift that keeps on giving.

## 2.4. *Kritikē Technē*

It is common to conceptualize *kritikē technē as* "art of distinction, art of judgement" (Gänshirt, 2007, p. 196). However, 'distinction' and 'judgement' do not have the exact same meaning. Distinction means distinguishing something from something else. The art of distinguishing is at the basis of knowledge: to know, in essence, is to be able to distinguish. When the art of distinguishing is associated with reading the Book of Nature – for example, going through the entrails of animals or looking at the positions of the stars – it is the same process of perceiving differences that we find in a dialogue where one person can distinguish themselves from the other person and each can distinguish between different sides of an issue. In this sense, *dialektikē technē* can be viewed as an art of distinction because it always analyzes everything by dividing it in two, as it were.

*Kritikē technē*, in its turn, is not so much an art of distinction as an art of judgment that consists in focusing on the very possibilities of knowledge. *Kritikē technē* is found (predominantly) not in natural science but in (critical) philosophy. Many people are not sure about the nature of philosophy, as shown by the title of a recent book *What Do Philosophers Do?* (Maddy, 2017). It is very easy to answer that question, though: philosophers philosophize or contemplate (Figure 7.7).

If we recall that, as Aristotle famously said, philosophy begins in wonder, then philosophers philosophize or contemplate anything that caused in them a feeling of amazement and admiration and calls for thinking deeply and fully about it. A more difficult and important question to ask would be What Do Philosophers Make? Obviously, the question does not refer to the median starting salary for philosophy majors – one of the first things brought up by a Google search. The question is what philosophers make in the sense of 'producing'.

As mentioned above, the nature of philosophy is criticism rather than discovery of knowledge through an art of distinguishing. Following Immanuel Kant, the task of critical philosophy is not inquiring into the nature of reality or meaning of cultural experiences, but, rather, enquiring about what makes it possible for us to inquire and to experience, in the first place, i.e., make judgments. In other words, the philosopher wonders how everything is possible – something that people rarely do when they go about their daily life. When the philosopher makes critical judgments (which also apply to

**Figure 7.7**   *The Thinker* by Auguste Rodin. This is a plaster version, created by Rodin in 1903, of the famous sculpture, exhibited in Rodin: the centennial exhibition in Grand Palais, Paris, from 22 March 2017 to 31 July 2017. Photo by Joe deSousa.

philosophy itself), they are both synthetic (combination of parts) and *a priori* (before experience). They are synthetic because their truth is not a result of analysis (division of parts) of the meaning of the words that make up the judgment. And they are *a priori* because their truth is independent from all particular experiences; instead, they grow out of intuition and *make possible* any and all experience.

*Kritikē technē* thus is a form of practice that maximally interrogates conscious reasoning. It does not take things apart in order to uncover the essence of something; rather, it postulates something that can be applied to knowledge overall. In other words, "the critic is not the one who debunks, but the one who assembles. The critic is not the one who lifts the rugs from under the feet of the naive believers, but the one who offers the participants arenas in which to gather" (Latour, 2004, p. 246).

It may appear as if this task is accomplished by *hermēneutikē technē*, which deals with interpretation and understanding. However, while it addresses a process of making meaning understandable, *hermēneutikē technē* deals with what it means to be a part of one's culture or humanity, in general. In both cases, it focuses on what is *sui generis*, i.e., of its own kind.

*Kritikē technē* addresses the conditions that make it possible to make meaning intelligible. Judgments in which such conditions are postulated are true universally and necessarily, unlike the laws of natural science which can only be general, let alone the attempts to understand what it means to be human. Only the philosopher has the luxury to articulate postulates whose nature is truly universal. 'General' means something that relates to a whole class, i.e., belongs to a certain kind. There is nothing wrong with generality; in fact, it is crucial for our life. In a way, one cannot not generalize because, if one can't generalize, one can't think. 'Universal', however, refers to something that is (constantly) turned into one: by definition, the Universe is one and only, including all kinds – human cultures, nature, consciousness, God(s), etc. By practicing *kritikē technē*, the philosopher makes the Universe go round.

*Hermēneutikē technē* operates in the sphere of variable cultures; it is here that we find the so-called field of intercultural communication. The reason is that when the focus is on the *relationships* "between cultures, similarities are downplayed for the sake of differences, closeness (in customs, mores, law, and socio-political institutions) is replaced by distance, and the identity or communality of belonging . . .[,] whilst not denied, lies rather in the background of the more prominent disjunctiveness of separate cultures separating truth and humanity within them. There is little room, if any, for any trans-cultural guidelines" (Hamrick, 1987, p. 10). It is only we start practicing *kritikē technē* that cultural differences are downplayed and the trans-human comes into the foreground. Philosophy reminds us that we are not only human, but all too human, our excess of meaning always pointing to something 'trans-', i.e., 'out there'– animal, strange, unknown.

Thus, culture as *technē* requires not only knowledge but also wisdom. If, as mentioned earlier, to know means being able to distinguish, wisdom means being able to postulate judgments with the universal appeal. Aristotle conceptualized wisdom (*sophia*) as the highest form of *technē* – *aretē technē* or artistic excellence (*Nicomachean Ethics*, VI.7, 1141a12), oriented "toward the most universal and theoretical form of knowledge,

**Table 7.1**   Culture as *technē*

| *Dialektikē technē* | *Rhētorikē technē* |
| --- | --- |
| Making a conversation | Making a speech |
| Making a plea | Making a claim |
| Making a discovery | Making a decision |
| *Hermēneutikē technē* | *Kritikē technē* |
| Making an expression | Making a judgment |
| Making an inference | Making a possibility |
| Making an interpretation (meaning) | Making the Universe intelligible (sense) |

which is the knowledge of the highest or 'most honorable' object, namely Being" (Rojcewicz, 2006, p. 64). It is Being that is the object of philosophy, operating through *kritikē technē*.

As we can see, the status of philosophy is unique. Philosophy is traditionally placed within the humanities and opposed to natural science. However, if we take a closer look at philosophy as *kritikē technē*, we will see that, on the one hand, it relates to a process of making cultural meanings intelligible and thus is a part of the humanities, and, on the other hand, postulates what makes the scientific inquiry possible; after all, all early philosophers were natural philosophers. And, all contemporary philosophers are humanists grounded in logic and mathematics. *Kritikē technē*, therefore, acts as an intermediary between the human sciences and the natural sciences, offering them 'arenas in which to gather'.

Thus, here is how the nature of culture can be presented in terms of the main forms of *technē* (Table 7. 1).

## 3. BACK TO CULTURE

*Kritikē technē* appears to be a weak and tentative form of practice; after all, it simply postulates something, suggesting some possibility as a basis for all our experience. However, in this seeming weakness lies its strength, since the critic is someone "for whom, if something is constructed, then it means *it is fragile, and thus in great need of care and caution*" (Latour, 2004, p. 246; emphasis added). Through *kritikē technē*, the philosopher reminds us that everything we make, however sturdy it may appear to be, is in fact delicate and vulnerable, and that every communicative act requires not only knowledge but also wisdom – careful judgment about it as a part of a whole.

It is important to remember that judgment is not just forming an opinion after careful thought: *"kritikē (technē)*, 'the art of judgement,' means to discern or to judge carefully *with a view to guarding oneself against error"* (Ulrich, 1983, p. 19; emphasis added). Similarly, intuition, which lies at the basis of making critical judgments, does not just mean the ability to know something immediately but also what watches over us, thus protecting us from unwise actions. Intuition does not really explain anything or help us to understand something, making its meaning intelligible; it simply points the way and we act accordingly. This often saves us from all kinds of disasters, large and small. Culture as a pattern that connects, is not just a model or a design: its meaning goes back to Latin *patronus* – 'defender, protector' (Latin: *pater* – 'father').

To view culture as a pattern is common; for instance, Ruth Benedict's well-known book, *Patterns of Culture* (1934), presents culture as a pattern of a recurrent design or a model for behavior. Such patterns are viewed as shaping human life in many ways: there are many different cultures, of course, hence the plural – 'patterns' – in the title. Culture overall, though, is not something that exists separately from humans; it is not 'as' (similar to) some design or model – it *is* the pattern that connects everything. Culture is a creative pattern: it does not simply shape human life but brings something forth into being while at the same time being a 'defender' and a 'protector'. Culture protects us not only from the harsh realities of nature, but also from ourselves. Even when we speak about 'protecting the surrounding environment', what is really meant is protecting nature from culture, i.e., from ourselves, for it is culture that surrounds nature and impacts it in innumerable ways, not vice versa (Groys, 1993).

Thus, culture is a pattern that connects: it brings us together into conversation – through *dialektikē technē* – the human with the other human (or the human and nature); it brings us together into society – through *rhētorikē technē* – the human with other humans; it brings us together into humanity – through *hermēneutikē technē* – the human with him/herself; and it brings us together into the Universe – through *kritikē technē* – the human with everything there is and there could be. *Hermēneutikē technē* best of all represents making as an inherently human cultural practice because all people try to understand their experiences, making their meaning understandable. This form of *technē* is best of all seen as perspectival, providing a horizon for our life journeys. *Rhētorikē technē* is another practice that most people can relate to since most people often speak to others in public settings. Notably, these two forms of *technē* are usually associated with the human sciences. It is not as easy to think of *dialektikē technē* and *kritikē technē* as cultural practices; most people do not find it easy to carry on a dialogue searching for truth or to philosophize. It is important to note, though, that all these forms of *technē* are cultural practices.

Thus, culture is what is made through various forms of *technē*. Because it is made, i.e., cultivated, it must be taken care of. If we take care of culture, culture will take care of us: this cannot be otherwise because culture *is* us. Often, we speak about 'everyday culture' (Trend, 2016). However, culture can't be 'every-other-day culture' or 'sometimes culture': culture is everywhere and everywhen. Because of its ubiquity, taking care of culture is something that is easy to forget. Yet, it is precisely because of its ubiquity that taking care of culture is crucial. As noted earlier, such key concepts as 'judgment', 'intuition' and 'pattern' all contain suggestions of watchful attention and protection. Culture is what we must always remember to handle with care (Klyukanov, 2008). Notably, "when we bring together culture and care, we arrive at a basic meaning that is found in the word 'memory', which connotes something vital for people but something that is lost in its earlier and initiatory presence" (Scott, 2007, p. 138).

While we (re)produce meaning each time we communicate, ritual is an especially important form of communication in this regard (Figure 7.8).

It is tempting to view ritual as a form of communication "not useful for specifically technical purposes" (Rothenbuhler, 1998, p. 11), when people seem to just go through the motions. However, ritual is one of the most important forms of communication because, through it, everything that is most meaningful – sacred – to a culture is reproduced, revived, unforgotten. The sacred meanings that are ritually reproduced are not argued about, debated, or postulated: "in any given cultural community, the sacred is whatever is treated as unquestionable, 'beyond interdiction,' as Durkheim puts it" (Rothenbuhler, 1998, p. 24). In a way, ritual is the best (to this point) answer that members of a certain culture have been able to come up with for a particular situation. It is important to note that "in a ritual . . . authors are unimportant" (Krippendorff & Bermejo, 2009,

**Figure 7.8**    Hindu priest officiating at a ritual for a Romuvan community in Lithuania. Romuvans are very active in ecumenical cooperation with Indian Hindus. Photo by Mantas LT.

p. 61); the author of the sacred meanings reproduced in rituals is culture, as such. Using the terminology from Coordinated Management of Meaning Theory, ritual has the strongest logical force because it represents the highest level of communication – that of cultural archetypes. In other words, ritual is the most natural form of communication. Notably, rituals are often (mostly) non-verbal when everything takes place without (a lot of) words. Cultural ritual, thus, is what goes without saying yet speaks volumes.

When 'the loss of culture' is lamented, it is first and foremost losing *technē* as the memory of making something: the disappearance of objects and actions is but a result of that. For instance, with all new technologies, we are losing our handicrafts, such as weaving, which is often considered the original meaning of *technē* as making something by joining together; for example, with all digital technologies, we are losing the art of handwriting, the patterned ritual of linking 'letters' into the community called 'words': the birth of meaning. Theodor W. Adorno lamented that we have forgotten how to close a door quietly and discreetly, yet firmly, leading to possible dramatic social consequences (Siegert, 2012, p. 7). However, this remains a possibility just by the virtue of our talking about it – of unforgetting: through cultural memory, we keep oblivion at bay. It is culture that keeps us alive and prevents everything from disappearing.

Ritual shows best of all that we can (re)produce culture only by going back to what is meaningful to us. There is no 'going back to nature' because we can talk about nature only insofar as it is cultivated ('culturized'). We can only move forward and make traces by going at the same time back to culture and retracing our steps. Thus, what we bring forth is ourselves: while natural-born, all humans are self-made. Culture "is that which is worthy of reverential homage" (Whitten, 1996, p. 204) – worthy because culture is human, because it is us. Humankind can continue only by cultivating itself, by paying homage to everything meaningful – publicly communicating special loyalty and respect to the pattern that connects. Whatever we make – discoveries, claims, sense, possibilities – we are making a reverential journey back home. And while we keep making this journey, we *are* home.

# 8

# The Wonder of Information

Key concepts:

Bit, channel, code, commemoration, creativity, cybernetics, data compression, entropy, feedback, freedom, imprint, information, materiality, meaning, memory, measurement, noise, non-summativity, observer, operation, operationalization, pragmatic, redundancy, receiver, reference, reflexivity, sense, sensible, semantic, source, system, transmission, transmitter.

Key names:

André-Marie Ampère, Gregory Bateson, Ray L. Birdwhistell, Søren Brier, Heinz von Foerster, R. V. L. Hartley, Katherine Hayles, James Gleick, Klaus Krippendorff, Richard L. Lanigan, Niklas Luhmann, John von Neumann, Plato, Claude Shannon, Paul Watzlawick, Warren Weaver, Norbert Wiener.


## 1. 'A SEMANTIC CHAMELEON'

Information is everywhere. We crave it, we acquire it, we save it, we exchange it, we process it, we delete it, we protect it, we retrieve it, we manage it, we use it, etc. At the same time, not only are we doing something with information, but information is changing our life, infiltrating and engulfing us.

As James Gleick, the author of *The Information: A History, A Theory, A Flood*, puts it, we are "creatures of the information" (2011, p. 426). Not creators, but creatures! Although the phrases 'We're creators of the information' and 'We're creatures of the information' have the same syntactical structure, their underlying meanings are very different: in the former case, the human is the agent, whereas in the latter, the agent is information, which appears to be a living creature in-forming our lives.

This creature, appears to be not only powerful but elusive. While the everyday concept of information is commonly associated with data, knowledge, facts, meaning, etc., it seems to be impossible to capture as it blends so well into the environment. Not surprisingly, it is viewed as "a semantic chameleon" (Thom, 1983, p. 277), and we are led to believe that "'information' is a hard word to get a handle on" (Nunberg, 2011). We should remember, though, that meaning has two sides – reference and sense. Or, in the words of Gottlob Frege, who suggested this distinction, "if words are used in the ordinary way, what one intends to speak of is their reference. It can also happen, however, that one wishes to talk about the words themselves or their sense" (Frege, 1993, p. 25). If we talk about the word 'information' itself, then its meaning is not that hard to capture, for we are dealing here with its definition or a statement of essence. In this sense (pun intended), 'information' is the way in which something manifests itself or what makes something what it is and thus distinguished from something else. When it comes to capturing the meaning of 'information' as reference, things get fuzzy; it is an abstract noun and does not refer to any concrete substance. However, precisely because it appears to be impossible to determine the meaning of 'information' in this respect, the opposite can be argued: what 'information' means is easy to figure out because it refers to anything that manifests itself in a certain (distinguished from everything else) way. In other words, information seems so hard to find because it is everywhere: if something has no form, we can't talk about it. For this reason, the definition of the phrase 'information age' is elusive, as well; it is impossible to date it or to determine if we're still in the information age or transitioning to another age. If theorized in this way, every age is an information age (Figure 8.1).

Just as it may appear as if 'information' evades understanding, we may be led to believe that its theorizing is a recent phenomenon. However, just as Monsieur Jourdain in Molière's famous play was surprised to find out that for forty years he'd been speaking in prose without knowing it, it will come as a surprise to many that we have been theorizing information for centuries. Not only were many attempts made to conceptualize information,

**Figure 8.1**    Information Age gallery at the Science Museum, London. Photo by Tyrobbo.

but people also learned how to deal with information overload, which, it turns out, is not a modern phenomenon but a byproduct of human culture. Long before the invention of the Internet and cloud computing, people had to manage information by using papyrus (Figure 8.2), codices, the printing press, etc. (Wright, 2008). People had to do it because they lived in fear of chaos, when nothing has form and so is beyond one's control; in a way, people through the ages have tried to in-form chaos, turning it into information, i.e., something 'signifying something'.

In the Western tradition, this goes back at least to Plato, as shown by Heinz von Foerster's article 'Circuitry of Clues to Platonic Ideation' (1962) in which he draws parallels between the concept of information and Plato's forms. For Plato, forms were the immutable ideas (Greek: *eidos*) that acted as defining forces for sensible objects. In a way, form is the character of an object; something cannot exist unless it is somehow characterized. Sensible things, therefore, are in-formed. Every form as idea, according to Plato, "goes together with knowledge, and is written in the soul of the learner" (*Phaedrus*, 276a). We should not be surprised reading this if we recall that the Greek *charaktēr* (χαρακτηρ) means 'symbol or imprint in the soul'. We should also remember that, in Plato's times, "oral communication still dominate[d] all

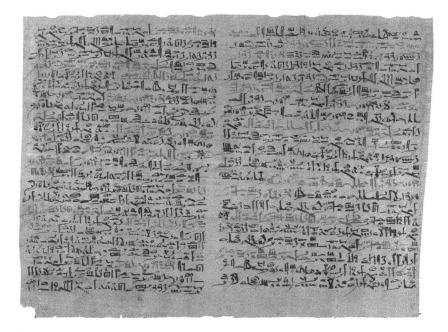

**Figure 8.2**    The Edwin Smith papyrus, the world's oldest surviving surgical document. Photo by Jeff Dahl.

the important relationships and valid transactions of life" (Havelock, 1963, p. 38). No advanced communication technologies yet existed, and writing was not yet wide-spread, so life experiences were imprinted mostly on the soul. Thus, ideas exist in the soul and are the formative force of both speech and writing. Forms cannot be identified with images: the latter are only copies of the former. By the same token, although 'to form' is often understood as 'to give shape', they are not the same: 'form' must be conceptualized as the guiding principle causing a thing to be what it is, whereas 'shape' is an external surface or outline. Shape is something one can see or feel and thus recognize; form is something that can be cognized.

As time went on, people dealt with more and more sensible objects. Besides, with the rapid development of writing systems and new communication technologies, it became easier to record experiences, i.e., give them external and stable shape. Rather than being imprinted on the soul, information came to be conceptualized more and more as an empirical phenomenon – something that can be observed and studied scientifically.

## 2. THE MAGNA CARTA OF THE INFORMATION AGE

In 1948, Claude Shannon published his paper 'A Mathematical Theory of Communication' in the *Bell Systems Technical Journal*. A year later, Shannon published those ideas in a book form together with Warren Weaver, a mathematician and science administrator who felt they needed to reach an audience beyond just communication engineers. The book was entitled *The Mathematical Theory of Communication* (Shannon & Weaver, 1949); the change from the indefinite to the definite article must be noted: it was as if the essence of information had been captured.

The scientific view presented was so groundbreaking that it was called by *Scientific American* 'The Magna Carta of the Information Age'. Elsewhere, it is labeled 'A Magna Carta for the Information Age' (Dyson et al., 1994). As we can see, there is an inherent tension in this view, reflected in the use of the article: in one case, it is taken as one instance out of many, and, in the other case, the definitive characterization. The latter is closer in meaning to the original Magna Carta, or 'The Great Charter', that almost a thousand years ago established the principle that everybody, including the king, was subject to law. Just as 'The Great Charter' brought everyone together before the rule of law, Shannon and Weaver's ideas were revolutionary in their unifying vision of information, which showed how every mode of communication, from text to pictures to sound, can be conceptualized within one framework. In a manner of speaking, just as everyone is equal before the rule of law, everyone is equal before information.

From the very start, Shannon made it clear that 'communication', found in the title of his paper, must be understood strictly in the engineering sense – as transmission of information. In the very first paragraph, he acknowledged that two important papers had provided a basis for his theory, one of which was 'Transmission of Information' by R. V. L. Hartley (1928). Based on those ideas, Shannon is interested in defining information in quantitative terms, rather than as content of the message. In his original paper, he states that "these semantic aspects of communication are irrelevant to the engineering problem" (Shannon, 1948, p. 379). Later, in his editorial in a volume of the *IRE Transactions on Information Theory*, he emphasizes that "the hard core of information theory is, essentially, a branch of mathematics, a strictly deductive system" (Shannon, 1956, p. 3).

This approach to communication, formulated by Shannon and further developed by Shannon together with Weaver, must be kept in mind when evaluating their theory. Often, we read that "it *ignores* any issue related to informational content" (Lombardi et al., 2014, p. 7; emphasis added) or that the birth of information theory can be identified with "the sacrifice of meaning" (Gleick, 2012, p. 416; see also: Nunberg, 2011). However, Shannon and Weaver were clearly aware of it: they simply found semantic aspects of communication irrelevant to their goal. In other words, they did not care about content "in the same way that a traffic engineer doesn't care what, if anything, the trucks on the highway are carrying" (Nunberg, 2011). The validity of every theory must be evaluated against its assumptions and goals; in other words, a theory cannot be blamed for not achieving what it did not claim it wanted to achieve. As noted previously, Shannon and Weaver's theory is based on the mathematical (statistical) concept of communication and had as its goal showing how information can be efficiently transmitted. Thus, the theory did not really 'ignore' informational content, i.e., refuse or fail to take notice of or acknowledge it. Shannon and Weaver did take notice of it; they simply chose not to take it into account when setting the goal for their theory.

Shannon and Weaver focused on communication as sending a message from one end, through a noisy channel, so it could be received on the other end. Their goal was to show how information can be transmitted without any error. It is stated that, in trying to do so, "information theorists *exclude* the self and other aspects of human vagueness" (Grant, 2003, p. 2; emphasis added). However, just as it can hardly be argued that informational content is ignored, Shannon and Weaver can hardly be blamed for excluding the self and other aspects of human vagueness, i.e., removing them from consideration. In fact, the opposite is the case: they were very much aware of such aspects and showed how they can be dealt with. According to Shannon and Weaver, all information can be presented in the form of recognizable patterns: the more such patterns can be compressed, the more information can be transmitted. Such patterns can be viewed as imprints of our experience; notably, Shannon's paper is sometimes labeled as a "blueprint for the digital age" (Waldrop, 2001). It is interesting to note that the Russian word for 'imprint' – *ottisk* – includes the meaning of 'squeezing' (Figure 8.3). Indeed, the goal of Information Theory is to show how everything related to the Self and other aspects of human vagueness can be turned or squeezed, as it were, into recognizable patterns.

Shannon showed how information can be coded: once represented digitally, it can then be transmitted without error. Any noise in the channel can be offset by introducing redundancy. The objective of source coding is to

**Figure 8.3**   Imprint of the Shugiin, the House of Representatives of the Japanese government.

remove uncertainty, which is achieved by compressing the message, i.e., squeezing more information into a smaller message, for example by creating a .ZIP file to attach and send with an email. According to Shannon, information can be conceptualized in terms of entropy, or the probability of occurrence of a certain state of affairs among all their possible combinations. High entropy means a more compressed message with less redundancy and thus more information.

Information can be measured in bits: one bit is the smallest unit of information, representing a choice between two equally likely probabilities. On the one hand, information can be transmitted through a channel in units without an error; on the other hand, every information channel has its own capacity: only a certain number of bits of information can be transmitted per a certain period without an error. In other words, information can be transmitted reliably only up to a limit: above that limit, to transmit error-free information is mathematically impossible. All digital innovations are aimed at pushing that limit further and expanding the channel capacity so that more information can be squeezed into a smaller message. Not everything, though, lends itself to data compression. Shannon was aware of the limitations inherent in his theory, noting that it is not very relevant to psychology, economics, and other social sciences. Emphasizing that his theory is aimed in a very specific direction and should not be artificially extended beyond its original goal, Shannon attempted "to inject a note of moderation in this situation" (1956, p. 3). Just as information in his theory can be measured, so, too, according to Shannon, must the understanding and application of the theory be done in moderation, i.e., kept within measures. In a way, he showed that we are capable of transmitting information free of error but this freedom is within limits.

## 3. THE SCIENCE OF GOVERNING

Although cybernetics became popular thanks to Norbert Wiener, who defined it as "the entire field of control and communication theory, whether in the machine or the animal" (1948, p. 19), the term itself was coined almost a hundred years earlier by André-Marie Ampère in his *Essay on the Philosophy of Science* (1834). Perhaps because Ampère listed 'la cyberné-tique' among the political sciences along with diplomacy and power theory, it is often translated into English as 'a science of government' (Mackay, 1991, p. 3); it is more appropriate, though, to speak about 'governing' rather than 'government' (Baumard, 2017, p. 2).

Cybernetics conceptualized communication as an information-processing mechanism that generates purposeful behavior (for an overview see: Geoghegan & Peters, 2014). Both living organisms (humans) and machines can be understood in terms of such mechanisms, as far as they are directed to a goal and control their behavior in the process of communicating with the environment – other living organisms and machines. The focus here, therefore, is not so much on the efficiency of information transmission, but rather on the functionality of such organisms and machines as systems.

One of the first concerted attempts to put systems thinking and cybernet-ics in the center of scientific discussion was made during the famous Macy Conferences (1943–1956) – meetings organized by the Josiah Macy Jr. Foundation (Figure 8.4). Those meetings brought together many leading

**Figure 8.4**    The Macy Conferences on Cybernetics: participants in the 10th Macy Conference (1953).

thinkers from a wide range of fields, including Norbert Wiener, a founder of cybernetics and a mathematician; William Ross Ashby, a psychiatrist and a pioneer in cybernetics; Heinz von Foerster, a biophysicist and a pioneer in cybernetics; Gregory Bateson and Margaret Mead, anthropologists; Ralph W. Gerard, a neurophysiologist and behavioral scientist; Paul Lazarsfeld, a sociologist; Kurt Lewin, a psychologist; John von Neumann, a mathematician; Walter Pitts, a logician; and Leonard J. Savage, a mathematician and statistician.

Those thinkers focused on functional analogies between machines and the central nervous system in humans, since both can store information and use it in controlling their behavior. It was not surprising, therefore, that the meetings drew the interest not only of scientists and mathematicians, but also psychologists, psychiatrists, sociologists, and anthropologists. They aimed to determine how mental disorders could be minimized and human behavior controlled, as well as the way the computing machine could be designed to generate adaptive behavior. Thus, despite a wide range of fields, all those attending the Macy Conferences spoke the same language of goal-directed behavior, information processing, control mechanism, etc. It was at these conferences that cybernetics took its shape as the science of governing.

The concept of information was of central importance to the development of cybernetics: "after all, the subject matter of cybernetics is not events and objects but the information 'carried' by events or objects. We consider the objects or events only as proposing facts, propositions, messages, percepts and the like" (Bateson, 1972, p. 407). Shannon and Weaver's Information Theory proved to be a cornerstone of cybernetics: it showed how information can be conceptualized, coded, and measured; how it can be efficiently transmitted through a channel; how redundancy can be introduced to offset noise; how the capacity of a channel can be calculated, etc.

While it owes much debt to Information Theory, cybernetics takes its approach to communication further. As mentioned earlier, cybernetics adopts a systemic view of communication; the same cannot be said of Information Theory. When discussing Information Theory, it is sometimes stated that "the communication system consists of an information source, a transmitter or encoder, a (possibly noisy) channel, and a receiver (decoder)" (Timpson, 2013, p. 16). However, a system is a complex whole in which all parts are interconnected and work toward a common goal; also, a system is qualitatively different from each of its parts, which is expressed by the concept of non-summativity. Information Theory views communication as information transmission, i.e., a process of sending a message from point A to point B, just like delivering a parcel by post. It is a mechanistic, not systemic, process. This process of transmission can be overseen, but it is not governed or controlled the way a system exercises influence over its behavior when communicating with its environment. While one can hardly speak about an information source, a transmitter, a channel, and a receiver forming a communication system, no one will argue that the goal of the transmission model of communication is "to map the flow of information *through systems*" (Craig, 1999, p. 127; emphasis added).

Communication as information transmission is not the same as the (systemic) activity of the central nervous system in humans. It is no accident that cybernetics drew the attention of psychologists and biologists, among others, while Information Theory is a matter of mathematics and engineering. Also, the goal of Information Theory is to show how communication can be efficiently conducted by compressing information; in this sense, it has an inward thrust. Cybernetics, however, presents communication as an information-processing mechanism that generates behavior toward a specified goal; in this sense, it is oriented toward an outside environment.

Thus, Information Theory presents communication as a one-way causal linear chain. Based on this view, many communication practices (as well as studies of communication) "continue to have cultural currency" (Craig, 1999, p. 127). At the same time, an inherent limitation of this linear cause-and-effect conceptualization of communication is overcome by cybernetics. This linear chain begins with an information source that is a 'point of no return', in the sense that no information comes back to it: once a message is sent, it is gone. And "any cyberneticist knows that such a one way communication channel lacks feedback and cannot behave 'intelligently'" (Wilson, 1988). Communication, therefore, is understood by cybernetics not as a chain but a loop.

Feedback loops originated in the ancient worlds, used by the Greeks and Arabs to control such devices as water clocks, oil lamps and the level of water in tanks (Bissell, 2009, p. 53). However, "it was not until the 1930s and 1940s . . . that the feedback loop was explicitly theorized as a flow of information" (Hayles, 1999, p. 8), used to design and control high-performance systems such as anti-aircraft weapons during WWII.

Feedback is any kind of signal that tells the source about the outcome of communication, i.e., whether the goal has or has not been reached. Feedback thus is information fed back into the system. As stated earlier, communication systems are characterized by purposeful behavior, i.e., designed and controlled with respect to a certain aim. Feedback is a central concept in cybernetics because it allows a system to compare the expected (designed) performance with the actual performance. If the difference between the expected and actual performances is decreasing, the information about it is known as negative feedback; if it is increasing, is is known as positive feedback. While cybernetics initially focused on negative feedback, a communication system needs to constantly balance both positive and negative feedback with respect to its certain aim.

Any difference between the expected performance and the actual performance of a system is meaningful: this information, fed back into the system, means that it must modify the original design. It is this flow of information that a system uses as a means of controlling itself. It is in this light that we must understand the well-known definition of information by Gregory Bateson: "what we mean by information – the elementary unit of information – is a difference which makes a difference" (Bateson, 1972, p. 453). Thus, control and communication go together and form the essence of cybernetics: it is no accident that Wiener put these three words in the title of his famous book (1948).

It should be emphasized that feedback must not be identified with constantly going through the same motion, i.e., reverting to the same pre-existing state. Information that returns to the source generates a new state, depending on the type of feedback (positive or negative); as a result, a system continuously changes. This way, a system explores and controls its communication with the environment: "in this regard, the hermeneutic circle might be viewed as a dynamic feedback loop that continually cycles" (Gould, 2003, p. 160).

Thus, the conceptualization of communication as a circular process allows for the explanation of self-generated properties in a system (Krippendorff, 1994). This conceptualization is different from a linear view of communication as a step-by-step process of transmitting information, which never returns to the source. Cybernetics provides a more complex view of communication than Information Theory: the latter only provides a basic framework for the former but cannot shed any new light on it. Cybernetics, however, being a higher-level view, allows one to take a new look at communication theorized as information transmission. This way, when one reexamines traditional research topics in communication, from mass communication to interpersonal influence, it appears that most linear processes of communication that have been studied are in fact embedded in larger circular flows and stem from arbitrary cuts of these flows.

*(Krippendorff, 1994, p. 61)*

To show how such processes are not isolated from information flows on a larger scale requires a change in approach to communication from a linear cause-and-effect view to a systemic view.

## 3.1. In the Eyes of the Beholders

Communication is often defined as the exchange (or transmission) of information (or meanings). Understood this way, all it takes for communication to occur is an interaction between two people with (supposedly) some information or meanings inside their heads. The problem with this conceptualization is that 'information' and 'meaning' are not operationally defined. It must be noted that sometimes transmission of information is identified with the delivery of message and called 'operationalization' (Harper, 1979). However, what is meant here is 'operation', i.e., an act or manner of functioning. 'Operationalization' includes 'operation' and refers to an act (operation) of defining a phenomenon that is not distinguishable and measurable, as such, though other phenomena point to its existence. Clearly, 'information' and 'meaning' are such phenomena. Meanwhile, "to operationalize these notions with the help of public criteria so as to make them investigable also by an outside observer would require the use of communication as the primary concept" (Sfard, 2008, p. 86). This cannot be done if we focus only on a pair of communicating individuals: they can see each other, while observation presupposes a meta-level – rising above the situation of interaction, as it were, and considering it in a more detached manner. To that end, we must focus on the "phenomena that are noticeable only at the level of the collective as a whole and become invisible when the focus shifts to individuals" (Sfard, 2008, p. 86). In other words, observation truly applies to group communication; it is at this level that cybernetics operates.

Every thing, of course, is 'the thing-in-itself', to use Kant's term: it cannot be known directly as we can only deal with a phenomenon as it manifests itself. Such appearances are always mediated and so can be observed indirectly. For instance, when "somebody observes the Moon through a telescope, . . . it is the object of the observation, mediated by the real image projected by the object glass in the interior of the telescope, and by the retinal image of the observer" (Frege, 1993, p. 26). We cannot be completely sure whether that thing really exists (perhaps it is just a piece of dirt on the lens of the telescope). And yet, "it is still objective, inasmuch as it can be used by several observers" (ibid.). The more often it is observed and the more observers are involved in this process, the more objective it appears. Frege notes that this way an idea itself can be taken as an object, as well, adding: "But to pursue this would take us too far afield" (Frege, 1993, p. 27). It can be mentioned that Charles S. Peirce did pursue this in his view of communication as continuous semiosis where an interpretant becomes a new object.

Thus, communication cannot be theorized from the cybernetic perspective without using the concept of observer. Based on this concept, two main orders of cybernetics are usually identified.

### 3.1.1. Observed Systems

In first-order cybernetics; the observer treats a communication system as objectively given and observes its dynamics from outside of the system. This classical view of observation is at the basis of the scientific method; if desired (by the observer), observation can be taken further toward the testing and manipulation of the system, i.e., experimenting with it to reach the observer's goal. The focus of first-order cybernetics, though, is on explaining and describing the goal of the system itself. As an example, we can imagine an alien using a telescope to observe the communication of the Earth's human inhabitants. While "the alien observer cannot possibly see any 'meanings' or 'information' passed from one person to another" (Sfard, 2008, p. 86), the observer can distinguish between their actions, such as gestures, and describe distinct patterns of human communication. This, of course, will provide a 'thin' description, using Clifford Geertz' term, i.e., superficial and lacking interpretive depth.

The closer the observer gets to the system observed, though, the 'thicker' the description becomes; an example would be that of human social interaction observed by the human observer who does not have to use a telescope and who understands the human language, etc. This way, the (cybernetic) description can provide a clarification of the formal aspects of relationships, using such concepts as organization, complexity, hierarchy, etc.

We find an example of such conceptual clarification in one of the most well-known books in communication theory – *Pragmatics of Human Communication: A Study of Interactional Patterns, Pathologies and Paradoxes* (Watzlawick et al., 1967). One might be led to believe that, since the book deals with interactional patterns of human communication, its approach is humanistic rather than scientific; however, this is not the case, which becomes clear early in the book where in the section entitled 'The Frame of Reference', the authors present such key concepts as 'information', 'information exchange', 'feedback', etc. Also, communication in the book is conceptualized as observable behavior; often, it is given in quotes. This approach to communication is further elaborated in a paper written by two authors of the book – Paul Watzlawick & Janet Beavin (1967). (The third author, Don D. Jackson, was an M.D. who provided his expertise on the issues of psychotherapy as they related to communication). In their paper, Watzlawick and Beavin state that their approach "to the study of human interaction . . . is based on the assumption that *communication* is synonymous with what is observable in such interaction" (Watzlawick & Beavin, 1967, p. 4). They also note the importance of interpretation in the interactional context, adding that it is difficult "to integrate with the investigator's . . . more monadic interpretation" (ibid.). Finally, they admit that, in any case, "such considerations take us beyond the aims of this paper" (ibid.). Thus, their aim is clearly to study interactional patterns of human communication from a scientific (cybernetic) perspective.

In their paper, Watzlawick and Beavin sympathetically quote Ray L. Birdwhistell, who emphasized that communication must be understood as a system, not as "a simple model of action and reaction, however complexly stated" (Birdwhistell, 1959, p. 104). Immediately after that, however, they write: "Herein our focus will be on dyadic, in-person communication, in which the cues exchanged emanate directly from the voice, the body, or the immediate context" (Watzlawick & Beavin, 1967, p. 4). They also say that they use the term pragmatics to refer to "an interpersonal relation" (ibid.), yet quote cases of social communication dynamics, e.g., experiments on independence and submission to group pressures. Also, they say that they try to avoid 'sender-receiver' language in order "to be able to focus on a reciprocal process in which *both (or all)* persons act and react, 'receive' and 'send'" (ibid.; emphasis added).

Herein lies a problem: on the one hand, they want to follow Birdwhistell's call for understanding communication as a system, while, on the other hand, they focus on dyadic communication, conceptualizing pragmatics as referring only to 'an interpersonal relation'. In other words, there is an internal contradiction in their approach to communication. This may explain, in part, why the Interactional Theory, associated with Watzlawick et al., is often presented within the framework of interpersonal communication. For instance, we read that *Pragmatics of Human Communication* "laid out an approach to interpersonal communication" (Courtright, 2007, p. 312) and that the book "had a profound effect on the subsequent study of interpersonal communication" (Knapp et al., 2002, p. 3). Elsewhere, however, we read that the authors' view of communication "was grounded in systems thinking" and that their book "was intended to focus on group interaction – and particularly family interaction with behavioral pathologies" (Dainton & Zelley, 2010, p. 81). The latter view is more consistent with the approach to communication presented in Watzlawick et al. (1967), despite some internal contradictions. A strictly cybernetic view of communication would be focused on group dynamics, rather than interpersonal interactions; this requires discussing interrelationships, rather than relationships, i.e., connections not just between two but among several individuals (or all).

### 3.1.2. Observing Systems

First-order cybernetics conceptualizes the observer as being outside the observed communication system. It seems that the information flowing from the system to the observer is completely objective and can be described 'the way it is'. However, Heinz von Foerster demonstrates the nonsensicality of this principle because "if the properties of the observer (namely to observe and describe) are eliminated, there is nothing left; no observation, no description" (2003, p. 289). Even without being so radical and eliminating the properties of the observer, there is always something that the observer cannot observe. Taking the example of the point of the retina where all fibers leading from the eye's light-sensitive surface converge to form the optic nerve, von Foerster notes that there is localized blindness in our visual field that "is not perceived at all, that is, neither as something present, nor as something absent" (ibid.). Or, as he put it, "We do not see that we do not see" (2003, p. 284) (Figure 8.5). If that is the case, there is always something missing in our observation, and we do not simply describe reality but construct it by bringing in a piece of our subjectivity. In other words, objectivity is a subject's delusion that "the

**Figure 8.5**   We do not see that we do not see. Image created by the authors.

properties of the observer shall not enter the description of his observations" (von Foerster, 2003, p. 288).

Thus, the observer does not exist in isolation from the system observed;
rather, the observer is a part of the system. In this sense, "systems that include
their own observers are essentially social systems. For example, a society . . .
consists of human individuals who observe each other and communicate
with each other about their observations" (Krippendorf, 1994, p. 63). This
view of communication is usually associated with Heinz von Foerster and
known as second-order cybernetics, showing how the principles of cybernetics apply to those who develop those principles. Von Foerster's ideas
are presented in his book *Observing Systems* (1981); the title is syntactically
ambivalent suggesting that, just as the observer can observe the system, the
observer can be observed by the system as well. When asked in an interview
to give the shortest description of the distinction between first-order cybernetics and second-order cybernetics, von Foerster formulated it as follows:
"first-order cybernetics is the cybernetics of observed systems, while second-
order cybernetics is the cybernetics of observing systems" (2003, p. 303).

That first-order cybernetics adhered to the principle of objectivity can be
justified, "and this justification was fear; fear that paradoxes would arise

when the observers were allowed to enter the universe of their observations" (von Foerster, 2003, p. 289). Social systems are inherently paradoxical because people are both observers and observed, in constant communication with one another. On the one hand, one aims at describing objectively whatever is observed, but, on the other hand, what is observed happens to be another person (a subject) and the very act of observation/description changes that person's behavior; also, the observer him/herself is changed as a result of observation. Von Foerster explains the paradoxical nature of communication very well by discussing the famous 'Liar's Paradox':

> What do you do when I say 'I am a liar,' do you believe me? If you do, then I must have spoken the truth; but if I had spoken the truth, I must have lied, etc., etc. What is the problem here? Lying? No, the problem is 'I,' the shortest self-referential loop. When speaking about oneself, using 'I', magic is performed. *One creates oneself by creating oneself. 'I' is the operator who is the result of the operation.*
>
> *(2003, pp. 303–304; emphasis added)*

Thus, the fear of first-order cybernetics becomes even more clear: not only is one afraid to admit that, as an observer, s/he cannot observe everything ('We do not see that we do not see'), but one is also afraid to be admitted into the system. In both cases, our control over the system is impacted: eliminated in the first case, and severely undermined in the second. As we can see, second-order cybernetics introduces to theorizing of communication the "subversive idea of reflexivity" (Hayles, 1999, p. 10), i.e., forces oneself to face oneself not only as an observer but also as an observed, i.e., as part of a system.

Second-order cybernetics has profound epistemological and ethical implications. Epistemologically, we do not simply gain knowledge about the outside world that exists separately from us; rather, we learn about ourselves as a part of that world, i.e., how we are all participants in constant social interactions. Ethically, objectivity can be seen "as a popular device for avoiding responsibility" (von Foerster, 2003, p. 293). In other words, it is easier to position oneself as a detached observer who has no responsibility for what happens within the system observed. In the case of second-order cybernetics, however, there are only mutually constitutive interactions between oneself and the system; any boundary between is arbitrary. Thus, just as 'Observing Systems' applies to both the observer (observing systems) and the system (observing the observer), the phrase 'One creates oneself by creating oneself' can apply to both the observer and the system: in both cases, we deal with *one* whole.

Second-order cybernetics presents a view of communication radically different from first-order cybernetics. Instead of feedback loops, communication is now conceptualized as informationally closed: "no information crosses the boundary separating the system from its environment. We do not see a world 'out there' that exists apart from us. Rather, we see only what our systemic organization allows us to see" (Hayles, 1999, pp. 10–11). In this sense, information cannot be observed separately from the mutually constitutive interactions between the components of a system; one can say that it either no longer exists or is indistinguishable from the system, as such (Hayles, 1999, p. 11). Such radical views of communication are found in the Theory of Radical Constructivism and, above all, the work of Niklas Luhmann as one of its main representatives. For him, there is no information outside of communication and "only communication can communicate" (1994, p. 371). While such views can be criticized for their lack of heuristic value and even for their nihilism, they capture the inherently uncertain and contingent nature of communication perhaps best of all, teaching us humility and patience.

Sometimes, in addition to first- and second-order cybernetics, attempts are made to identify third-order cybernetics, dealing with the phenomenon of emergence, by which something can "evolve spontaneously in directions the programmer may not have anticipated" (Hayles, 1999, p. 11). This seems to contradict the very nature of cybernetics with its focus on control of communication. One can recall what von Foerster said when asked if we can go on to third-order cybernetics:

> Yes, you could. But it would not create anything new, because by ascending into 'second-order', as Aristotle would say, one has stepped into the circle that closes upon itself. One has stepped into the domain of concepts that apply to themselves.
>
> *(2003, p. 301)*

So, for now, all we have is ourselves. Should some artificial creatures start evolving by themselves and without our control, we'll then need another name for the field within which to study them (if we still can).

## 4. THE HUMAN PRECONDITION

As late the 1950s, some scientists, including Francis Crick – the co-discoverer of the structure of DNA – were still putting 'information' in quotation marks (Nunberg, 2011). Today, this is no longer the case in the natural sciences, let alone the social sciences and humanities. Now natural processes, intelligent machines and humans can all be described in terms of information processing. Information is now everywhere. James Gleick entitles his book *The Information* (2011), with the definite article suggesting the totality and omnipresence of information. In other words, information is now ubiquitous. If we recall that 'ubiquitous' originally referred to a Lutheran theological position maintaining the omnipresence of God, we could say that information is our God – the omnipresent and all-powerful prime mover.

If that is the case, it is tempting to say that communication, like everything else, is also information, albeit under a different name. Most scholars believe, however, that information is only "perpetually masked as communication" (Catt, 2011, p. 140) and that, to understand how humans communicate, "information is not enough" (Brier, 2008). Thus, a distinction is made between Information Theory and Communication Theory, with their fundamental difference found in the basic unit under study – signals vs. signs, respectively (Lanigan, 2013a). Information Theory is a theory of signal transmission from a source to a destination using a shared code. Signals are simply recognized, unlike signs that require interpretation to be understood. "We have a *signal* when we perceive the presence and absence of signs" (Lanigan, 2013a, p. 61); in other words, signals signal, and what they signal (or point to) is a difference between something and something else. In this sense, information has no concern for what it points to: what matters is recognizing differences and selecting a message among many, whatever its content may be.

Even when we look at quantum, not classical, Information Theory, it turns out that they are similar in one fundamental way: communication is still conceptualized in terms of signals or signal states available, with the qubit being the main unit of quantum information (Timpson, 2013). Information, therefore, is a linear procedure where a choice is made bit by bit (or qubit by qubit), and "a 'no' . . . answer gives just as much 'information' as a 'yes'. . . answer" (Lanigan, 2013a, p. 62). Information does not discriminate: it is the same for everyone.

Thus, each time signals are transmitted, information is sent and received, i.e., "a difference which makes a difference" (Bateson, 1972, p. 453) is recognized. Human language can be treated as a code, and communication can be presented as a procedure of signal transmission; however, it cannot be completely equated with a formal (syntactical) algorithm of choices that disregards meaning – both semantic and pragmatic. In other words, we cannot understand human communication without "determining to whom [i.e., pragmatic meaning] or what [i.e., semantic meaning] a difference makes a difference" (Brier, 2008, p. 179). It can be said that, if information is a difference which makes a difference, then meaning is a difference which makes a difference to some specific individuals in some specific circumstances. Slightly paraphrasing Frege, we could say that one need have no scruples in speaking simply of information, whereas in the case of meaning "one must, strictly speaking, add to whom it belongs and at what time" (1993, p. 26). When speaking of meaning as 'belonging' to someone, though, we must remember that it is never a fixed object but rather something constituted in the process of communication; in other words, that meaning is a social phenomenon. Meaning is making something known to someone else, even when 'someone else' is you. While it takes just one to send or receive information, it takes (at least) two to mean. By definition, meaning is what is shared by several or all individuals.

Besides the fundamental difference in the basic unit of study, Information Theory and Communication Theory can be contrasted in other terms, including creativity, memory, measurement, and materiality.

Communication can be conceptualized as information transfer only if all the available choices for creating messages are given as data. In this light, communication is understood either as a linear process of reducing uncertainty (Information Theory) or as dynamics within an operationally closed system (Cybernetics). In both cases, communication is reduced to making choices that can only signify a difference which makes a difference, leading to the next choice, etc.: "thus, signification 'informs' how to choose, not what a choice means" (Lanigan, 2013a, p. 63). As mentioned earlier, meaning is a social undertaking: it is making something known to someone else. Meaning, therefore, is always created in every act of communication; it is this creativity that cannot be adequately conceptualized simply as information transfer. Data is what can be clearly defined: only this way can it be operated upon, i.e., an act of selecting and sending certain data. While creativity is sometimes seen as information (McGavin, 1997), it cannot be equated just with making choices within a defined situation. The essence of creativity is not definition but what can be called 'infinition' – an infinite process of defining something that cannot be fully or precisely defined, an endless list of possible definitions. 'To infine' means to suggest many possible definitions and to recognize that all of them fail to define the complexity or fluidity of the sub-ject (Epstein, 2012, p. 112). One can say that, whereas information is always defined, meaning can only be infined.

Just as information can be defined, it can be recorded, stored, and retrieved, hence the importance of a computer's memory. However, recording, stor-ing, and retrieving information "is only part of what human beings do when they enter into a memorious state" (Casey, 2000, p. 2). Such a state is differ-ent from the binary state or the qubit state of superposition: it includes the meanings of care, thought and even mourning. It must be emphasized that memory is not the content of a container; it "is not so much a thing as an act, . . . a shared consciousness. . . . [M]emory is the social act of remembering. It is commemoration" (Hobart & Schiffman, 2000, p. 15). Thus, an operation of information retrieval is not the same as an act of commemoration that "binds together the community as a living entity rather than passively stor-ing information about it" (Hobart & Schiffman, 2000, p. 16). Information is passively recorded and retrieved while meaning is actively remembered and commemorated (Figure 8.6).

In the case of information, it is only possible to speak about records or archives (collections of stored data). In the case of meaning, one must speak about history – descriptive accounts of human experiences. The com-puter's memory, large as it may be, is not the same as a history that can only be meaningful when lived. Also, once information has been recorded and stored, it cannot be forgotten. It can be lost, e.g. when a flash disk is lost or destroyed, but it cannot be forgotten. In its turn, human "life in any true sense is absolutely impossible without forgetfulness" (Nietzsche, 1957, pp. 6–7). Attempts are being made, though, to redefine the true sense of life; an example is the 'Total Information Awareness' program, which, as the name suggests, was aimed at developing a total recall system drastically changing people's personal, social and political lives (later, the program was renamed to 'Terrorism Information Awareness', becoming the '*Partial* Total Information Awareness' program). It must be noted that 'awareness' means only having a perception or recognizing a difference between some-thing and something else; in other words, it applies only to information, as the name of the program suggests. However, if people were aware of every-thing going on around them, they would suffer from information overload. That is why, just as it is only human to err, it is human to be unaware (of something). More importantly, just as information is not enough, it is not enough to simply be aware because one must be aware of being aware and

**Figure 8.6**    ONET (Organization of National Ex-Servicemen and Women) 52nd
Annual mass and wreath-laying ceremony. Dublin, Ireland, 9 November
2013. Photograph by the Irish Defence Forces.

be able to meaningfully understand and represent this awareness: only then
can we communicate and not just send and receive information.

As mentioned earlier, information is but a choice made from all possibilities
in a certain situation. Since it is a ratio between what is selected (a message)
and what could have been selected, information is measurable. Once coded
and measured, information then can be used in various technologies, e.g.
biometrics, aimed at fixing our identities so that they can be authenticated
(Martin & Whitley, 2013). Measuring information, however, is not simply
a matter of mathematical calculations, but also a meaningful action that

involves a joint decision; for instance, must we measure everything that can be measured, especially if "the ease of measuring may be inversely proportionate to the significance of what is measured" (Muller, 2018)? Moreover, we remember that error-free communication is mathematically impossible above a certain limit. Can such human concepts as 'love' or 'wonder' be measured? It is said that 'To err is human'. The second part of this phrase, as found in St. Augustine (*Sermons*, 164, 10.14), says: 'but to persist in error (out of pride) is diabolical.' Perhaps we should admit that such concepts as 'love' or 'wonder' are measureless: to try measuring them, and persist in that, would be diabolical.

Information is conceptualized as a non-substantial phenomenon – a difference that makes a difference. Hence, information theorists are not concerned with the material realization of information or the energy it requires. This is not to say, though, that energy and matter do not matter. Information may appear ethereal, but it can only be signified in the form of physical signals. We may find the freedom of information exhilarating, but we should remember that "within limits we are all free to say what we think; it is only the channels to the audience that cost money" (Wilden, 2013, p. 211). By the same token, while we can talk about information without any concern for its material realization, we should not forget that we can do so only because there is some medium, or intermediate substance, used for sending, receiving, storing and retrieving information. Also, that talking itself takes mental as well as physical effort. Thus, not only is matter in-formed; form is material-ized. In this light, the approach to communication "based on information theory is only functionalistic and does not have the capacity of encompassing meaning in a biological, not to say a human perspective" (Brier, 2003, p. 83). Information Theory focuses on how a series of signals functions, i.e., how it follows an algorithm. Communication Theory, in its turn, is "an account of how human beings . . . symbolize their interactive thinking, speaking, and bodily practices, i.e., behavior as culture" (Lanigan, 2013a, p. 63). Behavior or comportment is not the same as executing choices; it involves carrying oneself together with others, i.e. creating meaning together. Comportment is inherently interactive and intercorporeal: as mentioned in a previous chapter, meaning can be understood only by turning to one's speaking body.

So, while information is transmitted as signals, communication can only be experienced as meanings. Signal as indication of a certain state is coded, while meaning as symbolization of experience can only be (re)interpreted

in every situation of interaction. To equate communication and information would be to forget the uniqueness of communication and thus to forget
communication itself. "Rather than explaining communication into oblivion
by means of its ostensible identity with information, let us accept and appreciate the rich ambiguity of the *experience of communication*" (Catt, 2017,
p. 61; emphasis added). When Albert Einstein famously stated that information is not knowledge and that, to gain wisdom, we need experience, he was
effectively talking about the experience of communication. As experiences
are symbolized, i.e., accounted for, they form human history. Unlike data
that is recorded and stored, history is the living wisdom of all communication experiences, as witnessed by Greek *histōr*, meaning 'wise man, judge'.

Also, unlike information that explicitly requires a medium, the more immediate human experience, the more authentic and thus crucial it appears. In
this respect, for example, "the immediacy of pleasure and pain is lost with any
attempt to represent them discursively" (Cascardi, 1999, p. 17). Here, too,
Kant's view of art can be mentioned, representing "potentially threatening
kinds of experiences – including the 'wonder' and 'fear' that are the strongest forms of the pleasure and pain" (Cascardi, 1999, p. 107). Of course, we
cannot forget that which moves the sun and the other stars, i.e., love as pure
experience. In the words of Ludwig Feuerbach, "love should be immediate,
. . . only as such is it love" (1881, p. 268). The more immediate and pure love
is, the more likely to fail are the attempts at representing it discursively. One
can't give a rationally mediated account of love: just like a tautology, love is
true in every possible interpretation. As Lucetta says in Shakespeare's *The
Two Gentlemen of Verona*, "I have no other but a woman's reason; I think
him so because I think him so". It is through such human experiences as
pain, wonder, fear and love that communication reveals its ethical nature.
There is nothing ethical or unethical about information. So-called 'information ethics' deals with the behavioral rules about what is allowed or not to
be communicated in a society (Capurro, 2013). In other words, while it's
labeled 'information ethics', it is in fact the realm of communication ethics,
which is not surprising: ethics cannot not be a communication issue.

Although communication cannot be reduced to signal transmission, the
importance of information, as well as Information Theory, cannot be over-
stated. These ideas were inspired by the ideals of freedom, equality, reason
and progress. In this sense, "the post-World War II information of information theory is . . . a kind of post-Enlightenment pragmatism" (Schleifer,
2000, p. 85). In a way, the goal of the information theorists was not to denigrate

humans to the level of machines, but to raise machines up to the level of humans, thus demonstrating the power of human thought. For that purpose, information appears perfect: it is neutral and in principle available to all. Information is what can be used in the form of signals, i.e., recorded, stored, sent and received, independent of context: this can be done by anyone anywhere without any discrimination. However, it is important to emphasize that this can be done only if the intentions are clear and independent of the initial conditions (von Foerster 1995). This, of course, is a crucial caveat: in human communication, intentions are not always clear (even to the speaker him/herself), and actions are often taken on one condition or another. Because of this, we cannot *give* a complete account of something – we can only *take* it into account. To put it another way, we cannot simply control – we can only control *for*. Shannon and Wiener understood this very well. Shannon wrote: "It will be all too easy for our somewhat artificial prosperity to collapse overnight when it is realized that the use of a few exciting words like information, entropy, redundancy, do not solve all our problems" (Shannon, 1956, p. 3). And in his editorial in a volume of the *IRE Transactions on Information Theory*, Wiener wrote this: "I am pleading in this editorial that Information Theory . . . return to the point of view from which it originated: that of the general statistical concept of communication" (Wiener, 1956, p. 48). Even more than Shannon, perhaps due to his systems thinking, Wiener realized that communication can be used to manipulate and exploit people. "To make his views known on this, he wrote a passionately expressed book, *The Human Use of Human Beings*, which deplored nonegalitarian trends in a capitalist society. This was hardly read, while *Cybernetics* became an international bestseller" (Aleksander, 2001, p. 35). It is important not to forget that "Wiener saw himself as providing a triple synthesis of the probabilistic revolution in physics, an 'Augustinian' metaphysics and philosophy of science, and a theory of communication inspired by but going beyond mathematical communication theory" (Peters & Peters, 2016, p. 161).

So, the thinkers behind the ideas of Information Theory and Cybernetics clearly saw both their potential and their limitations (or dangers). That does not mean, though, that they were ready to give up their ideas and dismantle their theories; for them, information is a fundamental concept. Indeed, when it is stated that "information is not enough" (Brier, 2008), it must be emphasized that we still cannot do without information: it is just not enough, e.g., to conceptualize knowledge or understanding. There is no message without information, and so "information is a precondition for knowledge acquisition" (Dousa & Ibekwe-SanJuan, 2014, p. 1) and "information is a necessary condition for understanding" (Adriaans, 2012). Even wisdom requires information that is meaningfully fleshed out in various situations of human communication.

Message, however, is not the same as information, understood as a parcel to be sent and received. Message is a communicative act of in-forming, i.e., a releasing something, a letting something go, a setting something at liberty. It cannot take place in a vacuum, completely independent of any context, simply because we cannot remove ourselves from communication. Hence it is ourselves who are set free, by ourselves, in every act of communication. While it may appear to be far removed from human affairs, the role of information cannot in fact be overestimated. Information is not simply what challenges a channel's capacity; it is what tests us. Every act of in-forming is a test of whether "human beings could be trusted with freedom" (Hayles, 1999, p. 7). Each time we pass this test, we keep entropy at bay. In this sense, as Neil deGrasse Tyson, a famous American astrophysicist, has said, "all information is good, even when it is bad".

# 9

# The Wonder of Community

Key concepts:

Animality, becoming-animal, being-in-common, biopolitics, common being, community-in-the-making, ecology, ethics, gift, imagined communities, interspecies communication, hospitality, monstrosity, morality, natural community, life, the post-human.

Key names:

Aristotle, Giorgio Agamben, Benedict Anderson, Émile Benveniste, Martin Buber, Judith Butler, Gilles Deleuze, Jacques Derrida, John Dewey, Robert Esposito, Michel Foucault, Félix Guattari, Edmund Husserl, Karl Marx, George Herbert Mead, Jacques Lacan, Bruno Latour, Alphonso Lingis, Jean-Luc Nancy, Maurice Merleau-Ponty, John Peters, Plato, Frans de Waal, Ludwig Wittgenstein.

## 1. COMMUNITY AS LIKEMINDEDNESS

The notion of community has endured throughout many centuries. In the Western tradition, it can be found in the rise of the ancient Greek polis

(Starr, 1986), the oratory and politics of republican Rome (Steel & van der Blom, 2013), visions of community in the post-Roman world (Pohl et al., 2012), the construction of communities in the Middle Ages (Corradini et al., 2003), the idea of community in the Renaissance (Muir, 2002) and modernity (Parker & Bentley, 2007) when the idea of community became especially influential due to the insecure conditions of modern society (Delanty, 2013).

Today the term 'community' is used very frequently, by itself or combined with other words in various contexts, e.g. 'community health', 'community care', 'community charge', 'sense of community', 'community activism', 'community arts', 'community sports', 'community policing', 'community safety', 'community planning', 'community spirit', 'community building', etc. (Blackshaw, 2010). While used very frequently, the term 'community' is problematized and explicated much less often. Let us look at how community is conceptualized.

First of all, 'community' traditionally refers to a group of people actively engaged with one another in communicative practices (Figure 9.1).

**Figure 9.1**   Women from the Lord Howe Settlement community march in the opening parade for the campaign '16 Days of Activism Against Gender Based Violence'. Honiara, Solomon Islands. Photo by UN Women/ Marni Gilbert.

Here is one typical definition of community: "a *group* of *people* who are socially interdependent, who participate together in discussion and decision-making, and who share certain practices" (Bellah et al., 1985, p. 333). Even the so-called 'imagined communities' (Anderson, 2016) are theorized as a group of people who will never be able to see all of their fellow-members, as in the case of a nation, yet can still form in their minds the image of shared identity and practices.

Second, following Aristotle, community is seen as a group of people who divide political duties and contribute to the whole through functional role division; in this sense, a civic duty of every person is the "preservation of the *community* (*hē sōtēria tēs koinōnias*)" (*Politics*, III.4, 1276b28–31). This sense of community is still visible in the English word 'municipal' if we recall the Latin root of the word 'community' – *munus*, meaning the obligatory exchange with others as social duty.

Third, community can also refer to a group of 'political animals' held together by speech, understood as logos, which makes it possible for people to understand themselves "as citizens of a community held together by substantive bonds" (Poulakos, 1997, p. 34). According to Aristotle, unlike herd animals (*zōa agelaia*), or even 'social animals' (*zōa koinōnikē*), speech allows humans to coordinate and perform different functions toward a common end (Depew & Peters, 2001). The link between community and participation in shared communicative acts finds its manifestation in the well-known ritual view of communication, which shows how persons are drawn together "in fellowship and commonality" (Carey, 1989, p. 6).

Fourth, while communication is the means by which people are drawn together in a community, its common end is most often conceptualized as the "substance that is produced by their union" (Esposito, 2010, p. 2). This substance represents the essence or the indispensable quality which underlies and determines the existence of community. It is with such essence in mind that people create communities; for instance, it is asserted that "building of community is a religious task in the fundamental sense that religion is the art and discipline of dealing with the problems of relationship" (Jordan, 2003, p. 56). Once the plan has been fulfilled and a community built, it then becomes a property belonging to all members of a group – "the possession of a common faith" (Carey, 1989, p. 18). This view is sometimes referred to as "the proprietary conception of community" (Esposito, 2010, p. 1).

Fifth, the concept of community carries a certain evaluative weight. What is usually underscored is "the goodness of communication and community" (Shepherd & Rothenbuhler, 2001, p. xi). Raymond Williams, who chose 'community' as one of the keywords for his 'Vocabulary of Culture and Society' more than four decades ago, stated that it is "the warmly persuasive word" that "seems never to be used unfavourably" (Williams, 1976, p. 76). This conceptualization goes back to Aristotle, who noted that "every community is established for the sake of some good" (*Politics*, I.1, 1252a2–3). The positive valence and socially desirable qualities prevent it from categorizing ill-intentioned groups such as gangs or mafia as 'communities': here, it is more appropriate to speak about networks or organized crime groups or syndicates.

Sixth, and most importantly, a community must have something that is common and the same for each of its members. In the words of John Dewey:

> Men live in a community in virtue of the things which they have in common; and communication is the way in which they come to possess things in common. What they must have in common . . . are aims, beliefs, aspirations, knowledge – a common understanding – like-mindedness as the sociologists say.
>
> *(Dewey, 1980, p. 7)*

Herein, however, lies a possibility of seeing community in a very different light: "This is community that is cold: the summer of communality is an illusion, and so is warmth between people; the reality is that – like winter – community attempts to freeze-frame everything" (Blackshaw, 2010, p. 22). In this view, life is forced "into a sort of cage where not only our freedom gets lost but also the very meaning of our existence – that opening of existence outside itself that takes the name of *communitas*" (Esposito, 2013b, p. 85). Taken to its extreme, this view goes beyond noting the slipperiness of the notion of community as something too vague (Rapport & Amit, 2002, p. 13) or expressing skepticism about community as "a warm and cosy place" (Delanty, 2003, p. 118). For instance, the German philosopher Helmut Plessner in *The Limits of Community* (1999) "claimed that the idea of community is a dangerous one" (Plessner, 1999, p. 53) and that "community was an overvalued ideal and contained a latent authoritarianism" (Delanty, 2003, p. 22). According to Jacques Derrida, "the privilege granted to unity, to totality, to organic ensembles, to community as a homogenized whole – this is a danger – . . . for ethics, for politics" (1997: 13). This view addresses "the dark side of community" (Blackshaw, 2010, p. 22) or the danger of communities where "we find only ourselves" (Lingis, 1994, p. 6). It is no surprise, then, that there is another approach to community, which views it as a disruption and creation of new relationships.

## 2. 'LET US BEGIN BY THE IMPOSSIBLE'

The approach deconstructing the traditional conceptualization of community has a post-modern rather than modern orientation. Such thinkers as Jean-Luc Nancy, Giorgio Agamben, Maurice Blanchot, and Roberto Esposito argue that community cannot be identified with the essential substance possessed by a group of likeminded people. They all attempt to theorize how it may be possible to go beyond a 'common being', subsumed under a shared essence, and live together in terms of 'being-in-common'. In a way, they all strive to decenter and dis-contain community (Bird, 2017)

For instance, Jean-Luc Nancy does not view community as a shared goal or essence, achieved through work. For him, "a community is not a project of fusion, or in some general way a productive or operative project – nor is it a project at all" (Nancy, 1991, p. 15). In this view, community can't be made, produced, or instituted. Instead, community is 'inoperative' – a spontaneous exposure of singular beings to one another that communicate by not communing: "These places of *communication* are no longer places of fusion, even though in them one passes from one to the other; they are defined and exposed by their dislocation" (Nancy, 1991, p. 25). It is at such limits of communication that 'being-in-common' is experienced.

In a similar fashion, Judith Butler finds any community based on nation, language, territory, etc. to be exclusionary: its members may be protected at the expense of those who do not belong. She finds 'being-in-common' not in a certain essence but in the human condition of precariousness. Butler conceptualizes community in terms of vulnerability, loss and mourning, which applies to anyone instead of being limited to members of a bounded group. This "way of imagining community, one in which we are alike only in having this condition" (Butler, 2003, p. 16) is presented as more realistic and reveals its contingent nature.

Roberto Esposito takes this line of thinking further: for him, "what else is the 'common' if not . . . that which does not belong to anyone but instead is general, anonymous, indeterminate; that is not determined by essence . . .?"

(2013, pp. 45–46). In this sense, community is not so much what persons own as what they owe: "community takes the form of a collective debt that is owed to itself" (Bird & Short, 2015, p. 9). Community, therefore, reflects an unpayable debt: as Vanessa Lemm puts it, "community is a debt, a flaw, a lack. From this perspective, what we have in common by necessity is the impossibility of realizing community" (Lemm, 2013, p. 3).

Thus, community is theorized not as a certain substance owned by everyone but as the lack of 'one's own'. Just as we appreciate a community for providing a sense of security because we interact only with those whom we recognize as being 'like us', people feel "the deep urge for communication . . . [that is,] for contact with beings unlike ourselves" (Lingis, 2009, p. 121). In that respect, community appears as a process of "exposing oneself to expenditure at a loss, to sacrifice, . . . to forces and powers outside oneself" (Lingis, 1994, p. 12). Instead of being a mechanism of closure, community constantly embraces otherness and resists completion. While conceptualizing it as a debt and a lack, this approach still provides a constructive view of community, emphasizing its radical affirmation of life and an openness to difference. Without "a moment of wonder, of an openness to the newness and mystery of the other person, the creative energy of desire dissolves into indifference" (Young, 1997, p. 357) or turns into totalitarianism.

## 2.1. The Impossible Gift

The concept of community can be further theorized by turning to the origin of the word. 'Community' is derived from the Latin *munus*, and retains three of that word's possible meanings: 'debt', still visible in the English word 'remuneration'; 'public office', still visible in the English word 'municipal'; and 'gift', still visible in the English word 'munificent'. While the first two meanings do not cause any difficulty in interpretation as they clearly apply to community, the idea of gift-giving can be understood in two ways. Traditionally, the nature of gift-giving is seen as reciprocity, e.g. in the works of Marcel Mauss and Claude Lévi-Strauss. For some post-modern thinkers, however, if it is linked with exchange, there can be no pure or free gift. Instead of reciprocity underlying the gift economy, they see the principle of the gift in its gratuity (Esposito, 2010). The authentic gift consists in graciousness, done freely and without pay. Although the pure gift is impossible, this idea can break the cyclicality of economic rationality, which turns gifts into private property which circulates through an exchange of equivalents (Derrida, 1992). The pure gift defies exactness and is based on care. If people are motivated by the spirit of such a pure gift, then those who give will also receive free gifts from others: the pure gift is the gift that keeps on giving. It is such gift-giving that creates community.

## 2.2. The Impossible Hospitality

One more aspect of community needs to be examined, for, as Émile Benveniste points out, "an obvious connection joins the notion of the gift to that of hospitality" (Benveniste, 1997, p. 36). Just as with gift, hospitality has very positive connotations. Yet, it always posits some kind of limit that can't be trespassed, so, in a way, it exhibits a characteristic of being inhospitable. Thus, just like gift, hospitality can be institutionalized and turned into a service. This side of hospitality is found in the 'tourism industry' (Ng, 2017) and addressed in 'hospitality studies' (Lashley, 2017) where communication is discussed in such terms as 'strategic processes within workplaces', 'effective organizational structure' and 'well-defined job responsibilities'.

There is, however, another understanding of hospitality – as the absolute obligation to accept the Other. Such authentic hospitality involves risk-taking and vulnerability, pushing the boundaries and breaking through all conditions of the political and the juridical (Figure 9.2).

While it is impossible and can have no legal or political status, the spirit of unconditional hospitality motivates acts of hospitality and creates community, just as the idea of the pure gift does. In the words of Derrida,

> without at least the thought of this pure and unconditional hospitality, of hospitality *itself*, we would have no concept of hospitality in general. . . Without this thought of pure hospitality (a thought that is also, in its own way, an experience), we would not even have the idea of the other, of the alterity of the other, that is, of someone who enters into our lives without having been invited. We would not even have the idea of love or of 'living together (*vivre ensemble*)' with the other in a way that is not a part of some totality or 'ensemble'.
>
> *(Borradori, 2003, p. 129)*

If community is conceptualized as a homogenized whole, Derrida sees this as a danger for ethics, which can be avoided if community is motivated by the spirit of unconditional hospitality; after all, "what would an 'ethics' be

**Figure 9.2**    *Hospitality of Barbarians to Pilgrims* by Gustave Doré (1832–1883).
From J. P. Boyd, *Story of the Crusades* (P. W. Ziegler & Co.:
Philadelphia & St. Louis, 1892), p. 13.

without hospitality?" (Derrida, 2000, p. 129). On a related note, it is often mentioned how the study of communication suffers from an inherent identity crisis (Donsbach, 2006, p. 439). Another way to look at it, though, would be to emphasize its "virtue of hospitality" (Peters, 2012, p. 506). Just like gift-giving and hospitality, the study of communication is both impossible and necessary.

The conceptualization of community as openness to otherness which resists completion (and thus appears impossible) is normative. Just as the world is "a projection of the ideals created by the community" (Durkheim, 2009, p. 95), the concept of community itself is created by the ideal. Paraphrasing Derrida, one can ask: where would the real world be without the ideals, community being one of them? When Derrida says, "Let us begin by the impossible" (Derrida, 1997a, p. 248), this can apply to the motivating spirit of community.

## 2.3. Community in-the-Making

Thus, community can be conceptualized in two main ways.

In the traditional view, community is understood as a certain substance produced by the union of people who all share it as their common possession. Here, the emphasis is on sameness achieved through operative activity in which people consciously engage: only if "they were all cognizant of the common end and all interested in it, then they would form a community" (Dewey, 1980, p. 8). In the post-modern view, community is conceptualized as disruption and creation of new relationships by exposure to otherness. Here, the emphasis is on difference that can be understood only in terms of lack, vulnerability, and contingency.

These two views may lead to two extremes. "At one extreme it can be used to mean an all-embracing totalistic community of organic unity, which suffocates or annihilates difference" (Schwarzmantel, 2007, p. 461). In other words, taken to its extreme, this view leads to totality when individuality is eliminated and we end up with nothing but sameness and a complete lack of difference. "At the other extreme community can refer to much looser and evanescent forms of association" (Schwarzmantel, 2007, p. 461). When the second view is taken to its extreme, it leads to a complete lack of sameness, i.e., the only sameness a community has is its lack of sameness: in other words, community is 'inoperative', it is nothing but difference. As Nancy puts it, "community does not consist of anything other than the communication of 'singular beings,' which exist as such only through communication" (1991, p. 159).

We can see that each of these two views, taken separately and to its extreme, does not do justice to the nature of community. However, within each view, the other one is latently present. The traditional view foregrounds sameness while otherness is present in the background, i.e., community is theorized as the same identity shared by different individuals. The postmodern view foregrounds otherness while sameness is present in the background, i.e., community is theorized as different individuals sharing the same identity. Community, thus, is but a relation (Esposito, 2010), i.e., the Self being in relationship with the Other. Community can be close-knit or loose-knit but it is always a matter of 'being-with'. Community, therefore, always remains the same by being other than itself. Community never simply 'is' but always 'is-in-the-making' because "community . . . offers the opportunity to be otherwise" (Greene, 1995, p. 39).

It is important to remember that community affiliation can never be completed as 'a task project', since it is always in-the-making and "community-in-the-making includes the possibilities of a future-not-yet, where . . . possibility [is meant] . . . in a phenomenological sense, that which is phenomenally possible in excess over the calculable and explainable in terms of causes and present conditions" (Roth, 2009, p. 30). The possibility of community is contingent on the thought of the pure or impossible gift and hospitality. In the words of Derrida, "when the impossible makes itself possible, the event takes place (possibility of the impossible)" (2005, p. 90). Thus, there is a relation between the impossible and the possible that can be represented by linking the two words into one with a slash and showing its dual nature: im/possible. The slash shows the nature of community as it divides and connects.

## 3. 'BECOMING-ANIMAL'

As we saw earlier, community is traditionally understood as a group of people who form a unified identity; community, therefore, is implicitly *human* community. To understand what a community is is to answer "the question how individuals . . . come to be connected in just those ways which give human communities traits so different from those which mark assemblies of electrons, unions of trees in forests, swarms of insects, herds of sheep, and constellations of stars" (Dewey, 1984, p. 250). The separation of the human and the non-human is deeply entrenched. Humans are seen as standing apart from the physical and biological world because of their reflective capacity, among other things. In its turn, as Bruno Latour puts it, "'nature' is the unifying definition of 'non-human'" (Barron, 2003, p. 98).

However, the privileged ontological status of humans is being questioned more and more often. It is now stated that "the notion that there is something unique, essential, and universal about 'man' cannot be sustained, given that all the qualities that allegedly set humanity apart (such as language, reason, morality, art, altruism, technology) occur in the nonhuman world" (Weinstein & Colebrook, 2017, p. xx). Whether one agrees with this statement or not, the boundaries between the human and the non-human are blurred rather than clear-cut. Both human beings and non-human beings are living and sentient organisms; as such, they "are not just in the world, *they are of the world*, and this precisely because they are subjects and objects – perceiving and being perceived – at the same time" (Arendt, 1978, p. 20; emphasis added). The boundaries between the human and the non-human are inherently blurred because 'life' is first of all a concept. Life is not something that can be discovered by the natural sciences; rather, we must define what constitutes life, which is then presupposed by all, including natural sciences (Toadvine, 2015).

Our approach to community, therefore, must not be "just confined to the human but . . . concerned with the effects of our entanglements *with other kinds of living selves*" (Kohn, 2013, p. 4, emphasis added). Community cannot be conceptualized by separating the human and the non-human. As Maurice Merleau-Ponty reminds us, "for man, everything is constructed and everything is natural. . . everything breaks away from animal life and everything owes something to mere biological being" (Merleau-Ponty, 1962, p. 195). The 'animal' here must not be equated only with actual animals: "the animal . . . means above all multiplicity, plurality, assemblage with what surrounds us and with what always dwells inside us" (Esposito, 2012, p. 150). In this sense, community is never purely human, it is always "becoming-animal" (Deleuze & Guattari, 2007). This not only expands the scope of the concept of community but also makes it fluid and open-ended, for it

> brings into relationship completely heterogeneous terms – like a human being, an animal, and a micro-organism; but even a tree, a season, and an atmosphere: because what matters in the becoming-animal, even before its relationship with the animal, is especially the becoming of a life that only individuates itself by breaking the chains and prohibitions, the barriers and boundaries, that the human has etched within it.
> *(Esposito, 2012, p. 150)*

Let us look first at the relationship of the human with the animal taken literally – in the zoological sense.

### 3.1. Humans and Other Animals

The human interest in animals goes back thousands of years: in the oldest cave paintings we see animals, depicted in great detail, next to matchstick-style human hunters (Hurn, 2012). Although 'human' goes back to the Proto-Indo-European root *(dh)ghomon-*, meaning 'earthling, earthly being', as opposed to the gods, it is in opposition to animals that humans are most often conceptualized.

The ability of humans to identify with one another is usually attributed to our 'mindedness' and language competence. As discussed earlier, these two attributes behind human intersubjectivity are brought together in the theory of Symbolic Interactionism, which argues that the individual sense of 'self' arises through the process of using language symbols. According to George Herbert Mead, animals do not use language – they are only engaged in a 'conversation of gestures' because "the animal has no mind, no thought, and hence there is no meaning here in the significant or self-conscious sense" (Mead, 1964, p. 136).

This view is not universally shared, however. It is quite common to speak about the language of animals (Hart, 2014) – from chimpanzees to dolphins to dogs to crows. Some even state that rhetoric must be seen as an adaptive product of biology and culture and that animals practice rhetoric because their behavior is aimed at affecting others (Parrish, 2014). While others may find this statement too radical, clearly not all animal behavior can be explained by reflexes and conditioning: behaviors extending beyond the here-and-now are labelled 'emergent'. Those who still think of language as a specific human activity and are skeptical that it can be found in any species but humans, admit the existence of animal *communication*, which "is not language, although language can be used to communicate" (Deely, 2001, p. 5). Some even argue that all the major functions of communication proposed by Roman Jakobson – expressive, conative, phatic, referential, metalinguistic and poetic – can be applied by analogy in zoosemiotic contexts (Martinelli, 2017).

There is also a lot of evidence indicating that animals can consciously participate in intersubjective signal exchanges. As far as their cognitive abilities and social skills are concerned, animals exhibit cooperative behavior, self-recognition, triadic awareness, empathy, etc. According to Frans de Waal (2016), a famous primatologist and ethologist, there is no question whether animals are intelligent beings; rather, the question is whether we are smart enough to know how smart animals are.

Thus, when it comes to explaining animal behavior, the centrality of 'mindedness' as tied to language competence is questioned. Instead, animal behavior is conceptualized in terms of communication and "the interactional process of 'doing mind'" (Arluke & Sanders, 2009, p. xii). Just as the overall boundaries between the human and the non-human are blurred, there are intriguing commonalities between humans and other animals. We can recall how Aristotle noted that differences between humans and animals are more of degree than kind:

> In the great majority of animals there are traces of psychical qualities or attitudes, which qualities are more markedly differentiated in the case of human beings. For just as we pointed out resemblances in the physical organs, so in a number of animals we observe gentleness or fierceness, mildness or cross temper, courage, or timidity, fear or confidence, high spirit or low cunning, and, with regard to intelligence, something equivalent to sagacity. Some of these qualities in man, as compared with the corresponding qualities in animals, *differ only quantitatively: that is to say, a man has more or less of this quality, and an animal has more or less of some other*; other qualities in man are represented by analogous and not identical qualities: for instance, just as in man we find knowledge, wisdom, and sagacity, so in certain animals there exists some other natural potentiality akin to these.
>
> *(History of Animals, VIII.1, 588a18–31; emphasis added)*

Today, this view is supported by numerous scientific studies. As a result, we can speak about "the communicative behavior of non-human . . . communities" and see that "even on the animal level there exist patterns of signification which can, to a certain degree, be defined as cultural and social" (Eco, 1976, p. 9).

Thus, humans and other animals can form a community based on shared patterns of signification (Figure 9.3).

Ludwig Wittgenstein famously observed that "If a Lion could speak, we could not understand him" (1953, p. 223). Most likely, what Wittgenstein had in mind was that "to understand a species-specific utterance someone must be a specific part of the community" (Witzany, 2016, p. 42–43). However, the shared habits of behavior produced as a result of an embodied interspecies encounter can be seen as a 'language game', to use Wittgenstein's term. It is important to note that such language games are created by humans and animals together in the process of intersubjective experience. Here is, for example,

TWO PALS. THERE IS BETWEEN MAN AND DOG A KINSHIP OF SPIRIT THAT CANNOT BE DENIED.

**Figure 9.3**    *Two Pals.* From R. Dixon, *The Human Side of Animals* (Frederick A. Stokes: New York, 1918), facing p. 245. Image from the Biodiversity Heritage Library, contributed by the Library of Congress.

how Barbara Smuts describes such shared habits of behavior between her and her dog: "I can't explain how any of them came into being. Certainly, I did not invent them, and I don't think [Safi] did either. Rather, they developed spontaneously in the intersubjective space we inhabit together" (2001, p. 304). She goes on to say that these behaviors "simultaneously [reveal] a mutual past and an ongoing commitment to a common future in which the circle of shared experience and fellow feeling grows ever larger" (2001, p. 304). This is a good example of a community as 'being-in-common'.

In his exploration of the connections between animality and sovereignty, Derrida notes that what "so-called human living beings and so-called animal living beings . . . have in common is the fact of being living beings, . . . *supposing one has the right to exclude from it vegetables, plants and flowers*" (2011, p. 10; emphasis added). While he left vegetables, plants and flowers unexamined, there have been studies within the field of biocommunication, which includes "all the empires and kingdoms in biology (intraspecies communication, interspecies communication)" (Gebeshuber & Macqueen, 2017, p. 166). Studies of plant communication, understood as chemical exchange, now form "a robust emergent literature" (Nealon, 2016, p. xii; Baluška & Ninkovic, 2010). We hear about the re-discovery of plants and nature's wisdom (Gagliano, 2016) and plant-thinking or a philosophy of vegetal life including 'vegetal ontology' (Marder, 2013).

Some formulations for philosophy's abjection of plant life can be seen as too strong, e.g. the claim of "Husserl's failure to think the tree" (Marder, 2013, p. 78). Whatever the case, this charge does not apply to Martin Buber, e.g. his famous line "I consider a tree". Buber says that he can feel the tree as movement; moreover, "if will and grace are joined", he will be "drawn into a relation, and the tree ceases to be an It" (1958, pp. 98–99). This can be conceptualized as a case of quantum entanglement, in which it can't be determined whether the human first observes a tree or whether the tree first catches out attention (Mindell, 2000), pp. 271–272. What matters here is 'being-in-common'. As Buber so eloquently puts it, "Does the tree then have consciousness, similar to our own? I have no experience of that. But thinking that you have brought this off in your own case, must you again divide the indivisible?" (1958, pp. 58–59).

It is important to emphasize that plants use signals to communicate not only with one other, but also "with the broader neighborhood" (Gagliano, 2016, p. 23). This includes animals (Ruxton & Schaefer, 2011) as well as humans: "Human and plants have been interacting throughout all of human history" (Sommerer et al., 2016, p. 234). Of course, "the question remains how to characterize plant-human interaction beyond the human manipulation of a plant's phytochemical services" (Callicott, 2013, p. 38). Regardless of how this interaction is labeled, it is clear that "a natural community actually consists of its total population – plants, animals and human beings" (Thompson, 1949, p. 265).

### 3.2. 'Unnatural' Nature

When it comes to the separation of the human and the non-human, inorganic nature is the most non-human. While 'organic' is associated with naturalness and living processes, 'inorganic' carries the connotations of something that is non-living and even unnatural (Foster & Burkett, 2001). Inorganic components of nature, therefore, "were typically not included *as living* 'members' of the community" (DeWitt, 2006, p. 154). Meanwhile, that so little attention is paid to 'nonliving' aspects of nature can be attributed to "our natural human prejudices", as pointed out by Sir Arthur George Tansley – one of the most eminent botanists and ecologists of the 20th century, who emphasized the importance of constant exchange "between the organic and the inorganic" (1935, p. 299). It must be noted that Tansley viewed such exchange as an ecosystem rather than a community, which he considered just one level within the system made up of species populations living in a specific region (Sideris, 2012, p. 26). 'Community', however anthropomorphic, remains one of the key terms in ecology, going beyond its understanding only as all of the organisms in a prescribed area (Stroud et al., 2015).

The distinction between the organic and the inorganic is based on convention: the former refers to organisms considered living because they are composed of carbon compounds, while the latter do not form the complex molecular bonds that carbon makes possible and are thus considered 'non-living'. Due to its conventional nature, the distinction between the organic and the inorganic is blurred. It is interesting to note that, while this is now admitted by many scientists (Newman, 2009; Sheets-Johnstone, 2011), philosophers had earlier pointed out how this distinction implodes along with the conventional boundary between the human and non-human. For instance, Karl Marx saw an indivisible connection between the inorganic and the free human being: "The life of the species, both in man and in animals, consists physically in the fact that man (like the animal) lives on inorganic nature; and the more universal man (or the animal) is, the more universal is the sphere of inorganic nature on which he lives" (Marx, 1967, p. 70). In a similar vein, Mikhail Bakhtin wrote that our memory

> descends and disappears into the prehuman depths of matter and inorganic life, the experience of the life of worlds and atoms. And for this memory the history of the individual person begins long before the awakening of his consciousness (his conscious I).
>
> *(Shepherd, 2006, p. 41)*

Of course, even more than plant-human interaction, the question is how to characterize the shared experience of human and inorganic life. To that end, we need

new conceptions of the relation between self and other and new understandings of community, which in turn may necessitate new ways of
thinking about the relation between life and death and between the
human and the non-human, and even between the organic and the
inorganic.

*(Gere, 2012, p. 114)*

## 3.3. The Monstrous Other

Thus, community can be conceptualized as, to use Merleau-Ponty's phrase,
"a meeting of the human and the non-human" (2004, p. 203). In this sense,
what underlies community is interspecies communication, which has been
receiving more and more scholarly attention (Berea, 2018). On one end,
attention is paid to bacteria that, like humans, form communities (Popkin,
2017), as well as to the human-microbe symbiosis (Wilson, 2009). It is interesting to note that scientists speak about 'bacterial communities' more often
than, e.g., 'bacterial aggregates', as can be demonstrated by a Google search:
can it be that scientists feel some affinity with microbes while being drawn
to their otherness? On the other end, interspecies communication entails
talking to whales (Nollman, 2002) or forests (Kohn, 2013). Whether we view
a meeting of the human and the non-human on a small or large scale, it is
crucial to realize that "both macroscopic and microscopic are far from being
closed" (Derrida, 2013, p. 413). The very category of 'human' is spectral, like
all modern categories: humans derive from non-humans and are made from
non-humans such as bacteria and mitochondria (Morton, 2017). Also, the
more the scope of interspecies communication expands and the more we
think about such beings as "a tree, an ecosystem, a cloud – the more we
find ourselves obliged to think them not as alive or dead but as spectral"
(Morton, 2017, p. 272). There, we enter "the most unusual phase . . . for
which there is no scale" (Derrida, 2013, p. 413).

Interest in the unusual has existed since the ancient times. In his *Histories*,
the classical Greek historian Herodotus talks about all kinds of creatures
such as dog-headed men, headless people with eyes in their chest, a goat-
footed race, etc. Such creatures can be put into the category that the
Swedish botanist Linnaeus called *Homo monstrosus* – monstrous humans
or human–animal hybrids. Such creatures have the features of animals or
freaks but still resemble humans in other traits. Significantly, Herodotus
located those monstrous humans in actual geographic areas, e.g. the totally
bald Agrippaei can be found across the River Don (Metcalf, 2006). In ancient

China, there was a special genre called *zhiguai*, translated as 'tales of the miraculous', 'tales of the strange' or records of anomalies, which related the appearance of category-busters such as pygmies and giants, fishes shaped like oxen, dragons, immortals, the dead returned to life, elusive jade maidens, and ferns that turn into worms (Teiser, 2000).

One of the earliest attempts to conceptualize such creatures was made by Aristotle, who emphasized their elusive nature. He wrote that "in the case of monstrosities, whenever things occur contrary indeed to the established order but still always in a certain way and not at random, the result seems to be less of a monstrosity because even that which is contrary to nature is in a certain sense according to Nature" (*On the Generation of Animals*, IV.4, 770b13–16). Today, especially in post-human studies, numerous attempts are made to further theorize the phenomenon of monstrosity. It is noted that both the post-human and the monster refer to the unsettling of boundaries between nature and culture, human and machine, etc. (Castillo, 2014). Importantly, the monster is not viewed as an actual half-human creature tied to a specific geographic area; rather, its metaphysical nature is highlighted. In this sense, "the monster is neither before nor beyond the human, but an interrogation of the myth of human integrity, biologically and metaphysically" (MacCormack, 2016, p. 82).

The monstrous Other thus represents a unique dimension of the Other (Figure 9.4).

Using Jacques Lacan's term, it is the Other *qua* Real, "the impossible Thing, the 'inhuman partner,' which is the Other with whom no symmetrical dialogue, mediated by the symbolic Other, is possible" (Žižek, 2002, p. 70). The monster horrifies and fascinates us precisely because we can't fully identify with it. It is the most radical alterity, the otherness of the Other: "A monster is a species for which we do not have a name" (Derrida, 1995, p. 386).

Being inherently unstable and elusive, the monster keeps "showing itself in constantly novel and unexpected ways" (Camille, 1996, p. 200). This nature of the monster is explained by the origin of the word in Latin *monstrare*, which means 'to show'. The word 'monster' can be also traced back to *monere*, which means 'to warn'. Thus, 'the monster is an omen, foreboding, warning. At the same time, the word 'monstrosity' in Greek is *teras*, understood as 'wonder', 'marvel', and 'divinity'. A *teras* is a wondrous sign through which the divine shows itself in some manner. In other words, a

**Figure 9.4**   *Two Monsters* by Hieronimus Bosch (c. 1450–1516). Pen and bistre on paper. Berlin, Kupferstichkabinett. Scan by Jappalang.

*teras* is the appearance of something (divine) in something else to which it does not properly or naturally belong (human). "So understood, a monster is precisely the belonging together of a divine excess and the mundane thing through which such an excess shows itself" (Ewegen, 2014, p. 106). It is such 'belonging together' as a coming community that we feel, or fail to feel.

## 4. 'A POLITICAL AFFAIR'

Community as 'becoming-animal' consists in "the endless vitality of life" (Braidotti, 2006, p. 41); life, however, is always "a political affair" (Deleuze and Guattari, 1987, p. 292). These two characteristics combined in the single English word 'life' can be distinguished with the help of two words used in ancient Greek – *zōē* and *bios*. *Zōē* referred to being alive or the vitality of ever-living life, while *bios* referred to a way of life. This distinction lies at the basis of the concept of biopolitics: "a *bios* that is thoroughly oriented towards *zoe*, that is, a political community that elevates biological life to the status of a central political concern" (Hansen, 2010, p. 7).

The origins of Western biopolitics can be found in ancient Greek political and philosophical thought, particularly in the works of Plato and Aristotle for whom the nature of politics and government was inseparable from such themes as the regulation of the quantity and quality of population, their security and happiness, etc. (Ojakangas, 2016). Later, Christianity had an impact on classical biopolitical thought, and in the Middle Ages the natural way of life was one lived according to the word of God. The Renaissance saw a growing interest in biopolitics, and by the middle of the 20th century it became of a central political concern and a focus of scholarly attention.

It was Michel Foucault who introduced the term 'biopolitics' and who had a major influence on modern biopolitical thought. In his early works, such as *The Birth of the Clinic* (1973), Foucault showed how the human body and life can be governed and subject to administration in the areas of reproduction, illness, risk, etc. In his *History of Sexuality* (1979) Foucault shows how power can be wielded over life to discipline as well as to optimize the human body by regulating such biological processes as birth rates, life expectancy, mortality, etc.

Thus, biopolitics is concerned with the ways of governing humans as living beings and regulating their lives. The distinction between what life as living is and what it is as politically qualified, is constantly being blurred; this line is inherently fluid because life itself is not a thing but a flowing relation. Human individuals only appear as separate and distinct while, in fact, life is a community of bodies, "the endless contagion that combines, overlaps, soaks, coagulates, blends, and clones them" (Esposito, 2011, p. 151).

Biopolitics is literally everywhere life is found, its flows constantly governed and regulated, e.g. organ transplantation, reproductive surrogacy, human capital for the needs of the market, the flow of immigrants, etc. Human lives are categorized and authenticated by using surveillance technologies such as biometrics with the aim of fixing identities (Martin & Whitley, 2013) (Figure 9.5).

**Figure 9.5**    Data page of a Russian biometric passport. Image by Kostya0106.

Identities, of course, cannot be fixed once and for all; however, the communication flows that (re)create identities can be, and are, controlled. One can see the fluidity of identities first in symbolic terms and second in material terms: for example, in the flow of blood, because "in a community without limits, in which no precise border exists between one and the other, . . . the material and symbolic channel for its flow is blood" (Esposito, 2013a, p. 126). Blood donation comes closest to the pure gift (Farrell, 2006); significantly, an unpaid donor is called a "voluntary community donor" (Swanson, 2014, p. 139), and the (mostly non-profit) organizations that collect, test, label and distribute blood to hospitals, are known as 'community blood centers'.

Food is another area where regulation and administration constantly take place. Humans are the tasting species. *Sapiens* – the species in *Homo sapiens* – goes back to the Latin *sapere*, which means 'to have taste', 'to taste' and 'to be wise'. Thus, food is another example where the material and the symbolic converge. Also, its connection to hospitality is more obvious than that of blood: after all, hospitality is conviviality when one accepts a guest and the guest accepts what is given. The act of conviviality is sharing something with others, and what is shared in the first place is food. Food is considered to be the nexus of bioethics and biopolitics (Rawlinson & Ward, 2017). The biopolitics of food includes all areas of production, distribution, and consumption, e.g. provisioning, nutrition, genetic modification, food labeling, food sovereignty, etc.

Most food, of course, comes from animals; it is often argued that our humanity is determined by what we eat (Oliver, 2009). The question of whether it was natural for humans to eat animals came up already in ancient times. Aristotle, for instance, normalized this practice by saying that nature makes nothing in vain and so "the inference must be that she has made all animals for the sake of man" (*Politics*, I.8, 1256b21), including for the provision of clothing, instruments and food. There were other ways of approaching that question, emphasizing the moral and health benefits of a vegetarian diet. For instance, here is what Plutarch wrote about Pythagoras who was one of the first vegetarians:

> Can you really ask what reason Pythagoras had for abstaining from flesh? For my part I rather wonder both by what accident and in what state of soul or mind the first man who did so, touched his mouth to gore and brought his lips to the flesh of a dead creature, he who set forth tables of dead, stale bodies and ventured to call food and nourishment the parts that had a little before bellowed and cried, moved and lived.
>
> *(Plutarch,* On the Eating of Flesh, *I.1)*

In early tribes, animals were regarded as totemic ancestors; through various rituals, people showed respect for animals who gave themselves up for human consumption. In the modern world, the relations between humans and animals may exhibit different dynamics but the tensions are still there, calling for their regulation and normalization. The biopolitics of eating is one of the themes in the so-called 'animal studies' (Chrulew & Wadiwel, 2016; Kalof, 2017). If "the condition of animals has long served as a political allegory of the treatment of humans" (Peters, 1999, p. 242), its meaning is not so hidden anymore and is in need of interpretation. We see this condition in the faces of animals around us. No longer hidden, this condition has an ever stronger moral and political one meaning; significantly, it provided "a founding pathos for the animal rights movement" (Peters, 1999, p. 242).

Thus, biopolitics clearly shows that our concerns, both practical and theoretical, can't be focused on the ways of governing only the "vital capacities of human beings as living creatures" (Clarke et al., 2010, p. 7). Human lives are intertwined with those of non-humans, animals above all: we eat animals and perform experiments on them, but also form numerous psychological, social and physical relationships and bonds with them. In the light of all this, "how can the thought of another coming community not lead to a rethinking of the place of animals in community?" (Calarco, 2000, p. 96).

The original scope of biopolitics, aimed at the study of configurations of power used for the "control of life and the biological processes of man-as-species" (Foucault, 1997, p. 243), must be expanded to include all forms of biodiversity which allow and maintain the life of humans. Earlier, we quoted Derrida who, while concerned with the interrogation of animality, at the same time questioned the exclusion of vegetables, plants and flowers from the conceptualizion of the community of humans and other beings. Thus, he left the door open "for whatever we might have to say in the future about plants or other forms of biopolitical life" (Nealon, 2016, p. 149). In this light, plants have received special attention, perhaps because not only do we eat plants just as we eat animals, but because eating plants is now an established ('normalized') cultural practice, e.g. the 'plant-based diet'. It is argued that now "plants are the new animals – our new privileged figures for 'the other'" (Nealon, 2016, p. 149). As a result, the rethinking of a coming community cannot ignore the place of plants in it.

Based on Carl Linnaeus' accepted classification of nature, animals and plants are considered living matter, while minerals are considered non-living matter. However, as noted before, the line between what is considered to be living matter and what is considered non-living matter is not fixed and depends on the time-frame within which they are interpreted.

Sir Charles Scott Sherrington, an English neurophysiologist and Nobel laureate, stated that various types of organization of matter exhibit different
behaviors:

> A grey rock, said Ruskin, is a good sitter. That is one type of behav-
> iour. A darting dragon-fly is another type of behaviour. We call the
> one alive, the other not. But both are fundamentally balances of give
> and take of motion with their surround. To make 'life' a distinction
> between them is at root to treat them both artificially.
>
> *(Sherrington, 1940, p. 78)*

If that is the case, then the plants rights movement will be gaining momen-
tum, and such expressions as 'being stoned' will be met with resistance and
might be deemed politically incorrect and offensive to the mineral world.

Finally, let's not forget the monster that "is always alive" (Derrida, 1995,
p. 386). It must be remembered that the monster represents the most radical alterity with which we can't fully identify yet by which we are both
horrified and fascinated; "thus said, our neighborly proximity to the monster constitutes an urgent biopolitical and bioethical issue that calls for
much critical attention" (Huang, 2011, p. 46). Biopolitical decisions are very
hard to make here, though, because the monster is inherently unstable and
elusive; besides, the monster can appear anywhere. For instance, one article
(Ginn, 2013) addresses the appearances and disappearances of a domestic monster – the slug. The article describes how slugs and gardeners are
joined together by shared histories, curiosity and disgust. While gardeners
admit the vulnerability of slugs, they are at the same time transformed by
that recognition.

As the distinction between life as living and politically qualified life is constantly drawn and redrawn, there is always a question of who is worthy of
protection, security, care, etc. and who can be subject to nothing more than
'bare life' – or worse. "And this leads in turn . . . to the question of community – whom do we 'put to death'?'" (Borradori, 2003, p. 144). Here, 'putting
to death' is not necessarily identified with literally killing. Rather, following Derrida, it means any form of expulsion, rejection, or increasing risk of
death; in other words, killing the spirit of community. In this regard, "the
key question for . . . communication theory – a question at once philosophical, moral, and political – is how wide and deep our empathy for otherness
can reach" (Peters, 1999, p. 230). Empathy is evolutionarily advantageous

for various species, i.e., it is critical for successful interspecies communication, for instance, in sport dressage (Blokhuis & Lundgren, 2017) or in hunting, when it is important "to put oneself in someone else's shoes (or paws or hooves)" (Hurn, 2012, p. 119). A new discipline has even been proposed, called 'speculative psychology', that would go beyond human-animal interactions, e.g., imagining "What Is It Like to Be a Bat?" (Nagel, 1974), but probing toward what it is like "to be an atom, a grain of dust, an army, the Exxon Corporation, or France" (Harman, 2010, p. 15).

Of course, such questions can't remain only a matter of philosophy or psychology: the concepts of empathy, protection, expulsion, etc. all have strong moral connotations and are found at the basis of (bio)political decisions. Not surprisingly, the 'moral element' remains of profound significance in today's discourses of community" (Gold, 2005). In essence, any biopolitical view of community has a moral and normative character because it deals with our understanding and regulation of the nature and flows of life. More and more often, scholars raise this question: "Does our 'moral community' include non-human animals or not?" (Potter, 2005, p. 299). Morality is often understood in the deontological sense, in which judgments of actions are made based on rules. However, the nature of life being ever-flowing, it is impossible to limit morality (self-values) to a finite list of obligatory rules. Thus, it becomes crucial to move "beyond morality . . . to ethics, where we create and select those powers that expand life as a whole, beyond our limited perspectives" (Colebrook, 2001, p. 96). In this light, the traditional ethical (values with others) framework is being expanded to include animal ethics, interspecies ethics, and post-human ethics (Willett, 2014; Donovan, 2017; MacCormack, 2016). More and more often, community is theorized as the mutual entanglement of different kinds of beings, as shared lived reality. In this sense, community "is closer to the notion of the possibility of being in the place where the Other is" (Duranti, 2010, p. 16).

## 5. TO BE. CONTINUED

If community is theorized in broad terms – as shared, lived reality – it can be said that "the essence of community is life" (Henry, 2008, p. 119). The question 'What is life?', though, is an inherently philosophical and biopolitical question and cannot be answered by natural science alone. Regardless of how it is conceptualized and defined, life is something that is directly experienced; it is the life-world – something lived before all analysis and representation that follows. In this sense, as Edmund Husserl says, the world can be "equated with the life-world of humanity, *the all-embracing community*" (Husserl, 1973, p. 163; emphasis added). Although he talks about the human community, Husserl adds that "the world is, in the most comprehensive sense . . . our earth, which includes within itself all these different environing worlds with their modifications and their pasts" (Husserl, 1973, p. 163).

Earth, then, can be seen as the community of human and non-human beings that share the quality of 'living together'. It is important to emphasize that this quality includes "living together with the past of those who are no longer and will not be present or living, or with the unpredictable future to come . . . of those not yet living in the present" (Derrida, 2013, p. 20). To appreciate this aspect of the nature of community, one needs only to recall El Día de Los Muertos ('Day of the Dead') – a celebration in Mexico when those no longer living are awakened from their eternal sleep and become a part of the community sharing in all its celebrations, or to remember that community is always, in a way, a coming-community that doesn't exist. When understood this way, "'community' would break from its narrow human reference to gather in the rest of life, . . . and . . . would include '*all that participates in being*,' organic and inorganic, past, present, and future" (Rasmussen, 2013, p. 44; emphasis added).

So, community can be conceptualized as life, i.e., the experience of living-together on Earth. If we take into account that 'to live' goes back to the Proto-Indo-European root *leip-* ('to stick, to adhere'), forming words meaning 'to remain, to continue', then community can be theorized in terms of being, for "community is given to us with being and as being, well in advance of all our projects, desires, and undertakings" (Nancy, 1991, p. 35). Community in this sense is not so much 'a common being' as 'being-in-common'. This view de-emphasizes the shared quality of a community as its essence; instead, community is seen as the communication of any and all singular beings that exist only through communication. Thus, "decisive here is the idea of an inessential commonality, a solidarity that in no way concerns an essence. . . . [T]he communication of singularities . . . does not unite them in essence, but scatters them in existence" (Agamben, 1993, p. 18–19).

It is important to remember that community can be conceptualized not only as something that actually exists. If the 'common' is not what one owns but what one owes – an infinite lack, an unpayable debt (e.g. the concepts of 'pure gift' and 'pure hospitality'), then we must talk about "pure existence" (Esposito, 2013a, p. 46). In this sense, "community . . . is the very locus or, better, *the transcendental condition* of our existence" (Esposito, 2013a, p. 15; emphasis added). We must "not lose this originary condition" (Esposito, 2013a, p. 15) because, if we do, we lose ourselves, i.e., our very being – both as existence and as essence. And, we can only lose ourselves ourselves; *we* are the main threat to Earth. We must remember that community is our originary condition and "that we have always existed in common" (Esposito, 2013a, p. 14). Only this way – in/as community – can we continue to be.

# 10

# The Wonder
# of Space

Key concepts:

Astrobiology, astrocognition, exolinguistics, the 'Big Rip' scenario, CETI, Drake equation, inner space, intergalactic communication, interplanetary communication, interstellar communication, METI, outer space, proxemics, space-biased media, spatiality, SETI, technosignatures, time-biased media, xenology, Zipf's law.

Key names:

Aristotle, Giuseppe Cocconi, Nicolaus Copernicus, Frank Drake, Albert Einstein, Enrico Fermi, Edward Hall, Heinrich Hertz, Edmund Husserl, Harold Innis, Nikolai Kardashev, Guglielmo Marconi, Marshall McLuhan, Metrodorus of Chios, Philip Morrison, John Peters, Rudolph Pesek, Jill Tarter, Nikola Tesla, Alexander Zaitsev.

## 1. FROM THE STUDY OF SPACE TO SPATIAL STUDIES

Space is usually theorized as one type of nonverbal communication, along with body movements, touch, eye contact, artifacts, time, etc. This type of nonverbal communication is traditionally conceptualized within proxemics, which, following Edward Hall, is understood as the study of how human beings communicate through the use of space and associated with the "theories of man's use of space as a specialized elaboration of culture" (Hall, 1966, p. 1). Even when cultural differences in proxemics behavior are identified, e.g. different distances between communicators, the overall view is very straightforward: space spans everything in the external world, and people send and receive nonverbal messages in/through space. Since space is all around us ('out there') and thus conceptualized as objective, this view aims to be scientific.

Proxemics is presented as the study of how people communicate in/through space, in general. However, if one wants to be precise and keep the meaning of 'proximal' in mind, its focus should be on 'the area near or surrounding' the people engaged in communication. We can speak of 'proximal' only insofar as we can identify something 'distal'; in anatomy, for instance, there's a distinction between what is closer to the torso (proximal) and what is away from the torso (distal). This proximal-distal distinction appears in all languages (Piwek et al., 2008) and is employed in communication research: for instance, interpersonal communication is discussed in terms of 'proximal others' and 'distal others' in regard to medium preferences (Amit et al., 2013) or romantic relationships (Ghandour, 2004). So, technically, along with proxemics we should have 'distalics'; or, to cover both ends of the continuum, something like 'intervalics', which would be an inclusive term for the study of any 'space between'.

Thus, the role of space in communication can't be reduced only to the field of proxemics. Besides, proxemics focuses on the entire body as it moves through space; once the distance from public to intimate is crossed, however, communication often turns to touch, which is studied by haptics. If we take kinesics, we see that all visible arm and body movements, gestures, facial expression, posture and gait take place in space, as well. Verbal communication, also, cannot occur without space: there is always something 'out there' between the Self and the Other.

So, one can't communicate *not* in space: at best, communication can show a certain bias – either toward space or toward time, hence the well-known distinction between time- and space-biased media made by Harold Innis and elaborated by the Toronto school of communication theory (Cavell, 2003; Watson & Blondheim, 2007). As an economic historian, Innis' approach appeared scientific: he analyzed the role of media in the formation of civilizations and the rise and fall of empires. And yet, his approach also displayed a certain "moral-political pathos" (Peters, 2003, p. 398), which is reflected already in the term 'bias'. He connected the physical properties of materials, such as their weight and longevity – heavy and durable for time-biased, light and easily transportable for space-biased – to how knowledge is disseminated. And, when it comes "to the distribution of knowledge, it is effectively a political notion" (Frosh, 2007, p. 150). It is easy to see how such decisions lead to the distribution, uses and abuses of power. While emphasizing that societies need to strive for a balance between time- and space-biased communications media, Innis stated that "the balance between time and space has been seriously disturbed with disastrous consequences to Western civilization" (1971, p. 76). His own bias as a theorist was clearly toward the (time-based) oral tradition, for which he is said to have had a strong nostalgia (Kaestle, 1991).

As we can see, the study of space, even when it aims to be strictly scientific (objective), can't but reveal its humanistic (subjective) side; space, then, is not something that simply exists 'out there', but rather what is constituted in the dynamic relationships between people. Such conceptualization of space is found, for example, at the intersection of communication theory with geography, where communication is viewed as a process of spatial production (Lindell, 2016). This research is taken further by viewing space as a semiotic phenomenon (Gaines, 2006) which is understood as a part of semiosis and thus in relation to various social and cultural factors, e.g., mobility, place-making, memory, discursive struggle, ethics of recognition, etc. Similar to many disciplines that experienced the so-called 'spatial turn' (Warf & Arias, 2009), communication theory has moved from the study of space to spatial studies that do not view space as something taken-for-granted, focusing instead on the ways identity and power become located within a wide cultural context of social relations. This conceptualization of space does not aim to be scientific and falls under humanistic – most often critical – communication studies (Ewalt, 2017).

Thus, space is not something that objectively exists but is rather a form of spatiality. The newest form of spatiality, of course, is cyberspace: we're now living in the Global Village. Although mediated (e.g. by the Internet), communication appears immediate as people now can be instantly connected: to talk to someone across the globe on Skype or Viber is now a part of our common, everyday world.

## 2. BEYOND THE GOLDILOCKS WORLD OF SPATIALITY

All forms of our communication – regardless of cultural differences, degrees of mediation, figurative meanings or difficulties in understanding – appear normal when they take place at the human scale. We measure everything against ourselves, including the motor and sensory characteristics of the human body, our mental capabilities, or human social institutions. In other words, we live and communicate in the world in which everything is not too much/too large or too little/too small. The human world is a Goldilocks World where everything (for humans) is 'just right'.

The human scale can be seen as the default framework within which people are assumed to function. The default option comes into action when no other alternative is specified. This, however, does not mean that there *are* no other alternatives; on the contrary, it suggests that other options are available. The human scale represents a meso-level that falls between the micro- and macro-levels – everything that is too little/too small and too much/too large. As a result, the micro- and macro-scales

> are lopped off. . . For all intents and purposes, micro and macro phenomena no longer exist, and the meso scale becomes the only real world. This leaves us with an astoundingly impoverished awareness of the small and large systems that intimately affect our lives.
>
> *(Homer-Dixon, 2010, p. 90)*

Hence, important as the human scale is, we must not lose sight of the (sub) atomic scales and cosmological scales, which cannot but affect our lives situated in the middle and impacted from both ends. In this light,

> there is no particular reason why thinking about communication should be restricted to the human scale except that we are quite interesting to ourselves and find ourselves more or less at the midpoint in size between very small things like atoms and very large things like galaxies
>
> *(Peters, 2003, p. 400)*

Thus, communication theory must be concerned not only with proxemics, space-biased media, or the spatiality of the human world, but also with inner space and outer space (Kolb, 1986).

If we think of the Earth as a small world, then the world of the inner space is much, much, much smaller. In fact, we'd have to use the word 'much' as many times as the number of zeroes is needed to show by how many orders of magnitude the two words differ: a bacterium, for example, is about one-millionth of our human-sized stature. If we could shrink down to its size, we would find a complex world of millions of microbes many of which have not even been named (Fisher, 2016). More than half a century ago, Richard Feynman, a celebrated physicist, gave his famous talk entitled 'There's Plenty of Room at the Bottom' (2012), and today we're finding how complex and diverse life is in nanoscale. It has even been proposed that a civilization that can be compressed below the nanoscale may be capable of creating or entering black-hole-like environments (Smart, 2012).

The inner space may be our future, but our present everyday reality is still the human-sized world governed by classical mechanics, unlike the microworld of atoms and subatomic particles governed by quantum mechanics. If we could experience quantum behavior directly, we might be able to find out whether intelligence exists at such small scales. We cannot, however, directly interact with atoms and subatomic particles: all we can do is observe their behavior, e.g. through a quantum microscope. No matter how sophisticated our instruments, though, we cannot accurately measure their position and velocity simultaneously, in accordance with Heisenberg's Uncertainty Principle. In the human world everything appears immediate and is easy to measure; the body as an instrument works well for all kinds of purposes. What takes place in the microworld, however, calls for more and more instruments to 'save the appearances' – and still defies measure since it depends on our observation.

The more our observation affects the limits of what is observed, the greater our uncertainty about what it is. It is argued that, while in the studies of communication conducted within the social sciences "observer influences over phenomena are common, . . . such a limit may be less problematic in everyday (macro)physics, including astronomy, where the act of observation may not noticeably alter the observed" (Krippendorff, 2009, p. 14). Perhaps for this reason, among others, it is outer space – which is said to begin at about 180 km above the Earth where there is no air and the atmosphere disappears (Ilčev, 2016, p. 2) – that draws the attention of scholars from numerous fields, including communication theory. It must be noted that, while the study of communication is typically conducted within the social sciences or the humanities, the natural sciences are also full of considerations of "space, signals, distance, contact – central concerns and topics of communication theory" (Peters, 2003, p. 398). Of course, no 'Certainty Principle' can be claimed for understanding the workings of the outer space; besides, the Generalized Uncertainty Principle (GUP) takes into account the role of gravity and possible extra spatial dimensions, with novel implications for cosmology and black hole physics. Still, when such concepts as 'distance', 'signals', and 'contact' are discussed, what is usually meant is the distance between the Earth and other planets and galaxies; the signals we look for from those planets and galaxies and also send out to them; and possible contact with extraterrestrial intelligence. We can't, of course, disregard the studies of space and spatial studies of communication at the human scale; in fact, they foreshadowed the exploration of cosmological issues (Peters, 2003). Today, this research area is wide open – as open as outer space.

## 3. WONDERING WHERE EVERYBODY IS

Our Solar System is approximately 4.5 billion years old and the Universe is approximately 13.8 billion years old. There are billions of stars and galaxies in the Universe. And yet, no contact with extraterrestrial intelligence has been made. As the Italian physicist and Nobel laureate Enrico Fermi famously asked in the early 1950s, "Where is everybody?" (Webb, 2015). This later became known as Fermi's paradox. However, Fermi's question is not really a paradox: there is no logical contradiction between saying that no one has yet seen extraterrestrial intelligence and that it might still exist somewhere (Gray, 2016). Absence of evidence is not evidence of absence; of course, neither is it evidence of presence. Thus, the jury on this is still out – way out.

### 3.1. From Antiquity to Here

Humans have been wondering about the possibility of other worlds and life on them since antiquity. Already in the 4th century B.C., Metrodorus of Chios is reported to have stated that "it seems absurd, that in a large field one only stalk should grow, and in an infinite space one only world exist" (Ps.-Plutarch, *The Doctrines of the Philosophers*, I.5.4). In ancient Greece, the view of the plurality of worlds was held by many natural philosophers, e.g., by the atomists and the Stoics. The anti-pluralists such as Aristotle, however, placed Earth in the center of the Universe and viewed the heavens as a place of perfect circular motion: in Aristotle's words, "In the whole range of time past, so far as our inherited records reach, no change appears to have taken place either in the whole scheme of the outermost heaven or in any of its proper parts" (*On the Heavens*, I.3, 270b13–17). This geocentric view dominated for centuries until Nicolaus Copernicus put forward his heliocentric model in 1543: as a result, the Earth was no longer viewed as unique. Since the Earth was now a planet like any other, it was easier to speculate about the possibility of life and intelligence elsewhere. Extraterrestrial musings were further stimulated by the scientific developments in physics, astronomy, biology, chemistry, and mathematics.

From the beginning of the Enlightenment to the end of the 19th century, the interest in the possibility of extraterrestrial life continued to grow thanks, first of all, to the ideas of Johannes Kepler, Galileo Galilei, and Isaac Newton, and also to the works of fiction such as Jules Verne's *From the Earth to the Moon* and Herbert George Wells' *The First Men in the Moon* and *The War of the Worlds*. As is well known, Orson Welles' radio dramatization of the latter in 1938 caused a mild panic in some parts of the U.S.: many people believed that Martians had actually landed. It was clear that the human imagination, prepared by science and science fiction, had opened to the idea of our contact with extraterrestrial civilizations. New technologies were being developed to test that idea: in 1957 the Soviet Union launched *Sputnik 1* – the world's first artificial satellite (Figure 10.1), followed by *Sputnik 2*, and then, in 1958, by *Sputnik 3*. And, with that, we entered the Space Age.

In 1959 Giuseppe Cocconi and Philip Morrison published their paper entitled 'Searching for Interstellar Communications', which became a landmark for the systematic scientific inquiry into the possibility of extraterrestrial life. In the same year, space scientists George E. Mueller and John E. Taber gave a presentation entitled 'An Interplanetary Communication System', which described how long-distance digital transmissions in space can be set up using radio waves. In 1960, Frank Drake, then a radioastronomer at the National Radio Astronomy Observatory in Green Bank, West Virginia, used its 85-foot telescope to perform the world's first search for extraterrestrial intelligence. The search was named Project Ozma, after the queen of L. Frank Baum's imaginary land of Oz who lives in a place far away and populated by strange and exotic beings.

At a 1961 scientific conference in Green Bank where the feasibility of a search for extraterrestrial intelligence was discussed, Frank Drake proposed

**Figure 10.1**    Sputnik I exhibit in the Missile & Space Gallery at the National Museum of the United States Air Force. Photo by the U.S. Air Force.

a probabilistic model for estimating the number of actively communicative civilizations in our Milky Way galaxy, which became known as the Drake equation. Some of the factors in the model are more speculative than others, e.g. the fraction of intelligent sites that develop a technological communicating civilization, or the longevity of a communicative civilization (Tarter, 2011). The equation thus was open to different outcomes and aimed at generating the discussion on a probable number of extraterrestrial civilizations willing and able to communicate in the Milky Way.

In the mid-1960s, Rudolph Pesek, the Chairman of the Astronautics Commission of the Czechoslovak Academy of Sciences, coined an acronym

CETI for 'Communication with Extraterrestrial Intelligence', and proposed to establish an international symposium on the subject. More often, however, the term SETI ('Search for Extraterrestrial Intelligence') was used, since the search must precede the communication. In 1984, the SETI Institute was founded in the U.S. – a non-profit organization dedicated to scientific research of the possibility of life beyond the Earth. In addition to CETI and SETI, another acronym is used – METI, proposed by the Russian scientist Alexander Zaitsev who explained it as follows: "The scientifica program known as SETI endeavors as its main goal to search for any kind of electromagnetic radiation *from* aliens. In contrast, METI's main goal is to create and to send intelligent messages from humans *to* aliens" (2006, p. 399). Most recently, Dr. Jill Tarter, a leading astrophysicist in the search for extraterrestrial intelligence and SETI co-founder, stated that the acronym SETI is misleading because it is not the search for extraterrestrial intelligence but rather for evidence of someone else's technology; hence, the acronym must be dropped and we should talk instead about a search for 'technosignatures' (Cofield, 2018). Regardless of the name, scientific inquiry into the possibility of life and intelligence in outer space continues. While historically most of the scientists conducting such inquiry were physicists, astronomers and mathematicians, today it involves more and more scholars from the social sciences and humanities (Smith, 2018). Besides, many countries are now engaged in such research, including France, Argentina, Canada, Holland, Great Britain, China, Italy, Australia, Japan, Germany and Israel (Lemarchand et al., 2016). The history of scientific inquiry into the search for possible extraterrestrial civilizations is well-documented (Carroll, 2017; Dick, 1996; Raulin-Cerceau, 2010; Shuch, 2011).

Today, the relationship between outer space and communication is a very active area of research. It is common to speak about three types of possible extraterrestrial civilizations, based on the scale proposed by the Russian astrophysicist Nikolai S. Kardashev (1964). He proposed the classification of all civilizations according to the level of their capacity for communications technology, determined by the amount of energy at their disposal. Kardashev's scale has three categories, designated Type I, Type II and Type III civilizations: with each type, the amount of energy increases and so does the capacity for communication. Accordingly, three kinds of possible communication are identified.

*Interplanetary communication* is communication between civilizations of Type I. There are nearly 4,000 planets beyond our own, including some that astronomers believe might have the conditions necessary to support life (Greshko, 2018). The forerunners of scientific thought on interplanetary communication include Karl Gauss and Joseph Johann von Littrow, whose ideas were developed in the works of Camille Flammarion, Charles Cros, Nikola Tesla et al. (Raulin-Cerceau, 2010). The research of Konstantin Tsiolkovskii into propulsion dynamics and multistage rockets at the beginning of the 20th century was a breakthrough in the area of interplanetary communication, and the U.S.S.R. Society for Interplanetary Communications was established in Moscow in 1924. Tsiolkovskii's ideas form the basis for much of the spacecraft engineering today (Redd, 2013). Almost a century ago, Nikola Tesla stated: "I think that nothing can be more important than interplanetary communication" ("Tesla at 75", 1931). Recently, a car named after him was launched into space by Elon Musk, who also announced his plans to found a colony on Mars (Coppinger, 2016). We hear more and more often that the Earth won't sustain us forever and that the future of humanity is therefore connected with interplanetary communication (Kaku, 2018).

*Interstellar communication* is communication between civilizations of Type II. According to theoretical calculations, somewhere beyond the orbit of Pluto there should be a sharp boundary between the solar-system-generated magnetic field and the less dense field mostly made up of gas and dust. This boundary is called 'the heliopause', and it is beyond this boundary that interstellar communication is thought to occur. It can be recalled that Cocconi and Morrison's seminal paper, mentioned earlier, was dedicated to the search for interstellar communication. Since then, interstellar communication has drawn a lot of scientific attention (Harbeck, 2017; Vakoch, 2014). In 2012, after a 35-year, 13-billion-mile journey, NASA's *Voyager 1* spacecraft became the first human-made object to cross the heliopause and reach interstellar space. *Voyager 2*, which followed it, will likely cross that boundary in several years' time.

*Intergalactic communication* is communication between civilizations of Type III. While it is sometimes stated that "interplanetary travel is imminent, and intergalactic communication nearly so" (Mathur, 2001, p. 12), the latter for now seems to be more wishful thinking. Not only is intergalactic space extremely hot, but it is also much less dense than interstellar space: the vacuousness of intergalactic space is said to be much more than the best vacuums we can create at the present time (Choudhuri, 2010). Just as intergalactic space is more sparse, so is the field of its scientific research.

Intergalactic space is just too far and too empty: it does not lend itself to rigorous scientific study. That is why, perhaps, some work in this area appears way 'out there'; for instance, the pyramid complex in Bosnia has been suggested to be a network based on a 'cosmic Internet' which bridges remote places in the galaxy (Woodard, 2009). Similarly, the Rtanj mountain situated in eastern Serbia and shaped like a pyramid is claimed to be an integral element of an intergalactic communication network (Marianović, 2017; Osmanagich, 2017). That such claims are more speculative than scientific is not surprising: there is just too much we don't know.

## 4. 'LIFE AS WE DON'T KNOW IT'

So, "communication theory should not be afraid to depart the human scale" (Peters, 2006b, p. 219). And yet, it is not easy to come to terms, for example, with nonlocal interaction such as quantum entanglement in which particles are mutually affected no matter how far they are from each other – what Albert Einstein called 'spooky action at a distance' (Letter to Max Born, March 3, 1947; see Born, 2005, p. 155). Naturally, when it comes to the Universe, its scale is truly overwhelming for the human mind: there are several hundred billion galaxies in the visible universe alone! So, when Heidegger talks about our 'being-thrown-in-the-world' ('in-die-Welt-Geworfen-Sein'), it may appear even comforting compared to what Peter Sloterdijk represents as 'being-thrown-in-the-cosmos' – 'in-den-Weltraum-Geworfen-Sein' (Davis, 2013: viii). This kind of 'thrownness' is not just spooky, but terrifying: Blaise Pascal, for instance, was terrified by the eternal silence of the infinite spaces of the heavens (1909, III, 206), and Mikhail Bakhtin spoke of cosmic terror and the fear of the immeasurable (Last, 2013). So, it is not easy to depart the human scale and find one's "naked self confronting the universe" (Peters, 1999, p. 179).

Confronting the Universe is not the same as confronting a species or one of its representatives. 'Species' in Late Latin meant 'a special case' and was related to *specere* – 'to look at, to see, behold', from Proto-Indo-European root *spek- – 'to observe'. In the case of the Universe, though, there is no species to observe, just whatever part of it is visible (the substantivized noun 'extraterrestrial(s)' is often used to avoid using 'species'). It is often stated that we will not share similar physical realities (such as bodies) with extraterrestrials, and that these circumstances will have far-reaching consequences for our possible communication with them (Dunér, 2013). But we can't say even *that* with any certainty because what we have to deal with is "life as we don't know it" (Koerner & LeVay, 2000, p. 195).

We must conceptualize something that is literally alien to us, in the sense that it is not part of our evolutionary heritage. Sometimes, the terrestrial and extraterrestrial worlds are viewed as radically different, and this is presented as the "incommensurability problem" (Vakoch, 1999). However, to present incommensurability as an insurmountable obstacle is oxymoronic, because even discussing in/commensurability presupposes some conceptual common ground, e.g. the concept of measure. As such, we can take steps toward knowing the life that we don't know. Let's see which areas of scholarship help us along that way.

*Astrobiology.*    Also known as exobiology, astrobiology is an interdisciplinary field drawing on knowledge from biology, chemistry, physics, geology and astronomy. Astrobiology speculates about the forms of life that could exist on other planets (Cockell, 2018; Dunér et al., 2013; Hanslmeier, 2013). To imagine where else life may be found in the solar system and beyond, astrobiology must take as its starting point terrestrial biology, exploring the origin of life on the Earth and how its development influenced the course of biological evolution. For instance, it's generally assumed that extraterrestrial civilizations will be carbon-based, need the presence of liquid water, and exist on a planet around a sun-like star (Ransford, 2008).

*Astrocognition.*    It is important to understand the emergence and evolution of our cognitive capacities because this knowledge can be used to formulate various theories of extraterrestrial intelligence. Such explorations are brought together in the field of astrocognition as the study of human cognitive processes in extraterrestrial environments: "Central here is the view of the mind as embodied, situated, enactive, and distributed, in other words, the coevolution of cognition and environment" (Dunér, 2017, p. 436). Thus, while astrobiology studies the necessary and sufficient conditions for life in the Universe, astrocognition seeks the necessary and sufficient conditions for awareness and self-awareness. Also included in astrocognition is the question of what may happen to human cognition when people encounter a physically, biologically and culturally different environment (Dunér et al., 2013).

*Cybernetics.*    Developed with the help of cognitive science, cybernetics forms one of the traditions in communication theory studying the significance of consciousness and analogies between living and nonliving systems (Craig, 1999). Possible communication with extraterrestrials is often discussed using the framework of cybernetics. For example, a recent paper notes the rapidly developing artificial intelligence and addresses the prospect of interspecies cybernetic communication between humankind and post-humans designed for space exploration and space settlement (Robinson, 2017).

*Ethology.*   Communication with extraterrestrial civilizations is less a scientific-technological matter than a communicative-semiotic one (Dunér et al, 2013). In this light, focusing on natural language as a system of signs and other semiotic systems can provide insights into possible communication with extraterrestrials. It is assumed that our communication with animals is in some ways comparable to possible communication with species on other planets: hence, studies of animal communication can contribute to our understanding of methods for communicating with extraterrestrial civilizations. Most often, dolphins are taken as a model for alien intelligence (Figure 10.2). In fact, Carl Sagan is even quoted as saying that "it will be much easier to understand interstellar messages, if we ever pick them up, than dolphin messages" (Czajkowski, 2001, p. 349).

One well-known example of such research was the so-called 'Order of the Dolphin', founded in 1961 at a meeting of SETI at the National Radio Astronomy Observatory in Green Bank, West Virginia. One of the participants

**Figure 10.2**   Dolphin communication. Photo by Serguei S. Dukachev.

was John Lilly, who conducted extensive research on dolphin communication (Lilly, 1967), and the name 'The Order of the Dolphin' was chosen to honor his work on interspecies communication. We find his research continued today, e.g., in the work of Laurance Doyle and his colleagues, who apply Information Theory to animal communication aiming to develop more sophisticated detectors for possible extraterrestrial intelligent signals (Doyle et al., 2011).

*Cryptology.*    In the sci-fi film *Arrival,* the aliens make contact with humans and Louise Banks, an accomplished linguist, decodes their mysterious language. In Sue Burke's recent novel entitled *Semiosis* (2018), humans make contact with sentient plants on a far-away planet. The ideas for such films and novels, as well as for inquiry into the possibility of communication with extraterrestrial civilizations, come from real-life explorations. For instance, it is suggested that we may gain clues to decoding extraterrestrial messages by examining past attempts to decode dead languages here on Earth (Finney & Bentley, 1998). Although extinct, such languages are not a product of imagination: at some point, they really existed.

Of special interest in this respect is the area of cryptology that deals with situations where communication is prevented or limited (Denning, 2014). The importance of cryptology for the study of possible messages from extraterrestrial civilizations has been noted by communication theorists (Peters, 1999). In this respect, the Rosetta Stone is frequently invoked, which was deciphered by Jean-François Champollion – a French philologist and orientalist. Carl Sagan writes in *Cosmos*: "What a joy it must have been [for Champollion] to open this one-way communication channel with another civilization, to permit a culture that had been mute for millennia to speak of its history, magic, medicine, religion, politics and philosophy" (1980, p. 296). This feat of cryptoanalysis is inspiring today when "we are again seeking messages from an ancient and exotic civilization, this time hidden from us not in time, but in space" (ibid.). It must be remembered, though, that in cryptology an original text (plaintext) is encrypted via a keytext to create a cryptotext. For the plaintext to be decoded, the cryptotext must contain some indirect information about the keytext. This may not be the case in extraterrestrial communication, in which there would be no bilingual texts. Besides, cryptoanalysis as a process of semiosis takes place in a certain context: for instance, in deciphering the Rosetta Stone, some other factors played a role, e.g. some inscriptions from other artifacts, such as the Philae Obelisk, and also Champollion's knowledge of ancient Greek and Coptic Egyptian (Denning, 2014).

The universal language, according to most scholars, is found in mathematics. Carl Sagan spoke of a cosmic Rosetta Stone and believed that all technical civilizations, no matter how different, must have a common language and "that common language is science and mathematics" (Rasmussen, 1991, p. 73). Following Sagan, many scholars have proposed that mathematics is the best system of signs to use for communicating with extraterrestrials. Yet, mathematics rests on human ways of experiencing the world and thus is a cultural product like any other language.

*Exolinguistics.*    Since none of the naturally evolved languages that existed or exist, including mathematics, seem to be good enough for communicating with extraterrestrials, artificial languages are created for that purpose. Such synthetic languages, sometimes called 'exolanguages', designed for maximum efficiency, are a part of the field of exolinguistics, also called astrolinguistics or xenolingusitics, which focuses on hypothetical languages. Some examples of such languages include Astraglossa, created by the English biologist Lancelot Hogben in 1954 as a means of communication via short and long radio pulses (Dunér et al., 2013), and LINCOS ('Lingua Cosmica'), created by Hans Freudenthal in 1960, with a recently updated version called NEW LINCOS (Firneis & Leitner, 2013). Also, a forthcoming book edited by Douglas Vakoch, entitled *Xenolinguistics: Toward a Science of Extraterrestrial Language*, aims to explore the nature of language when compared with non-human communication systems: some of the confirmed topics include the place of Universal Grammar in the Universe, the likely nature of alien language, a view from multimodal interactional linguistics, etc.

*Hermeneutics.*    While we have not yet had any contact with extraterrestirals, we can observe and contemplate stars, planets and galaxies, and this is already an experience. Distant as it may be, such experience can be seen as a small part of the hermeneutic circle, the whole of which is unknown. And, as noted earlier, "a spiritual or intellectual journey may imaginatively originate at any point on the hermeneutical circle" (Paparella, 2012, p. 11). Our possible communication with extraterrestrial civilizations can be seen as a hermeneutic circle and so it requires an art of understanding. And one can obviously understand only something that exists – in hermeneutics, usually texts. Since no texts have been written by extraterrestrials, human attempts to understand their possible intelligence and capacity for communication are mostly speculative, found in literary works, such as Stanislaw Lem's novel *His Master's Voice* (1968) – "a brilliantly dizzying meditation on the hermeneutic undecidabilities of a letter from the stars, a text outside any known relationship" (Peters, 1999, p. 249). One could also place astrology in the hermeneutic tradition and view planets as cosmic symbols calling for our understanding (Mazzucchelli, 2000). While astrology is usually rejected by the scientific community, it can hardly be completely dismissed for generating ideas and expectations to be tested, whenever possible, by empirical methods. Significantly, we come across attempts to develop astrological hermeneutics, including a theory of unwritten texts (Colilli, 2015). Sometimes, a real text is taken as a basis for contemplating the relationship between humans and extraterrestrial civilizations; for instance, extraterrestrial biblical hermeneutics views the Bible as a scientific report of aliens interacting with terrestrial life as its creators (Zeller, 2010). Naturally, religious and spiritual aspects of these relationships present a special challenge for communication with extraterrestrials, since these are the most subjective experiences that cannot be empirically verified. Theology and science, though, stand in relationship of contrariety rather than contradiction; for example, one of the oldest astronomical institutes in the world is the Vatican Observatory – a scientific research institute of the Holy See subject to the Governorate of Vatican City State – where they see no conflict between science and the possibility of extraterrestrial 'brothers' as part of creation (Archdiocese of Baltimore, 2012).

*Phenomenology.*    Edmund Husserl, to whom phenomenology as a method for exploring conscious experience of one's lived world owes its existence, emphasized that the phenomenon of space, in general, is a crucial part of our perception because "the same thing appears for each in a different way in accordance with the different place in space" (Husserl, 2006: 7). In this respect, locomotion is central since we constantly change spatial spots with one another and so our experiences change continuously: communication thus is an intersubjective experience. Husserl wrote that "the earth is not the 'whole of Nature'; it is one of the stars in the infinite space of the world" (Merleau-Ponty, 2002, p. 118). In the case of confronting the Universe, the object of one's experience is 'the infinite space of the world'. So, when it comes to possible communication with extraterrestrial objects such as stars, says Husserl, we are "able to 'experience' them, to apprehend them indirectly as bodies", and for that "I must already be a human being for myself on the earth as my source-ground" (Husserl, 2002, p. 125). Notice that the word 'experience' is put in quotation marks, which suggests its extremely mediated character. Husserl also talks about the possibility of flying arks as 'airships' or 'spaceships' of the Earth: with respect to them, we can only draw inferences as if they were bodies like any others.

> Only when we think of our stars as secondary arks with their eventual humanities, etc., only when we figure ourselves as transplanted there among these humanities, perhaps flying there, is it otherwise. Then it is like children born on ships, but with some differences.
>
> *(Merleau-Ponty, 2002, p. 127)*

Although today the words 'airships' and 'spaceships' do not need any quotation marks, we still only rely on indirect apprehending and cannot actually *experience* those differences. Communication, though, is not only about apprehension, representation, or computation: ultimately it is "our phenomenological experiences of the Lifeworld" (Dunér, 2017, 442).

Sometimes, attempts are made to bring all the research outlined above under one umbrella of "xenology – the science of studying ETI" (Ashkenazi, 2017, p. 5). The importance of all this knowledge cannot be denied as we must get ready for possible contact with extraterrestrial intelligence. Yet, while we must get ready, we can never be completely prepared: "perhaps finding extraterrestrial life will be more like falling in love than confirming a specific hypothesis. When it happens, we'll know" (Grinspoon, 2004, pp. 98–99).

## 4.1. The Medium and the Message

As we can see, many disciplines join forces in exploring possible communication with extraterrestrial civilizations. There is one controversial issue, though, that has a decisive impact on such explorations, known as the METI/SETI debate, i.e., whether to send messages into outer space or simply to search for extraterrestrial intelligence. In other words, do we actively try to contact aliens or passively wait to receive signals from them? Communication is a risky experience: its meaning goes back to the Proto-Indo-European root *per- – 'to try, risk'. Trying to communicate with extraterrestrials gives a new meaning to the concept of 'risk communication' (Korbitz, 2014). In fact, it is more appropriate to speak here not about risk but existential threat.

Those in favor of the passive approach (SETI) are concerned that, if we break the 'Great Silence' (Brin, 1983), the outcome for us may be devastating. It is likely that an extraterrestrial civilization will be more technologically advanced and the Earth will be colonized or humankind will be annihilated. Those in favor of the active approach (METI) argue that it is too late to keep quiet: if we're afraid of alerting aliens to our presence, that ship sailed more than two billion years ago (Greshko, 2018). As pointed out by Frank Drake, we're leaking large amounts of information into outer space, and an advanced civilization could easily pick it up. Besides, in the spirit of technological determinism, if contacting an extraterrestrial civilization is technically possible, someone will try to establish it sooner or later (Johnson, 2017).

The METI/SETI debate cannot settle itself: it calls for a human decision. The big question here is, "Who gets to decide?" This rarely brought up question is more political than scientific and presents a problem of the commons, if not *the* problem of the commons (Denning, 2014). This problem cannot be addressed without ideas drawn from rhetoric, discourse analysis, psychology of social interaction, cultural studies and other disciplines and fields that deal with agency, voice, power, identity, etc.

Whatever side in the METI/SETI debate one takes, one cannot discuss the possibility of extraterrestrial communication without two key concepts – a medium and a message. In human communication, we very often do not think much of a medium because we interact mostly either orally face-to-face or electronically on social media: in both cases, we take the medium for granted (more so in the former case than in the latter, due to the invisibility of air). We think more of *what* to say rather than *how* to get it across. In extraterrestrial communication the situation is reversed because possible civilizations are very far away – in outer space – and we must first think of *how* to contact them (or how they can contact us) and then think of *what* to say: "after all, communication . . . requires that a medium exist with which to convey the message" (Williams, 2017).

### 4.1.1. The Medium

Following Marshall McLuhan, we conceptualize "media as extensions of our senses" (1994, p. 53) that make our physical and nervous systems more powerful and efficient. We do not know what evolutionary path extraterrestrials may have followed: it may be that their intelligence is rooted in some sense(s) more advanced than human. Naturally, we must discuss the media that can be used for communication with extraterrestrial civilizations based on the five human senses, which are usually divided into the contact senses (touch, smell, and taste) and the remote senses (seeing and hearing). On this basis, such factors can be addressed as the amount of transmitted/received information, the range, rate and efficiency of transmission/reception, the ease and cost of communication, etc.

The best contact with extraterrestrials would be through the contact senses, as it would provide the maximum richness of information. Reports of such intercorporeal communication are given today by those claiming to have been abducted by aliens and by self-proclaimed mediums, i.e., those who converse with the dead; for instance, former nurse Kerrie-Ann Thornton, a Sydney-based medium, has recently alleged an encounter with an extraterrestrial telling her that the Earth is dying and that we must go somewhere else (Palin, 2017). Needless to say, such reports are not embraced by the scholarly community. Thus, it is the media which are the extensions of the remote senses that are used for communication with extraterrestrial civilizations.

The most obvious choice is sound waves, since they are a wide-spread means of communication for humans and many non-humans; indeed, one of the first known examples of human communication over large distances was by drums. It can be assumed that extraterrestrial civilizations will also possess an atmosphere through which vibrations can travel. Indeed, sound as a medium of extraterrestrial communication was used even before the advent of the space age. In the early 20th century, Heinrich Hertz and Nikola Tesla saw the future of interplanetary communication in using radio waves. At about the same time, Guglielmo Marconi picked up some unusual radio signals and tried to determine if they might have come from Mars (Garber, 2014). Radio waves can be used for both transmitting messages from the Earth and listening to messages from outer space. Most of the early SETI searches are examples of the former as they were based on radio astronomy. The most recent case of the latter is the project called 'Breakthrough Listen' – a network of telescopes and computers listening for signs of intelligence in deep space and encompassing the 1,000,000 closest stars and 100 closest galaxies (Williams, 2017). Sound as a medium has advantages: it is easy to generate; it can travel through space without much interference; certain 'magical frequencies' have been proposed that the aliens would most likely use (e.g. 1420 MHz – the emission frequency of hydrogen, which is the most abundant element in the universe), etc. At the same time, sound has disadvantages: its transmission speed is fairly low; it does not travel well in thin atmospheres; it can be distorted by noise such as a stormy environment, etc.

Other efforts to establish contact with extraterrestrial civilizations may include optical means of communication, e.g., visible light such as emitted by lasers

(Cofield, 2018). An example on the transmitting end is the 'Breakthrough Starshot' project, which plans to fit a tiny chip to a lightweight sail and send it through space with a 100-billion-watt laser. An example on the receiving end is the project known as 'Optical SETI' (OSETI), scanning the sky for laser light. As a visual medium, light has clear advantages over sound: it can carry more information, it experiences less interference, it is less expensive than radio waves, it can cover long distances in space, etc.

Today, we are entering the era of multimessenger astronomy, when gravitational waves from the merger of two neutron stars can be both seen and heard by the combined arsenal of technological 'eyes' and 'ears'.

### 4.1.2. The Message

At the heart of contact with extraterrestrials lies, of course, the message or *what* is communicated. The possibility of such communication, though, is based on the presupposition that the message will be recognized as an invitation for contact. For example, we read in a recent article about a message of radio signals set to reach the planet GJ273b in 2029; its inhabitants, if any, may not understand all the symbols of mathematics and physics, however, "the import of the message . . . will be clear: 'Let's talk!'" ("Nanoo nanoo", 2017, p. 70). Yet, there is no guarantee that the message will be recognized at all. So, the essential question here, often lost in discussions, "is *not* to find out what the messages means: it is to realise that there is a message" (Sonesson, 2013, p. 188). To that end, the so-called Zipf's law could be used to determine if signals possess any marks of a message. According to this law, proposed by George Kingsley Zipf and widely used in computational linguistics, the frequency of any word is inversely proportional to its rank. If each word is equally likely to occur, their distribution would be represented by a flat line. For signals to have syntax and meaning, the relationship among their frequencies must yield a line with a slope of -1, which is found in most written and spoken languages. Thus, for signals to/from outer space to be identified as a message, they should at a minimum conform to Zipf's law (Dumas, 2011).

Once recognized as a message, all attention will be paid to its content. Ideally, rather than attempting to represent basic ideas of human evolution, e.g. "encoding chemistry" (Vakoch, 2011b, p. 381), a message itself would be a living record and not just a trace of such living experience. For instance, studying extremophiles – microorganisms such as tardigrades or water bears, which live in environments inhospitable to all other life as we know it – is said to be getting as close as we can to studying alien civilizations (Ransford, 2008). It is hypothesized that bacteria are microscopic data storage systems that could carry vast amounts of information through interplanetary atmospheres (Zubrin, 2001).

In reality, all messages to outer space have been auditory or visual. The first auditory message in the history of the humankind was the radio broadcast from the Evpatoria Planetary Radar in 1962. The message was transmitted using Morse code and contained the words 'MIR' (Russian for both 'peace' and 'world'), 'LENIN' (the leader of the 1917 Bolshevik Revolution) and 'SSSR' (Russian for 'U.S.S.R.', the Union of Soviet Socialist Republics) (Kutuza & Rhziga, 2012; for other examples of interstellar radio messages see: Hanslmeier, 2013, p. 192). Some messages sent to outer space have been musical. For example, in 2001, a 'Concert for ET' was transmitted from Evpatoria to six nearby Sun-like stars; the music included Gershwin's 'Summertime', the finale of Beethoven's Ninth Symphony, and the melody of the Russian folksong 'Kalinka-Malinka' performed on a solo instrument known as a theremin (Zaitsev, 2002). Music was also a part of the famous message on the *Voyager* spacecraft launched by NASA in 1977. In addition to music from around the world, the message included a 12-minute sequence of selected sounds of the Earth based on a proposal prepared by Jon Lomberg, who recommended that the sounds follow the evolution of life, from natural sounds to sounds of non-human life to sounds of human life (Lemarchand & Lomberg, 2011) (Figure 10.3).

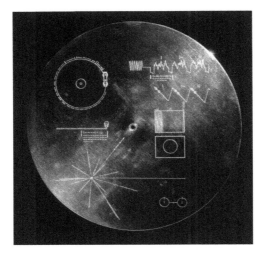

**Figure 10.3**   *The Sounds of Earth* record cover. NASA/JPL.

The first visual messages go farther back in history than the auditory ones. Some believe that mysterious ancient geoglyphs such as the Nazca Lines of coastal Peru (Figure 10.4) are not just examples of artistic expression but attempts to communicate with God or extraterrestrials (McAuliffe, 2015, p. 95).

In the same vein, Karl Friedrich Gauss suggested constructing massive geometric figures on the surface of the Earth, for example, cutting a giant triangle in the Siberian forest. Also in the 19th century, Joseph Johann von Littrow came up with the idea of pouring kerosene into a 30-kilometre-wide circular canal as a signal of our presence to extraterrestrials (Schirber, 2009). In the 20th century, more realistic proposals were developed and put into practice. Carl Sagan and Frank Drake designed a small gold-anodized

**Figure 10.4**   Aerial view of the "Owlman" aka "Astronaut", the most enigmatic geoglyph of the Nazca Lines, the Nazca Desert, southern Peru. Photo by Diego Delso, delso.photo, License CC-BY-SA.

aluminum plaque for *Pioneer 10* and *Pioneer 11*, launched by NASA in 1972 and 1973. The plaque depicts the nude figures of a man and a woman and diagrams of the solar system with the sun's position in space (Figure 10.5). In 1977, the *Voyager 2* spacecraft was launched with a gold-plated copper disk that contained many images depicting scientific knowledge, human anatomy, human endeavors and the terrestrial environment.

Some messages are explicitly in the form of a narrative. As mentioned above, the message on *Voyager* contained a sequence of sounds following the evolution of life. Visual images are also used for the purpose of creating a message in the form of a story. For example, it is suggested that cosmic storytelling take the form of image-only, cartoon narratives transmitted in frame-by-frame progression. Simple message strings, such as a Phoid (a human-like creature) catching rain in hands or a cup and drinking, are woven into a cinematic story. It is proposed that this way the basics of human knowledge and behavior can be communicated (Letaw, 2011).

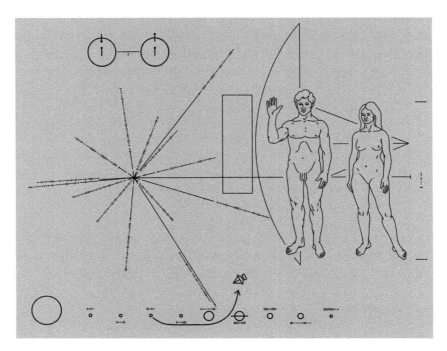

**Figure 10.5**   *Pioneer 10*'s famed Pioneer plaque. Designed by Carl Sagan and Frank Drake. Artwork prepared by Linda Salzman Sagan. Photo by NASA Ames Resarch Center (NASA-ARC).

In 2006, the *New Horizons* spacecraft was launched, for which images are being crowd-sourced from people all over the planet; based on them, a new message will be formed and uploaded on the spacecraft. Labeled 'One Earth Message', it is presented on the project's Facebook page as "a digital, crowd-sourced 'selfie of Earth' intended for any beings who find NASA's *New Horizons* spacecraft". Similarly, the SETI Institute's online project 'Earth Speaks' invites people from around the world to propose their own messages to an extraterrestrial civilization. People are invited to submit ideas in both auditory and visual media so that they can be used in the same message.

There are many questions we face when thinking about the message for extraterrestrial communication. For instance, there is the ongoing debate about the 'unified message', i.e., should the message represent the Earth speaking with one voice or should it highlight different perspectives presenting a diversity of views? (Ashkenazi, 2017; Vakoch, 2011b). Also, should we try to send as much information as possible? The contents of a major library such as the Library of Congress could be transmitted in under an hour with the highest-speed optical signaling link (Shostak, 2009). At the same time, suggestions are made to do something elegant and design the simplest message that captures human achievements as a species (Johnson, 2017). In the same vein, should we send an abstract message using complex symbols or should we be very concrete and focus on possible intersubjective experiences, for example, some astronomical landmarks likely to be observable to both terrestrials and extraterrestrials? Also, since it is most likely that it will be quite a while until extraterrestrial communication becomes a dialogue in the usual sense (DeVito, 2011, p. 160; Sagan, 1973), should we send a series of messages a few days or weeks apart, each containing more information than the last, but also some redundancy as a check on understanding (DeVito, 2011, p. 161)? If we receive a message from outer space, how do we announce this? Another question is whether we should focus on the message to outer space and not worry about the messages we daily exchange on Earth. For example, it is common to speak about "the hunt for alien life" (Lindell, 2016). If aliens could be listening to our communication, should we perhaps think about our language more carefully and use different metaphors?

## 5. 'OUMUAMUA

It is sometimes argued that spending money in trying to contact extra-terrestrial civilizations is money badly spent (Ashkenazi, 2017). After all, humankind may not survive long enough to receive a reply. So, why spend any effort at all on theorizing possible communication with extraterrestrials? Fermi's question – "Where is everybody?" – still has no answer, and all we can do is speculate on possible locations, possible mediums, possible messages, etc. The topic of communication with outer space seems to be too far-fetched, too far 'out there'. And yet, this topic is highly relevant in many ways. Let's see how it helps to bring together and highlight the ideas discussed in the previous chapters.

*Time* (chapter 1) can only be discussed in relation to space. The exploration of space helps us to understand the nature of time and their interrelationship: we can only talk about space-time (or even spacetime) as a four-dimensional continuum. Communication, therefore, is never a simple mechanical transmission through space but also a process of unfolding over time. We cannot *not* consider this historical aspect of communication. Significantly, the last factor of Drake's equation – *L*, or the longevity of a communicative civilization – is crucial, yet difficult to answer. At the moment, we know just one such civilization – our own, which is changing rapidly. Will people be around a thousand years from now? If yes, will the people living then be able to understand the response from another civilization to a message sent by those who lived a thousand years ago?

*Polis* (chapter 2), as an open space for communication and decision-making, is critical today just as it was several thousand years ago. As noted, extraterrestrial communication is not just a scientific but also a political problem and so directly pertains to the nature of the polis. Any controversial issue, e.g. the METI/SETI debate, must be open for public deliberation in which people come forth to present their views, leading to a decision on a course of action. We all should identify with Diogenes who considered himself to be a *kosmopolitēs* – 'a citizen of the cosmos.'

*God* (chapter 3) is mysterious, and people are drawn to God just as they are drawn to the cosmos. Outer space, as heaven, is often considered God's realm. In the words of John Glenn – a former astronaut and the first American to orbit the Earth – "to look up out at this kind of creation and not believe in God is . . . impossible" (Zauzmer, 2016). It can be recalled that the origins of the transmission view of communication lie in religious ideas transported across space for the purpose of control and the extension of God's kingdom on Earth. With space expanding beyond the Earth, people must pause and think about God and the purpose of their possible communication with extraterrestrials.

*The body* (chapter 4) is the nexus of our existence: we experience the world, including ourselves, through the body. Thinking about extraterrestrial civilizations, we acutely realize that communication cannot be conceptualized only in terms of data and technologies. Not simply a process of sending and receiving signals, communication is an intersubjective and intercorporeal experience. Hence, genuine contact between terrestrial bodies and extraterrestrial bodies must result in sensorimotor contact, i.e., be a tactile experience – a matter of touch.

*Mind* (chapter 5) is not localized in our brain or even body. While cognition depends on the physical and biological environment of the Earth, no sharp line can be drawn between the body and the world, and so our mind extends not only into the terrestrial environment but also outer space: "interstellar messages are in fact distributed thoughts outside our brains" (Dunér, 2011, p. 457). And, if it is not a stand-alone and localized entity, then the mind can be conceptualized as an unbounded field in which everything in the Universe is interconnected.

*Language* (chapter 6) is, of course, the main prerequisite for communication between humans and extraterrestrials. Since language is any system of symbols and rules for their combination, "the interstellar communication problem is very much a semiotic problem" (Dunér, 2011). Often, such communication is presented as 'conversation'. It is argued that "we need . . . to look carefully at conversations (even delayed over centuries) to understand some of the complexities inherent in communicating with ETI" (Ashkenazi, 2016, p. 113). However, as noted earlier, conversation is an intimate and most spontaneous form of interaction; to call communication with extraterrestrials 'conversation' would be stretching its meaning. At least for the foreseeable future,

> there will never be a conversation of that character between two inhabited planets. You will be able to say, 'Hello, how are you?', but 200 [years] from now it will be a descendant of his, many times removed, who says, 'I'm fine, [how] are you, he was fine'. Thus the communication that we are discussing is of an entirely different nature.
> *(Bracewell, 1974)*

Here, we deal with an intergroup communication situation. At this level, language fully reveals its nature as a practical activity: in this respect, communicating with the extraterrestrials will be a socializing practice (Dunér, 2017). Since all limits of language are not constraints but openings, communication at this level will be a new form of life and a new dwelling place in which humans and extraterrestrials can belong.

*Culture* (chapter 7) is a form of practice that leaves meaningful traces. It can be recalled that one of the first practical human acts was clearing out a place from wilderness, i.e., making space and thus opening up some opportunity. Searching for extraterrestrial intelligence, in essence, is searching for such new traces and thus opportunities; significantly, it is now suggested that the acronym SETI be replaced with 'technosignatures'.

*Information (*chapter 8) is most directly identified with extraterrestrial communication, which is conceptualized in the engineering sense as sending and receiving signals. By exploring extraterrestrial communication in this sense, we see how information can be coded, measured, and efficiently transmitted through a channel, etc. At the same time, we come to understand that a message cannot be limited to information sent and received, for it is always a communicative act of in-forming that takes place in a certain context.

*Community* (chapter 9) is one of the central concerns in exploring extraterrestrial intelligence. We are eager to learn about other civilizations and partake of their knowledge to our benefit; thus, it is easy to become fixated on "the quest for communication with aliens . . . those creatures from outer and inner space" (Peters, 1999, p. 257). However, all communication is search for Otherness: "There is no other kind of communication" (ibid.). And so we gain something even if we never receive a reply from outer space because it's not only about aliens, it's about us. This is captured very well in the title of a talk given in July 2018 by Dr. Jill Tarter at the Florida Institute of Technology Cross-Cultural Management summit: 'A Cosmic Perspective: Searching for Aliens, Finding Ourselves'. In other words, thinking about extraterrestrial civilizations helps us to focus on our own, which is now threatened by another great extinction – and not at the hands of aliens but due to human intervention. Saving our terrestrial civilization is a goal that can be accomplished by all those engaged in communicative practices toward a common end, i.e., by the Earth community. To accomplish this goal, all must step back and look at the big picture, i.e., to appreciate how small the Earth is when viewed from cosmos – just "a small blue dot', in Sagan's words (1997).

The importance of exploring diverse human experiences around the globe in order to discover our commonality cannot be overemphasized. As stated in the 'Draft Declaration of Principles Concerning Sending Communications with Extraterrestrial Intelligence', proposed by the SETI Committee of the International Academy of Astronautics, all messages to extraterrestrial intelligence "should be sent on behalf of all Humankind" and "reflect a careful concern for the broad interests and wellbeing of *Humanity*" (1995, emphasis added). However, all forms of communication among beings on Earth must be examined, since its community cannot be conceptualized by separating the human and the non-human. It must be recalled that animals helped humans to explore outer space (Dohrer, 2017). The Soviet Union launched *Sputnik 2* in 1957 with a small dog, Laika, on board. In 1960, the Soviet Union sent two dogs, Belka and Strelka: they were the first animals to orbit the Earth and return alive (Figures 10.6 and 10.7). Thus, thinking about possible communication with extraterrestrials helps us to fully appreciate the Earth as the community of human and non-human beings living together.

**Figure 10.6**    Belka in the Memorial Museum of Cosmonautics in Moscow. Photo by Armael.

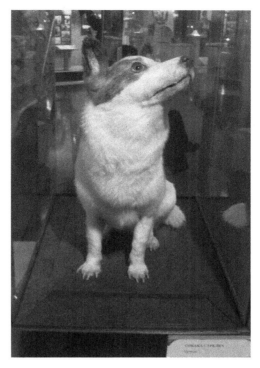

**Figure 10.7**    Strelka in the Memorial Museum of Cosmonautics in Moscow.
Photo by Armael.

We must remember that community can be conceptualized not only as a common substance shared by everyone like us, but also as a deep urge for contact with those unlike ourselves and as the lack of 'one's own'. And "what else is the 'common' if not . . . that which does not belong to anyone . . .?" (Esposito, 2013a, pp. 45–46). Can there be a better description of outer space than that?! In this sense, our community is held together by a lack, by what we can never own. Perhaps we can continue avoiding another great extinction here on Earth as long as we feel the urge for communication with extraterrestrials.

Thinking about possible communication with extraterrestrials is not, of course, something that most people often do. We're too busy living in what appears to be a perpetual present, especially now that "we are in the epoch of simultaneity" (Foucault, 1986, p. 22). It seems that we can be instantaneously present anywhere and co-present with anyone. And yet, "'now' can stretch only as far as our signals carry" (Peters, 2015, p. 367). This is something that is easy to forget in our day-to-day communication, especially oral face-to-face interaction. However, when it comes to sending a message, "even on earth, there is technically no true simultaneity" as there is "an infinitesimal delay between departure and arrival" (Peters, 2015, p. 367). Obviously, with sending a message to outer space, the delay is anything but infinitesimal; for instance, "a message sent to Andromeda would take 2 million years to arrive . . . and another 2 million years for a response to return" (Stunkel, 2015, p. 21).

Thus, thinking about outer space helps us to understand the nature of communication in general. While interaction at the human scale may appear instantaneous, "dealing in an enormous universe has taught us that all emanations come out of the past" and "the farther we see into the universe, the farther we see into deep history" (Peters, 2015, p. 363). Communication is always a process of trying to cross some gaps – sometimes barely noticeable, sometimes vast. When Foucault says that the anxiety of our era has more to do with space than with time (Foucault, 1986), we must remember that space and time go hand-in-hand as the Universe is one space-time continuum. Today we must be more anxious given its accelerated expansion: the Universe is said to be running away from us. Scientists believe that, if such expansion continues and dark energy doesn't degrade over time, then distant galaxies will be dragged farther and farther:

> Light emitted by such galaxies will therefore fight a losing battle to traverse the rapidly widening gulf that separates us. The light will never reach Earth. . .Because of this, when future astronomers look to the sky, they will no longer witness the past. The past will have drifted beyond the cliffs of space.
>
> *(Greene, 2011)*

Since the Earth is a part of the Universe, the Universe is running away not just from us but from itself. Or, to put it more accurately, dark energy is tearing things in the Universe apart instead of pulling them together. If the Universe keeps expanding faster and faster, all matter in it will eventually be torn apart – what is known as 'the Big Rip' scenario.

Thus, "the universe is in incomplete communication with itself" (Peters, 2003, p. 397). Hence, we must keep filling gaps in communication – completing it, as it were. While scientists speculate there may be some previously unsuspected force-field that could reverse its expansion, there is something that actually exists and keeps the Universe alive: "The only thing that holds it together is its common history – what every eye in the universe can see in common" (ibid.). Since there can be no common history without communication, we can say that what holds the Universe together is communication: only this way can we save ourselves from eternal darkness and the Universe from disappearing. As noted earlier, every message – whether sent to or from outer space – comes out of the past, aimed at bridging a gap and arriving at its destination.

Recently, in October of 2017, astronomers at the University of Hawaii discovered an object flying through our solar system at a very high speed and potentially carrying such a message – the first known interstellar asteroid that they dubbed 'Oumuamua, which means 'a messenger from afar arriving first' in Hawaiian. The astronomers found the asteroid's cigar-like shape and orbital characteristics unusual and so wondered if it might be an extraterrestrial spacecraft (Figure 10.8).

When they examined it, however, they didn't discover any signals that might have been transmitted by intelligent life, at least on the frequencies examined.

**Figure 10.8**    An artist's impression of the first interstellar asteroid 'Oumuamua. Image by ESO/M. Kornmesser. Source: http://www.eso.org/public/images/eso1737a/.

Still, scientists now speculate that extraterrestrial civilizations may possess the capabilities to launch ships over interstellar distances. In fact, "new research suggests these exotic objects are more abundant than we thought" (Dvorsky, 2018).

We must remember, though, that, just as such objects appear exotic to us, our spacecraft, e.g. *Voyager 1*, would likely appear exotic to aliens. As noted earlier, if we think of others and not ourselves as 'exotic', we fail to recognize the true nature of communication (Peters, 1999, p. 260). Aliens observing our ship flying through the outer space may find it just as strange and dub it – in their own language – 'a messenger from afar arriving first'. Both their spacecraft and our spacecraft, while moving in opposite directions, are arriving from the past. And it does not really matter which one arrives first because this is not a competition in which one wins and the other loses. In this scenario, as soon as a messenger from afar – whichever it is – arrives, contact is established, and we all win for we can now communicate and learn about the Other and ourselves. For instance, we may finally learn the meaning of life, which has always been in plain sight – but only if one can see it from millions of light years away. We may also learn something crucial about the Universe, e.g. why it has been running away from us: we may be surprised to hear that it was because of something we'd said – 'hunting for aliens'. More importantly, we will have a common history and so can take better care of our common destiny. Thus, "we should act as if our choices shape the universe" (Peters, 1999, p. 257).

Communication, though, is never over: if completed, it ceases to be communication. Hence, once we have caught up with the Universe, or, rather, once the Universe has caught up with itself, communication will still continue, the whole Universe becoming a messenger (Peters, 1999). New chasms will emerge and will need to be crossed, this time through interversal communication, i.e., communication among different universes. At one point, the concept of multiple universes could be found only in science fiction, but now quantum theory speculates that many versions of our universe exist. Moreover, if they remain weakly coupled (e.g., by gravity), it is possible to speak about "communication between parallel universes" (Anderson, 2015, p. 124). We must continue speculating about new instruments that could send/receive signals to/from that far out; theorizing about communication ceases once we stop wondering about its nature. As Aristotle writes in his *Metaphysics*, it is owing to their wonder that men both now begin and at first began to philosophize; they wondered originally at the obvious difficulties, then advanced little by little and stated difficulties about the greater matters, e.g. about the phenomena of the moon and those of the sun and of the stars, and about the genesis of the universe.

*(I.2, 982b11–28)*

So, let's keep wondering. Let's keep communicating. Let's keep the wonder of communication alive.

# Bibliography

Abbas, N. (1999, May 25). The posthuman view on virtual bodies. *CTheory*. Retrieved from www.ctheory.net/articles.aspx?id=266

Aczel, A. (2014). *Why science does not disprove God*. New York: William Morrow.

Addey, C. (2014). *Divination and theurgy in Neoplatonism: Oracles of the Gods.* Farnham & Burlington, VT: Ashgate.

Adriaans, P. W. (2012). Information. In E. N. Zalta (Ed.). *The Stanford Encyclopedia of Philosophy* (Winter 2012 Edition). Retrieved from https://plato.stanford.edu/entries/information/

Agamben, G. (1993). *The coming community* (M. Hardt, Trans.). Minneapolis, MN & London: University of Minnesota Press.

Agamben, G. (2017). *The omnibus Homo Sacer*. Stanford, CA: Stanford University Press.

Aiello, G. & Tosoni, S. (2016). Going about the city: Methods and methodologies for urban communication research. *International Journal of Communication, 10*, 1252–1262.

Aitken, J. E. and Shedletsky, L. J. (1997). *Intrapersonal communication processes.* Plymouth, MI: Hayden-McNeil Publishers.

Albano, C. (2005). Seeing the mind: considerations on visual metaphors of the mind in Western thought (16th–18th centuries). *Developmental Medicine and Child Neurology, 47*(12), 843–848.

Alderson-Day, B., Weis, S., McCarthy-Jones, S., Moseley, P., Smailes, D., & Fernyhough, C. (2016). The brain's conversation with itself: Neural substrates of dialogic inner speech. *Social Cognitive & Affective Neuroscience, 11*(1), 110–120.

Aleksander, I. (2001). *How to build a mind. Toward machines with imagination.* New York: Columbia University Press.

Alerby, E., Hagström, E., & Westman, S. (2014). The embodied classroom: A phenomenological discussion of the body and the room. *Journal of Pedagogy, 5*(1), 11–23.

Allen, J. (2001). *Inference from signs: Ancient debates about the nature of evidence.* Oxford: Clarendon Press.

Allen, M. (Ed.) (2017). *The SAGE encyclopedia of communication research methods.* Milwaukee, WI: University of Wisconsin-Milwaukee.

Allmer, T. (2015). *Critical theory and social media: Between emancipation and commodification.* London: Routledge.

Alloa, E. (2015). Getting in touch. Aristotelian diagnostics. In R. Kearney & B. Treanor (Eds.), *Carnal hermeneutics* (pp. 195–213). New York: Fordham University Press.

Althusser, L. (1971). *Lenin and philosophy, and other essays.* New York and London: Monthly Review Press.

Amit, E., Wakslak, C., & Trope, Y. (2012). The use of visual and verbal means of communication across psychological distance. *Personality and Social Psychology Bulletin, 39*(1), 43–56.

Ampère, A.M. (1834). *Essai sur la philosophie des sciences* [Essay on philosophy of science]. Tome 2. Paris: Bachelier.

*The Ancient Egyptian Book of the Dead* (2006). (R. Faulkner, Trans.). Austin, TX: University of Texas Press.

Anderson, A. A. (2004). *Mythos, logos,* and *telos*: How to regain the love of wisdom. In A. A. Anderson, S. V. Hicks, & L. Witkowski (Eds.), *Mythos and logos: How to regain the love of wisdom* (pp. 61–74). New York &Amsterdam: Rodopi.

Anderson, B. (2006). *Imagined communities: Reflections on the origin and spread of nationalism*. London & New York: Verso.

Anderson, G. (2003). *The Athenian experiment: Building an imagined political community in ancient Attica, 508–490 B.C.* Ann Arbor, MI: University of Michigan Press.

Anderson, J. (2000). The 'third generation' of the Frankfurt School. *Intellectual History Newsletter 22*. Retrieved from www.phil.uu.nl/~joel/research/publications/3rdGeneration.htm

Anderson, R. W. (2015). *The cosmic compendium: The ultimate fate of the Universe*. Morrisville, NC: Lulu.com

Aquinas, Thomas (1946). *The commentary of St. Thomas Aquinas on Aristotle's Treatise on the soul*. (R. A. Kocourek, Trans.). St. Paul, MN: College of St. Thomas.

Archdiocese of Baltimore. (2012, January 19). *Vatican astronomers says if aliens exist, they may not need redemption*. Retrieved from www.archbalt.org/vatican-astronomer-says-if-aliens-exist-they-may-not-need-redemption/

Arendt, H. (1978). *The life of the mind. Vol. 2. Willing*. San Diego, etc.: Harcourt Brace Jovanovich.

Arendt, H. (1998). *The human condition*. 2nd ed. Chicago, IL: University of Chicago Press.

Arluke, A., & Sanders, C. (2008). Introduction to part one: Thinking with animals. In A. Arluke, & C. Sanders (Eds.), *Between the species: Readings in human-animal relations* (pp. 1–4). Boston, MA: Allyn & Bacon.

Arnett, R. (2016). Dialogue theory. In K.B. Jensen, R. Craig, J. Pooley, & E. Rothenbuhler (Eds.), *The international encyclopedia of communication theory and philosophy*. Malden, MA: Wiley-Blackwell. doi.org/10.1002/9781118766804.wbiect008

Ashcraft, K. L., & Mumby, D. K. (2004). *Reworking gender: A feminist communicology of organization*. Thousand Oaks, CA: SAGE.

Ashkenazi, M. (2017). *What we know about extraterrestrial intelligence. Foundations of xenology*. Berlin: Springer.

Assmann. J. (2003). *The mind of Egypt: History and meaning in the time of the pharaohs* (A. Jenkins, Trans.). Cambridge, MA: Harvard University Press.

Austin, J.L. (1975). *How to do things with words*. Oxford: Oxford University Press.

Avramides, A. (2017). Wittgenstein and ordinary language philosophy. In H. G. Glock & J. Hyman (Eds.), *A companion to Wittgenstein* (pp. 718–730). Chichester, UK: Wiley-Blackwell.

Ayee, E. (2013). Human communication revisited: A biblical perspective. *Koers: Bulletin for Christian Scholarship, 78*(1), Art. #549, 16 pages. dx.doi.org/10.4102/koers.v78i1.549

Bacon, F. (1861). *The philosophical works of Francis Bacon, with prefaces and notes by the late Robert Leslie Ellis, together with English translations of the principal Latin pieces, vols 1–15.* J. Spedding (Ed.). London: Longman & co.

Bailey, L. (2005). *The enchantments of technology.* Urbana, IL & Chicago, IL: University of Illinois Press.

Bakhtin, M. (1984). *Rabelais and his world* (H. Iswolsky, Trans.). Bloomington, IN: Indiana University Press.

Ballard, B. (2003). Through language to learning: Preparing overseas students for studies in Western universities. In H. Coleman (Ed.), *Society and the language classroom* (pp. 148–168). Cambridge, UK: Cambridge University Press.

Baluška, F. & Ninkovic, V. (Eds.). (2010). *Plant communication from an ecological perspective.* Berlin: Springer.

Bandura, A. (2001). Social cognitive theory of mass communication. *Mediapsychology, 3*, 265–299.

Banet-Weiser, S. (2010). Afterword: Traces in social worlds. In H. Gray & M. Gómez-Barris (Eds.), *Toward a sociology of the trace* (pp. 289–292). Minneapolis, MN: University of Minnesota Press.

Barbour, I. (1992). *Ethics in an age of technology. The Gifford lectures, volume 2.* New York: Harper Collins.

Barnes, E. (2017). *The minority body: A theory of disability.* Oxford: Oxford University Press.

Barnlund, D. (1968). *Interpersonal communication: Survey and studies.* Boston, MA: Houghton Mifflin.

Barthes, R. (1972). *Mythologies* (A. Lavers, Trans.). New York: Farrar, Straus & Giroux.

Barron, C. (Ed.). (2003). A strong distinction between humans and non-humans is no longer required for research purposes: A debate between Bruno Latour and Steve Fuller. *History of the Human Sciences, 16*(2), 77–99.

Bateson, G. (1972). *Steps to an ecology of mind: Collected essays in anthropology, psychiatry, evolution, and epistemology.* Chicago, IL and London: University of Chicago Press.

Bates, K., Goodley, D., & Runswick-Cole, K. (2017). Precarious lives and resistant possibilities: The labour of people with learning disabilities in times of austerity. *Disability & Society, 32*(2), 160–175.

Bauman, Z. (1993). *Postmodern ethics.* Oxford: Blackwell.

Baumard, P. (2017). *Cybersecurity in France.* Berlin: Springer.

Beiner, R. (1983). *Political judgement.* London: Methuen.

Bellah, R. N., Madsen, R., Sullivan, W. M., Swidler, A., & Tipton, S. M. (1985). *Habits of the heart: Individualism and commitment in American life.* Berkeley, CA: University of California Press.

Benedict, R. (1934). *Patterns of culture.* Oxford: Houghton Mifflin.

Benedict, K. (2004). *Empowering collaborations: Writing partnerships between religious women and scribes in the Middle Ages.* New York & London: Routledge.

Benson, B. E., & Wirzba, N. (Eds.). (2005). *The phenomenology of prayer.* New York: Fordham University Press.

Benveniste, E. (1997). Gift and exchange in the Indo-European vocabulary. In A. D. Schrift (Ed.), *The logic of the gift: Toward an ethic of generosity* (pp. 33–43). New York: Routledge.

Berea A. (2018). *Emergence of communication in socio-biological networks.* Berlin: Springer.

Berger, A. A. (2000). The meanings of culture. *M/C: A Journal of Media and Culture, 3*(2). Retrieved from www.api-network.com/mc/0005/meaning.php/

Berger, J. (2014). Word of mouth and interpersonal communication: A review and directions for future research. *Journal of Consumer Psychology, 24*(4), 586–660.

Berko, R. M., Wolvin, A. & Wolvin, D. (2004). *Communicating: A social and career focus.* 9th ed. Boston, MA: Houghton Mifflin.

Bernays, E. (1928). *Propaganda.* New York: Boni & Liveright.

Berry, D. (2007). *Health communication: Theory and practice.* Maidenhead, UK: Open University Press.

Bhabha, H. (1994). *The location of culture.* New York: Routledge.

Bhandar, B., & Goldberg-Hiller J. (Eds.). (2015). *Plastic materialities: Politics, legality, and metamorphosis in the work of Catherine Malabou.* Durham, NC: Duke University Press.

Bialostosky, D. (2004). Aristotle's rhetoric and Bakhtin's discourse theory. In W. Jost & W. Olmsted (Eds.), *A companion to rhetoric and rhetorical criticism* (pp. 393–408). Malden, MA: Blackwell.

Bilansky, A. (1999) Rhetoric, democracy, and the deliberative horizon. In C. J. Swearingen & D. S. Kaufer (Eds.), *Rhetoric, the polis, and the global village: Selected papers from the 1998 thirtieth anniversary Rhetoric Society of America* (pp. 221–230). Mahwah, NJ: Erlbaum.

Binding, L., & Tapp, D. (2008). Human understanding in dialogue: Gadamer's recovery of the genuine. *Nursing Philosophy, 9*(2), 121–130.

Bird, G. (2017). *Containing community: From political economy to ontology in Agamben, Esposito, and Nancy.* Albany, NY: SUNY Press.

Bird, G., & Short, J. (2015). *Community, immunity and the proper: Roberto Esposito.* Abingdon, UK & New York: Routledge.

Birdwhistell, R. L. (1952). *Introduction to kinesics: An annotation system for analysis of body motion and gesture.* Louisville, KY: University of Louisville.

Birdwhistell, R. L. (1959). Contribution of linguistic-kinesic studies to the understanding of schizophrenia. In A. Auerback (Ed.), *Schizophrenia. An integrated approach* (pp. 99–123). New York: Ronald Press.

Bissell, C. (2009). A history of automatic control. In S. Y. Nof (Ed). *Springer handbook of automation.* (pp. 53–69). Berlin: Springer.

Bizzell, P., & Herzberg, B. (2001). Enlightenment rhetoric: Introduction. In P. Bizzell & B. Herzberg (Eds.), *The rhetorical tradition: Readings from classical times to the present* (pp. 791–813). 2nd ed. Boston: Bedford St. Martin's.

Blackman, L. (2008). *The body: The key concepts.* Oxford and New York: Berg.

Blackshaw, T. (2010). *Key concepts in community studies.* Los Angeles, CA & London: SAGE.

Blair, D. (2006). *Wittgenstein, language and information: "Back to the rough ground!"* Berlin: Springer.

Blake, R. H., & Haroldsen, E. (1975). *A taxonomy of concepts in communication.* New York: Hastings House.

Bleeker, M., Sherman, J.F., & Nedelkopoulou E. (2015). *Performance and phenomenology: Traditions and transformations*. New York and London: Routledge.

Bliss, J. (2008). *Naming and namelessness in medieval romance*. Woodbridge, UK & Rochester, NY: Boydell & Brewer.

Bloch, M. (1977). The past and the present in the present. *Man, n.s. 12*(2), 278–292.

Blokhuis, M. Z., & Lundgren, C. (2017). Riders' perceptions of equestrian communication in sports dressage. *Society & Animals, 25*(6), 573–591.

Blumer, H. (2004). *George Herbert Mead and human conduct* (T. J. Morrione, Ed.). Walnut Creek, CA: AltaMira Press.

Boletsi, M. (2013). *Barbarianism and its discontents*. Stanford, CA: Stanford. University Press.

Boorstin, D. (1983). *The discoverers: A history of man's search to know his world and himself*. New York: Vintage.

Boorstin, D. (1992). *The creators: A history of the heroes of the imagination*. New York: Random House.

Borenstein, S. (1998, November 7). Astronauts' faith isn't lost in space. *Orlando Sentinel*. Retrieved from http://articles.orlandosentinel.com/1998-11-07/life style/9811060642_1_astronauts-john-glenn-faith

Bormann, E.G. (1982). The symbolic convergence theory of communication: Applications and implications for teachers and consultants. *Journal of Applied Communication Research, 10*(1) 50–61.

Born, M. (2005). *The Born–Einstein letters, 1916–1955: Friendship, politics, and physics in uncertain times* (I. Born, Trans.). New York: Macmillan.

Borradori, G. (2003). *Philosophy in a time of terror: Dialogues with Jürgen Habermas and Jacques Derrida*. Chicago, IL & London: University of Chicago Press.

Bracewell, R. N. (1974). Interstellar probes. In C. Ponnampernuma & A. G. W. Cameron (Eds.), *Interstellar communication: Scientific perspectives* (pp. 102–117). Boston: Houghton Mifflin.

Braidotti, R. (2006). *Transpositions: On nomadic ethics*. Cambridge, UK: Polity Press.

Brandon, S. G. F. (1972). The deification of time. In J. T. Fraser, F. C. Haber & G. H. Müller (Eds.), *The study of time: Proceedings of the First Conference of the International Society for the Study of Time Oberwolfach (Black Forest) - West Germany* (pp. 370–382). Berlin & Heidelberg: Springer-Verlag.

Brefczynski-Lewis, J. (2011). Neuroimaging: Directions and potentials for communication research. *Communication Research Reports, 28* (2), 196–204.

Brettler, M. (2004). Cyclical and teleological time in the Hebrew Bible. In R. M. Rosen (Ed.), *Time and temporality in the ancient world* (pp. 111–128). Philadelphia, PA: University of Pennsylvania Museum of Archeology and Anthropology.

Brier, S. (2003). The cybersemiotic model of communication: An evolutionary view on the threshold between semiosis and informational exchange. *tripleC 1*(1): 71–94. doi.org/10.31269/tripleC.v1i1.6

Brier, S. (2008). *Cybersemiotics: Why information is not enough*. Toronto: University of Toronto Press.

Brin, D. (1983). The "great silence": The controversy concerning extraterrestrial intelligent life. *Quarterly Journal of the Royal Astronomical Society, 24*(3), 283–309.

Broadhurst, S. & Price, S. (2017). *Digital bodies: Creativity and technology in the arts and humanities*. London: Palgrave MacMillan.

Brockmeier, J. (2005). The text of the mind. In C. Emeling & D. M. Johnson (Eds.), *The mind as a scientific object: Between brain and culture* (pp. 435–452). New York: Oxford University Press.

Brody, A. (1985). *The face of the centre: Papunya Tula paintings, 1971–84.* Melbourne, Australia; National Gallery of Victoria.

Brooke, C. G. (2000). Forgetting to be (post)human: Media and memory in a Kairotic Age. *JAC: A Journal of Composition Theory, 20*(4), 775–795.

Brooke, H. (2010). *The symptom and the subject: The emergence of the physical body in ancient Greece.* Princeton, NJ: Princeton University Press.

Bruner, E. M. (2005, October 7–8). Role of narrative in tourism. Paper presented at the conference 'On Voyage: New Directions in Tourism Theory'. Berkeley, CA. Retrieved from www.nyu.edu/classes/bkg/tourist/narrative.doc

Buber, M. (1958). *I and Thou* (R. G. Smith, Trans.). New York: Scribner.

Buber, M. (1965). *Between man and man* (R. G. Smith, Trans.). New York: Macmillan.

Buck, R. (1997). From DNA to MTV: The spontaneous communication of emotional messages.In J. O. Greene (Ed.), *Message production: Advances in communication theory* (pp. 313–340). New York & London: Routledge.

Bueno, O. (2013). Perception and conception: Shaping human minds. *Biosemiotics, 6*(3), 323–336.

Burke, K. (1966). *Language as symbolic action: Essays on life, literature, and method.* Oakland, CA: University of California Press.

Burke, K. (1969a). *A grammar of motives.* Berkeley, CA: University of California Press.

Burke, K. (1969b). *A rhetoric of motives.* Berkeley, CA: University of California Press.

Burke, K. (1973). *The philosophy of literary forms: Studies in symbolic action.* Berkeley, CA: University of California Press.

Burke, K. (1989). *On symbols and society* (J. R Gusfield, Ed.). Chicago, IL & London: University of Chicago Press.

Burkert, W. (1987). Die antike Stadt als Festgemeinschaft. In P. Hugger, W. Burkert & E. Lichtenhahn (Eds.), *Stadt und Fest: Zu Geschichte und Gegenwart europäische Festkultur* (pp. 25–44). Stuttgart, Germany: J. B. Metzler.

Butler, J. V. (2003). Mourning, politics. *Studies in Gender and Sexuality, 4*(1), 9–37.

Buttrick, D. (1988). *Homiletic: Moves and structures.* Philadelphia, PA: Fortress Press.

Cacioppo, J., & Freberg, L. (2016). *Discovering psychology: The science of mind.* Boston, MA: Cengage.

Cairns-Smith, A.G. (1971). *The life puzzle: On crystals and organisms and on the possibility of a crystal as an ancestor.* Toronto: University of Toronto Press.

Calarco, M. (2000). On the borders of language and death: Agamben and the question of the animal. *Philosophy Today, 44*, 91–97.

Calero, H. (2005). *The power of nonverbal communication: How you act is more important than what you say.* Los Angeles, CA & Aberdeen, WA: Silver Lake Publishing.

Callicott, C. (2013). Interspecies communication in the Western Amazon: Music as a form of conversation between plants and people. *European Journal of Ecopsychology, 4*, 32–43.

Camille, M. (1996). Prophets, canons, and promising monsters. *Art Bulletin, 78*(2), 198–201.

Candlish, S., & Wrisley, G. (2014). Private language. In E. N. Zalta (Ed.), *The Stanford Encyclopedia of Philosophy* (Fall 2014 edition). Retrieved from https://plato.stanford.edu/archives/fall2014/entries/private-language/.

Cappon, L. J. (Ed.) (1959). *The Adams-Jefferson letters: The complete correspondence between Thomas Jefferson and Abigail and John Adams. Vol. 2: 1812–1826.* Chapel Hill, NC: University of North Carolina Press.

Capurro, R. (2013) Information ethics. In B. Kaldis (Ed.) *Encyclopedia of philosophy and the social sciences* (pp. 471–473). Los Angeles, CA: SAGE.

Carey, J. (1989). *Communication as culture: Essays on media and society.* New York & London: Routledge.

Carilli, T. & Campbell, J. (Eds.) (2005). *Women and the media: Diverse perspectives.* Lanham, MD & Oxford: University Press of America.

Carlyle, T. (1831). *Sartor Resartus: The life and opinions of Herr Teufelsdrockh.* New York: Scribner's.

Carpenter, E., & McLuhan, M. (Eds.). (1960). *Explorations in communication: an anthology.* Boston, MA: Beacon Press.

Carr, N. (2017, October 6). How smartphones hijack our minds. *The Wall Street Journal.* Retrieved from www.wsj.com/articles/how-smartphones-hijack-our-minds-1507307811

Carroll, M. (2017). *Earths of distant suns: How we find them, communicate with them and maybe even travel there.* Berlin: Springer.

Carruthers, P. (2006). *The architecture of the mind: Massive modularity and the flexibility of thought.* Oxford: Oxford University Press.

Cascardi, A. (1999). *Consequences of enlightenment.* New York, NY: Cambridge University Press.

Casey, S. (2000). *Remembering: A phenomenological study.* 2nd ed. Bloomington, IN: Indiana University Press.

Cassirer, E. (1996). The philosophy of symbolic forms (J. M. Krois, Trans.). In J. M. Krois & D. P. Verene (Eds.), *The philosophy of symbolic forms, vol. 4: The metaphysics of symbolic forms.* New Haven, CT: Yale University Press.

Castells, M. (1996). *The rise of the network society.* Oxford: Blackwell.

Castells, M. (2007). Communication, power and counter-power in the network society. *International Journal of Communication, 1,* 238–266.

Castells, M., Fernández-Ardèvol, M., Qiu, J.L., & Sey, A. (2006). *Mobile communication and society: A global perspective.* Cambridge, MA: The MIT Press.

Castillo, D, R. (2014). Monsters for the age of the post-human. Writing monsters: Essays on Iberian and Latin American cultures. *Hispanic issues on line, 15,* 161–178. Retrieved from https://conservancy.umn.edu/bitstream/handle/11299/184485/hiol_15_09_castillo_monsters_for_the_age_of_the_post_human.pdf?sequence=1

Catt, I. E. (2011). The signifying world between ineffability and intelligibility: Body as sign in communicology. *The Review of Communication, 11*(2), 122–144.

Catt, I. E. (2017). *Embodiment in the semiotic matrix: Communicology in Peirce, Dewey, Bateson, and Bourdieu.* Madison, NJ: Fairleigh Dickinson University Press.

Catt I.E., & Eicher-Catt, D. (Eds.). (2010). *Communicology: The new science of embodied discourse.* Madison, NJ: Fairleigh Dickinson University Press.

Cavell, R. (2003). *McLuhan in space: A cultural geography.* Toronto, Canada: University of Toronto Press.

Cayley, D. (2004) *The rivers north of the future: The testament of Ivan Illich, as told to David Cayley, foreword by Charles Taylor.* Toronto: Anansi Press.

Charles, A. (2016). *A critical analysis of the representation of female body image in women magazines*. Munich: GRIN Verlag.

Chatwin, B. (1988). *The songlines*. London: Penguin Books

Cherry, S. (2007). *Torah through time: Understanding bible commentary from the rabbinic period to modern times*. Philadelphia, PA: Jewish Publication Society.

Chomsky, N. (1997, October). What makes mainstream media mainstream. *Z Magazine*. Retrieved from https://chomsky.info/199710__/

Choudhuri, A. R. (2010). *Astrophysics for physicists*. New York: Cambridge University Press.

Chrulew, M., & Wadiwel D. J. (Eds.). (2016). *Foucault and animals*. Leiden, Netherlands & Boston, MA: Brill.

Cioffi, R. (2014). Seeing Gods: Epiphany and narrative in the Greek novels. *Ancient Narrative, 11*, 1–42.

Cisney, V.W., & Morar, N. (Eds.). (2016). *Biopower: Foucault and beyond*. Chicago, IL & London: University of Chicago Press.

Clarke, A. E., Mamo, L., Fosket, J. R., Fishman, J.R., & Shim, J. K. (Eds) (2010). *Biomedicalization: Technoscience, health and illness in the US*. Durham, NC: Duke University Press.

Clarke, D. (2003). *Descartes's theory of the mind*. Oxford: Clarendon Press.

Coats, B. (2012). *Voices in concert: Communication ethnography of Pentecostal worship*. Doctoral dissertation. Milwaukee: Marquette University.

Cockell, C. (2018). *The equations of life. How physics shapes evolution*. New York: Basic Books.

Cofield, C. (2018, January 25). "Search for extraterrestrial intelligence" needs a new name, SETI Pioneer Says. *Space.com*. Retrieved from www.space.com/39474-search-for-extraterrestrial-intelligence-needs-new-name.html

Cohen, Y. (2014). Jewish communication theory: Biblical law and contemporary media practice. In R. Fortner & M. Fackler. (Eds.). *The handbook of media and mass communication theory* (pp. 859–873). New York: Wiley-Blackwell.

Colaiaco, J. (2001). *Socrates against Athens: Philosophy on trial*. New York: Routledge.

Combs, S. (2005). *The Dao of rhetoric*. Albany, NY: SUNY Press.

Colebrook, C. (2001). *Gilles Deleuze*. London: Routledge.

Colilli, P. (2015). *Agamben and the signature of astrology as: Spheres of potentiality*. Lanham, MD: Lexington Books.

Cooley, C. H. (1998). *On self and social organization*. Chicago, IL: University of Chicago Press.

Cooley, C. H. (2017). *Life and the student: Roadside notes on human nature, society, and letters*. London & New York: Routledge.

Coppinger, R. (2017, September 27). Elon Musk outlines Mars colony vision. *BBC.com*. Retrieved from www.bbc.com/news/science-environment-37486372

Corradini, R., Diesenberger, M., & Reimitz, H. (Eds). (2003). *The construction of communities in the Early Middle Ages: Texts, resources, artifacts*. Leiden, Netherlands & Boston, MA: Brill.

Cort, J. (2010). *Framing the Jina: Narratives of icons and idols in Jain history*. Oxford: Oxford University Press.

Coulter-Harris, D. M. (2016). *Chasing immortality in world religions*. Jefferson, NC: McFarland & Company.

Courtright, J. A. (2007). Relational communication: A view from the pragmatic perspective. In B. Whaley & W. Samter (Eds.), *Explaining communication: Contemporary theories and exemplars* (pp. 311–332). Mahwah, NJ: Erlbaum.

Coward, H. (1995). Introduction. In H. Coward (Ed.) *Population, consumption, and the environment: Religious and secular responses* (pp. 1–26). Albany, NY: SUNY Press.

Craig, R. (1999). Communication theory as a field. *Communication theory, 9*(2), 119–161.

Craig, R. (2005). How we talk about how we talk: Communication theory in the public interest. *Journal of Communication, 55*(4), 659–667.

Crosby, J. (2009). Liminality and the sacred: Discipline building and speaking with the other. *Liminalities: A Journal of Performance Studies, 5*(1), 1–19.

Crossley, N. (2012). Phenomenology of the body. In B. Turner (Ed.), *The Routledge handbook of the body* (pp. 130–143). Abingdon, UK & New York: Routledge.

Croucher, S., & Cronn-Mills, D. (2015). *Understanding communication research methods: A theoretical and practical approach.* New York: Routledge.

Croucher, S., Sommier, M., Kuchma, A., & Melnychenko, V. (2016). A content analysis of the discourses of "religion" and "spirituality" in communication journals: 2002–2012. *Journal of Communication and Religion, 38,* 42–79.

Crusius, T. (1999). *Kenneth Burke and the conversation after philosophy.* Carbondale, IL: Southern Illinois University Press.

Cunningham, S. (1995). Intrapersonal communication: A review and critique. In J. E. Aitken & L. Shedletsky (Eds.) *Intrapersonal communication processes* (pp. 3–18). Fall Church, VA: Speech Communication Association.

Cushman, D. P., & Kincaid, D. L. (1987). Introduction and initial insights: Asian perspectives on communication theory. In D. L. Kincaid (Ed.), *Communication theory: Eastern and Western perspectives* (pp. 11–22). San Diego, CA: Academic Press.

Cutié, Albert R. (2016). *Talking God: Preaching to contemporary congregations.* New York: Morehouse Publishing.

Czajkowski, W. (2001). *Philosophies of man: A study on/in a meta-anthropology.* Gliwice: Wydawnictvo Politechniki Śląskiej.

Czitrom, D. (1982). *Media and the American mind: From Morse to McLuhan.* Chapel Hill, NC: University of North Carolina Press.

Dainton, M., & Zelley, E. (2010). *Applying communication theory for professional life.* Los Angeles, CA: SAGE.

Daly, A. (2016). *Merleau-Ponty and the ethics of intersubjectivity.* London: Palgrave Macmillan.

D'Antonio, W. V., Davidson, J. D., Hoge, D. R., & Meyer, K. (2001). *American Catholics: Gender, generation, and commitment.* Walnut Creek, CA: AltaMira Press.

Darwin, C. (1872). *The expression of the emotions in man and animals.* London: John Murray.

Darwin, C. (1909). *The voyage of the Beagle.* New York: P. F. Collier & Son.

Davis, C. (2013). Foreword. In P. Sloterdijk, *Philosophical temperaments: From Plato to Foucault* (T. Dunlap, Trans.) (pp. vii–xv). New York: Columbia University Press.

De Waal, F. (2016). *Are we smart enough to know how smart animals are?* New York: W. W. Norton.

Deely, J. (2001). *Four ages of understanding: The first postmodern survey of philosophy from ancient times to the turn of the twenty-first century.* Toronto: University of Toronto Press.

DeMello, M. (2000). *Bodies of inscription: Cultural history of the modern tattoo community.* Durham, NC: Duke University Press.

Delanty, G. (2003). *Community.* London: Routledge.

Deleuze, G., & Guattari, F. (1987). *A thousand plateaus: Capitalism and schizophrenia* (B. Massumi, Trans.). Minneapolis, MN: University of Minnesota Press.

Denning, K. (2014). Learning to read interstellar message decipherment from archaeological and anthropological perspectives. In D. Vakoch, D. (Ed.), *Archaeology, anthropology, and interstellar communication* (pp. 95–112). Washington, DC: NASA.

Depew, D., & Peters, J. D. (2001). Community and communication: The conceptual background. In G. J. Shepherd & E. W. Rothenbuhler (Eds.), *Communication and community* (pp. 3–21). Mahwah, NJ: Erlbaum.

Derrida, J. (1982). *Margins of philosophy.* (A. Bass, Trans.). Chicago, IL: University of Chicago Press.

Derrida, J. (1991). A *Derrida reader: Between the blinds.* P. Kamuf (Ed.). New York: Columbia University Press.

Derrida, J. (1992). *Given time: I. Counterfeit money* (P. Kamuf, Trans.). Chicago, IL: University of Chicago Press.

Derrida, J. (1995). Passages – from traumatism to promise. In E. Weber (Ed.), *Interviews, 1974–1994* (P. Kamuf, Trans.) (pp.386–387). Stanford, CA: Stanford University Press.

Derrida, J. (1997a). *Deconstruction in a nutshell: a conversation with Jacques Derrida.* J. D. Caputo (Ed.). New York: Fordham University Press,

Derrida, J. (1997b). *Of grammatology* (C. G. Spivak, Trans.). Baltimore, MD: Johns Hopkins University Press.

Derrida, J. (2000). *Of hospitality: Anne Dufourmantelle invites Jacques Derrida to respond* (R. Bowlby, Trans.). Stanford, CA: Stanford University Press.

Derrida, J. (2005). *Paper machine* (R. Bowlby, Trans.). Stanford, CA: Stanford University Press.

Derrida, J. (2009). *The beast and the sovereign, Volume I* (G. Bennington, Trans.). Chicago IL & London: University of Chicago Press.

Descartes, R. (1911). *The philosophical works of Descartes* (E. S. Haldane & G. R. T. Ross, Eds.). 2 vols. Cambridge, UK: Cambridge University Press.

Descartes, R. (1954). *Philosophical writings: A selection* (E. Anscombe & P. T. Geach, Ed. & Trans.). Edinburgh: Nelson.

DeVito, C. (2011). Cultural aspects of interstellar communication. In D. A. Vakoch & A.A. Harrison (Eds.), *Civilizations beyond Earth: Extraterrestrial life and society* (pp.159–169). New York : Berghahn Books.

Dewey, J. (1967). *The early works of John Dewey, 1882–1898. Volume 2: 1887: Psychology.* J. A. Boydston (Ed.).Carbondale, IL & Edwardsville, IL: Southern Illinois University Press.

Dewey, J. (1980). *The middle works of John Dewey, 1899–1924. Volume 9: 1916: Democracy and education.* J. A. Boydston (Ed.). Carbondale, IL: Southern Illinois University Press.

Dewey, J. (1984). *The later works of John Dewey, 1925–1953. Volume 2: 1925–1927. Essays, reviews, miscellany, and 'The public and its problems'*. J. A. Boydston (Ed.). Carbondale, IL: Southern Illinois University Press.

DeWitt C. B. (2006). Stewardship: responding dynamically to the consequences of human action in the world. In R. J. Berry (Ed.), *Environmental stewardship: Critical perspectives—past and present* (pp. 145–158). New York & London: T&T Clark.

Dick, S. J. (1996). *The biological universe: The twentieth-century extraterrestrial life debate and the limits of science*. Cambridge, UK: Cambridge University Press.

Dilthey, W. (1990). *Die geistige Welt: Einleitung in die Philosophie des Lebens. Erste Hälfte: Abhandlungen zur Grundlegung der Geisteswissenschaften. Gesammelte Schriften, V. Band* (K. Gründer, Ed.). Stuttgart/Göttingen: Teubner/Vandenhoeck & Ruprecht.

Dilthey, W. (2010). The formation of the historical world in the human sciences. In R.F. Rodi & R.A. Makkreel (Eds.), *Selected works, volume III: The formation of the historical world in the human sciences* (pp.101–209). Princeton, NJ: Princeton University Press.

Dinwoodie, D. W. (2006). Time and the individual in native North America. In S. A. Kan & P. Turner Strong (Eds.), *New perspectives on native North America* (pp. 327–348). Lincoln, NE: University of Nebraska Press.

Dixon, T. L. (2006). Psychological reactions to crime news portrayals of black criminals: Understanding the moderating roles of prior news viewing and stereotype endorsement. *Communication Monographs, 73*(2), 62–187.

Dohrer, E. (2017, May 30). Laika, the dog, and the first animals in space. *SPACE.com*. Retrieved from www.space.com/17764-laika-first-animals-in-space.html

Donovan, J. (2017). Interspecies dialogue and animal ethics: The feminist care perspective. In L. Kalof (Ed.), *The Oxford handbook of animal studies* (pp. 208–226). New York & Oxford: Oxford University Press.

Donsbach, W. (2006). The identity of communication research. *Journal of Communication, 56*, 437–448.

Doob, L. W. (1989). Propaganda. In E. Barnouw (Ed.), *International encyclopedia of communications, Vol. 3* (pp. 374–378). New York & Oxford: Oxford University Press.

Dosse, F. (2011). *Gilles Deleuze and Felix Guattari: Intersecting lives* (D. Glassman, Trans.). New York: Columbia University Press.

Dossey, L. (2013). The millennium of consciousness: Reflections on the one mind. *Explore: The Journal of Science and Healing, 9*(2), 67–74.

Dousa, T. M., & Ibekwe-SanJuan, F. (2014). Introduction. In T. M Dousa & F. Ibekwe- SanJuan (Eds.), *Theories of information, communication and knowledge: A multidisciplinary approach* (pp. 1–21). Berlin: Springer.

Doyle, L. R., McCowan, B., Johnston, S., & Hanser, S. F. (2011). Information theory, animal communication and the search for extraterrestrial intelligence. *Acta Astronautica, 68*(3–4), 406–417.

Draaisma, D. (2000). *Metaphors of memory: A history of ideas about the mind* (P. Vincent, Trans.). Cambridge, UK: Cambridge University Press.

duBois, P. (1991). *Torture and truth*. New York & London: Routledge.

duBois, P. (2014). *A million and one gods: The persistence of polytheism*. Cambridge, MA: Harvard University Press.

Dumas, S. (2011). A proposal for an interstellar Rosetta Stone. In D. A. Vakoch (Ed.), *Communication with extraterrestrial intelligence (CETI)* (pp. 403–411). Albany, NY: SUNY Press.

Dunér, D. (2011). Cognitive foundations of interstellar communication. In D. A. Vakoch (Ed.), *Communication with extraterrestrial intelligence (CETI)* (pp. 449–468). Albany, NY: SUNY Press.

Dunér, D. (2017). On the plausibility of intelligent life on other worlds : A cognitive-semiotic assessment of $f_i \cdot f_c \cdot L$. *Environmental Humanities, 9*(2), 433–453.

Dunér, D., Parthemore, J., Persson, E., & Holmberg, G. (Eds.). (2013). *The history and philosophy of astrobiology: Perspectives on extraterrestrial life and the human mind.* Newcastle upon Tyne, UK: Cambridge Scholars Publishing.

Duranti, A. (2010). Husserl, intersubjectivity and anthropology. *Anthropological Theory, 10*(1), 1–20.

Durkheim, É (1954). *The elementary forms of the religious life: A study in religious sociology* (J. W. Swain, Trans.). London: Allen & Unwin.

Durkheim, É. (2009) *Sociology and philosophy* (D. F. Pocock, Trans.). Abingdon, UK & New York: Routledge.

Durkheim, É., Lukes, S., & Scull, A. T. (2013). *Durkheim and the law.* Basingstoke, UK: Palgrave Macmillan.

Dvorsky, G. (2018). Interstellar asteroids like 'Oumuamua could rewrite the origins of life on Earth. *Gizmodo.com.* Retrieved from https://gizmodo.com/interstellar-asteroids-like-oumuamua-could-rewrite-the-1822837006

Dyson, E., Gilder, G. F., Keyworth, G., & Toffler, A. (1994, August). A Magna Carta for the knowledge age. *The Progress & Freedom Foundation.* Retrieved from www.pff.org/issues-pubs/futureinsights/fi1.2magnacarta.html

Eagleton, T. (1996). *The illusions of postmodernism.* Oxford, UK: Basil Blackwell.

Eberle, G. (1994). *The geography of nowhere: Finding one's self in the postmodern world.* Kansas City, MO: Sheed & Ward.

Eby, F., & Arrowood, F. (1946). *The development of modern education in theory, organization and practice.* New York: Prentice-Hall.

Ecks, S. (2009). Welcome home, Descartes! Rethinking the anthropology of the body. *Perspectives in Biology and Medicine, 52*(1), 153–158.

Eco, U. (1976). *A theory of semiotics.* Bloomington, IN: Indiana University Press.

Eco, U. (1986). *Travels in hyperreality: Essays* (W. Weaver, Trans.). San Diego, CA: Harcourt Brace Jovanovich.

Eggins, S., & Slade, D. (2005). *Analysing casual conversation.* Sheffield, UK: Equinox Publishing.

Ehala, M. (2015). Ethnolinguistic vitality. In K. Tracy, C. Ilie, & T. Sandel (Eds.), *The international encyclopedia of language and social interaction* (pp. 1–7). Chichester, UK & Malden, MA: John Wiley and Sons.

Ekman, P & Friesen, W. V. (2008). Hand movements. In C. D. Mortensen (Ed.), *Communication theory* (pp. 273–292). New Brunswick, NJ: Transaction Publishers.

Eliot, T. S. (1943). *Four quartets.* New York: Harcourt, Brace.

Entman, R.M. (1991). Symposium framing U.S. coverage of international news: Contrasts in narratives of the KAL and Iran air incidents. *Journal of Communication, 41*(4), 6–27.

Epstein, M. (2012). *The transformative humanities: A manifesto.* London: Bloomsbury.

Ercolini, G. L. (2016). *Kant's philosophy of communication*. Pittsburgh, PA: Duquesne University Press.

Erickson, D.L. (2011). Intuition, telepathy, and interspecies communication. *NeuroQuantology*, *9*(1), 145–152.

Esposito, R. (2010). *Communitas: The origin and destiny of community* (T. Campbell, Trans.). Stanford, CA: Stanford University Press.

Esposito, R. (2011). *Immunitas: The protection and negation of life* (Z. Hanafi, Trans.). Cambridge, UK: Polity Press.

Esposito, R. (2012). *Third person: Politics of life and philosophy of the ompersonal* (Z. Hanafi, Trans.). Cambridge, UK: Polity Press.

Esposito, R. (2013a). *Terms of the political: Community, immunity, biopolitics* (R. N. Welch, Trans.). New York: Fordham University Press.

Esposito, R. (2013b). Community, immunity, biopolitics (Z. Hanafi, Trans.). *Angelaki: Journal of the Theoretical Humanities*, *18*(3), 1–12.

Ewalt, J. (2017, October). Mapping and spatial studies. In J. F. Nussbaum (Ed.), *Oxford research encyclopedia of communication*. doi.org/10.1093/acrefore/9780190228613.65

Ewegen, S. M. (2014). *Plato's Cratylus: The comedy of language*. Bloomington, IN & Indianapolis, IN: Indiana University Press.

Eugenides, J. (2011). *Middlesex*. Toronto: Vintage.

Evans, V. (2004). *The structure of time: Language, meaning and temporal cognition*. Amsterdam & Philadelphia, PA: John Benjamins.

Fabian, J. (2014). *Time and the other: How anthropology makes its object*. New York: Columbia University Press.

Fackler, M. (2014). God still speaks: A Christian theory of communication. In R. Fortner & M. Fackler (Eds.), *The handbook of media and mass communication theory* (pp. 874–888). New York: Wiley-Blackwell.

Fagg, L. W. (1985). *Two faces of time*. Wheaton, IL: The Theosophical Publishing House.

Fahnestock, J., & Secor, M. (1985). Toward a modern version of stasis theory. In C. W. Kneupper (Ed.), *Oldspeak/Newspeak: Rhetorical transformations* (pp. 217–226). Arlington, TX: Rhetoric Society of America.

Farrell A. M. (2006). Is the gift still good? Examining the politics and regulation of blood safety in the European Union. *Medical Law Review*, *14*(2), 155–179

Ferguson, N. (2017). *The square and the tower: Networks and power from the Freemasons to Facebook*. London: Penguin.

Feuerbach, L. (1881). *The essence of Christianity*. Boston, MA: Houghton Mifflin.

Feynman, R. (2012). There's plenty of room at the bottom: An invitation to enter a new field of physics. In W. A. Goddard, D. Brenner, S. E. Lyshefski & G. J. Iafrate (Eds.) *Handbook of nanoscience, engineering, and technology* (pp. 3–12). Boca Raton, FL: CRC Press.

Finnegan, R. (2002). *Communicating: The multiple modes of human communication*. Abingdon, UK & New York: Routledge.

Finney, B., & Bentley, J. (1998). A tale of two analogues: Learning at a distance from the ancient Greeks and Maya and the problem of deciphering extraterrestrial radio transmissions. *Acta Astronautica*, *42*(10), 691–696.

Firneis, M., & Leitner, F. (2013). The evolution of LINCOS: A language for cosmic interpretation. In D. Dunér et al. (Eds.), *The history and philosophy of astrobiology:*

*Perspectives on extraterrestrial life and the human mind* (pp. 201–212). Newcastle upon Tyne, UK: Cambridge Scholars Publishing.

Fischer, K. R. (2004). *Imaging life after death: Love that moves the sun and stars*. New York & Mahwah, NJ: Paulist Press.

Fischer-Lichte, E. (2014). *The Routledge introduction to theatre and performance studies* (M. Armojand & R. Mosse, Eds., M. Armojand, Trans.). Abingdon, UK & New York: Routledge.

Fisher, A. (1978). *Perspectives on human communication*. New York & London: Macmillan.

Fisher, B. A. (1970). Decision emergence: Phases in-group decision-making. *Speech Monographs, 37*, 53–66

Fisher, P. (2016, August 12). Small world: Does ecology reach all the way down to the subatomic scale? *The Conversation*. Retrieved from https://theconversation.com/small-world-does-ecology-reach-all-the-way-down-to-the-subatomic-scale-52471

Flanagan, O. (1996). *Self-expressions: Mind, morals, and the meaning of life*. New York: Oxford University Press.

Foer, F. (2017). *World without mind: The existential threat of Big Tech*. London: Penguin.

Fortner, R.S. (2014). Lewis Mumford: Technics, civilization, and media theory. In R. Fortner & M. Fackler (Eds.), *The handbook of media and mass communication theory* (pp. 210–224). New York: Wiley-Blackwell.

Foster, J.B., & Burkett, P. (2001). Marx and the dialectic of organic/inorganic relations: A rejoinder to Salleh and Clark. *Organization and Environment, 14*(4), 451–462.

Foti, V. M. (1999). Heidegger, Hölderlin, and Sophoclean tragedy. In J. Risser (Ed.), *Heidegger toward the turn: Essays on the work of the 1930s* (pp. 163–186). Albany, NY: SUNY Press.

Foucault, M. (1970). *The order of things: An archaeology of the human sciences* (A. Sheridan, Trans.). New York: Random House.

Foucault, M. (1973). *The birth of the clinic* (A. Sheridan, Trans.). New York: Pantheon Books.

Foucault, M. (1979). *The history of sexuality. Volume 1: An introduction* (R. Hurley, Trans.). London: Allen Lane.

Foucault, M (1983, October-November). *Discourse and truth: The problematization of parrhesia. Six lectures given by Michel Foucault at the University of California at Berkeley, CA, Oct.–Nov. 1983*. Retrieved from https://foucault.info/parrhesia/

Foucault, M. (1986). Of other spaces (J. Miskowiec, Trans.). *Diacritics, 16*, 22–27.

Foucault, M. (1997). *Society must be defended. Lecture at the Collège de France, 1975–76* (M. Bertani & A. Fontana, Eds., D. Macey, Trans.). New York: Picador.

Foucault, M. (2005). T*he hermeneutics of the subject: Lectures at the Collège de France, 1981–1982* (F. Gros, Ed.), G. Burchell, Trans.). New York: Palgrave Macmillan.

Frampton, K. (2001). *Studies in Tectonic culture. The poetics of construction in nineteenth and twentieth century architecture*. J. Cava (Ed.). Cambridge, MA: The MIT Press.

France, J. & Kramer S. (Eds.). (2001). *Communication and mental illness: Theoretical and practical approaches*. London: Jessica Kingsley.

Francis (2013). *Evangelii gaudium* [The joy of the Gospel]. Retrieved from http://w2.vatican.va/content/francesco/en/apost_exhortations/documents/papa-francesco_esortazione-ap_20131124_evangelii-gaudium.html

Frege, G. (1993). On sense and reference (M. Black, Trans.). In A.W. Moore (Ed.) *Meaning and reference* (pp. 23–42). Oxford: Oxford University Press.

Friend, T. (2004). *Animal talk: Breaking the codes of animal language.* New York: Free Press.

Fromm, E. (2013). *Marx's concept of man, including "economic and philosophical manuscripts".* London and New York: Bloomsbury.

Frosh, P. (2007). The bias of bias: Innis, Lessing, and the problem of space. In R. Watson & M. Blondheim (Eds.), *The Toronto school of communication theory: Interpretations, extensions, applications* (pp. 147–169). Toronto: University of Toronto Press.

Frow, J. (1997). *Time and commodity culture: Essays in cultural theory and postmodernity.* Oxford, UK: Clarendon Press.

Fuchs, C. (2016). *Critical theory of communication: New readings of Lukács, Adorno, Marcuse, Honneth, and Habermas in the age of the Internet.* London: University of Westminster Press.

Fuller. S. (2016). Social epistemology. In K.B. Jensen, R.T. Craig, J. D. Pooley, & E. W. Rothenbuhler (Eds), *The international encyclopedia of communication theory and philosophy.* Chichester, UK: Wiley-Blackwell.

Gabora, L. (2007). Mind. In R. A. Bentley, H. D. G. Maschner, & C. Chippendale (Eds.), *Handbook of theories and methods in archaeology* (pp. 283–296). Walnut Creek, CA: AltaMira Press.

Gadamer, H.-G. (2004). *Truth and method* (J. Weinsheimer & D. G. Marshall, Trans.). London & New York: Continuum.

Gadamer, H.-G. (2007). *The Gadamer reader: A bouquet of the later writings* (R. E. Palmer, Ed. & Trans.). Evanston, IL: Northwestern University Press.

Gagliano, M. (2016). Seeing green: The re-discovery of plants and nature's wisdom. In P. Vieira, M. Gagliano & J. Ryan (Eds.), *The green thread: Dialogues with the vegetal world* (pp. 147–157). Lanham, MD: Lexington Books.

Gaines, E. (2006). Communication and the semiotics of space. *Journal of Creative Communication, 1*(2), 173–181.

Galison, P. (2004). *Einstein's clocks, Poincaré's maps: Empires of time.* New York: W. W. Norton.

Gallagher, S. (2005). *How the body shapes the mind.* Oxford: Clarendon Press.

Gallois, C., Cretchley, J., & Watson, B.M. (2012). Approaches and methods in intergroup communication. In H. Giles (Ed.), *The handbook of intergroup communication* (pp. 31–43). Abingdon, UK & New York: Routledge.

Gänshirt, C. (2007). *Tools for ideas: Introduction to architectural design.* Basel, Switzerland: Birkhäuser.

Garber, M. (2014, January-February). Saving the lost art of conversation. *The Atlantic.* Retrieved from www.theatlantic.com/magazine/archive/2014/01/the-eavesdropper/355727/

Garber, S. (2014). A political history of NASA. In D. Vakoch (Ed.), *Archaeology, anthropology, and interstellar communication* (pp. 23–48). Washington, DC: NASA.

Gardner, A. (2008). Conversation analysis. In A. Davies & C. Elder (Eds.), *The handbook of applied linguistics* (pp. 262–284). Malden, MA: Blackwell.

Gasché, R. (2007). *The honor of thinking: Critique, theory, philosophy.* Stanford, CA: Stanford University Press.

Gaudio, R. (2003). Coffeetalk: Starbucks™ and the commercialization of casual conversation. *Language in Society, 32*(5), 659–691.

Gebeshuber, I. C., & Macqueen, M. O. (2017). Superfast evolution via trans- and interspecies biocommunication. In R. Gordon & J. Seckbach (Eds.), *Biocommunication: Sign-mediated interactions between cells and organisms* (pp. 165–185). Hoboken, NJ: World Scientific.

Gebser, J. (1985). *The ever-present origin* (N. Barstad & A. Mickunas, Trans.). Athens, OH: Ohio University Press.

Geertz, C. (1973). *The interpretation of cultures*. New York: Basic Books.

Geoghegan, B. & Peters, B. (2014). Cybernetics. In M.-L. Ryan, L. Emerson & B. J. Robertson (Eds.), *The Johns Hopkins guide to digital media* (pp. 109–112). Baltimore, MD: Johns Hopkins University Press.

George, V. (2008). *Paths to the divine: Ancient and Indian*. Washington, DC: Council for Research in Values and Philosophy.

Gerbner, G., & Gross, L. (1976). Living with television: The violence profile. *Journal of Communication, 26*(2), 173–199.

Gere, C. (2012). *Community without community in digital culture*. London and New York: Palgrave Macmillan.

Ghandour, B. M. (2004). *Proximal versus distal romantic relationships: An analysis of construal differences*. Masters Thesis. Retrieved from https://scholarworks.umass.edu/theses/2413

Gheituri A., & Golfam A. (2009). God-man communication in the Quran: A semiological approach. *International Journal of Humanities, 16*(1), 45–62.

Gibson, W. (1984). *Neuromancer*. New York: Ace Books.

Giddens, A. (1991) *Modernity and self-identity: Self and society in the late modern age*. Stanford, CA: Stanford University Press.

Gilchrist-Petty, E. S., & Long, S. D. (Eds.). (2016). *Contexts of the dark side of communication: A reader*. New York: Peter Lang.

Giles, H. (2012). Principles of intergroup communication. In H. Giles (Ed.), *The handbook of intergroup communication* (pp. 3–18). Abingdon, UK & New York: Routledge.

Giles, H., Reid, S., & Harwood, J. (Eds.) (2010). *The dynamics of intergroup communication*. New York: Peter Lang.

Ginn, F. (2013). Sticky lives: Slugs, detachment and more-than-human ethics in the garden. *Transactions of the Institute of British Geographers, 1*(39), 532–544.

Glasser, A. (1967). *Extrasensory perception*. New York: Essandess Special Editions.

Gleick, J. (2012). *The Information: A history, a theory, a flood*. New York: Vintage.

Gold, A. (2005). *Conceptualizing community: Anthropological reflections. The Collaborative Initiative for Research Ethics in Environmental Health*. Retrieved from www.brown.edu/research/research-ethics/sites/brown.edu.research.research-ethics/files/uploads/Conceptualizing%20Community%20-%20Gold.pdf

Gorman, M. (1962). *General semantics and contemporary Thomism*. Lincoln, NE: University of Nebraska Press.

Goudeli, K. (2002). *Challenges to German idealism: Schelling, Fichte and Kant*. New York, NY: Palgrave Macmillan.

Gould, S. J. (2001). Introduction. In C. Zimmer, *Evolution: The triumph of an idea* (pp. ix–xiv). New York: Harper Collins.

Gould, S. J. (2003). Toward a theory of advertising lovemaps in marketing communications: Overdetermination, postmodern thought, and the advertising hermeneutic circle. In Reichert & J. Lambiase (Eds.) *Sex in advertising: Perspectives on the erotic appeal* (pp. 151–172). Mahwah, NJ: Erlbaum.

Gräb, W. (2011). Doing theology in a globalized world: Religion, diversity, and conflicts in films. In Foley, E. (Ed.), *Religion, diversity and conflict* (pp. 163–174). Zurich & Berlin: LIT Verlag.

Graeser, A. (1977). On language, thought, and reality in Ancient Greek philosophy. *Dialectica, 41*, 360–388.

Grafton, A. (2011, May 13). Review of J. Gleick, *The Information: A history, a theory, a flood. Washington Post.* Retrieved from www.washingtonpost.com/entertain ment/books/james-gleicks-the-information/2011/04/26/AFMxqr2G_story. html?noredirect=on&utm_term=.602e9bfd374e

Granfield, P. (1973). *Ecclesial cybernetics: A systems analysis of authority and decision-making in the Catholic Church, with a plea for shared responsibility.* New York: Macmillan.

Grant, C. B. (2003). Destabilizing social communication theory. *Theory, Culture and Society, 20*(6), 95–119+154.

Grant, S. (2018). *Talking to my country.* London: Scribe.

Graves-Brown, P. (2015, February 23). Review of L. Malafouris, *How things shape the mind: A theory of material engagement. Journal of Contemporary Archaeology Book Reviews.* Retrieved from www.equinoxpub.com/home/jca-book-reviews-things-shape-mind-theory-material-engagement-lambros-malafouris/

Gray, R. (2016). The Fermi paradox is neither Fermi's nor a paradox. *Astrobiology, 15*(3), 195–199.

Green, J. (2014). *Drawn from the ground: Sound, sign, and inscription in Central Australian sand stories.* Cambridge, UK: Cambridge University Press.

Greene, B. (2011, January 1). Darkness on the Edge of the Universe. *New York Times.* Retrieved from www.nytimes.com/2011/01/16/opinion/16greene.html

Greene, M. (1995). *Releasing the imagination: Essays on education and social change.* San Francisco: Jossey-Bass.

Greer, J. M. (2005). *A world full of Gods: An inquiry into polytheism.* Tucson, AZ: ADF Publishing.

Greif, H. (2017). What is the extension of the extended mind? *Synthese, 194*, 4311.

Greshko, M. (2018, March 27). Aliens could detect life on Earth: Here's how. *National Geographic.* Retrieved from https://news.nationalgeographic.com/2018/03/how-aliens-could-discover-life-on-earth-one-strange-rock-science/

Grice. P. (1989). *Studies in the way of words.* Cambridge, MA: Harvard University Press.

Griffiths, J. G. (1966). Hecataeus and Herodotus on 'A gift of the river'. *Journal of Near Eastern Studies, 25*(1), 57–61.

Grinspoon, D. (2004) *Lonely planets: The natural philosophy of alien life.* New York: Ecco/Harper Collins.

Griswold, C. L. (2010). *Self-knowledge in Plato's Phaedrus.* University Park, PA: Pennsylvania State University Press

Grondin, J. (1994). *Introduction to philosophical hermeneutics.* New Haven, CT: Yale University Press.

Groys, B. (1993). *Utopia and exchange* [Utopiya I obmen]. Moscow: Znak.

Gumbrecht, H. U. (2004). *Production of presence: What meaning cannot convey.* Stanford, CA: Stanford University Press.

Gumperz, J. (1982). *Discourse strategies.* Cambridge, UK: Cambridge University Press.

Gusfield, J. R. (1989). Introduction. In K. Burke, *On symbols and society* (J. R. Gusfield, Ed.) (pp. 1–49). Chicago, IL & London: University of Chicago Press.

Haas, L. (2008). *Merleau-Ponty's philosophy.* Bloomington, IN: Indiana University Press

Habermas, J. (1989). *The structural transformation of the public sphere: An inquiry into a category of bourgeois society* (T. Burger & F. Lawrence, Trans.). Cambridge, UK: Polity Press.

Habermas, J. (1994). Three normative models of democracy. *Constellations, 1*(1), 1–10

Habermas, J. (1998). *Inclusion of the other: Studies in political theory* (C. Cronin & P. De Greiff, Eds.). Cambridge, MA: The MIT Press.

Habermas, J. (2001). Reflections on the linguistic foundations of sociology: The Christian Gauss Lectures (Princeton University, February-March 1971). In J. Habermas, *On the pragmatics of social interaction* (B. Fultner, Trans.), (pp.1–103). Cambridge, MA: MIT Press.

Haeri, N. (2013). The private performance of *Salat* prayers: Repetition, time, and meaning. *Anthropological Quarterly, 86*(1), 5–34.

Hahee, D. (2004). *Bodily arts: Rhetoric and athletics in Ancient Greece.* Austin, TX: University of Texas Press.

Hall, B. J. (1992). Theories of culture and communication. *Communication Theory, 2*(1), 50–70.

Hall, E. T. (1959). *The silent language.* Greenwich, CT: Fawcett Publications.

Hall, E. T. (1966). *The hidden dimension.* Gardeii. City, NY: Doubleday.

Hall, E. T. (1983). *The dance of life: The other dimension of time.* Garden City, NY: Anchor Press/Doubleday.

Hallett, T., Shulman, D., & Fine G. A. (2009). Peopling organizations: The promise of classic symbolic interactionism for an inhabited institutionalism. In P. S. Adler (Ed.), *The Oxford handbook of sociology and organization studies: Classical foundations* (pp. 486–509). Oxford: Oxford University Press.

Hamrick, W. (1987). *An existential phenomenology of law: Maurice Merleau-Ponty.* Berlin: Springer.

Hanna, J.L (1987). *To dance is human: A theory of nonverbal communication.* Chicago, IL: University of Chicago Press.

Hansen, S. K. (2010). *Zoe, bios and the language of biopower.* Doctoral thesis. Nashville, TN: Vanderbilt University.

Hansen, C. H. & Hansen, R. D. (1988). How rock music videos can change what is seen when boy meets girl: Priming stereotypic appraisal of social interactions. *Sex Roles, 19*(5), 287–316.

Hanslmeier, A. (2013). *Astrobiology, the search for life in the universe.* Sharjah: Bentham Science Publishers.

Haraway, D. (1988). Situated knowledges: The science question in feminism and the privilege of partial perspective. *Feminist Studies, 14*(3), 575–599.

Haraway, D. (1999). Cover endorsement. In K. Hayles, *How we became posthuman. Virtual bodies in cybernetics*. Chicago, IL: University of Chicago Press.

Harbeck, C. (2017). *Interstellar communications*. Scotts Valley, CA: CreateSpace Independent Publishing Platform.

Harman, G. (2010). Time, space, essence, and eidos: A new theory of causation. *Cosmos and History: The Journal of Natural and Social Philosophy*, 6(1).

Harper, N. (1979). *Human communication theory: The history of a paradigm*. Rochelle Park, NJ: Hayden Book Company.

Harris, S. (2005). *The end of faith: Religion, terror, and the future of reason*. New York & London: W.W. Norton.

Harrison, P. (2007). *Original sin and the origins of modern science*. Cambridge, UK: Cambridge University Press.

Harrison, R. P. (1992). *Forests: The shadow of civilization*. Chicago, IL & London: University of Chicago Press.

Harrison, R. P. (2014). *Juvenescence: A cultural history of our age*. Chicago, IL & London: University of Chicago Press.

Hart, S. (2014). *The language of animals*. New York: Henry Holt.

Hartley, R.V.L. (1928) Transmission of information. *Bell System Technical Journal*, 7, 535–563.

Hartwig, M. (2015). Style. In M. K. Hartwig (Ed.), *A companion to ancient Egyptian art* (pp. 39–59). Malden, MA: Wiley-Blackwell.

Haugeland, J. (1998). *Having thought: Essays in the metaphysics of mind*. Cambridge, MA: Harvard University Press.

Haugen, E. (1972). *The ecology of language: Essays*. A. S. Dil (Ed.). Stanford, CA: Stanford University Press.

Havelock, E. (1963). *Preface to Plato*. Oxford: Blackwell.

Hayles, K. N. (1999). *How we became posthuman: Virtual bodies in cybernetics*. Chicago, IL: University of Chicago Press.

Heath, R. L., & Bryant, J. (200). *Human communication theory and research: Concepts, contexts, and challenges*. Mahwah, NJ: Erlbaum.

Heidegger, M. (1966). *Being and Time: A translation of Sein und Zeit* (D. J Schmidt, Ed., J. Stambaugh, Trans.). New York: SUNY Press.

Heidegger, M. (1971). *On the way to language* (P. D. Hertz, Trans.) New York: Harper & Row.

Heidegger, M. (1977). *The question concerning technology and other essays* (W. Lovitt, Trans.). New York: Harper & Row.

Heidkamp, B., & Kergel, D. (Eds). (2017). *Precarity within the digital age: Media change and social insecurity*. Berlin: Springer.

Heinrich, F. (2012). Flesh as communication: Body art and art theory. *Contemporary Aesthetics, 10*.

Henry, M. (2008). *Material phenomenology*. (S. Davidson, Trans.). New. York: Fordham University Press.

Herbert, N. (1987). *Quantum reality: Beyond the new physics*. New York: Anchor Books.

Herman, E. S., & Chomsky, N. (1988). *Manufacturing consent: The political economy of the mass media*. New York: Pantheon.

Hexter, R. (1993). *A guide to the Odyssey: A commentary on the English translation of Robert Fitzgerald*. New York, NY: Vintage Books.

Higgins, E. T., Bargh, J. A., & Lombardi, W. J. (1985). Nature of priming effects on categorization. *Journal of Experimental Psychology: Learning, Memory, and Cognition, 11*(1), 59–69.

Hirst, W., Coman, A., & Coman, D. (2014). *Putting the social back into human memory.* In T. J. Perfect & D. S. Lindsey (Eds.), The SAGE handbook of applied memory. Washington, DC: SAGE. dx.doi.org/10.4135/9781446294703.n16

Hittinger, J. (2013). Plato and Aristotle on the family and the polis. *The Saint Anselm Journal, 8* (2), 1–22.

Hobart, M. E., & Schiffman, Z. S. (2000). *Information ages: Literacy, numeracy, and the computer revolution.* Baltimore, MD: John Hopkins University Press.

Hoffman, K. (2009). Culture as text: hazards and possibilities of Geertz's literary/ literacy metaphor. *The Journal of North African Studies, 14* (3/4), 417– 430.

Holland, D., & Lachicotte, W. Jr. (2007). Vygotsky, Mead, and the new sociocultural studies of identity. In H. M. Daniels, H., M. Cole, & J. V. Wertsch (Eds.), *The Cambridge companion to Vygotsky* (pp. 101–135). New York: Cambridge University Press.

Holzer, H. (2017). The forgotten Marxist theory of communication & society. *Journal for a Global Sustainable Information Society, 15*(2).

Homer-Dixon, T. (2010). *The ingenuity gap: Can we solve the problems of the future?* Toronto: Vintage.

Hopkins, J. C. (1898). *Canada: An encyclopedia of the country.* (Vol.1). Toronto: The Linscott Publishing Company.

Horsfield, P. (2016). Christianity. In K. B. Jensen, R. T. Craig, J. D. Pooley, & E. W. Rothenbuhler (Eds.), *The international encyclopedia of communication theory and philosophy.* Malden, MA: Wiley-Blackwell.

Huang, H. (2011). Risk, fear and immunity: Reinventing the political in the age of biopolitics. *Concentric: Literary and Cultural Studies, 37*(1), 43–71.

Huchingson, J. (2003). Chaos, communications theory, and God's abundance. *Zygon: Journal of Religion and Science, 37*(2), 395–414.

Humboldt, W. von (1999). *On language: On the diversity of human language construction and its influence on the mental development of the human species* (M. Losonsky, Ed., P, Heath, Trans.). Cambridge, UK: Cambridge University Press.

Hurn, S. (2012). *Humans and other animals: Cross-cultural perspectives on human-animal interactions.* London: Pluto Press.

Husserl, E. (1970). *The crisis of European sciences and transcendental philosophy* (D. Carr, Trans.). Evanston, IL: Northwestern University Press.

Husserl E. (1973). *Experience and judgment: Investigations in a genealogy of logic* (L. Landgrebe, Ed., J. S. Churchill & K. Ameriks, Trans.). Evanston, IL: Northwestern University Press.

Husserl E. (1981). *Shorter works* (P. McCormick & F. A. Elliston, Eds.). Notre Dame, IN: University of Notre Dame Press.

Husserl, E. (1989). *Ideas pertaining to a pure phenomenology and to a phenomenological philosophy. Second book: Studies in the phenomenology of constitution* (R. Rojcewicz & A .Schuwer, Trans.). Dordrecht, Netherlands: Kluwer.

Husserl E. (2006). *The basic problems of phenomenology: From the lectures (Winter Semester, 1910–1911)* (I. Farin & J.G. Hart, Trans.). Berlin: Springer.

Hustwit, J.R. (2014). *Interreligious hermeneutics and the pursuit of truth.* Lanham, MD: Lexington Books.

Ilčev, S. D. (2016). *Global mobile satellite communications theory: For maritime, land and aeronautical applications.* Berlin: Springer.

Ime, U. (2013). *Behind the listening position.* Bloomington, IN: WestBow Press.

Imhausen, A., & Pommerening T. (Eds.). (2016). *Writings of early scholars in the ancient Near East, Egypt, Rome, and Greece: Translating ancient scientific texts.* Berlin and New York: De Gruyter

Immink, F.G. (2016). The sense of God's presence in prayer. *HTS Teologiese Studies / Theological Studies, 72*(4). Retrieved from http://dx.doi.org/10.4102/hts.v72i4.4122

Ingham, I. (2007). *Neuroimaging in communication sciences and disorders.* San Diego: Plural Publishing.

Inglis, D. (2013). *An invitation to social theory.* New York: John Wiley & Sons.

Innis, H. A. (1971). *The bias of communication.* Toronto: University of Toronto Press.

Irigaray, L. (1999). *The forgetting of air in Martin Heidegger* (M. B. Mader, Trans.). Austin, TX: University of Texas Press.

James, W. (1890a). *The principles of psychology: Volume one.* New York: Henry Holt.

James, W. (1890b). *The principles of psychology: Volume two.* New York: Henry Holt.

James, W. (1903). *The varieties of religious experience.* New York: Longman.

James, W. (1907). *Pragmatism, a new name for some old ways of thinking.* New York: Longman.

James, W. (1909). *A pluralistic universe: Hibbert lectures at Manchester College on the present situation in philosophy.* New York: Longman.

Jameson, F. (1998). *The cultural turn: Selected writings on the postmodern, 1983–1998.* London & New York: Verso.

Jameson, F. (2002). *A singular modernity: Essay on the ontology of the present.* London & New York: Verso.

Jameson, F. (2003). The end of temporality. *Critical Inquiry, 29*(4), 695–718.

Jastrow, J. (1935). *Wish and wisdom: Episodes in the vagaries of belief.* New York: Appleton-Century.

Johnson, C. (2007). *Socrates and the immoralists.* Lanham, MD: Lexington Books.

Johnson, G. A. (Ed). (1993). *The Merleau-Ponty aesthetics reader: Philosophy and painting* (M. B. Smith, Trans.). Evanston, IL: Northwestern University Press.

Johnson, S. (2017, June 28).). Greetings, E.T. (Please don't murder us.). *New York Times.* Retrieved from www.nytimes.com/2017/06/28/magazine/greetings-et-please-dont-murder-us.html

Johnson Thornton, D. (2016). Rhetorical construction of bodies. In J. F. Nussbaum (Ed.), *Oxford research encyclopedia of communications.* doi.org/10.1093/acrefore/9780190228613.013.57

Jordan, J. W. (2004). The rhetorical limits of the "plastic body". *Quarterly Journal of Speech, 90*(3), 327–358.

Jordan, W. R. (2003). *The Sunflower forest: Ecological restoration and the new communion with nature.* Berkeley, CA: University of California Press.

Kaebnick, G. E. (2014). *Humans in nature: The world as we find it and the world as we create it.* Oxford & New York: Oxford University Press.

Kaestle, C. F., Damon-Moore, H., Stedman,L. C., & Tinsley, K. (1991). *Literacy in the United States: Readers and reading since 1880.* New Haven, CT: Yale University Press.

Kaku, M. (2018). *The future of humanity: Terraforming Mars, interstellar travel, immortality, and our destiny beyond.* New York: Doubleday.

Kalof, Linda (Ed.). (2017). *The Oxford handbook of animal studies.* New York & Oxford: Oxford University Press

Kant, I. (1888). *The philosophy of Kant: As contained in extracts from his own writings* (J. Watson, Ed. & Trans.). London: Macmillan.

Kant, I. (1899). *Critique of pure reason* (J. M. D. Meiklejohn, Trans.). New York: Wiley.

Kant, I. (1991). *Kant: Political writings* (H. S. Reiss, Ed.), (H. B. Nisbet, Trans.). Cambridge, UK: Cambridge University Press.

Kant, I. (1996). *Practical philosophy* (M. Gregor, Ed.). Cambridge, UK: Cambridge University Press.

Kappeler, W. (2009). *Communication habits for the pilgrim church: Vatican teaching on media and society.* New York: Peter Lang.

Kardashev, N. (1964). Transmission of information by extraterrestrial civilizations. *Soviet Astronomy, 8,* 217.

Katona, V. (2010). Reconsidering the tectonic: On the sacred ambivalence of the tectonic in the light of Martin Heidegger and relevant theoretical studies on architecture. *Architecture, 41*(1), 19–25.

Kaylor, B. T. (2011). Accounting for the divine: Examining rhetorical claims of God's inspiration. *Journal of Communication and Religion, 34,* 75–88.

Kearney, R. (2015). The wager of carnal hermeneutics. In R. Kearney & B. Treanor (Eds.), *Carnal hermeneutics* (pp. 15–56). New York: Fordham University Press.

Kearney, R. & Treanor, B. (Eds.). (2015). *Carnal hermeneutics.* New York: Fordham University Press.

Kearns, M. (1987). Metaphors and the humanizing of the mind. *Metaphor & Symbolic Activity, 2*(2), 115–138.

Keblusek, L., Giles, H., & Maass, A. (2017). Communication and group life: How language and symbols shape intergroup relations. *Group Processes & Intergroup Relations, 20*(5), 632–643.

Keegan, P. (2014). *Graffiti in antiquity.* London & New York: Routledge.

Kenner, H. (1992). Shem the textman. In R. M. Bollettieri Bosinelli, C. Marengo, & Christine van Boheemen (Eds.), *The languages of Joyce: Selected papers from the 11th international James Joyce Symposium Venice 2008* (pp. 145–145). Amsterdam & Philadelphia, PA: John Benjamins.

Kirsch, S. (2016). Democracy and disclosure: Edward Bernays and the manipulation of the masses. In G. L. Henderson & M. J. Braun (Eds.), *Propaganda and rhetoric in democracy: History, theory, analysis* (pp. 29–50). Carbondale, IL: Southern Illinois University Press.

Kittler, F. (2006). Number and numeral. *Theory, Culture & Society, 23* (7–8), 51–61.

Kiverstein, J., Farina, M. & Clark A. (2013). The extended mind thesis. In D. Pritchard (Ed.). *Oxford bibliographies online. Philosophy* (pp. 1–20). Oxford: Oxford University Press.

Kluger, J. (2012, August 31). We never talk anymore: The problem with text messaging. *CNN.com.* Retrieved from www.cnn.com/2012/08/31/tech/mobile/problem-text-messaging-oms/index.html

Klyukanov, I. (2008). A Communicology of culture: Handle with care. *Atlantic Journal of Communication, 16*(3–4), 211–225.

Klyukanov, I. (2012). Communication – that which befalls us. *Empedocles: European Journal for the Philosophy of Communication, 4*(1), 15–27.

Knapp, M. L., Daly, J. A., Albada K. F., & Miller, G. R. (2002). Background and current trends in the study of interpersonal communication. In M. L. Knapp & J. A. Daly (Eds.), *Handbook of interpersonal communication* (pp. 3–20). Thousand Oaks, CA: SAGE.

Koerner, D. W., & LeVay, S. (2000). *The scientific quest for extraterrestrial life.* Oxford: Oxford University Press.

Kohn, E. (2013). *How forests think: Toward an anthropology beyond the human.* Berkeley, CA: University of California Press.

Kolb, E. (1986). *Inner space/outer space: The interface between cosmology and particle physics.* Chicago, IL: University of Chicago Press.

Korbitz, A. 2014. Toward understanding the active SETI debate: Insights from risk communication and perception. *Acta Astronautica, 105*(2), 517–520.

Korngold, J. S. (2011). *The God upgrade. Finding your 21st-century spirituality in Judaism's 5,000-year-old tradition.* Woodstock, VT: Jewish Lights Publishing.

Korzybski, A. (1958). *Science and sanity. An introduction to non-Aristotelian systems and general semantics.* Brooklyn, NY: Institute of General Semantics.

Kramarae, C. (2009). Muted group theory. In S. W. Littlejohn & K. A. Foss (Eds.), *Encyclopedia of communication theory, vol. 1* (pp. 668–669). Thousand Oaks, CA: SAGE.

Kraft, C. (1991). *Communication theory for Christian witness.* Maryknoll, NY: Orbis Books.

Krippendorff, K. (1990). Models and metaphors of communication. *University of Pennsylvania Scholarly Commons. Departmental papers.* Retrieved from http://repository.upenn.edu/asc_papers/276

Krippendorff, K. (1993). Major metaphors of communication and some constructivist reflections on their use. *Cybernetics & Human Knowing, 2*(1), 3–25.

Krippendorff, K. (1994). A recursive theory of communication. In D. Crowley & D. Mitchell (Eds.), *Communication theory today* (pp. 78–104). Cambridge, UK: Polity Press.

Krippendorff, K. (2009). *On communicating: Otherness, meaning, and information* (F. Bermejo, Ed.). London: Routledge.

Kutuza B.G., & Rzhiga O.N. (2012). Radio physical studies of planets and the Earth at the Institute of Radio Technology and Electronics of the USSR Academy of Sciences. In S. Braude et al. (Eds), *A brief history of radio astronomy in the USSR. A collection of scientific essays.* Berlin: Springer.

Kyle, D. G. (2015). *Sport and spectacle in the ancient world.* Chichester, UK: Wiley-Blackwell.

Lacan, J. (1981). *Séminaire* III. Paris: Le Seuil.

Lamm, C., & Majdandžić J. (2015). The role of shared neural activations, mirror neurons, and morality in empathy: A critical comment. *Neuroscience Research, 90*, 15–24

Landes, D. A. (2013). *Merleau-Ponty and the paradoxes of expression.* London & New York: Bloomsbury.

Landry, R., & Bourhis, R. Y. (1997). Linguistic landscape and ethnolinguistic vitality: An empirical study. *Journal of Language and Social Psychology, 16*, 23–49.

Lanigan, R. (2010). The verbal and nonverbal codes of communicology: The foundation of interpersonal agency and efficacy. In I. E Catt & D. Eicher-Catt (Eds.),

*Communicology: The new science of embodied discourse* (pp. 102–128). Madison, NJ: Fairleigh Dickinson University Press.

Lanigan, R. (2013a). Information theories. In P. Cobley & P. J. Schultz (Eds.), *Theories and models of communication* (pp. 58–83). Berlin: De Gruyter Mouton.

Lanigan, R. (2013b). Communicology and culturology: Semiotic phenomenological method in applied small group research. *Public Journal of Semiotics, 4*(2), 71–103.

Lanigan, R. (2015). Communicology. In Donsbach, W. (Ed.), *The concise encyclopedia of communication* (pp. 102–103). Malden, MA: Wiley Blackwell.

Lanigan, R., & Strobl, R. L. (1981). A critical theory approach. In D. Nimmo & K. Sanders (Eds.), *The handbook of political communication* (pp. 141–167). Beverly Hills, CA: SAGE.

Lashley, C. (Ed.). (2017). *The Routledge handbook of hospitality studies*. Abingdon, UK & New York: Routledge.

Last, A. (2013). Negotiating the inhuman: Bakhtin, materiality and the instrumentalisation of climate change. *Theory, Culture & Society, 30*(2), 60–83.

Latour, B. (1993). *We have never been modern.* (C. Porter, Trans.). Cambridge, MA: Harvard University Press.

Latour, B. (1999). Body, cyborgs, and the politics of incarnation. In S. Sweeney & I. Hodder (Eds.), *The body* (pp. 127–141). Cambridge, UK: Cambridge University Press.

Latour, B. (2004). Why has critique run out of steam? From matters of fact to matters of concern. *Critical Inquiry, 30*(2), 225–248.

Latour, B. (2010). *On the modern cult of the factish gods*. Durham, NC: Duke University Press.

Latour, B., & Woolgar, S (1979). *Laboratory life: The social construction of scientific facts*. Princeton, NJ: Princeton University Press.

Leane, J. (2010). Aboriginal representation: Conflict or dialogue in the Academy. *The Australian Journal of Indigenous Education, 39*(51), 32–39.

Lecheler, S., & Vreese, C. H. (2012). News framing and public opinion: A mediation analysis of framing effects on political attitudes. *Journalism and Mass Communication Quarterly, 89* (2), 185–204.

Lee, H., & Liebenau, J. (2000). Time and the Internet at the turn of the millennium. *Time & Society, 9*(1), 43–56.

Leibniz, G. W. F. von (1890). *The philosophical works of Leibnitz*. New Haven, CT: Tuttle, Morehouse & Taylor.

Leiss, W. (1990). *Under technology's thumb*. Montreal: McGill-Queen's University Press.

Lemarchand G. A., Leck, E. & Tash, A. (2016). *Mapping research and innovation in the state of Israel*. Paris, UNESCO. Retrieved from http://unesdoc.unesco.org/Ulis/cgi-bin/ulis.pl?catno=244059&set=00574422E1_2_96&gp=0&lin=1&ll=1

Lemarchand, G. A. & Lomberg, J. (2011). Communication among interstellar intelligent species: A search for universal cognitive maps. In D. A. Vakoch (Ed.), *Communication with extraterrestrial intelligence (CETI)* (pp. 371–395). Albany, NY: SUNY Press.

Lemm, V. (2013). Introduction: Biopolitics and community. In R. Esposito, *Terms of the political: Community, immunity, biopolitics* (R. N. Welch, Trans.) (pp. 1–13). New York: Fordham University Press.

Leont'ev, A.N. (2009). *The development of mind: Selected works of Aleksei Nikolaevich Leontyev with a preface by Mike Cole*. Ohio: Bookmasters, Inc. Retrieved from http://marxists.anu.edu.au/archive/leontev/works/development-mind.pdf

Leski, K. (2015). *The storm of creativity: A storm's eye view*. Cambridge, MA: The MIT Press.

Letaw, H. (2011). Cosmic storytelling: primitive observables as Rosetta analogies. In D. A. Vakoch & A. A. Harrison (Eds.), *Civilizations beyond Earth: Extraterrestrial life and society*. New York: Berghahn Books.

Lévi-Strauss, C. (1969). *The elementary structures of kinship* (J. H. Bell, J. R. von Sturmer & R. Needham, Trans.). Boston, MA: Beacon Press.

Levitin, D. (2017, March 3). Inside the theater of the mind. *The Wall Street Journal*, Retrieved from www.wsj.com/articles/inside-the-theater-of-the-mind-1488580315

Lewis, R. D. (2006). *When cultures collide: Leading across cultures*. 3rd ed. Boston, MA & London: Nicholas Brealey International.

Lewis, S. (1996). *News and society in the Greek polis*. Chapel Hill, NC: University of North Carolina Press.

Lilly, J. (1967). *The mind of the dolphin: A nonhuman intelligence*. New York: Doubleday.

Lindell, J. (2015) Mediapolis, where art thou? Mediated cosmopolitanism in three media systems between 2002 and 2010. *International Communication Gazette*, *77*(2), 189–207.

Lindell, J. (2016). Communication as spatial production: Expanding the research agenda of communication geography. *Space and Culture*, *19*(1), 56–66.

Lingis, A. (1994). *The community of those who have nothing in common*. Bloomington, IN & Indianapolis, IN: Indiana University Press.

Lingis, A. (2009). Contact and communication. In A. J. Mitchell & J. K. Winfree (Eds.), *The obsessions of Georges Bataille: community and communication* (pp. 119–132). Albany, NY: SUNY Press.

Lipari, L. (2010). Listening, thinking, being. *Communication Theory*, *20*(3), 348–362.

Littlejohn S., Foss, K. A., & Oetzel, J.G. (Eds.) (2017). *Theories of human communication*. Long Grove, IL: Waveland Press.

Lock, M. M. & Farquhar, J. (2007). Introduction. In M. M. Lock & J. Farquhar (eds.), *Beyond the body proper: Reading the anthropology of material life*. (pp. 1–18). Durham, NC & London: Duke University Press.

Lombardi, O., Holik, F. & Vanni, L. (2014). What is Shannon information? *Synthese*, *193*, 1983–2012. doi.org/10.1007/s11229-015-0824-z

Louchakova-Schwartz, O. & Crouch, C. (Eds.) (2017). *Topical issue: Phenomenology of religious experience. Open Theology*, *3*(1). Retrieved from www.degruyter.com/view/j/opth.2017.3.issue-1/issue-files/opth.2017.3.issue-1.xml

Lowenthal, L. (1944). Biographies in popular magazines. In P. F. Lazarsfeld & F. M. Stanton (Eds.), *Radio research 1942–43* (pp. 507–548). New York: Duell, Sloan & Pearce.

Luhmann, N. (1994). How can the mind participate in communication? In H.-U. Gumbrecht & K. L. Pfeiffer (Eds.), *Materialities of communication* (W. Whobrey, Trans.) (pp. 371–388). Stanford, CA: Stanford University Press.

Luhrmann, T. M. (2012). *When God talks back. Understanding the American Evangelical relationship with God*. New York: Knopf.

Luhrmann, T., Padmavati, R., Tharoor, H., & Osei, A. (2015). Hearing voices in different cultures: A social kindling hypothesis. *TopiCS: Topics in Cognitive Science* *7*(4), 646–663.

Lyotard, J.-F. (1984). *The postmodern condition: A report on knowledge* (G. Bennington & B. Massumi, Trans.). Manchester, UK: Manchester University Press.

Macey, S. L. (Ed.). (1994). *Encyclopedia of time*. New York: Garland.

Mackay, A. (1991). *A dictionary of scientific quotations*. Boca Raton, FL: CRC Press.

MacCormack, P. (2016). *Posthuman ethics: Embodiment and cultural theory*. New York & London: Routledge.

MacDonald, P. (2013). Paleo-philosophy: Archaic ideas about space and time. *Comparative Philosophy*, *4*(2), 82–117.

Macke, F. J. (2014). Intrapersonal communicology: Reflection, reflexivity, and relational consciousness in embodied subjectivity. *Atlantic Journal of Communication*, *16*, 122–148.

Macke, F. J. (2015). *The experience of human communication: Body, flesh, and relationship*. Madison, NJ: Fairleigh Dickinson University Press.

Maddy, P. (2017). *What do philosophers do? Skepticism and the practice of philosophy*. New York: Oxford University Press.

Mandelshtam, O. (1991). *Selected poems* (J. Greene, Trans.). London: Penguin.

Manville, P.B. (1990). *The origins of citizenship in ancient Athens*. Princeton, NJ: Princeton University Press.

Marder, M. (2013). *Plant-thinking: A philosophy of vegetal life*. New York Columbia University Press.

Marianović, G. (2017, April). *Magnetoteluric and electrodynamics research, April 2017, the mission "Rtanj", Serbia*. Retrieved from http://sbresearchgroup.eu/index.php/en/?option=com_content&view=category&layout=blog

Martin, A.K., & Whitley, E. A. (2013). Fixing identity? Biometrics and the tensions of material practices. *Media, Culture and Society*, *35*(1), 52–60.

Martinelli, D. (2017). Zoosemiotics, typologies of signs and continuity between humans and other animals. In R. Gordon & J. Seckbach (Eds.), *Biocommunication: Sign-mediated interactions between cells and organisms* (pp. 63–86). Hoboken, NJ: World Scientific.

Martinez, J. (2011). *Communicative sexualities: A communicology of sexual experience*. Lanham, MD: Lexington Books.

Martland, T.R. (1975). On "the limits of my language mean the limits of my world". *The Review of Metaphysics*, *29*(1), 19–26.

Marvin, C. (2006). Communication as embodiment. In G. J. Shepherd, J. St. John, & T. Striphas (Eds.), *Communication as ...: Perspectives on theory* (pp. 67–74). Thousand Oaks, CA: SAGE.

Marx, K. (1967). *Economic and philosophic manuscripts of 1844* (M. Milligan, Trans.). Moscow: Progress Publishers.

Marx, K., & Engels, F. (1970). *The German ideology* (C. J. Arthur, Ed.). New York: International Publishers.

Mason, S.F. (1953). *Main currents of scientific thought: A history of the sciences*. New York: Abelard-Schuman.

Mathur, K. (2001). *Intercultural communication: An agenda for developing countries*. New Delhi: Allied Publishers.

Matsumoto, D., Frank, M. G., & Hwang, H. S. (2013). *Nonverbal communication: Science and applications*. Los Angeles, CA: SAGE.

Maynard, D. W. (1988). Language, interaction, and social problems. *Social Problems, 35*(4), 311–344.

Mazzucchelli, A. (2000). Celestial weathercock, Diagrams & metaphorical web: Some semiotic considerations on Western astrology. *European Journal for Semiotic Studies, 12*(4).

McAuliffe, Joseph. (2015). Desert soils. In S. J. Phillips, P. W. Comus, M. A. Dimmitt, & L. M. Brewer (Eds.), *A natural history of the Sonoran desert* (pp. 87–104). Berkeley, CA: University of California Press.

McChesney, R. W., & Nichols, J. (2016). *People get ready: The fight against a jobless economy and a citizenless democracy*. Washington, DC: Nation Books.

McCombs, M. E., & Shaw, D. L. (1972). The agenda-setting function of mass media. *Public Opinion Quarterly, 36*(2), 176–187.

McCormick, M. (2010). The lived body: The essential dimension in social work practice. *Qualitative Social Work, 10*(1), 66–85.

McCoy, M. (2007). *Plato on the rhetoric of philosophers and sophists*. Cambridge, UK & New York: Cambridge University Press.

McGavin, L.H. (1997). Creativity as information: Measuring aesthetic attractions. *Nonlinear Dynamics, Psychology, and Life Sciences, 1*(3), 203–226.

McGlew, J. (1993). *Tyranny and political culture in Ancient Greece*. Ithaca, NY & London: Cornell University Press.

McKenna, W. (2012). *Husserl's introductions to phenomenology: Interpretation and critique*. The Hague, Netherlands & Boston: Martinus Nijhoff.

McLuhan, M. (1962). *The Gutenberg galaxy: The making of typographic man*. Toronto: University of Toronto Press.

McLuhan, M. (1994). *Understanding media: The extensions of man*. Cambridge, MA: The MIT Press.

McLuhan, M. (1997). *Media research: Technology, art and communication* (M. Moos, Ed.). New York & London: Routledge.

McLuhan, M. (2004). Visual and acoustic space. In C. Cox & D. Warner (Eds.), *Audio culture: Readings in modern music* (pp. 67–72). New York & London: Continuum.

McLuhan, M., & Fiore, Q. (1967). *The medium is the massage*. New York: Bantam.

McQuail, D. (2002). *McQuail's reader in mass communication theory*. London: SAGE.

Mead, G.H. (1934). Wundt and the concept of gesture. In G. H. Mead, *Mind, self and society from the standpoint of a social behaviorist* (C. W. Morris, Ed.) (pp. 42–51). Chicago, IL: University of Chicago Press.

Mead, G.H. (1964). *On social psychology: selected papers*. Chicago, IL: University of Chicago Press.

Mead, G. H. (1982). *The individual and the social self: Unpublished essays by G. H. Mead* (D. L. Miller, Ed.). Chicago, IL: University of Chicago Press.

Mead, G.H. (2015). *Mind, self, and society: The definitive edition* (C. W. Morris, D. R. Huebner and H. Joas. Chicago, IL & London: University of Chicago Press.

Mehrabian, A. (1971). *Silent messages*. Belmont, CA: Wadsworth.

Meier, C. (1990). *The Greek discovery of politics* (D. McLintock, Trans.). Cambridge, MA: Harvard University Press.

Meijer, D.K.F., & Geesink, H.J.H. (2017). Consciousness in the universe is scale invariant and implies the event horizon of the human brain. *NeuroQuantology, 15*(3), pp. 41–79.

Meline, T. J. (2010). *A research primer for communication sciences and disorders.* Boston, MA: Pearson.

Merchant, C. (2006). The scientific revolution and the death of nature. *Isis, 97,* 513–533.

Merchant, C. (2008). Francis Bacon and the "vexations of art": Experimentation as intervention. *British Journal for the History of Science, 46*(4), 551–599.

Merleau-Ponty, M. (1964a). *Signs* (R. C. McCleary, Trans.). Evanston, IL: Northwestern University Press.

Merleau-Ponty, M. (1964b). *Sense and non-sense* (H. L. Dreyfus & P. Allen Dreyfus, Trans.). Evanston, IL: Northwestern University Press.

Merleau-Ponty, M. (1993). Eye and mind. In G. Johnson, (Ed.), *The Merleau-Ponty aesthetics reader: Philosophy and painting* (pp. 121–149). Evanston, IL: Northwestern University Press.

Merleau-Ponty, M. (2002). *Husserl at the limits of Phenomenology: Including texts by Edmund Husserl.* (L. Lawlor, Ed., B. Bergo, Trans.). Evanston, IL: Northwestern University Press.

Merleau-Ponty, M. (2004). *Basic writings* (T. Baldwin, Ed.). London & New York: Routledge.

Merleau-Ponty, M. (2012). *Phenomenology of perception* (D. A. Landes, Trans.). London & New York: Routledge.

Metcalf, P. (2006). *Anthropology: The basics.* London & New York: Routledge.

Mifsud, M. (2007). On rhetoric as gift/giving. *Philosophy & Rhetoric, 40*(1), 89–107.

Miller, B. (2008). *Why the passion? Bernard Lonergan on the cross as communication.* Doctoral dissertation. Boston, MA: Boston College. Retrieved from https://dlib.bc.edu/islandora/object/bc-ir:101393

Miller, C. (1993). The polis as rhetorical community. *Rhetorica, 11*(3), 211–240.

Miller, M. (2006). Transforming leadership: What does love have to do with it? *Transformation, 23*(2), 94–106.

Miller, R. (2011). *Vygotsky in perspective.* Cambridge, UK: Cambridge University Press.

Mindell, A. (2000). *Quantum mind: The edge between physics and psychology.* Portland: Lao Tse Press.

Mithen, S. (1999). *The prehistory of the mind: The cognitive origins of art, religion and science.* London: Thames and Hudson.

Mithen, S. (20050. *The singing Neanderthals: The origins of music, language, mind and body.* London: Weidenfeld & Nicolson.

Molina-Markham, E. (2014). Finding the "sense of the meeting": Decision making through silence among Quakers. *Western Journal of Communication, 78*(2), 155–174.

Moon, L. (2011). Prostitution and date rape: The commodification of consent. In A. L. McEvoy (Ed.), *Sex, love, and friendship: studies of the society for the philosophy of sex and love, 1993–2003* (pp. 67–74). Amsterdam & New York: Rodopi.

Morand, D.A., & Ocker, R.J. (2003). Politeness theory and computer-mediated communication: A sociolinguistic approach to analyzing relational Messages. *Proceedings of the 36th Annual Hawaii International Conference on System Sciences (HICSS '03), 1*(1), 17.2. doi.org/10.1109/HICSS.2003.1173660

Morris, W. (Ed.). (1982). *The American heritage dictionary of the English language*. Boston, MA: Houghton Mifflin.

Mortensen, C. D. (Ed.). (2008). *Communication theory*. New Brunswick, NJ: Transaction Publishers.

Morton, A. (2005). Mind. In T. Honderich (Ed.), *The Oxford companion to philosophy* (pp. 569–570). 2nd ed. Oxford: Oxford University Press.

Morton, T. (2017). Specters of ecology. In E. Hörl & J. Burton (Eds.), *General ecology: The new ecological paradigm* (pp. 303–321). New York: Bloomsbury.

Mozeson, I. (2018). *Edenics: Origins of languages*. Retrieved from www.ancient-hebrew.org/language_edenics.html

Muir, E. (2002). The 2001 Josephine Waters Bennett lecture: The idea of community in Renaissance Italy. *Renaissance Quarterly, 55*(1), 1–18.

Muller, J. Z. (2018, January 12). A cure for our fixation on metrics. *The Wall Street Journal*. Retrieved from www.wsj.com/articles/a-cure-for-our-metric-fixation-1515772238

Mumby, D. (2012). *Organizational communication: A critical approach*. Thousand Oaks, CA: SAGE.

Mumford L. (1944). *The condition of man*. London: Secker and Warburg.

Mumford, L. (2010). *Technics and civilization*. Chicago, IL & London: University of Chicago Press.

Muraoka, H. (2009). A typology of problems in contact situations. In J. Nekvapil & T. Sherman (Eds.), *Language management in contact situations: Perspectives from three continents* (pp. 151–168). New York: Peter Lang.

Nagel, T. (1974). What is it like to be a bat? *The Philosophical Review, 83*(4), 435–450.

Nagy, G. (1996). *Greek mythology and poetics*. Ithaca, NY: Cornell University Press.

Nancy, J.-L. (1991). *The inoperative community* (P. Connor, Ed.). Minneapolis, MN: University of Minnesota Press.

Nanoo nanoo (2017, November 18th). *The Economist*. Retrieved from https://biblio.helmo.be/opac_css/doc_num.php?explnum_id=7703

Nealon, J. (2016). *Plant theory: Biopower & vegetable life*. Stanford, CA: Stanford University Press,

Nerlich, B. (1992). *Semantic theories in Europe, 1830–1930: From etymology to contextuality*. Amsterdam & Philadelphia, PA: John Benjamins.

Neuvonen, P. J. (2016). *Equal citizenship and its limits in EU law: We the burden?* London: Hart Publishing.

Newman, M. C. (2009). *Fundamentals of ecotoxicology*. 3rd ed. Boca Raton, FL: CRC Press.

Newton, I. (1934). *Principia* (F. Cajori, Trans.). 3rd ed. Berkeley, CA: University of California Press.

Neyrey, J. (2004). *Render to God: New Testament understandings of the divine*. Minneapolis, MN: Fortress Press.

Ng, R. (2017). *Intercultural communication in the hospitality and tourism industry: A study of message design logic across two cultures*. Bachelor's thesis. Ithaca, NY: Cornell University. Retrieved from http://scholarship.sha.cornell.edu/honorstheses/5

Nietzsche, F. (1957). *The use and abuse of history* (P. Preuss, Trans.). New York: Library of Liberal Arts.

Nietzsche, F. (1974). *The gay science ... with a prelude in rhymes and an appendix of songs* (W. Kaufmann, Trans.). New York: Random House.

Nightingale, A.W. (2004). *Spectacles of truth in Classical Greek philosophy: Theoria in its cultural context*. Cambridge, UK: Cambridge University Press.

Nollman, J. (2002). *The man who talks to whales: The art of interspecies communication*. Boulder, CO: Sentient Publications.

Nöth, W. (1995). *Handbook of semiotics*. Bloomington, IN & Indianapolis, IN: Indiana University Press.

Nowotny, H. (2005). *Time: The modern and postmodern experience* (N. Plaice, Trans.). Cambridge, UK: Polity Press.

Nunberg, G. (2011, March 18). Review of J. Gleick, *The Information. A History. A Theory. A Flood. New York Times*. Retrieved from www.nytimes.com/2011/03/20/books/review/book-review-the-information-by-james-gleick.html

Ober, J. (2001). *Political dissent in democratic Athens: Intellectual critics of popular rule*. Princeton, NJ: Princeton University Press.

Ogden, C.K., & Richards, I. A. (1989). *The meaning of meaning: A study of the influence of language upon thought and of the science of symbolism*. New York: Harcourt Brace Jovanovich.

Ojakangas, M. (2016). *On the Greek origins of biopolitics: A reinterpretation of the history of biopower*. Abingdon, UK & New York: Routledge.

Oliver, K. (2009). *Animal lessons: How they teach us to be human*. New York: Columbia University Press.

Olson, L. N., Baiocchi-Wagner, E. A., Kratzer, J. M. W., & Symonds, S. E. (2012). *The dark side of family communication*. Cambridge, UK & Malden, MA: Polity Press.

Ong, W. J. (1982). *Orality and literacy: The technologizing of the world*. London & New York: Methuen.

Osmanagich, S. (2017, January 24). Exclusive: Discovery of Tesla's Torsion fields above the Bosnian Pyramids. *Sarajevo Times*. Retrieved from www.sarajevotimes.com/exclusive-discovery-teslas-torsion-fields-bosnian-pyramids/

Pace, E. (2011). *Religion as communication: God's talk*. Farnham, UK & Burlington, VT: Ashgate.

Padula, A. (2009). Kinesics. In S. W. Littlejohn & K. A. Foss (Eds.), *Encyclopedia of communication theory* (pp. 582–584). Thousand Oaks, CA: SAGE.

Pafumi, G. R. (2013). *God Is dead! Don't blame Nietzsche: It was Carl Sagan and Stephen Hawking who killed him*. Scotts Valley, CA: CreateSpace Independent Publishing Platform.

Palin, M. (2017, April 3). Psychic medium Kerrie-Anne Thornton claims she can talk to aliens. *News.com.au*. Retrieved from www.news.com.au/technology/science/aliens-use-my-body-sydneybased-medium-claims-to-communicate-with-extraterrestrials/news-story/ca5641cb4b9396f7627a547030e8c555

Palmer, R. E. (1980). The liminality of Hermes and the meaning of hermeneutics. *Proceedings of the Heraclitean Society, 5*, 4–11.

Paparella, E. (2012). *Essays on the origins of the EU's cultural identity and its present economic-political crisis*. New York: Xlibris Books.

Parker, C.H., & Bentley, J. H. (Eds.). (2007). *Between the Middle Ages and modernity: Individual and community in the early modern world*. Lanham, MD: Rowman & Littlefield.

Parret, H. (1993). *The aesthetics of communication: Pragmatics and beyond.* Dordrecht, Netherlands & Boston, MA: Kluwer.

Parrish, A. C. (2014). *Adaptive rhetoric: Evolution, culture, and the art of persuasion.* New York: Routledge.

Pasanek, B. (2015). *Metaphors of mind: An eighteenth-century dictionary.* Baltimore, MD: Johns Hopkins University Press.

Pascal, B. (1909). *Pensées* (L. Brunschvicg, Ed.). Paris: Hachette.

Pearce, W. B. (2009). *Making social worlds: A communication perspective.* Malden, MA: Blackwell.

Pease, B., & Pease, A. (2008). *The definitive book of body language: The hidden meaning behind people's gestures and expressions.* Buderim, Australia: Pease International.

Peck, J. (1995), TV talk shows as therapeutic discourse: The ideological labor of the televised talking cure. *Communication Theory, 5,* 58–81.

Peirce, C. S. (1935). *Collected papers of Charles Sanders Peirce, volumes V and VI: Pragmatism and pragmaticism and scientific metaphysics* (P. Weiss & C. Hartshorne, Eds). Cambridge, MA: Belknap Press.

Peirce, C. S. (1967) *Manuscripts in the Houghton Library of Harvard University.* Amherst, MA: University of Massachusetts Press

Peirce, C. S. (1992). *The essential Peirce: Selected philosophical writings* (N. Houser & C. Kloesel, Eds.). Bloomington, IN & Indianapolis, IN: Indiana University Press.

Penprase, B. E. (2011). *The power of stars: How celestial observations have shaped civilization.* New York: Springer.

Peters, J. D (1995). Historical tensions in the concept of public opinion. In T. L. Glasser & C. T. Salmon (Eds.), *Public opinion and the communication of consent* (pp. 3–32). New York,: Guilford.

Peters, J. D. (1999). *Speaking into the air: A history of the idea of communication.* Chicago, IL: University of Chicago Press.

Peters, J. D. (2003). Space, time, and communication theory. *Canadian Journal of Communication, 28,* 397–411.

Peters, J. D. (2005). *Courting the abyss: Free speech and the liberal tradition.* Chicago, IL & London: University of Chicago Press.

Peters, J. D. (2006a). Technology and ideology: The case of the telegraph revisited. In J. Packer & C. Robertson (Eds.), *Thinking with James Carey: Essays on communication, transportation, history* (pp. 137–155). New York: Peter Lang.

Peters, J. D. (2006b). Communication as dissemination. In G. J. Shepherd, J. St. John & T. Striphas (Eds.), *Communication as ...: Perspectives on theory* (pp. 211–222). Thousand Oaks, CA: SAGE.

Peters, J. (2012). Afterword: Doctors of philosophy. In J. Hannan (Ed.), *Philosophical profiles in the theory of communication* (pp. 499–510). New York: Peter Lang.

Peters, J. (2015). *The marvelous clouds: Toward a philosophy of elemental media.* Chicago, IL & London: University of Chicago Press.

Peters, J. D. & Peters, B. (2016). Norbert Wiener as pragmatist. *Empedocles: European Journal for the Philosophy of Communication, 7*(2), 157–172.

Petersen, A. (2014). Uncertainty and God: A Jamesian pragmatist approach to uncertainty and ignorance in science and religion. *Zygon, 49*(4), 808–828.

Pettman, D. (2016). *Infinite distraction: Paying attention to social media.* Cambridge, UK: Polity Press.

Petzinger, G. von (2016). *The first signs: Unlocking the mysteries of the world's oldest symbols*. New York: Simon and Schuster.

Pew Research Center (2014). *Religious landscape study: Belief in God*. Retrieved from www.pewforum.org/religious-landscape-study/belief-in-god/

Pickering, M. (2006). *Auguste Comte, volume 1: An intellectual biography*. Cambridge, UK: Cambridge University Press.

Pinchevski, A. (2005). *By way of interruption: Levinas and the ethics of communication*. Pittsburgh, PA: Duquesne University Press.

Piwek, P., Beun, R. J., & Cremers, A. (2008). "Proximal" and "distal" in language and cognition: Evidence from deictic demonstratives in Dutch. *Journal of Pragmatics*, *40*(4), 694–718.

Plessner, H. (1999). *The limits of community: A critique of social radicalism*. Amherst, NY: Humanity Books.

Poe, M. T. (2011). *A history of communications: Media and society from the evolution of speech to the internet*. Cambridge, UK: Cambridge University Press.

Pohl, W., Gantner, C. & Payne, R. (Eds.) (2012). *Visions of community in the post-Roman world. The West, Byzantium and the Islamic world, 300–1100*. Farnham, UK & Burlington, VT: Ashgate.

Polanyi, M. (1962). *Personal knowledge*. Chicago, IL: University of Chicago Press.

Popkin, G. (2017, September 9). Bacteria use brainlike bursts of electricity to communicate. *Scientific American*. Retrieved from www.scientificamerican.com/article/bacteria-use-brainlike-bursts-of-electricity-to-communicate/

Popper, K. (1963). *Conjectures and refutations: The growth of scientific knowledge*. London: Routledge & Kegan Paul.

Potter, N. (2005). Kant on duties to animals. *Jahrbuch für Recht und Ethik*, *13*, 299–311.

Poulakos, T. (1997). *Speaking for the polis: Isocrates' rhetorical education*. Columbia, SC: University of South Carolina Press.

Pratkanis, R. (1997). The social psychology of mass communications: An American perspective. In D. F. Halpern & A. Voiskounsky (Eds.), *States of mind: American and Post-Soviet perspectives on contemporary issues in psychology* (pp. 126–159). New York: Oxford University Press.

Price, M. (2007). Religious communication and its relation to the state: Comparative perspectives. In A. Sajo (Ed.), *Censorial sensitivities: Free speech and religion in a fundamentalist world* (pp. 85–106). The Hague, Netherlands: Eleven International.

Putsch, RW III, & Joyce, M. (1990). Dealing with patients from other cultures. In H. K. Walker, W. D. Hall, & J.W. Hurst (Ed.), *Clinical methods: The history, physical, and laboratory examinations* (pp.1050–1065). Boston, MA: Butterworths.

Rae, G. (2011). *Realizing freedom: Hegel, Sartre, and the alienation of the human being*. London, UK: Palgrave Macmillan.

Ransford, M. (2008, June 17). The search for extraterrestrial life: A brief history. *Popular Science*. Retrieved from www.popsci.com/military-aviation-space/article/2008-06/et-phone-earth

Ramsey, R.E., & Miller, D. J. (Eds.). (2012). *Experiences between philosophy and communication: Engaging the philosophical contributions of Calvin O. Schrag*. Albany, NY: SUNY Press.

Rapport, N. & Amit, V. (2002). *The trouble with community: anthropological reflections on movement, identity and collectivity*. London: Pluto Press.

Rasch, W. (2000). *Niklas Luhmann's modernity: The paradoxes of differentiation.* Stanford, CA: Stanford University Press.

Rasmussen, L. (1991). *Earth-honoring faith: Religious ethics in a new key.* New York: Oxford University Press.

Rasmussen, R. M. (1991). *Extraterrestrial life.* San Diego, CA: Lucent Books.

Raulin-Cerceau, F. (2010). The pioneers of interplanetary communication: From Gauss to Tesla. *Acta Astronautica, 67*(11), 1391–1398.

Rawlinson, M. & Ward, C. (Eds.). (2017). *The Routledge handbook of food.* New York: Routledge.

Redd, N. T. (2013, February 27). Konstantin Tsiolkovsky: Russian father of rocketry. *Space.com.* Retrieved from www.space.com/19994-konstantin-tsiolkovsky.html

Renson, R. (1997, June 18). Rebellion of the body: Human movement in a post-modern perspective. *Playthegame.* Retrieved from www.playthegame.org/news/news-articles/1997/rebellion-of-the-body-human-movement-in-a-postmodern-perspective/

Richard, I. A. (1928). *Principles of literary criticism.* London: Kegan Paul.

Richter, D. S. (2011). *Cosmopolis: Imagining community in late classical Athens and the early Roman empire.* Oxford & New York: Oxford University Press.

Rickert,T. (2013). *Ambient rhetoric: The attunements of rhetorical being.* Pittsburgh, PA: University of Pittsburgh Press.

Ricoeur, P. (1984). *Time and narrative, volume 1.* Chicago, IL & London: University of Chicago Press.

Riemer, N. (2010). *Introducing semantics.* Cambridge, UK: Cambridge University Press.

Robbins, R., & Dowty, R. (2016). *Cultural anthropology: A problem-based approach.* Boston, MA: Cengage Learning.

Roberts, N. (Ed.). (2008). *The age of direct citizen participation.* Armonk, NY: M. E. Sharpe.

Robertson, G. (1886). *Hobbes.* London: Blackwood and Sons.

Robinson, G. (2017). The prospect of interspecies cybernetic communication between humankind and post-humans designed and created for space exploration and space settlement. *Journal of Space Philosophy, 6*(1), 95–112.

Robson, E. (2004). Scholarly conceptions and quantifications of time in Assyria and Babylonia, c. 750–250 BCE. In Rosen, R. (Ed.), *Time and temporality in the ancient world* (pp. 45–90). Philadelphia, PA: University of Pennsylvania Museum of Archeology and Anthropology.

Rodriguez, A. (Ed.). (2001). *Essays on communication & spirituality: Contributions to a new discourse on communication.* Lanham, MA: University Press of America.

Rogers, C., & Campbell, L. (2015). Endangered languages. In M. Aronoff (Ed.), *Oxford research encyclopedia of linguistics.* doi.org/10.1093/acrefore/9780199384655.013.21

Rojcewicz, R. (2006). *The gods and technology: A reading of Heidegger.* Albany, NY: SUNY Press.

Ross, M. (1986). Australian Aboriginal oral traditions. *Oral Tradition, 1*(2), 231–271.

Roth, W. M. (2009). Identity and community: Differences at heart and futures-to-come. *Education & didactique, 3*(3), 99–118.

Rothenbuhler, E. (1998). *Ritual communication: From everyday conversation to mediated ceremony.* Thousand Oaks, CA: SAGE.

Rothman, L. (2016, April 9). Is God dead? TIME's iconic cover at 50. *Time*. Retrieved from http://time.com/isgoddead/

Ruben, B., & Stewart L. (2006). *Communication and human behavior*. Boston, MA: Allyn & Bacon.

Rubin, J. (1998). *A psychoanalysis for our time: Exploring the blindness of the seeing I*. New York: New York University Press.

Ruesch, J., & Bateson, G. (1951). *Communication: The social matrix of psychiatry*. New York: W.W. Norton.

Russell, B. (2009). *The basic writings of Bertrand Russell*. London: Routledge.

Ruxton, G. D., & Schaefer, H. M. (2011). Resolving current disagreements and ambiguities in the terminology of animal communication. *Journal of Evolutionary Biology, 24*(12), 2574–2585.

Sabourin, T. (2003). *The contemporary American family: A dialectical perspective on communication and relationships*. Thousand Oaks, CA: SAGE.

Sagan, C. (Ed.). (1973). *Communication with extraterrestrial intelligence(CETI)*. Cambridge, MA: The MIT Press.

Sagan, C. (1980). *Cosmos*. London: Book Club Associates.

Sagan, C. (1997). *Pale blue dot: A vision of the human future in space*. New York: Ballantine Books.

Sanneh, L. (1989). *Translating the message: The missionary impact on culture*. Maryknoll, NY: Orbis.

Sartre, J.-P. (1995). *Being and nothingness. An essay on phenomenological ontology* H. Barnes (Transl.). London: Routledge.

Sartwell, C. (2002). Community at the margin. In P. Alperson (Ed.), *Diversity and community: An interdisciplinary reader* (pp. 47–57). Hoboken, NJ: Blackwell.

Saussure, F. de (1986). *Course in general linguistics* (C. Bally & A. Sechehaye, Eds., A. Riedlinger, Trans.). LaSalle, IL: Open Court.

Schaefer, M., Rotte, M., Heinze, H.J., & Denke, C. (2015). Dirty deeds and dirty bodies: Embodiment of the Macbeth effect is mapped topographically onto the somatosensory cortex. *Scientific Reports, 5*(18051). doi.org/10.1038/srep18051

Scheufele, D. A. (2000). Agenda-setting, priming, and framing revisited: Another look at cognitive effects of political communication. *Mass Communication and Society, 3*(2), 297–316.

Schirber, M. (2009, January 29). Attempts to contact aliens date back more than 150 years. *Space.com*. Retrieved from www.space.com/6370-attempts-contact-aliens-date-150-years.html

Schlegel, F. (1971). *Lucinde and the fragments* (P. Firchow, Trans.). Minneapolis, MN: University of Minnesota Press.

Schleiermacher, F. D. E. (1977). *Hermeneutics: The handwritten manuscripts* (J. Duke & J. Forstman, Trans.). Missoula, MT: Scholars Press.

Schleifer, R. (2000). *Analogical thinking: Post-Enlightenment understanding in language, collaboration, and interpretation*. Ann Arbor, MI: University of Michigan Press.

Schnabel, E. J. (2008). *Paul the missionary: Realities, strategies and methods*. Downers Grove, IL: IVP Academic.

Schrift, A. (Ed.). (1997). *The logic of the gift: Toward an ethic of generosity*. New York: Routledge.

Schroeder, C. O. (2001). *History, justice, and the agency of God: A hermeneutical and exegetical investigation on Isaiah and Psalms*. Leiden, Netherlands & Boston, MA: Brill.

Schuetz, J. (2009). Religious communication theories. In S. W. Littlejohn & K. A. Foss (Eds.), *Encyclopedia of communication theory* (pp. 847–850). Thousand Oaks, CA: SAGE.

Schultze, Q. J. (2005). The "God-problem" in communication studies. *Journal of Communication and Religion, 28,* 1–22.

Schwab, G. (1994). Nonsense and metacommunications: Reflections on Lewis Carroll. In R. Bogue & M. I. Spariosu (Eds.), *The play of the Self* (pp. 157–178). Albany, NY: SUNY Press.

Schwarzmantel, J. (2007). Community as communication: Jean-Luc Nancy and "being-in-common". *Political Studies, 55,* 459–476.

Scott, C. (2007). *Living with indifference.* Bloomington, IN: Indiana University Press.

Seamon, D. (2013). Lived bodies, place, and phenomenology: Implications for human rights and environmental justice. *Journal of Human Rights and the Environment, 4*(2), 143.

Seife, C. (2000). *Zero: The biography of a dangerous idea.* New York: Viking.

Sereno, K. K., & *Mortensen,* C. D. (1970). *Foundations of communication theory.* New York: Harper & Row.

Sfard, A. (2008). *Thinking as communicating: Human development, the growth of discourses, and mathematizing.* Cambridge, UK: Cambridge University Press.

Shaffer, T. S., Allison, J. M., & Pelias, R. J. (2015). A critical history of the "live" body in performance within the National Communication Association. In P. J. Gehrke & W. M. Keith (Eds.), *A century of communication studies: The unfinished conversation* (pp. 187–206). New York: Routledge.

Shanahan, J., & Morgan, M. (1999). *Television and its viewers: Cultivation theory and research.* Cambridge, UK: Cambridge University Press.

Shannon, C. E. (1948). A mathematical theory of communication. *The Bell System Technical Journal.* (*27*), 379–423, 623–656.

Shannon, C. E. (1956). The bandwagon. *IRE Transactions on Information Theory.* (2)*1,* 3.

Shannon, C. E., & Weaver, W. (1949). *The mathematical theory of communication.* Urbana, IL: The University of Illinois Press.

Shaw, D., & Van Engen, C. (2003). *Communicating God's word in a complex world: God's truth or hocus pocus?* Lanham, MD: Rowman & Littlefield Publishers.

Sheets-Johnstone, M. (2011). *The primacy of movement.* Philadelphia, PA: John Benjamins Publishing Company.

Shepherd, G. J. (1993). Building a discipline of communication. *Journal of Communication, 43*(3), 83–91.

Shepherd, G. J., & Rothenbuhler, E. W. (2001). Preface. In G. J. Shepherd & E. W. Rothenbuhler (Eds.), *Communication and community* (pp. 3–21). Mahwah, NJ: Erlbaum.

Shepherd, S. (2006). A feeling for history? Bakhtin and the problem of "great time". *The Slavonic and East European Review, 8* 4(1), 32–51.

Sheridan, T. (2014). *What Is God? Can religion be modeled?* Washington, DC: New Academia Publishing.

Sherrington, C. (1940). *Man on his nature.* Cambridge, UK: Cambridge University Press.

Shilling, Ch. (2012). *The body and social theory.* London: SAGE.

Shiner, L. (2003). *The invention of art: A cultural history.* Chicago, IL: University of Chicago Press

Shorris, E. (2000). *Riches for the poor: The Clemente course in the humanities.* New York: W. W. Norton.

Shostak, S. (2009). *Confessions of an alien hunter: A scientist's search for extraterrestrial intelligence.* Washington, DC: National Geographic.

Shuch, H. P. (2011). *Searching for extraterrestrial intelligence: SETI past, present, and future.* Berlin: Springer.

Siegert, B. (2012). Doors: On the materiality of the symbolic (J. D. Peters, Trans.). *Grey Room, 47,* 6–23.

Sideris, L. (2012). *Environmental ethics, ecological theology and natural selection: Suffering and responsibility.* New York: Columbia University Press.

Sigler, J. E. (2014). First "What is knowing?" and then "How'd they know?": Epistemological and phenomenological considerations in the study of direct divine communication (DDC). *Journal of Communication and Religion, 37*(1), 145–170.

Sloterdijk, P. (2013). *Philosophical temperaments: From Plato to Foucault* (T. Dunlap, Trans.). New York: Columbia University Press.

Smart, J. M. (2012). The transcension hypothesis. Sufficiently advanced civilizations invariably leave our universe, and implications for METI and SETI. *Acta Astronautica, 78,* 55–68.

Smith, A. R. (Ed.). (2016). *Radical conflict: Essays on violence, intractability, and communication.* Lanham, MD: Lexington Books.

Smith, A. R., Catt, I. E., & Klyukanov, I. E. (Eds.). (2017). *Communicology for the human sciences: Lanigan and philosophy of communication.* New York: Peter Lang.

Smith, K. C. (2018). Got humanities? *Astrobiology, (18)*4, 465–467.

Smith, P. K., Pepler, D., & Rigby, K. (Eds.). (2004). *Bullying in schools: How successful can interventions be?* New York,: Cambridge University Press.

Smuts, B. (2001). Encounters with animal minds. *Journal of Consciousness Studies, 8*(5), 293–309.

Snyder, L. (2017, October 20). Review of O. Sacks, *The river of consciousness. The Wall Street Journal.* Retrieved from www.wsj.com/articles/review-oliver-sacks-travels-down-the-river-of-consciousness-1508522780

Soliz, J., & Colaner, C. W. (2014). Familial solidarity and religious identity: Communication and interfaith families. In L. Turner & R. West (Eds.), *The SAGE handbook of family communication* (pp. 401–416). London: SAGE.

Sommerer, C., Mignonneau, L., & Weil, F. (2015). The art of human to plant interaction. In P. Vieira, J. Ryan & M. Gagliano (Eds.), *The green thread: Dialogues with the vegetal world* (pp. 233–254). Lanham, MD: Lexington Books.

Sonesson, G. (1996/1997). Approaches to the lifeworld core of pictorial rhetoric. *Visio: La Revue de l'association Internationale de Semiótique Visuelle, 1*(3), 49–76.

Sonesson, G. (2013). Preparations for discussing constructivism with a Martian (the second coming). In D. Dunér, J. Parthemore, E. Persson & G. Holmberg (Eds.), *The history and philosophy of astrobiology: Perspectives on extraterrestrial life and the human mind* (pp. 185–200). Newcastle upon Tyne, UK: Cambridge Scholars Publishing.

Sowards, W.M. (2017). *In defense of communicating God's word: Conversational preaching. How an understanding of interpersonal communications theory can improve our preaching.* Doctoral dissertation. Sewanee, TN: University of the South. Retrieved from https://dspace.sewanee.edu/bitstream/handle/11005/3692/SowardsInDefenseSOT20

Sperber, D., & Wilson, D. (2002). Pragmatics, modularity and mind-reading. *Mind & Language, 17*(1–2), 3–23.

Spitzberg, B. H., & Cupach, W. R. (2007). *The dark side of interpersonal communication.* Mahwah, NJ: Erlbaum.

Stanner, W. E. H. (1979). *White man got no Dreaming. Essay, 1938–1973.* Canberra, Australia: Australian National University.

Stark, R. & Glock, C. (1974). *American piety: The nature of religious commitment.* Berkeley, CA: University of California Press.

Starr, C. G. (1986). *Individual and community: The rise of the polis, 800–500 B.C.* New York: Oxford University Press.

Staten, H. (2006). A critique of the will to power. In K. Pearson (Ed.), *A companion to Nietzsche* (pp. 565–582). Hoboken, NJ: John Wiley & Sons

Stawarska, B. (2015). *Saussure's philosophy of language as phenomenology: Undoing the doctrine of the course in general linguistics.* New York: Oxford University Press.

Steel, C. & van der Blom, H. (2013). *Community and communication: Oratory and politics in republican Rome.* Oxford: Oxford University Press.

Stegmüller, W. (1970). *Main currents in contemporary German, British, and American philosophy* (A. E. Blumberg, Trans.) Bloomington, IN: Indiana University Press.

Stehr, N. & Ericson R. (Eds.). (1992). *The culture and power of knowledge: Inquiries into contemporary societies.* Berlin & New York: Walter de Gruyter.

Stepanov, Y. (2004). Konstanty. Slovar' russkoj kultury. [Constants: A vocabulary of Russian culture]. Moscow: Akademicheski Proekt.

Stetsenko, A. (2016). *The transformative mind: Expanding Vygotsky's approach to development and education.* Cambridge, UK: Cambridge University Press.

Stewart, J.(1998). Historical frames of relational perspectives. In R. L. Conville & L. E. Rogers (Eds.), *The meaning of 'relationship' in interpersonal communication* (pp. 23–46). Westport, CT & London: Praeger.

Stewart, J. (Ed.). (1996). *Beyond the symbol model: Reflections on the representational nature of language.* Albany, NY: SUNY Press.

Stewart, C. (2008). Prayer among the Benedictines. In R. Hammerling (Ed.), *A history of prayer* (pp. 201–222). Leiden, Netherlands & Boston, MA: Brill.

Stibbe, A. (1996). The metaphorical construction of illness in Chinese culture. *Journal of Asian Pacific Communication, 7*(3), 177–188.

Stroud J. T., Bush M. R., Ladd M. C., Nowicki R. J., Shantz A. A., & Sweatman J. (2015). Is a community still a community? Reviewing definitions of key terms in community ecology. *Ecology & Evolution, 5*(21), 4757–4765.

Stueber, K. R. (2010). *Rediscovering empathy: Agency, folk psychology, and the human sciences.* Cambridge, MA: The MIT Press.

Stunkel, K. (2015). *Ideas and art in Asian civilizations: India, China and Japan.* Armonk, NY: M. E. Sharpe.

Swanson, K. (2014). *Banking on the body: The market in blood, milk, and sperm in modern America*. Cambridge, MA: Harvard University Press.

Susina, J. (2010). Playing around in Lewis Carroll's "Alice" books. *American Journal of Play, 2*(4), 419–428.

Suto, T. (2012). *Boethius on mind, grammar and logic: A study of Boethius' commentaries on Peri Hermeneias*. Leiden, Netherlands & Boston, MA: Brill.

Tannen, D. (1984). The pragmatics of cross-cultural communication. *Applied Linguistics, 5*(3), 189–195.

Tansley, A.G. (1935). The use and abuse of vegetational concepts and terms. *Ecology, 16*, 284–307.

Tarter, J. (2011). The search for extraterrestrial intelligence (SETI). *Annual Review of Astronomy and Astrophysics, 39*, 511–548.

Taylor, C. (1995). Liberal politics and the public sphere. In A. Etzioni (Ed.), *The new communitarian thinking* (pp. 183–217). Charlottesville, VA: University Press of Virginia.

Taylor, C. (2016). Preface to this edition. In P. Ricoeur, *Hermeneutics and the human sciences* (J. B. Thompson, Ed. & Trans.) (pp. vii–ix). New York: Cambridge University Press.

Teiser, S. F. (2000). Review of R. F. Campany, *Strange writing: Anomaly accounts in early medieval China. History of Religions, 39*(3), 308.

Tekdemir, H. (2007). *Humpty Dumpty's fall: Failing to see the writing on the wall*. In I. Baş & D. C. Freeman (Eds.), *Challenging the boundaries* (pp. 203–210) Amsterdam & New York: Rodopi.

TenHouten, W. (2005). *Time and society*. Albany, NY: SUNY Press.

Tesla at 75. (1931, July 20). *Time, 18*(3). Retrieved from https://teslauniverse.com/nikola-tesla/articles/nikola-tesla-75

Timpson, C. G. (2013). *Quantum information theory and the foundations of quantum mechanics*, Oxford: Oxford University Press.

Thom, R. (1983). *Mathematical models of morphogenesis*. Chichester, UK: Ellis Horwood.

Thompson, L. (1949). The relations of men, animals, and plants in an island community (Fiji). *American Anthropologist, 51*, 253–267.

Thompson, N. (2003). *Communication and language: A handbook of theory and practice*. Basingstoke, UK: Palgrave Macmillan.

Thorogood, J. (2016). Satire and geopolitics: Vulgarity, ambiguity and the body grotesque in South Park. *Geopolitics, 21*(1), 215–235

Toadvine, T. (2015). Biodiversity and the diacritics of life. In R. Kearney & B. Treanor (Eds.), *Carnal hermeneutics* (pp. 325–250). New York: Fordham University Press.

Todorov, T. (1999). *The conquest of America: The question of the other*. Norman, OK: University of Oklahoma Press.

Tratnik, P. (2017). *Conquest of body: Biopower with biotechnology*. Berlin: Springer.

Trend, D. (2016). *Everyday culture: Finding and making meaning in a changing world*. New York: Routledge.

Tsatsou, P. (2009). Reconceptualising "time" and "space" in the era of electronic media and communications. *Platform: Journal of Media and Communication, 1*(1), 11–32.

Turkle, S. (2011). *Alone together: Why we expect more from technology and less from each other*. New York: Basic Books.

Turner, B. (Ed.). (2012). *Routledge handbook of body studies*. New York: Routledge.

Turner, L. & West, R. (2013). *Perspectives on family communication*. New York: McGraw-Hill.

Turner, L. & West, R. (Eds.) (2014). *The SAGE handbook of family communication*. Thousand Oaks, CA: SAGE.

Ulrich, W. (1983). *Critical heuristics of social planning: A new approach to practical philosophy*. New York: John Wiley & Sons.

Vakoch, D. (1999). The view from a distant star. *Mercury, 28*(2), 26–39.

Vakoch, D. (Ed.), (2011a). *Communication with extraterrestrial intelligence (CETI)*. Albany, NY: SUNY Press.

Vakoch, D. (2011b). What's past is prologue: Future messages of cosmic evolution. In H. P. Shuch (Ed.), *Searching for extraterrestrial intelligence: SETI past, present and future* (pp. 373–398). Berlin: Springer.

Vakoch, D. (Ed.), (2014). *Archaeology, anthropology, and interstellar communication*. Washington, DC: NASA.

Violi, P. (2008). Beyond the body: Toward a full embodied semiosis. In R. M. Frank, R. Dirven, T. Ziemke, & E. Bernárdez (Eds.), *Body, language and mind, vol. 2: Sociocultural situatedness* (pp. 53–76). Berlin: Walter de Gruyter.

Visser, M. (2002). *Beyond fate*. Toronto: Anansi Press.

Vivian, B. (2004). *Being made strange: Rhetoric beyond representation*. Albany, NY: SUNY Press.

Vizenor, G. (1999). *Manifest manners: Narratives on post-Indian survivance*. Lincoln, NE: University of Nebraska Press.

Vocate, D. (Ed.). (1994). *Intrapersonal communication: Different voices, different minds*. Hillsdale, NJ: Erlbaum.

Volkman, L. (2003). Extensions of the battle zone: Ian McEwan's cult novel *The cement garden*. In K. Stierstorfer (Ed.), *Beyond postmodernism: Reassessment in literature, theory, and culture* (pp. 303–318). Berlin: Walter de Gruyter.

von Foerster, H. (1962). Circuitry of clues to Platonic ideation. In C. A. Musés (Ed.), *Aspects of the theory of artificial intelligence. The proceedings of the First International Symposium on Biosimulation, Locarno, June 29–July 5, 1960*. New York: Springer.

von Foerster, H. (1981). *Observing systems*. Seaside, CA: Intersystems.

von Foerster H. (1995). Ethics and second-order cybernetics. Opening address for the International Conference, Systems and Family Therapy: Ethics, Epistemology, New Methods, held in Paris, France, October 4th, 1990. *Stanford Humanities Review, 4*(2), 308–319. Retrieved from https://web.stanford.edu/group/SHR/4-2/text/foerster.html

von Foerster H. (2003). *Understanding understanding: Essays on cybernetics and cognition*. New York: Springer.

Vygotsky, L. (1980). *Mind in society: Development of higher psychological processes*. Cambridge, MA: Harvard University Press.

Vygotsky, L. (1997). *The collected works of L. S. Vygotsky: The history of the development of higher mental functions* (R. W. Rieber, Ed.). New York: Springer.

Vygotsky, L. (2004). *The essential Vygotsky* (R. W. Reiber & D. K. Robinson, Eds.). New York: Springer.

Waldenfels, B. (2007). *The question of the other*. Hong Kong: Chinese University Press.

Waldrop, M. (2001). Claude Shannon: Reluctant father of the digital age. *MIT Technology Review, 104*(6), 64–71.

Walker, J. (2000). *Rhetoric and poetics in antiquity*. New York: Oxford University Press.

Waller, B. M., Hope, L., Burrowes, N. & Morrison, E. R. (2011). Twelve (not so) angry men: Managing conversational group size increases perceived contribution by decision makers. *Group Processes & Intergroup Relations, 14*(6), 1–9.

Warf, B., & Arias, S. (Eds.). (2009). *The spatial turn: Interdisciplinary perspectives*. New York: Routledge.

Watson, R., & Blondheim, M. (Eds.). (2007). *The Toronto School of Communication theory: Interpretations, extensions, applications*. Toronto: University of Toronto Press.

Watzlawick, P. & Beavin, J. (1967). Some formal aspects of communication. *American Behavioral Scientist, 10*(8), 4–8.

Watzlawick, P., Beavin, J., & Jackson, D.D. (1967). *Pragmatics of human communication: A study of interactional patterns, pathologies and paradoxes*. New York: W.W. Norton.

Weaver, W. (1949). The mathematics of communication. *Scientific American, 181*(1), 11–15.

Webb, S. (2015). *If the universe is teeming with aliens... Where is everybody? Seventy-five solutions to the Fermi paradox and the problem of extraterrestrial life*. New York: Springer.

Weinberg, D. (2012). Social constructionism and the body. In B. Turner (Ed.), *The Routledge handbook of body studies* (pp. 144–56). London: Routledge.

Weinstein, J., & Colebrook, C. (Eds.). (2017). *Posthumous life: Theorizing beyond the posthuman*. New York, NY: Columbia University Press.

Weisman. A. (2007). *The world without us*. Basingstoke, UK: Macmillan.

Wertsch, J. V. (1985). *Vygotsky and the social formation of mind*. Cambridge, MA: Harvard University Press.

Wesley, J. (1831). *The works of the Reverend John Wesley, AM*, vol. 3. New York: J. Emory & B. Waugh.

West, R., & Turner, L. (2008). *Understanding interpersonal communication: Making choices in changing times*. Boston, MA: Wadsworth.

Whitten, N., Jr (1996). The Ecuadorian Levantiamento Indígena of 1990 and the epitomizing symbol of 1992: Reflections on nationalism, ethnic-bloc formation, and racialist ideologies. In J. D. Hill (Ed.), *History, power, and identity: Ethnogenesis in the Americas, 1492–1992* (pp. 193–218). Iowa City: University of Iowa Press.

Wiener, N. (1948). *Cybernetics, or control and communication in the animal and the machine*. New York: John Wiley & Sons.

Wiener, N. (1950). *On the human use of human beings: Cybernetics and society*. Boston, MA: Houghton Mifflin.

Wiener, N. (1956). What is information theory? *IRE Transactions on Information Theory, 2*(2), 48.

Wilczek, F. (2017, June 23). No, truth isn't dead. Science plays a vital role in defining the boundaries of rational discourse. *The Wall Street Journal*. Retrieved from www.wsj.com/articles/no-truth-isnt-dead-1498235984

Wilden, A. (2013). *System and structure: Essays in communication and exchange*. London: Routledge.

Wilkie, R., & McKinoon, A. (2013). George Herbert Mead on humans and other animals: Social relations after human-animal studies. *Sociological Research Online, 18*(4), 19.

Willett, C. (2014). *Interspecies ethics.* New York: Columbia University Press.

Williams, B. (2008). *The sense of the past: Essays in the history of philosophy* (M. Burnyeat, Ed.). Princeton, NJ: Princeton University Press.

Williams, M. (2017, June 1). Are Aliens Communicating with Neutrino Beams? *Universe Today.* Retrieved from www.universetoday.com/135813/aliens-communicating-neutrino-beams/

Williams, R. (1976). *Keywords: A vocabulary of culture and society.* Glasgow, UK: Croom Helm.

Wilson, D. (2003). The future of comparative and international education in a globalized world. In M. Bray (Ed.), *Comparative education: Continuing traditions, new challenges, and new paradigms* (pp. 15–33). Dordrecht, Netherlands: Kluwer.

Wilson, M. (2009). *Bacteriology of humans: An ecological perspective.* Malden, MA: Blackwell.

Wilson, R.A. (1988). *Coincidence: A head test.* Santa Monica, CA: New Falcon Publications.

Winslow, C.E. (1980). *The conquest of epidemic disease: A chapter in the history of ideas.* Madison, WI: University of Wisconsin Press.

Winthrop-Young, G. (2015). Siren recursions. In S. Sale & L. Salisbury (Eds.), *Kittler now: Current perspectives in Kittler studies* (pp.71–95). Cambridge, UK: Polity Press.

Wittgenstein, L. (1953). *Philosophical investigations* (G. E. M. Anscombe, Trans.). Oxford: Blackwell.

Wittgenstein, L. (1969). *On certainty* (G. E. M. Anscombe & G. H. von Wright, Eds, D. Paul & G. E. M. Anscombe, Trans.). Oxford: Blackwell.

Wittgenstein, L. (1979). *Notebooks 1914–1916* (G. E. M. Anscombe & G. H. von Wright, Eds, G. E. M. Anscombe, Trans.). Oxford: Blackwell.

Wittgenstein, L. (2002). *Tractatus logico-philosophicus* (D. F. Pears & B. F. McGuinness, Trans.). London and New York: Routledge.

Witzany, G. (2016). The biocommunication method: On the road to an integrative biology. *Communicative & Integrative Biology, 9*(2). doi.org/10.1080/19420889.2016.1164374

Wood, J. (2015). *Interpersonal communication: Everyday encounters.* Boston, MA: Wadsworth.

Woodard, C. (2009, January 14). The mystery of Bosnia's ancient pyramids. *Smithsonian Magazine.* Retrieved from: www.smithsonianmag.com/history-archaeology/The-Mystery-of-Bosnias-Ancient-Pyramids.html

Woodall, W. G., & Burgoon, J. K. (1981). The effects of nonverbal synchrony on message comprehension and persuasiveness. *Journal of Nonverbal Behavior, 5*(4), 207–223.

Wright, A. (2008). *Glut: Mastering information through the ages.* Ithaca, NY: Cornell University Press.

Wright, T. (2017). Garfinkeling. In M. Allen (Ed.), *The SAGE encyclopedia of communication research methods* (pp. 608–610). Los Angeles, CA: SAGE.

Young, I.M. (1997). *Intersecting voices: Dilemmas of gender, political philosophy, and policy.* Princeton, NJ: Princeton University Press.

Yunis, H. (2010). Plato's rhetoric. In I. Worthington (Ed.), *A companion to Greek rhetoric* (pp. 75–89). Malden, MA: Blackwell.

Zaitsev, A. (2002, March 17). Design and implementation of the 1st Theremin concert for aliens. 6th International Space Arts Workshop "The Collaborative Process in Space Art". Retrieved from www.cplire.ru/html/ra&sr/irm/Theremin-concert.html.

Zaitsev, A. L. (2011). METI: Messaging to extraterrestrial intelligence. In H. Shuch (Ed.), *Searching for extraterrestrial intelligence: SETI past, present, and future* (pp. 399–428). Berlin: Springer.

Zanatta, F., Dein, S., & Littlewood, R. (2011). Communication as magic: An ethnographic study on child-God communication in Northern Italy. *World Cultural Psychiatry Research Review, 6*(1), 61–74.

Zauzmer, J. (2016, December 8). In space, John Glenn saw the face of God. "It just strengthens my faith." *Washington Post.* Retrieved from www.washingtonpost.com/news/acts-of-faith/wp/2016/12/08/in-outer-space-john-glenn-saw-the-face-of-god/?utm_term=.26b79a76421c

Zeller, B. (2010). Extraterrestrial biblical hermeneutics and the making of Heaven's gate. *Nova Religio: The Journal of Alternative and Emergent Religions, 14*(2), 34–60.

Zimbardo, P. G., & Boyd, J. N. (1999). Putting time in perspective: A valid, reliable individual-differences metric. *Journal of Personality and Social Psychology, 77*(6), 1271–1288.

Zimmer, C. (2013, July 13). Genes are us. And them. *National Geographic.* Retrieved from http://thenextdeal.org/nat-geo-genes-are-us-and-them/

Žižek, S. (2002). The real of sexual difference. In S. Barnard & B. Fink (Eds.), *Reading Seminar XX: Lacan's major work on love, knowledge, and feminine sexuality* (pp. 57–76). Albany, NY: SUNY Press.

Zubrin, R. (2001) Interstellar panspermia reconsidered. *Journal of the British Interplanetary Society, 54*, 262–269.

# Index